INFANCY AND EARLIEST CHILDHOOD IN THE ROMAN WORLD

Infancy and Earliest Childhood in the Roman World

'A Fragment of Time'

MAUREEN CARROLL

OXFORD
UNIVERSITY PRESS

Great Clarendon Street, Oxford, OX2 6DP,
United Kingdom

Oxford University Press is a department of the University of Oxford.
It furthers the University's objective of excellence in research, scholarship,
and education by publishing worldwide. Oxford is a registered trade mark of
Oxford University Press in the UK and in certain other countries

First Edition published in 2018

Published in the United States of America by Oxford University Press
198 Madison Avenue, New York, NY 10016, United States of America

British Library Cataloguing in Publication Data
Data available

Library of Congress Control Number: 2017954181

ISBN 978–0–19–968763–3

Preface and Acknowledgements

The research for this book developed out of my earlier work on infant death and burial in Roman Italy, and it expands on that foundation to explore a range of aspects of life and death in earliest childhood across the empire and over several centuries. The book isolates the age group of the under one-year-olds to gain insight into the developing personhood and social role of children in this stage of life in the Roman world. It integrates archaeological evidence, material culture, and imagery with social and cultural history to reach a more nuanced and critical understanding of the historical and cultural influences on the relationships between infants, their families, and the societies in which they lived.

During the writing of this book I have enjoyed the support of various organizations and individuals, and it is my pleasure to acknowledge them here. I am grateful to the Leverhulme Trust and the Pamela Staunton Bequest for financial support which allowed me to travel, collect data, and meet the costs of procuring images for this book. I have benefited greatly from using the excellent research facilities at the British School at Rome, the Römisch-Germanische Kommission in Frankfurt, and the Institute for Classical Studies in London. I am grateful also to the University of Sheffield for two periods of study leave. I would like to thank Rebecca Gowland for reading and commenting on the bioarchaeological part of my draft manuscript. OUP's reviewers also made helpful comments on my book proposal, and the feedback of the manuscript reviewer was most encouraging.

I am grateful to various museums and institutions for facilitating my data collection, supplying photos, and granting permission to reproduce images of artefacts and monuments. These include the Allard Pearson Museum (Amsterdam); Augusta Raurica (Augst); the Museo Nazionale Romano, the Museo dell'Ara Pacis, the Musei Capitolini, Centrale Montemartini, and the Sovrintendenza Capitolina ai Beni Culturali (Rome); The British School at Rome; the Ormož Regional Museum (Ptuj); the Landesmuseum Mainz; the Hungarian National Museum (Budapest); the Ägyptisches Museum und Papyrussammlung (Berlin); the Musée Carnavalet (Paris); the Metropolitan Museum of Art (New York); the Harvard Art Museums (Boston); the Dakhleh Oasis Project; The British Museum and the Science Museum (London); the Fitzwilliam Museum (Cambridge); York Museums Trust; the Manchester Museum; the Colchester Archaeological Trust; and Pre-Construct Archaeology. Photos also were provided by the Rheinisches Bildarchiv in Cologne, the Deutsches Archäologisches Institut in Rome, the image library of *ubi erat lupa*, and Agence Roger Viollet, Paris.

I am deeply indebted to my two wonderful and talented illustrators, Irene de Luis and Jerneja Willmott. And I am grateful to the following colleagues for their assistance in acquiring photos: Laura Baiges Sotos, Elizabeth Bray, Jonathan Butler, Angela Carbonaro, Jean-Christophe Clamagirand, Nina Crummy, Emma Darbyshire, Alessio De Cristofaro, Isabella Donadio, Maria Daniela Donninelli, Cäcilia Fluck, Bastien Gissinger, Mojca Vomer Gojkovič, Emma-Jayne Graham, Ortolf Harl, Jamilla Hawa, Justin Hobson, Daria Lanzuolo, Sébastien Lepetz, Natasha Logan, Nicola Lyons, Zsolt Mrav, Pia Nystrom, Markus Peter, Stefania Peterlini, Tracy Prowse, Ellen Riemer, Susanne Schenker, Martina Schwarz, Bryan Sitch, Alastair Small, Jeremiah Solak, Chris Streek, William van Andringa, René van Beek, Petra Verlinden, Sandra Wheeler, Ruth Whitehouse, and Olivia Zorn.

I am also indebted to Simon Clark, Head of School for Paediatrics in Yorkshire and Humber, for allowing me access to the neonatal wing of the Royal Hallamshire Hospital in Sheffield and for thoughtful discussions on earliest life.

Finally, I am grateful to Charlotte Loveridge, Commissioning Editor for Classics and Archaeology, and Georgina Leighton, Assistant Commissioning Editor, in particular, for their guidance and support.

Contents

List of Figures

Figures

The publisher and the author apologize for any errors or omissions in the permissions and acknowledgements for the above illustrations. If contacted they will be pleased to rectify these at the earliest opportunity.

List of Abbreviations

AE	*L'Année Épigraphique.*
CIL	*Corpus Inscriptionum Latinarum.* Berlin: Berlin-Brandenburgische Akademie der Wissenschaften, 1863–.
Digest	Watson, A. (1985), *The Digest of Justinian*, Vols. 1–2. Philadelphia: University of Pennsylvania Press.
FIRA 2	Riccobono, S., Raviera, G., Ferrini, C., Furlani, J., and Arangio-Ruiz, V. (1940), *Fontes Iuris Romani Anteiustiniani.* Florence: Barbera.
ICUR	*Inscriptiones Christianae Urbis Romae.* Rome: Ex Officina Libraria Pontificia, 1922–92.
IG	*Inscriptiones Graecae.* Berlin: Berlin-Brandenburgische Akademie der Wissenschaften, 1924–.
ILS	Dessau, H. (1892–2016), *Inscriptiones Latinae Selectae.* Berlin: Weidmann.
RIC	*Roman Imperial Coinage.* London: Spink, 1923–94.
RIU	*Die römischen Inscriften Ungarns.* Amsterdam and Bonn: Habelt, 1972–2001.

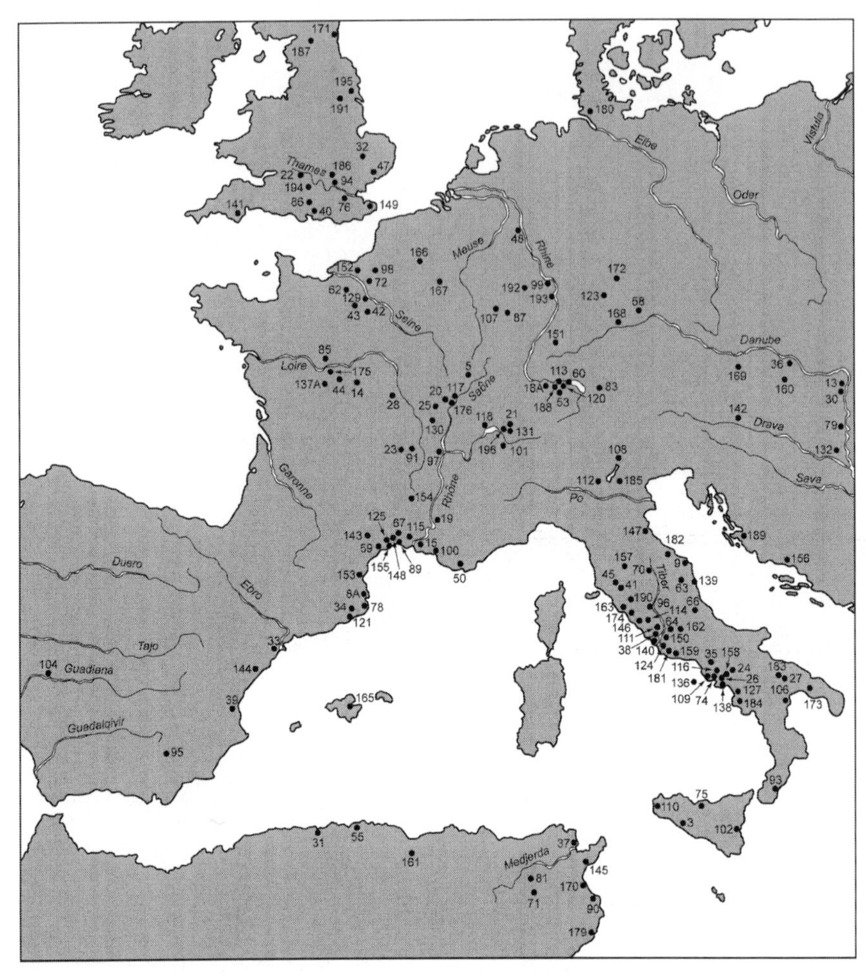

Map 1. Sites in Italy and the western Roman provinces, including pre-Roman sites discussed in the text.

Drawing: Irene de Luis.

3. Agrigento
5. Alesia
8A. Ampurias (Empúries)
9. Ancona
13. Aquincum
14. Argenton
15. Arles
18A. Augst
19. Augusta Tricastinorum (Saint-Paul-Trois-Châteaux)
20. Autun
21. Avenches
22. Barton Court
23. Beaumont
24. Benevento
25. Bibracte
26. Boscoreale
27. Botromagno
28. Bourges
30. Budapest
31. Caesarea Mauretaniae (Cherchell)
32. Cambridge
33. Camí de la Platja del Cossis
34. Camp de les Lloses
35. Capua
36. Carnuntum
37. Carthage
38. Castel Malnome
39. Castellet de Bernabé
40. Chichester
41. Chiusi
42. Chantambre
43. Chartres
44. Chauvigny
45. Chianciano
47. Colchester
48. Cologne
50. Costebelle
53. Dietikon
55. Draria-el-Achour
58. Ellingen
59. Ensérune
60. Eschenz
62. Évreux
63. Ficana
64. Fidene
66. Fossa
67. Gailhan
69. Gravisca
70. Gubbio
71. Haïdra
72. Halatte
74. Herculaneum
75. Himera
76. Holborough
78. Illa d'en Reixac
79. Intercisa
81. Kef (El Kef)
83. Kempten
85. Langeais
86. Lankhills
87. Laquenexy
89. Lattes
90. Leptiminus (Lemta)
91. Lezoux
93. Lokri Epizephyri
94. London
95. Los Villares
96. Lugnano
97. Lyon
98. Lyons-la-Forêt
99. Mainz
100. Marseille
101. Martigny
102. Megara Hyblaea
104. Mérida
106. Metaponto
107. Metz
108. Mezzocorona
109. Misenum
110. Mozia
111. Narce
112. Nave
113. Neftenbach
114. Nepi
115. Nîmes
116. Nola
117. Nuits-Saint-Georges
118. Nyon
120. Oberwinterthur
121. Olèrdola
123. Osterburken
124. Ostia
125. Ouveillan
127. Paestum
129. Paris
130. Pâtural
131. Payerne
132. Pecs
136. Pithekoussai
137A. Poitiers
138. Pompeii
139. Portorecanati
140. Portus
141. Poundbury
142. Ptuj
143. Puech de Mus
144. Puig de la Nau
145. Pupput
146. Pyrgi
147. Ravenna
148. Rec de Ligno à Valros
149. Reculver
150. Rome
151. Rottweil
152. Rouen
153. Ruscino
154. Salces
155. Sallèles d'Aude
156. Salona
157. Sanguineto
158. Sarno
159. Satricum
160. Scarbantia
161. Sétif
162. Settecamini
163. Settefinestre
165. S'Illot des Porros
166. Soissons
167. Sommesous
168. Sontheim
169. Sopron
170. Sousse
171. South Shields
172. Stettfeld
173. Taranto
174. Tarquinia
175. Tavant
176. Tavaux
179. Thina
180. Tofting
181. Tusculum (Frascati)
182. Urbino
183. Vagnari
184. Velia
185. Verona
186. Verulamium (St. Albans)
187. Vindolanda
188. Vindonissa (Windisch)
189. Vrana
190. Vulci
191. Wattle Syke
192. Wederath-Belginum
193. Worms
194. Yewden
195. York
196. Yverdon-les-Bains

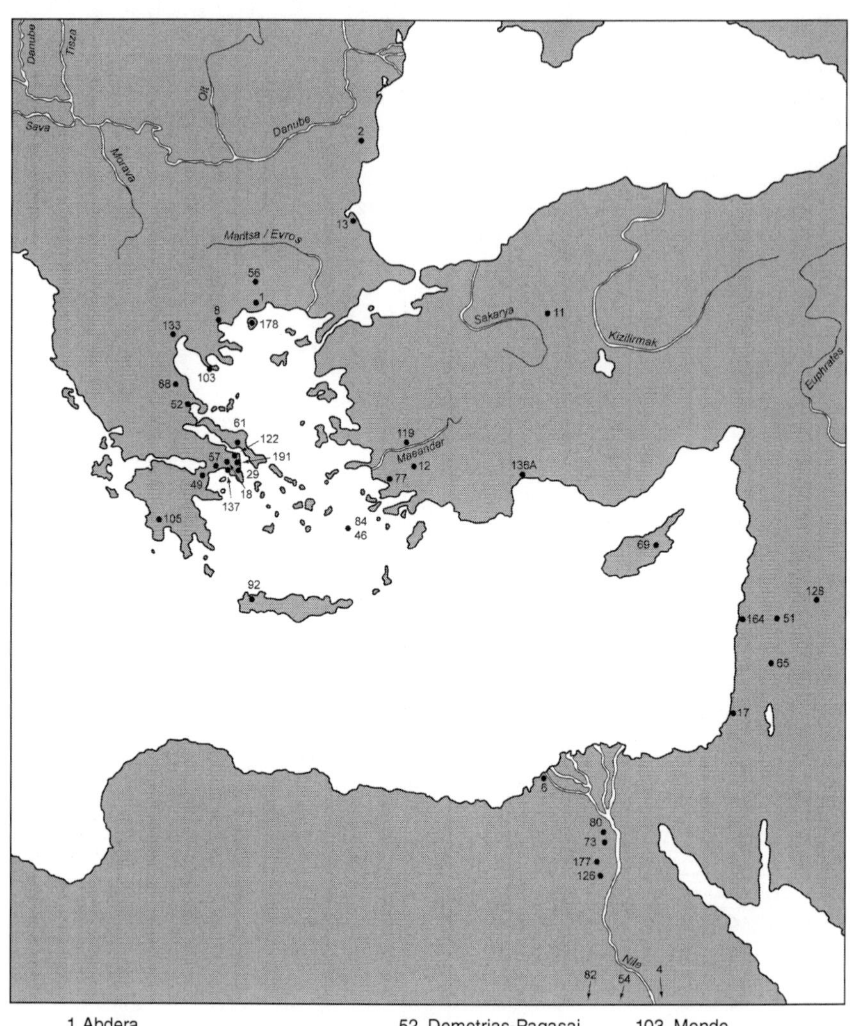

1. Abdera
2. Adamklissi
4. Akhmim
6. Alexandria
8. Amphipolis
11. Ankara
12. Aphrodisias
13. Apollonia Pontica (Sozopol)
17. Ashkelon
18. Athens
29. Brauron
46. Chora
49. Corinth
51. Daraya
52. Demetrias-Pagasai
54. Douch
56. Echinos
57. Eleusis
61. Eretria
65. Fiq
69. Golgoi
73. Hawara
77. Iasos
80. Karanis
82. Kellis
84. Kylindra
88. Larissa
92. Lissos
103. Mende
105. Messene
119. Nysa
122. Oropos
126. Oxyrhynchus
128. Palmyra
133. Pella
136A. Perge
137. Piraeus
164. Sidon
177. Tebtunis
178. Thasos

Map 2. Sites in the eastern Roman provinces, including pre-Roman sites discussed in the text.

Drawing: Irene de Luis.

1

Introduction

LOCATING CHILDREN IN THE ROMAN FAMILY

The Roman family has developed in the last quarter century as a distinct and dynamic research theme in ancient social history, an important impetus having been provided by the series of *Roman Family Conferences* initiated in 1981 by Beryl Rawson. Multi-authored, edited volumes emerged from these conferences in Australia, North America, and Europe dealing with various aspects of the family, generally with a focus on Rome and Italy and on historical sources.[1] Significant regional, chronological, methodological, and subject-specific advances in family studies in Classical antiquity have been made since then, to which Rawson's edited *Companion to Families in the Greek and Roman Worlds*, published in 2011, is testament.[2] More recently, the papers of a conference held in 2009 in Gothenburg, and published in 2012, not only present new and diverse topics on ancient families and households, but also aim to redefine approaches to the family in Greek and Roman antiquity in the twenty-first century.[3]

Whilst several of these publications have touched on aspects of children, few focus specifically on childhood, although the growing interest in children in Classical antiquity is apparent. Grete Lillehammer's call for archaeologists to see children "as human beings in their own right, albeit ones on small feet" has not gone unheeded.[4] Rawson's *Children and Childhood in Roman Italy*, published in 2003, stood out in its time, and the broader topic of childhood in the Roman world was pursued in 2006 by Christian Laes in his *Kinderen bei den Romeinen*, later translated into English as *Children in the Roman Empire: Outsiders Within*.[5] Several multi-authored books on children in the Greek and

[1] Rawson 1986 (republished 1992); Rawson 1991; Rawson and Weaver 1997; George 2005b.
[2] Rawson 2011.
[3] Harlow and Larsson Lovén 2012.
[4] Lillehammer 2000, 24. For a multi-period synthesis of the archaeology of childhood and a plea for researchers to investigate children as social actors, see Baxter 2005.
[5] Rawson 2003a; Laes 2011a.

the Roman worlds have since appeared.[6] The last *Roman Family Conference* volume published in 2010 was the first one in that series to have a greater emphasis on children, as is reflected in its title, *Children, Memory and Family Identity in Roman Culture.*[7]

The topic of child death and mortuary behaviour in antiquity has also been explored extensively, first in 2008 in a volume edited by a Spanish team with a rich and interesting collection of papers by international contributors, and later in 2010 and 2012 in three volumes of papers from conferences in Athens, Arles, and Alexandria, all part of the research programme *L'Enfant et la mort dans l'Antiquité.*[8] Furthermore, The Society for the Study of Childhood in the Past, founded in 2007 for historical research into childhood of all periods, has been influential in establishing not only a journal for multi-period studies, but also in facilitating workshops, meetings and publications, such as *Children, Spaces and Identity.*[9] The latter contains papers ranging from prehistory to the nineteenth century, primarily based on material from the Iberian peninsula.

Although research on children in Roman culture clearly is flourishing, the role and significance of the very youngest children are topics that are still very underdeveloped in archaeological and historical research. In this context, French-language scholarship has been trail-blazing with two volumes of essays accompanying a museum exhibition in Bourges and a conference in Fribourg devoted entirely to maternity, birth, and earliest childhood.[10] The most recent multi-authored volume on the health and death of Roman infants in Italy and beyond, edited by myself and Emma-Jayne Graham in 2014, takes a multidisciplinary approach to a variety of topics relevant to infancy, such as religion, feeding practices, disability, infanticide, and infant burial and funerary commemoration.[11]

ROMAN INFANCY: DEVELOPING A RESEARCH THEME

In 2011, Rawson heralded the study of birth and infancy in Classical antiquity as a "newly emerging field".[12] Two years later, Véronique Dasen, who has done much to further research into ancient childhood, also referred to the

[6] Cohen and Rutter 2007; Evans Grubbs, Parkin, and Bell 2013. See also Lillehammer 2010; Lally and Moore 2011; and Coşkunsu 2015 for a multi-period approach to the archaeology of childhood.

[7] Dasen and Späth 2010.

[8] Gusi et al. 2008; Guimier-Sorbets and Morizot 2010 ; Hermary and Dubois 2012; Nenna 2012.

[9] Sánchez Romero et al. 2015. See Crawford and Lewis 2008 on the society and its remit.

[10] Gourevitch et al. 2003; Dasen 2004.

[11] Carroll and Graham 2014.

[12] Rawson 2011, 5.

topic as "un nouveau champ de recherches".[13] My book is situated firmly in this developing field of research. Children who had only just been born or were in their first year of life were rarely mentioned in Roman literary sources, and, when they were, they could be referred to in dismissive terms. According to Cicero, for example, people who complained about dying before their time (*mors immatura*) felt that the loss of an infant in the cradle could be tolerated without protest, because such youngsters had not yet "tasted the sweets of life" or been able to conceive of a future.[14] For Seneca, talking down the death of a child was the best way to deal with such loss. His consolatory advice to his contemporaries was to consider children as being merely on loan, their longevity being determined by fickle fate; they should be remembered, but not mourned.[15]

Such letters, dialogues, and philosophical treatises have had an adverse effect on our modern understanding of ancient parent–infant relationships, and they have even helped to generate misleading assumptions. Roman texts have prompted historians to claim that Roman parents had little emotional attachment to their offspring, or that the Romans had culturally ascribed notions of infants as non-persons, placing a "relatively low social value... on small children".[16] The Roman father has been portrayed as a severe figure who inspected his newborn child, lifting the infant off the ground if he decided to let it live, although this harsh version of the circumstances surrounding new life appears much more to be a myth propagated by modern scholars.[17]

Current understanding of infant death has led to statements such as "infants rarely received proper burial in Roman times" or "deceased infants were often not even buried properly".[18] This notion has been dispelled clearly by my own research on Roman infant death and burial in Italy.[19] Other scholars have flagged up the under-representation of graves and funerary monuments for babies under one year.[20] The Romans are said to have viewed "children in the first month or two of life" as "not yet really human beings", because they were sometimes buried in and around settlements, rather than in the communal cemetery.[21] Even more negative is the claim that the Romans exhibited "an indifference to burying children, especially infants, carefully", suggesting that they found expressions of grief for the very young inappropriate and irrelevant.[22]

But the pertinent Roman texts were written by elite men in the empire's capital whose Stoic philosophical views were an endorsement of public self-control and composure in the face of adversity and loss. Such writers paid

[13] Dasen 2013a, 2. [14] Cicero, *Tusculan Disputations* 1.39.
[15] Seneca, *Moral Essays* 99; Seneca, *Consolation to Marcia* 6.21. [16] Dixon 1988, 104.
[17] B. D. Shaw 2001a. [18] Sallares et al. 2004, 319; Krause 2011, 642.
[19] Carroll 2011a and 2012a. [20] McWilliam 2001, 79; Hänninen 2005, 54.
[21] Wileman 2005, 77. [22] Russell 1985, 49.

comparatively little attention to newborns and babies because they were of little relevance to the agendas of the socio-political elite. It would be inadvisable to accept these texts as an accurate reflection of what Romans of both sexes and of all social classes and geographic origins felt about their children, or to believe that they convey public opinion. Moreover, the Roman Empire was vast, incorporating many ethnic groups, regional histories, and social systems, and very different practices could exist even within a shared overarching political body. Roman literature on aspects of infancy and society's perception of infants generally reflects only the attitudes of the (male) elite in Rome. It does not take into account that cultural differences might contribute to widely varying responses to infants in a geographic, historical, and social sense.

Of course, with perhaps as many as 30 per cent of babies dying within the first month of life in the Roman period, it is easy to assume that parents rarely formed close bonds with the newest members of their family. High infant mortality is cited as a reason why Roman parents might not have invested emotionally in the high-risk gamble of reproduction, the supposed indifference with which they dealt with infant death having been a protective mechanism against loss and sorrow.[23] This is to take liberties with the ancient evidence. In regions of the world where still today neonatal mortality rates are high and stillbirths remain common, few people would automatically claim that modern parents in those regions are indifferent to infant death, but they feel free to make this assertion regarding ancient parents.[24] High infant mortality cannot fail to have an effect on the family and society as a whole, and superficial coping mechanisms may simply mask the deep emotional trauma of infant loss. In the Roman world, as now, the death of a baby will have triggered a range of responses, and bereaved mothers and fathers may well have had an experience that they found transformative, even if we cannot always recognize them.[25]

I neither have children of my own, nor had I ever seen a premature baby or one that might be too weak to survive after birth. For the purposes of researching this book, I wanted to understand what being premature means physically, how parents deal emotionally with conditions and circumstances that threaten the lives of their newborn infants, and to reflect on human responses to infant death. In 2013, Simon Clark, Head of School for Paediatrics in Yorkshire and Humber, allowed me to visit the neonatal unit of the Jessop Wing of the Royal Hallamshire Hospital in Sheffield. Many of these

[23] Bradley 1986, 220. This is clearly still a popular notion, as witnessed by the statement by Pascal-Emmanuel Gobry in the April 2015 online edition of *The Week*: "High infant mortality rates created a cultural pressure to not develop emotional attachments to children" (http://theweek.com/articles/551027/how-christianity-invented-children).

[24] Zupan 2005, 2047; Cacciatore and Bushfield 2007, 61.

[25] Lovell 1997; Riches and Dawson 1997.

babies had been born at less than thirty weeks gestation, which, in Roman times, would have been incompatible with survival. Some of them, after my visit, will have survived premature birth and the associated health complications, others probably not, but most parents I witnessed were putting on a brave face and hoping for the best, even against all odds. Some just looked numb with grief. I was shocked at how viscerally distressing I found the experience of seeing such tiny bodies and so much vulnerability; no amount of cultural conditioning or cool academic reasoning prepared me for this. It seemed to me a natural reaction and a human experience to be so distraught, and I found it difficult to believe that Roman parents could have reacted less naturally to the illness and death of small, helpless beings.

It made me wonder whether we are hard-wired as humans to react physically and emotionally to new life, the distress of infants, and the loss of young life, now and in the past. And scientific studies appear to support this. A recent MRI scan study of maternal brain activation in response to infants either crying or smiling showed highly elaborate neural mechanisms mediating maternal love and complex behaviours for protectiveness.[26] Another scientific study suggested that caring for children awakens a parenting network in the brain, and that the neural underpinnings of maternal instinct can be developed by anyone who chooses to be a parent, putting fathers also in the picture as sensitive caregivers.[27] Furthermore, it has been shown that parents experience a whole range of emotional reactions to infant death, including depression, anxiety, interpersonal sensitivity, and aggression, and these can last for years after the death of the infant.[28] Mothers and fathers may grieve in different ways, with men possibly experiencing constraints in resolving grief because of their masculine role expectations, but, despite cultural and social variations, the loss of an infant remains one of the most painful events in parents' lives.[29] This pertains as much to the loss of an infant shortly after birth as it does to the experience of losing a baby through miscarriage or stillbirth.[30]

A month after my visit to the neonatal unit, I attended the annual memorial service at a church in Sheffield for families who had lost babies at various stages. The church was full of people (parents, grandparents, siblings) who had been coming to this event for years, and it was clear that the experience of losing a baby still deeply affected them all. The pain and sorrow was tangible. Both the hospital visit and the memorial service gave me a rare insight into neonatal birth, death, and medical care, as well as the ways in which families coped with grief.

[26] Noriuchi et al. 2008. [27] Abraham et al. 2014.
[28] Rogers et al. 2008; Murphy and Thomas 2013; Murphy and Shevlin 2014.
[29] Cordell and Thomas 1990; Riches and Dawson 1997; Thompson 1997.
[30] Lovell 1997; Turton et al. 2006.

The coping strategies of parents and families in the face of adversity, illness, or death, of course, will differ, depending on social context, cultural environment, and period. Nancy Scheper-Hughes's work in the 1960s and 1980s in the shantytown of Alto do Cruzeiro in Timbaúba is particularly useful in exploring coping mechanisms to deal with frequent infant death in twentieth-century Brazil.[31] The behaviour of mothers in this context might help us also to understand and contextualize Roman social reactions, especially the restraint in grieving publicly as seemingly recommended by Roman authors. In Alto, in the face of extreme poverty and violence, and with an infant mortality rate of up to 40 per cent (higher than the estimate of the Roman period), the apparent resignation of mothers to "too much loss, too much death" masks the symptoms of depression resulting from the death of their babies: "a continual exposure to trauma obliterated rage and protest, it also minimized attachment so as to diminish sorrow".[32] Scheper-Hughes notes that mother love emerges strongly if newborns survive the most perilous beginnings and begin to develop strength and vitality; these are the children worth investing in emotionally and physically, because they are thought to have a future. The mothers of Alto simply cannot allow themselves to become overly attached immediately to their newborns, because the grief at repeated loss would otherwise become overwhelming.

Perhaps in the Roman world, as in Alto, there was the recognition that not all of one's children could be expected to live—Bradley calls it "a foreseeable loss"—but that does not mean that Romans did not find early death very difficult and that grief and loss were not felt acutely.[33] The responses of Roman parents to infant death were conditioned by social expectations and circumstances that helped them cope when death occurred.[34] Moses Finley is certain that the intensity and duration of parental responses in the Roman past were not like our modern ones, but he knows of "no way to measure or even to identify the differences".[35] Paradoxically, although Roman Stoic treatises on how to react to the death of infants and very young children are sometimes interpreted as true reflections of Roman parental indifference, the fact that they were written in the first place to console bereaved parents rather highlights how people struggled emotionally to come to terms with their loss.[36]

In fact, as I argue in this book, a nuanced reading of the archaeological remains and the written sources help clarify the relationship between the daily realities of and the literary rhetoric about earliest childhood. This approach

[31] Scheper-Hughes 1989. [32] Scheper-Hughes 2013, 27. [33] Bradley 1986, 220.

[34] George 2000, 204. A novel explanation for the so-called regulation of funerary rituals for infants was put forward by Krauße 1998, 342: with high child mortality, such regulations prevented parents being driven to financial ruin.

[35] Finley 1981, 159.

[36] See the valuable discussion on Stoic ideas of parenthood and grieving in Reydams-Schils 2005, 134–41.

allows us to recognize the investment by the family and society in general in the health, well-being, and future of the very young, even while still *in utero*. It also enables us to differentiate accurately between public and private manifestations of grief at the death of children. The displays of mourning so frowned upon by Stoic society were public, performative, and competitive in the context of the elite, whereas private expressions of genuine loss and grief felt by all social classes, including the poor, are recognizable in the choices they made regarding the treatment of their dead infants and young children and the material culture given to them in death. The study of infant burials allows us also to contextualize and put into perspective Roman legal texts recommending the length of mourning periods for various age groups. They state that a child who lived for a year should be mourned for a month, but for any infant younger than this there would be no mourning period at all, seemingly supporting the notion that Roman society assigned no value at all to its youngest children.[37] But the archaeological evidence makes it clear that there was a significant difference between *public* mourning (referenced in legal texts) and *private* expressions of grief (recognizable in the burial assemblages).

The evidence from archaeology, funerary epigraphy, and material culture marshalled in this study dispels the long-held notion that the very youngest infants were insignificant beings without a social persona whose lives were treated with indifference. It is, of course, difficult to define what a person is and at what age personhood commences. As recently as 2013, medical ethics researchers argued controversially that "both a fetus and a newborn certainly are human beings and potential persons, but neither is a 'person' in the sense of 'subject of a moral right to life'".[38] On my train journey to work on 5 December 2014, I was struck by the headline in the *Metro* newspaper in which a child left disabled, due to her mother's drinking during pregnancy, was refused compensation by the court, "because the girl was 'not a person' at the time". Clearly our own perception of personhood is not fixed, although there may be differences between private and legal views.

For the ancient Roman world, there are various indications in the material record that infants within the first year of their life—and even within the first weeks and months—were invested with identities and a persona of various kinds. Here I would like to flag up just three examples of material culture, to be discussed in more depth in the relevant sections of the book, that give us

[37] Ulpian, *Fontes Iuris Romani Anteiustiniani* (*FIRA*) 2.536; Paulus, *Opinions* 1.21.13; Pliny, *Natural History* 7.16.68, 72.

[38] Giubilini and Minerva 2013. The article elicited many responses, as to be expected, including a paper by Di Nucci (2013) who makes a case for a relevant moral difference between foetuses and newborns. One of the authors, Francesca Minerva, even received death threats after the publication of her paper: http://www.ibtimes.com/dr-francesca-minerva-after-birth-abortion-article-defended-after-death-threats-419638.

insight into the developing and invested personhood of children younger than one year old. Terracotta *ex votos* of swaddled babies that were commonly dedicated in central Italian sanctuaries from the fourth to the second centuries BC, for example, reflect the specific anxiety felt by parents in the first two or three months of an infant's life (Fig. 1.1). Once the baby had successfully negotiated this dangerous postnatal period and was released from its swaddling bands, its effigy as an individual in society and in the religious

Fig. 1.1 Terracotta votive infant in swaddling clothes from a sanctuary in Italy.
Photo: Allard Pierson Museum, Amsterdam.

community was dedicated by its relieved parents in gratitude for divine assistance.[39] Another illuminating artefact is the gravestone of an infant boy in Spain, L. Helvius Lupus, whose epitaph records him as being eight months old, a Roman citizen, and an official inhabitant of the Roman town of Emerita Augusta.[40] As an *Emeritensis*, therefore, this very young child already had a civic identity as a Roman citizen and a corporate identity as a registered member of this community. My third example is a miniature *gladius*, deposited in the late first or early second century AD with an infant between three and six months of age in the cemetery at Tavant in Roman Gaul (see Fig. 9.1).[41] The *gladius* is only nine centimetres long, and is a miniature version of the short fighting sword included in the kit of an adult male Roman soldier. The small size of the *gladius* here is relative to the tender age of the infant, but its inclusion in the burial indicates that a masculine identity had already been fixed for this very young child.

I am not naively claiming that *all* children were *always* wanted by Roman parents; some mothers and fathers, for example, would not have been able to afford to feed a constantly expanding family and may have been reluctant to take on more responsibilities, although when a child died at a very tender age and was said to have been "most desired" (*desiderantissima*), the parent's emotional attachment is very clear.[42] Nor am I claiming that infants, for one reason or another, might not have been rejected, abandoned, or even outright killed, a theme which runs through some genres of Latin literature and which I discuss at some length later in the book. Neither do I want to ignore the fact that children could suffer abuse or work as child labourers, although at least the very young would not have been suitable for the latter. What I oppose is the uncritical assumption that high infant mortality necessarily conditioned Roman parents not to invest in the early life of their children or to view them, or their deaths, with indifference. Indeed, Margaret King concludes that Roman parents certainly were not unconcerned about the welfare of infant children, and that attitudes and behavioural patterns "were in general child-oriented".[43]

To understand what very young children experienced or how they were treated in their short lives, and precisely how risky the first weeks and months of life really were, the skeletal remains of infants are an immensely valuable resource which can be read. Infant remains not only shed light on

[39] Graham 2013 and 2014; see also Derks 2014.

[40] *L'Année Épigraphique* (*AE*) 1965, 298; Rothenberg and Blanco-Freijeiro 1981, 18, fig. 3; Edmondson et al. 2001, 139–41, cat. no. 10, pls. 10A–C.

[41] Riquier and Salé, 2006, 34–6, figs. 34–6.

[42] This is expressed in an epitaph commemorating Eutychia from Rome who was one year and an illegible number of months old: *Corpus Inscriptionum Latinarum* (*CIL*) VI.17426.

[43] King 1996.

Fig. 1.2 The author with the skeleton of a premature infant (thirty weeks' gestation), from an historical reference collection curated by the Department of Archaeology, University of Sheffield.

Photo: Petra Verlinden.

the life of children and the conditions under which they lived, but they also, in a very visible way, impress on us the vulnerability and delicate nature of infants of the tenderest age (Fig. 1.2). In the last decade, important advances have been made in the bioarchaeology of children of all ages and in different periods of antiquity, although there are still limitations to the study of human remains.[44] For example, there is no truly reliable way to sex skeletons of individuals below the age of puberty, so that we cannot be certain if infants and very young children were male or female based only on their bones. Nevertheless, these children, as I hope to show, often appear to have been given a gendered identity during their brief lives which can be reflected in the choice of objects that accompanied them in burial. Scientific studies of children's skeletons from archaeological and forensic contexts shed light on the health, disease, and physical development of children during different periods of the life-course, in different regions and social environments. A particular area of bioarchaeological research pertaining to earliest childhood is the age at which Roman infants began to be weaned off mother's milk and how this might have affected growth and the health of individuals who lived into adulthood.[45]

The skeletal data, however, are not always presented in published reports in a way that allows a nuanced understanding of infant mortality in the first year of life, especially when all children under the age of six or seven years are grouped together in age-at-death profiles for particular cemetery populations, rather than being presented as pre-term, perinatal, neonatal, and infant up to the age of one year.[46] Fortunately, however, there is an increasing body of published data that presents more precise ages for the skeletons examined, and these publications are important for mapping out the circumstances and conditions of earliest life.

In antiquity, pregnancy was measured in lunar months, with an infant being born in the tenth lunar month, i.e. at full-term or nine months in conventional modern calculations. For the purposes of this book, I have adopted Sandra Wheeler's definitions for the terms "foetal", "perinate", and "infant".[47] She defines a foetus as an individual aged under thirty-six weeks' gestation, a perinate as an individual aged around birth (thirty-nine to forty weeks' gestation), and an infant as an individual aged from around birth to one year.[48] For those infants who are no older than one month, I use the term newborn. These are biological ages, but a variety of words were used for children in a cultural sense that perhaps are not closely related to the biological ages.[49] Some of these

[44] Baker et al. 2005; M. E. Lewis 2007; Gowland and Redfern 2010; Fox 2012 ; Redfern and Gowland 2012.

[45] Katzenberg et al. 1996; Dupras et al. 2001; Prowse et al. 2008; Keenleyside et al. 2009; Powell et al. 2014.

[46] Scattarella et al. 2006; Catalano et al. 2012; Minozzi et al. 2012.

[47] Wheeler 2012, 219.

[48] There are other definitions: Redfern 2007, 176: pre-term, less than 37 weeks old; full-term, 37–42 weeks; infant, more than 42 weeks old and up to 3 years old. Lazer 2009: foetal applies to any time prior to birth; infant applies to the period from birth to 3 years of age. For Beaumont 2012, 38, an infant is a child up to the third year of life.

[49] For a discussion on the variability and different definitions of terms relating to childhood, see Halcrow and Tayles 2008.

words express the small size or incompleteness of an individual, such as *infans*, *impubes*, *puer*, *puella*, *parvus*, *pupus*, and *pusus*; other terms are associated with age or ancestry, such as *filius*, *gnatus*, *natus*, *nepos*, and *stirps*.[50] None of them is obviously related to an infant specifically in his or her first year of life, or to what we could call a baby; in fact, *infans*, meaning literally someone who is not speaking or is not able to speak, referred to all children up to the age of seven.[51] As Mark Golden notes for Classical Athens, stages of childhood were not delineated by single words, even though artists and writers showed an awareness of infancy and other stages in the child's life-course.[52] The same is true of the Romans. Neither does the lack of a Latin word for baby or infant in its first year mean that this phase of life was not appreciated as something special. In fact, the first year of life was marked by many milestones, from the naming day at eight or nine days, the official registration of birth by the thirtieth day, the release from swaddling bands at forty to sixty days, and the beginning of teething at six months, to the achievement of the child's first birthday. All these milestones were associated with the successful negotiation of the early life-course, the precarious nature of which would have been all too obvious to Roman families.

AIM AND ORGANIZATION OF THIS STUDY

This book aims to fill a lacuna on the subject of infancy and earliest childhood, isolating the age group of the under one-year-olds because of the very particular historical circumstances that affected this period in the life cycle and attitudes toward it. The book integrates archaeological evidence, material culture, and the iconography of infancy with social and cultural history, an approach for which this subject matter is especially well suited. The burial evidence assessed in many places in the book gives us a particular lens through which to explore such issues. The material culture is privileged in a way that brings new insights to the debate and raises new questions, breaking with the older tradition of using material culture to support ideas taken from primary texts. Far from disregarding the texts, I have included quotes from them when they are immediately relevant to the material culture presented in the book, and this pertains especially to Greek and Roman medical texts. But the written sources do not dominate, nor do they simply provide the background noise for

[50] Kepartová 1984. Parkin 2010, 97–101, discusses the ancient Greek and Latin names for children.

[51] This is the equivalent of the Greek *paidion*, according to Golden 2015, 11. He points out that the Greeks had a word for the newborn—*brephos*—but later the word could mean a child up to the age of six.

[52] Golden 2015, 11.

the material remains. Instead, I have saved the relevant and influential primary texts for Chapter 9, where they are discussed in their own right. The wider chronological and geographic framing of the Roman evidence, roughly the fourth century BC to the fourth century AD in all regions throughout the empire in which evidence has survived, makes the point that the Romans are not just about Rome, or indeed Italy, but a far wider world in which cultural influences were reflected in the way infants and young children were raised, socialized, cared for, buried, and mourned.

In order to contextualize and set the scene for the Roman evidence, and to understand regional and cultural trends that may have continued to influence how infants were treated in the Roman period, Chapter 2 surveys burial data and a range of material evidence for the youngest children in the pre-Roman Iron Age and early Roman period in and around the Mediterranean, from about the eighth century BC. Chapter 3 evaluates skeletal studies and Roman medical treatises to gain insight into pregnancy, birth, and differing weaning practices and regimes of care. Furthermore, it examines artefactual and religious evidence to understand how Roman parents sought divine assistance to safeguard maternal health and ensure the survival of their children. Chapter 4 explores the things with which babies were surrounded in life, and identifies a material culture of infancy, such as toys, feeding bottles, apotropaic jewellery, and swaddling clothes by evaluating artefacts of various types and materials. Chapter 5 looks into images of infants and very young children, particularly those that portray them in the social context of the Roman family and extended household. It also explores the ways in which Roman and barbarian children are contrasted and symbolically charged with meaning in public art.

The next three chapters focus primarily on Roman funerary evidence. Chapter 6 investigates data from Roman cemeteries across the empire in order to consider infant mortality and to investigate the location of infant burials, either within or outside the communal burial grounds. It also discusses intramural burial and evaluates the evidence for practices such as infanticide and infant exposure. Chapter 7 attempts to gain insight into the family's investment in and attachment to infants, as expressed in funerary ritual. It explores the various ways in which the bodies of dead infants were treated and prepared for burial and the deposition of an array of grave goods that accompanied infants. The focus of Chapter 8 is the diversity in the funerary commemoration of the youngest members of Roman society, the portrayal of infants in funerary art and inscriptions being a means by which the status, gender, ethnicity, and citizenship of the commemorators could be negotiated and expressed for contemporary society and posterity.

After discussing a wide range of different types of physical evidence, Chapter 9 brings together Roman literary sources, such as philosophical treatises, private letters, legal documents, and poems, to compare and contrast the messages conveyed by elite male texts with the archaeological, pictorial, and artefactual evidence for infants in Roman society. The literature is, thereby, contextualized within a larger and more diverse framework, and by privileging the picture created by the material culture new insights can be gained into the context of the texts and their potential for a more nuanced understanding of social and behavioural patterns that might have influenced relationships between adults and their infants.

2

Infants and Children in Pre-Roman Mediterranean Societies

INFANT DEATH AND BURIAL

In his study of early Iron Age cemeteries in the Abruzzo region of Italy, Vincenzo D'Ercole claims that infants between six months and a year of age were at "a 'critical' age" before they had "been received into the community of adults".[1] His claim is based on the fact that infants in this age group in the Abruzzo were not buried with grave goods, unlike older children and adults. But once they had completed their first year of life, according to D'Ercole, children assumed a social identity and fully entered the adult community, at which point they were buried in the same manner as all others in the community. His conclusions suggest a social unimportance of the youngest children in Iron Age societies in this region. In a similar vein, Christiane Sourvinou-Inwood argues that small children in ancient Greece had no social persona and no relationships beyond their closest family, their deaths having had an impact only on the family and not on society in general.[2] Bernard Dedet goes a step further, claiming that newborns and infants in southern Gaul in the Iron Age were not considered human in contemporary society because of their mode of deposition at death: naked, in the foetal position, and excluded from the communal cemetery.[3] But are these claims truly valid for these particular regions or those further afield?

One way to explore how people reacted to the death of their infants is to assess the mortuary treatment of them, and it is here that we have a broad evidential base for south-west Europe and the western, central, and eastern Mediterranean regions. It is possible to recognize two broad cultural groups that responded in different ways to infant death and burial from the eighth to the second centuries BC: the cultures that buried their babies in the buildings of their settlements and excluded them from the communal cemetery (Gaul,

[1] D'Ercole 1999, 38–9. [2] Sourvinou-Inwood 1983, 42, 44–5.
[3] Dedet 2008, 159; and 2013, 44.

Spain, Britain), and the cultures that included their infants in the cemeteries with other age groups in the community (Greece, Italy).

The archaeological evidence does not allow any sweeping statements about infant mortality rates for these periods or regions, and it is very difficult to determine with any degree of certainty what the situation might have been. This may be explained by possible differences in regional location, climate, lifestyles, and social organization, but it also may be related to the under-representation of infantile skeletons at some sites. For example, in an Iron Age necropolis at S'Illot des Porros on Majorca, infants under the age of one year were virtually absent, very likely because these children were buried somewhere other than the communal cemetery.[4] The opposite extreme of over-representation is apparent at Abdera in northern Greece, where infants under the age of one accounted for 66 per cent of the burials in the Ammolofos-Koum Tepe cemetery between 650 and 570 BC.[5] Clearly, excavated cemeteries will not necessarily be an accurate reflection of the number of infants under one who died in a community, as there may be many factors responsible for their presence or absence in this context. Based on other general data from pre-industrial populations, however, the infant mortality rate might be estimated to range from roughly 25 per cent to between 30 and 50 per cent.[6]

Location and Method of Disposal: Cultural Differences

In Languedoc and Provence in southern Gaul, the deposition of newborns and infants under the age of one in communal cemeteries is a rarity in the Iron Age, with only 0.3–0.4 per cent representation in the relevant cemeteries.[7] With a possible 25 per cent mortality rate for children up to the age of one year, this represents only a tiny percentage of this vulnerable cohort; if infant mortality was higher, the attested percentage is even more minimal. Although cremation was the primary burial rite for older children and adults from the fifth to the second centuries BC, all infants younger than a year were inhumed.[8] Furthermore, these are all infants older than six months, and there is also no evidence for any separate areas in cemeteries just for babies.[9] If burial in the cemetery is indicative of membership in the community, the rarity of babies in this context may indicate that the youngest children were not considered part of the wider community. However, there is a sense of belonging at family level,

[4] Alesan et al. 1999, 290, 298. It is also possible that in the 1960s they were not recognized, according to Alesan et al. 1999, 293–4.

[5] Kallintzi and Papaikonomou 2010, 133.

[6] Alesan et al. 1999, 291; Dedet, Gruat, and Marty 2001, 149.

[7] Dedet 2012, 151.

[8] Dedet and Schwaller 2010.

[9] Dedet 2008, 146, 152, 163–5, figs. 3, 8.

because sometimes infants were buried with other individuals, almost always with a female adult who may well have been the mother.[10]

The familial connection is also indicated by the fact that children under the age of one appear regularly within and around family dwellings and in workshop areas in settlements, where they were inhumed in simple pits and, in very rare cases, in a ceramic urn.[11] These are always located near the walls of structures. About three quarters of those known died at full term; the rest were only eight or nine lunar months of age, the equivalent of seven or eight gestational months.[12] Foetuses less than six gestational months are extremely rare in the archaeological record, but they do exist. A double burial of foetuses, possibly twins, only four or five lunar months old, at Lattes in southern Gaul in the early first century BC is a good example here.[13] Also, in central Switzerland and Britain, very young infants were interred in and around domestic dwellings in settlements, indicating that the custom was rather widespread in northern and western Europe at this time.[14]

Occasionally, as at Lattes, these infant burials tended to concentrate in certain rooms within the houses.[15] In the *oppidum* at Gailhan in Languedoc, ten infants ranging from premature to six months were buried in the last quarter of the fifth century in shallow pits in the courtyards of houses, and a further twelve or thirteen were deposited here in the early fourth century (Fig. 2.1).[16] With five domestic dwellings recognizable, Dedet, Duday, and Tillier estimate that each household would have consisted of a nuclear family

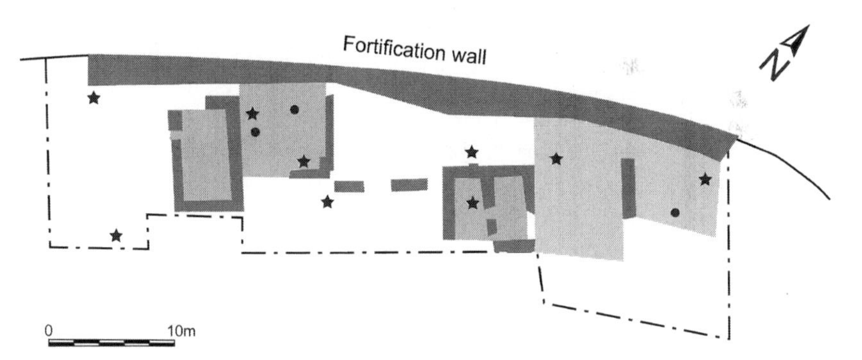

Fig. 2.1 Plan of houses in the *oppidum* at Gailhan with infant burials, fourth century BC. Dots = skeletons; stars = bones.

Drawing: Irene de Luis.

[10] Dedet 2008, 153.
[11] Dedet 2008, 156, fig. 6: Lattes tomb 4.
[12] Dedet 2008, 148.
[13] Dedet 2008, 157; Dedet and Schwaller 2010, 279.
[14] Curdy et al. 1993, 143–4, fig. 13; Fabre 1995; Tibbetts 2008.
[15] Dedet 2008, 150–1.
[16] Dedet et al. 1991.

of mother, father, and seven or eight children, two of which would have died as infants (and were buried in the houses) and two of which died before the age of twelve (and were buried elsewhere).[17] At the southern Gaulish *oppidum* of Puech de Mus in the second half of the fifth century, premature infants and newborns were buried not only in houses, but also, and more frequently, in shallow pits in or around buildings in which metalworking took place, as indicated by hearths, finished and unfinished iron and bronze artefacts, metal scrap, and crucibles.[18] As in all other cases mentioned here, these burials are located close to the walls of structures.

In the neighbouring eastern Pyrenees, in Catalunya, there is further evidence for the burial of perinatal infants in domestic and workshop spaces.[19] At the *oppidum* of Illa d'en Reixac, for instance, at least nine perinatal infants were buried in the fourth century BC in pits in the floors of houses; only one of them was in a container consisting of the base of an amphora.[20] At Olèrdola, a nearby settlement occupied from the fourth to the early second centuries BC, at least eleven babies of this age were buried in a row of structures used for tanning and metal working (Fig. 2.2).[21] All of them were interred in shallow pits under the floors and close to the base of the walls of the buildings. A pair of twins were buried together with three other perinatal infants in room UH4. Further south, at Puig de la Nau and Castellet de Bernabé on the east coast of Spain, infant burials in domestic dwellings also are attested.[22] At the latter site, a relatively wide range of ages is represented, with one premature infant, five perinatal infants, three babies only weeks old, and two children between four and six months of age being present.[23] Whilst most infants were buried in pits, a baby five to seven months old was interred in the fourth century BC in a painted ceramic urn and accompanied by various objects, including a miniature axe head, a little bell, bronze rings, and a sea shell.[24]

These, and other infant burials in houses, have been interpreted as potential ritual burials, and even as building sacrifices, but such theories fail to convince, as there is nothing about these burials that looks different from apparently normal infant burials with grave goods relevant for this age group anywhere else.[25] In fact, all the small trinkets found with the infant at Castellet de Bernabé were either pierced or made so that they could be strung from a cord or string, suggesting that these are simply apotropaic amulets given to the baby in life. Neither is evidence of ritual activity or domestic cult in the same buildings as the infant burials a reliable indication that the two are connected,

[17] Dedet et al. 1991, 95, 97.
[18] Dedet et al. 2001.
[19] Subirà and Molist 2008, 374–6.
[20] Agustí et al. 2008, 118–20.
[21] Subirà and Molist 2008, 365–74.
[22] Guérin et al. 1989; Chapa-Brunet 2008, 622–8.
[23] Guérin et al. 1989; Chapa-Brunet 2008, 626.
[24] Chapa-Brunet 2008, 626–7, fig. 5; Muriel and Playà 2008, 647, fig. 2; López-Bertran and Vives-Ferrándiz 2015, 84–5, fig. 5.
[25] Subirà and Molist 2008, 380–1; Ruiz 2013, 1001, 1003–4.

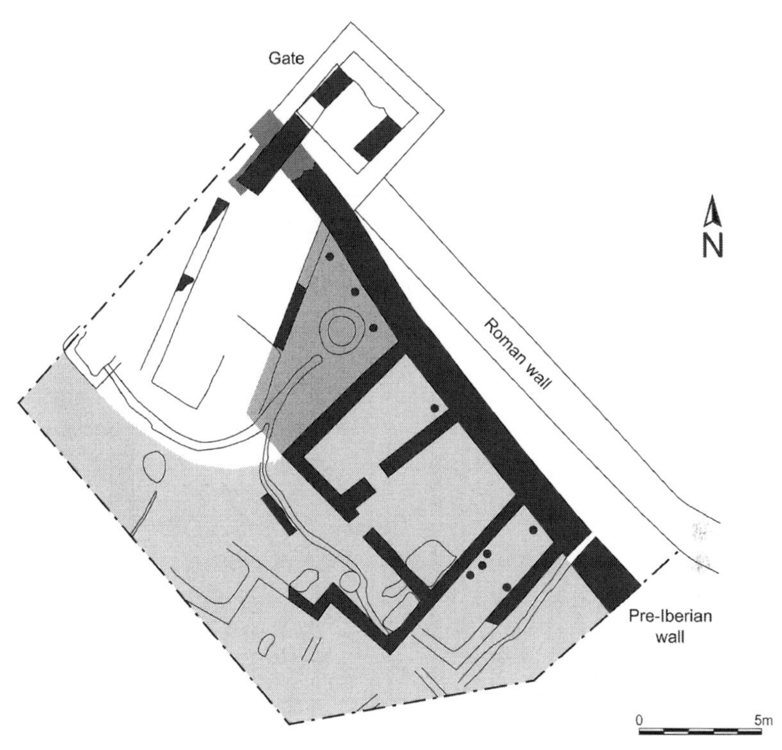

Fig. 2.2 Plan of houses in the settlement at Olèrdola with infant burials (black dots), fourth to early second century BC.
Drawing: Irene de Luis.

especially when votive deposits and infants are found in different rooms, as in Building B at Camp de les Lloses near Barcelona.[26]

Against the background of the burial of infants typically in settlements in these regions, and particularly in Languedoc and Provence, the Greek colony of Marseille on the southern Gaulish coast stands out as an anomaly (see Table 1).[27] Here, between the fourth and the middle of the second centuries BC, infants under the age of one year were not buried in houses, but inhumed in the communal cemetery in the Sainte-Barbe quarter of the modern city, along with adults and other individuals of all age categories. In addition to that, the custom of burying babies in pots in Greek Marseille contrasts sharply with the rarity of infant burials in ceramic containers elsewhere in Iron-Age Gaul.[28] The custom of pot burial, *enchytrismos*, appears in Greece and in the Greek eastern Mediterranean around the eighth and early seventh centuries BC, a

[26] Ruiz 2013, 1001. [27] Moliner et al. 2003.
[28] Moliner et al. 2003, 53; Dedet and Schwaller 2010.

time during which infants, who earlier had been buried in houses and settlements, increasingly began to be interred in communal cemeteries. Morris and Mazarakis Ainian relate this change in the formal and visible burial of a whole cross-section of the population to the beginning of the Greek city state and the principle of citizenship, and they see it in conjunction with the separation of public and private spaces.[29] But the change in burial location must also mean that the very youngest children were now acknowledged members of the community and shared that social link in death. From the end of the eighth to the end of the fifth centuries BC in Athens, for example, the number of infant burials rose dramatically, reflecting a change in social and political attitudes towards infants and small children in the Greek city state.[30]

From the late eighth to early seventh centuries BC, *enchytrismos* burials for infants and young children appear in Greek communal cemeteries also in Eretria in Euboea; at Mende, an Eretrian colony on the Chalkidiki peninsula; at Abdera, an Ionian colony on the Thracian seaboard; at Oropos in Euboea; and at Kylindra on the island of Astypalaia, to name but a few.[31] *Enchytrismos* burials also are widespread in the Greek-settled regions of southern Italy, for example at Agrigento on Sicily, and on their fringes at sites such as Botromagno in Puglia (Fig. 2.3).[32] Between the seventh and fifth centuries, 55 per cent of the burials of neonates at Himera on Sicily were *enchytrismos* burials, with a further 11 per cent of *enchytrismos* burials belonging to infants up to the age of one.[33] The infant burials at Marseille, a western 'outpost' of Greek social and cultural customs, fit in very well with this trend. The vessels used as ceramic funerary containers in *enchytrismos* burials differ regionally, from local wine amphorae at Marseille to storage jars (*pithoi*, *stamnoi*) and water vessels (*hydriai*) at Agrigento.[34] At Oropos, infants were buried in reused one-handled jugs, whereas children one to five years of age were placed in coarse storage jars, *pithoi*, or at the bottom of cist and shaft graves, indicating differential treatment according to age group.[35] An even wider range of ceramic containers is in evidence in the sixth and fifth centuries BC in Himera, where locally manufactured *chytrai* (cooking pots), *pithoi*, *hydriai*, and

[29] Morris 1987; Mazarakis Ainian 2010, 75. See also Langdon 2007, 173.

[30] Houby Nielsen 2000, 155.

[31] Eretria: Crielaard 1998; Mende: Vokotopoulou 1994; Abdera: Kallintzi and Papaikonomou 2010; Oropos: Vlachou 2007; Astypalaia: Hillson 2009; Michalaki-Kollia 2010 and 2013.

[32] Whitehouse et al. 2000, 69–71, figs. 25–7 (tomb 13); 82–6, fig. 38 (tomb 7). Both ceramic vessels—a *situla* and a *pithos* at Botromagno—had their mouth sealed with a large tile or stone. See also Caminneci 2012a.

[33] In Himera's Pestavecchia cemetery, the total given for *enchytrismos* burials is 65 per cent: Vassallo 1993–4, 1247–9. See also Vassallo 2014, 262–5.

[34] Moliner et al. 2003, 53–5; Caminneci 2012a, 122. A *hydria* of local manufacture was used in a single case in the fourth century for a perinatal baby burial at Marseille: Moliner et al. 2003, 57, 272, pl. 139 (tomb 254).

[35] Vlachou 2007, 215, 225, figs. 4–7.

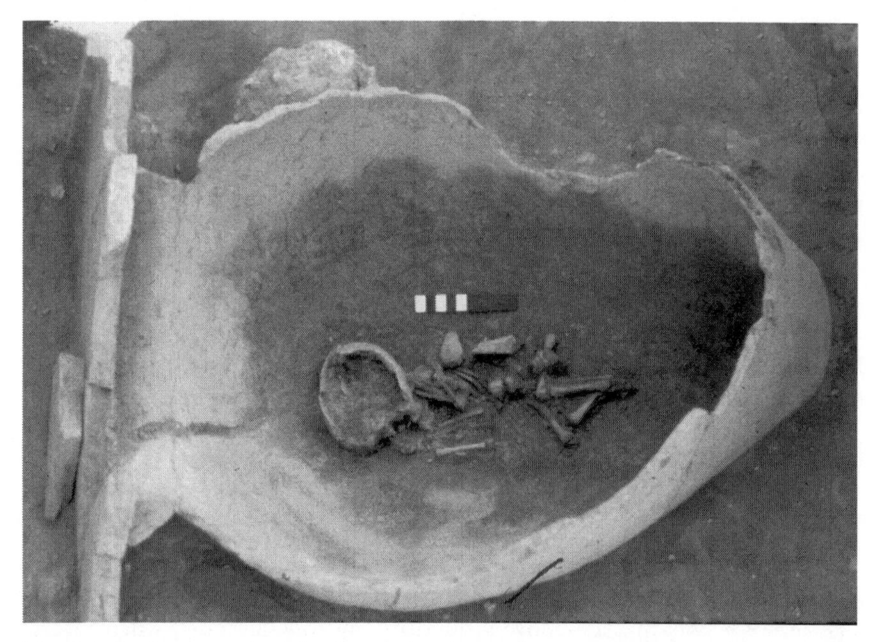

Fig. 2.3 *Enchytrismos* burial of an infant in tomb 7 at Botromagno, sixth to fifth centuries BC.
Photo: Ruth Whitehouse and John Wilkins.

stamnoi, painted amphorae from the centre of the island, and transport amphorae from various Mediterranean origins (Corinth, Attica, Samos, Etruria, Phoenicia) were used as coffins, primarily for newborns.[36] In general, ceramic containers with narrow necks, such as amphorae and small jugs, were cut open on the shoulder or belly, and the infant was inserted, before the neck was stopped up with a stone, a tile, or a piece of another vessel.

In some places in central and southern Italy, it became customary from the seventh century BC to contain the infant body in roof tiles, particularly long, rectangular ridge tiles about fifty to sixty centimetres in length with a C-shaped profile. This type of tile is referred to variously as a Laconian tile or a *coppo*; the Latin word is *imbrex*, and we find these tiles used much later as infant coffins in Roman Gaul (see Chapter 7). A coffin was created by turning two tiles to face each other, one under the infant's body, one on top of it, creating a tube-like container. Cesarano's study of *coppi* shows that 132 of the 551 burials (24 per cent) from the mid-sixth to the fourth centuries BC in the *necropolis* at Fossa in the Abruzzo were infants buried in *coppi*.[37] Three such

[36] Vassallo 1993–4, 1249–51, figs. 3–5; Vassallo 2010, 53, fig. 10; Vassallo and Valentino 2012, 53–4, figs. 100–7, 122–3; Vassallo 2014, 283–4, fig. 29.
[37] Cesarano 2010–11, 159–60, fig. 6.

containers contained two infants, possibly twins. Interestingly, these infant burials were always closely associated with adult male burials. In the second half of the sixth century at Ficana near Ostia and Narce north of Rome, newborns and babies only weeks old were also buried in this manner.[38] Newborns in a necropolis north of Nola in Campania were interred in *coppi* in the fourth century, and these are comparable in size to *coppi* used for infant burials elsewhere.[39] *Coppi* were used primarily in the fifth century for newborn burials at Pithekoussai on the west coast of Italy, although in the following century small children also were contained in them.[40] When older children were buried in *coppi*, the tiles chosen were considerably longer, as at Ficana, where those used for a child two to four years of age were up to ninety-five centimetres in length.[41] The Laconian tiles used for infant and child burials in rural cemeteries in the territory of Metaponto on the southern Italian coast are, for some reason, often rather larger and up to over a metre in length.[42] Flat roof tiles, or *tegulae*, also appear from the fifth century BC in Metapontine burials of children and even newborn infants, the tiles being positioned upright to make a box or coffin for the body, a so-called burial *alla cappuccina*.[43]

There is very little evidence that the burial places of infants in Iron-Age Gaul were visibly marked above ground in any way, although when several burials are found in the same room or courtyard in settlements without the individual graves being disturbed by subsequent burials, it may seem evident that something on the surface reminded people of the site. There is ambiguous evidence for this at Puech de Mus, where two infant burials may have been marked by a dressed stone in a vertical position.[44] One of these, measuring twenty-eight centimetres in height, was of oolitic limestone which is not indigenous to the area and must have been brought in from elsewhere, although it is unclear whether it was simply reused here or if its primary purpose was to mark this grave. On the other hand, infant burials at Gailhan were intercut, which speaks against any surface markers at that site.[45] Even though cremation burials at Ensérune were marked above ground by worked blocks of shelly limestone, none of these pertains to infants.[46]

The evidence for above-ground markers associated with infant burials is clearer in Greece and Italy. At Oropos, small stone cairns were found above

[38] Jarva 1981; Cesarano 2010–11, 157–8.

[39] Cesarano 2010–11, 161–2. *Coppi* were used even earlier for infant burials, from the seventh and sixth centuries BC: Modica 2007, 135–7, pls. 110a–c, 111a (tombs III, IV, VI).

[40] Buchner and Ridgway 1993, tomb 36, tomb 63; Cesarano 2010–11, 161–2; Elia and Meirano 2015, 318, fig. 22.6. See also a one-year-old in a *coppo* at Himera: Vassallo 2014, 281, fig. 28.

[41] Cesarano 2010–11, 158. He does not rule out the possibility that the infant burials may have been associated with houses, the remains of which have disappeared.

[42] Carter 1998, 323 (tomb 269); 324 (tomb 271).

[43] Carter 1998, 426, tomb 192 (newborn).

[44] Dedet et al. 2001, 135–6, 151.

[45] Dedet et al. 1991, 94.

[46] Dedet and Schwaller 2010, 279, fig. 15a.

some of the pits with infant and child burials, but it is unclear whether they marked all of them.[47] At Fossa, a stone slab sometimes signalled the site of an infant grave, and a block of tufa marked the surface of a mid-sixth-century infant burial at Narce.[48] *Enchytrismos* burials at Himera were marked by a single stone, usually a river boulder, with one end driven into the ground.[49] None of these stones was inscribed with any information. This lack of commemorative texts contrasts sharply with Classical Athens, the Greek East, and the Greek settlements in Magna Graecia (southern Italy) which saw a floruit of stone monuments erected to the dead from the fifth century BC, although, unlike the situation in the Roman period (see Chapter 8), no gravestones set up specifically to the memory of an infant in its first year survive in Greek funerary commemoration of this era.

In those regions in which infants were interred in communal cemeteries, it is relevant to consider the proportion of them and to what extent they were integrated with other individuals in this location. In central and southern Spain, for example, newborns are found in pre-Roman cemeteries only when they are buried with an adult female, and it is often presumed that she was the mother.[50] An unambiguous connection between a mother and her infant is apparent in the rich burial of a pregnant woman in her thirties in Athens in the mid-ninth century BC.[51] The cremated remains of the mother were found in 1967, but it was not until the contents of the burial were re-examined that the bones of a foetus between thirty-four and thirty-six gestational weeks old were recognized, as they were mixed with the cremated bones of the mother. The condition of the foetal bones suggests that the child within the mother's body had been partially protected from burning.[52] Equally unambiguous is the cremation burial of a pregnant woman in Amphipolis in the third quarter of the fourth century.[53] Her cremated remains, and those of her foetus, were deposited in a red-figure *hydria* closed with a drinking cup (*skyphos*) and draped with a funerary wreath in gilt bronze. A closer 'integration' between adult and infant is hard to imagine.

Children account for almost 87 per cent of the occupants of the Ammolofos-Koum Tepe cemetery at Abdera where the new incoming colonists from Ionian Klazomenai were buried between 650 and 570 BC.[54] Of the 231 skeletons

[47] Vlachou 2007, 219. [48] Cesarano 2010–11, 157, 164.

[49] Vassallo and Valentino 2012, 50, figs. 61–2. [50] Chapa-Brunet 2008, 628.

[51] Liston and Papadopoulos 2004.

[52] Liston and Papadopoulos 2004, 19. For another possible double burial of mother and infant at Vari in the sixth century, the mother dying in childbirth, see Alexandridou 2012, 43–6, fig. 5. The baby buried in a pot that lies on the legs of an inhumed mother at Abdera may have something to do with death in childbirth or with later complications for mother and baby, but a specific age is not cited for the infant, so it is unclear: Koukouli-Chrysanthaki 1994, 40, fig. 8.

[53] Malamidou and Papaikonomou 2013, 32–3.

[54] Kallintzi and Papaikonomou 2010.

anthropologically examined from this site in this period, 66 per cent belong to infants under the age of one year, with a peak in infant mortality at birth (15 per cent) and between birth and six months (39 per cent). Adolescent and older children up to eighteen, as well as some adults, are also buried in this necropolis, so the area was not reserved for the very youngest, even though they dominate in numbers. Interestingly, during the subsequent period of settlement by colonists from Teos, scattered burial mounds for family interments are the norm, with no infants younger than a year. This may suggest that the two population groups dealt with infants in different ways, but the problem here is that the adult burials of the Klazomenian period have not yet been discovered, and if an infant cemetery exists for the Tean period, it, too, has not yet been found, so perhaps the two sites and situations cannot really be compared for information on infant death and burial or differing cultural attitudes.[55]

At Mende in northern Greece, in the cemetery of the eighth and seventh centuries BC, 177 pot burials were deposited among pit burials and a few cist graves, with a very high 97.6 per cent of the burials being those of infants and small children, suggesting to Vokotopoulou that this peripheral part of the cemetery might have been reserved for these age groups.[56] But evidence for anything that could be called a baby cemetery is everywhere still elusive, except at Astypalaia, where almost 3000 infants have been found interred in domestic ceramic vessels as well as a wide variety of amphorae from the mid-eighth century BC to about AD 100, with the majority of burials dating to the period between *c.*600 to *c.*400 BC.[57] These *enchytrismos* vessels were converted into coffins by cutting out a piece of the pot wall, inserting the tiny corpse, replacing the cut-out piece, and blocking the pot neck with another piece of amphora, a ceramic vessel, or a stone. Roughly 77 per cent of newborns buried here had died at or very shortly before birth, while about 9 per cent are foetuses or premature births (younger than thirty-seven gestational weeks) and 14 per cent are infants that had already lived for a short while.[58] Only two older children, a two-year-old and a three-year-old, were included in this burial ground. The neighbouring Katsalos cemetery, in contrast, contained the remains of both adults and children and, therefore, was a place in which the whole community was represented.

There are other locations that are associated with multiple infant burials, and these are wells; in Greece, such deposits go back to the early Bronze Age.[59] The two main sites relevant here are Athens and Messene, both wells referred to as a "specialized deposit".[60] The well in Athens lay just outside the agora, and within a period of about fifteen years in the second century, roughly 165–150 BC, 499 infants were deposited in it, all but two of which were

[55] Massar 2012. [56] Vokotopoulou 1994, 92–4. [57] Hillson 2009.
[58] Michalaki-Kollia 2010; Michalaki-Kollia 2013.
[59] Bourbou and Themelis 2010, 112–13. [60] Fox 2012, 414.

newborn or full-term foetuses.[61] Many of the infants show evidence of congenital abnormalities and infections that were common and deadly to this vulnerable age cohort. Almost all of the ceramic vessels found in the well were large open shapes, such as basins, bowls, wine-mixing vessels, and mortars, and many of them were whole, leading Liston and Rotroff to suggest that each of the vessels could have been used to carry a tiny body and associated afterbirth to the well, possibly by the midwives who cleaned up after the birth.[62] Approximately thirty infants were deposited annually in this well in a fifteen-year span of use, and Liston and Rotroff hypothesize that this number of perinatal deaths would be in keeping with a small number of midwives attending Athenian women during childbirth.[63] Interesting is the inclusion of as many as 150 dogs in this deposit which may be associated with purification following childbirth and the pollution associated with untimely death.[64]

The well at Messene is also an intramural site associated with the agora of the city and was in use for infant deposits in the third and second centuries BC.[65] At least 262 (or 284, depending on counting method) perinatal infants were recognized in the deposit. As in the well in Athens, human remains (but no adults), dog skeletons, and discarded pottery were comingled, the latter, in the main, being local amphorae and cooking pots. Elsewhere at Messene, outside a Hellenistic funerary monument (K3) of an elite family, ceramic containers were used for infant *enchytrismos* burials, leading Bourbou and Themelis to suggest that the perinatal infants in the well had been interred originally in amphorae and cooking pots in a burial site such as this, but they had been dug up and deposited secondarily in the well once the initial place of interment had undergone a change of use.[66] Four dogs were buried among the *enchytrismos* burials outside monument K3, allowing further parallels to be drawn with the well assemblage. But there is no archaeological evidence, to my knowledge, to suggest that the infants in the well were not put there in the first place as a primary deposit, as in Athens, rather than having been removed from a consecrated location such as a cemetery to be redeposited in the well. Although the infants in both wells in Athens and Messene are in a location perhaps not normally chosen for burial, i.e. outside the cemetery, these children, far from being worthless or of no social significance, were united in an age-related cohort of the dead that occupied a place in the heart of the community of the living and continued to be sought out by families for some time.

[61] Liston and Rotroff 2013a; Liston and Rotroff 2013b. Two exceptions were an adult and an eight-year-old child.

[62] Liston and Rotroff 2013a, 66, fig. 3.3.

[63] Liston and Rotroff 2013a, 77.

[64] Liston and Rotroff 2013a, 67–8.

[65] Bourbou and Themelis 2010.

[66] Bourbou and Themelis 2010, 117. See also Bourbou 2013, 335–9.

Grave Goods for Infants

Characteristic of burials for premature and perinatal infants in southern Gaul (apart from Greek Marseille) is the absence of grave goods, although to interpret this lack of personal items or vessels for food or drink as an indication that these very young children were "êtres sans importance, hors de l'humanité, encore sauvages en quelque sorte" is far too strong.[67] Infants older than six months were given grave goods occasionally, although there seems to be no particular age-related pattern in the inclusion of items such as a simple ring or an amulet necklace. Particularly interesting is a necklace of amulets accompanying an infant between six and twelve months of age in the sixth century at Ruscino in the eastern Pyrenees.[68] These consisted of five bronze rings, three amber beads, a coral bead, and a relict deer canine. Sometimes other infants in this age category were provided with objects that suggest a gendered identity, such as arm rings or even a spindle whorl.[69]

In the Greek east, Magna Graecia, and central Italy, there is no generally uniform set of grave goods for infants. They range from pottery vessels, coins, and jewellery of various kinds, to figurines and other objects of potential symbolic significance.[70] These appear in more generous numbers with children over six months, but newborns were also recipients of various items. A *fibula*, hair spirals, glass beads, and a pig's tooth were amongst the grave goods of a newborn buried in *coppi* at Narce in the mid-sixth century BC.[71] The two-month-old infant in tomb 7 at Botromagno in Puglia, buried in the sixth century, had a very rich assemblage of grave goods, including a bronze *fibula*, two silver *fibulae*, three bronze beads, two amber pendants, and one amber bead (Fig. 2.3).[72] An infant a few months old in the Pestavecchia cemetery at Himera was given lunate earrings and a ring made of bronze.[73] Another perinatal infant buried in a painted *stamnos* at the same site was accompanied by seven small limestone balls which have been interpreted as toys or part of a game, but such a young baby would have had no need for games, unless the family was projecting a future childish activity that was stopped by death.[74] Two *coppi* burials of infants at Nola contained a small cup and another pouring or feeding vessel.[75] At Metaponto, newborns were provided with ceramic vessels, such as cups, oil flasks (*aryballoi*, *lekythoi*), and terracotta figurines.[76] In the Sainte-Barbe cemetery at Marseille, two perinatal infants had a ceramic vessel buried with them, in one case a spouted feeding bottle.[77]

[67] Dedet 2012, 151.
[68] Dedet 2008, 158, 162, fig. 7B; Dedet 2012, 151–3, fig. 4.
[69] Dedet 2012, 153, figs. 5B and 5E.
[70] Dubois 2012.
[71] Cesarano 2010–11, 157.
[72] Whitehouse et al. 2000, 82–6, figs. 38–43.
[73] Vassallo 1993–4, fig. 1; Vassallo 2014, 284, fig. 31.
[74] Vassallo 2014, 283–4, fig. 29.
[75] Cesarano 2010–11, 164.
[76] Carter 1998, 280 (tomb 29); 417 (tomb 191); 426 (tomb 292); see also a feeding bottle (*askos*) in the burial of a newborn in the Punic cemetery at Palermo: Spatafora 2014, 300.
[77] Moliner et al. 2003, 113, 254, 265, fig. 97, pl. 10 (tombs 36, 118).

Feeding bottles and feeding cups also appear in child graves in the Greek colonies of Himera and Taranto.[78] Daniel Graepler includes them in his group of age-specific items for infants, although he acknowledges their presence also in the grave assemblages of older children, possibly as items that had been used by them in their infancy or as vessels to administer nourishment to children too ill to feed themselves.[79] Feeding bottles were also found in the graves of infants from the fifth to the third centuries BC at Botromagno.[80] There are few studies on Greek weaning practices, using the skeletal material for isotopic analysis, but a recent assessment of the children in the Greek colony of Apollonia Pontica on the Black Sea has shown that babies began to be taken off the breast at about six months and introduced to other foods, the process usually being completed by the age of three.[81] Feeding bottles, like those at Taranto or Himera, filled with liquids other than mother's milk, may have been used in weaning babies at Apollonia Pontica, although, without such bottles in funerary assemblages at the site, we can only speculate. Although these bottles have also been interpreted as lamp fillers or funerary libation vessels, among other things, a Greek terracotta figurine of the fifth century BC, now in Geneva, is particularly important as it illustrates the use and purpose of these vessels: a seated mother holds a spouted cup to the lips of a baby on her lap, thus not feeding her child directly from the breast (Fig. 2.4).[82] Of the few objects deposited with the foetuses and perinatal infants in the Hellenistic well in the Athenian agora, a spouted feeding bottle is perhaps the single most poignant and relevant to babies.[83] Feeding bottles continued to be used in the Roman period in many places (see Chapters 4 and 7), and the analysis of residues in a group of these in Roman Cologne demonstrates that they once held milky substances, rather than other non-edible contents.[84]

In the Greek-period cemetery at Marseille, objects other than sea shells are rare in the graves of the very youngest children (see Table 1).[85] Such shells seem to have had some popularity in Greek culture, as they are found also in the graves of infants and very young children, although not in large numbers,

[78] Graepler 1997; Dubois 2013; Vassallo 2014, 271, fig. 12; 283–4, fig. 29.

[79] Graepler 1997, 173–7.

[80] Whitehouse et al. 2000, 125–7, 180–3, figs. 109–11 (tomb 12); 192, 219–21, fig. 139 (tomb 1).

[81] Schmidt et al. 2016.

[82] Gourevitch and Chamay 1992; Beaumont 2012, 55, fig. 3.8; Dubois 2013, 66. For interpretations of these vessels as something other than feeding bottles, see Carter 1998, 189–90, 229. See also the Bronze Age Egyptian feeding bottles in the shape of a woman squeezing her breast to feed a baby on her lap: Budin 2011, 142–5. Hellenistic Greek terracotta figurines are more likely to represent a female, possibly a nurse, holding an infant on her lap, without the baby being fed: Uhlenbrock 1990, 122–3, cat. nos. 15–16.

[83] Liston and Rotroff 2013a, 65–6, fig. 3.2; Liston and Rotroff 2013b, 74.

[84] Huttmann et al. 1989; Graepler 1997, 176.

[85] Moliner et al. 2003, 164–5, 183. Although these are usually local Mediterranean species, one of the shells in the grave of a child around nine months old was a scallop shell of Atlantic origin: 183, 263, fig. 141, pl. 9 (tomb 105).

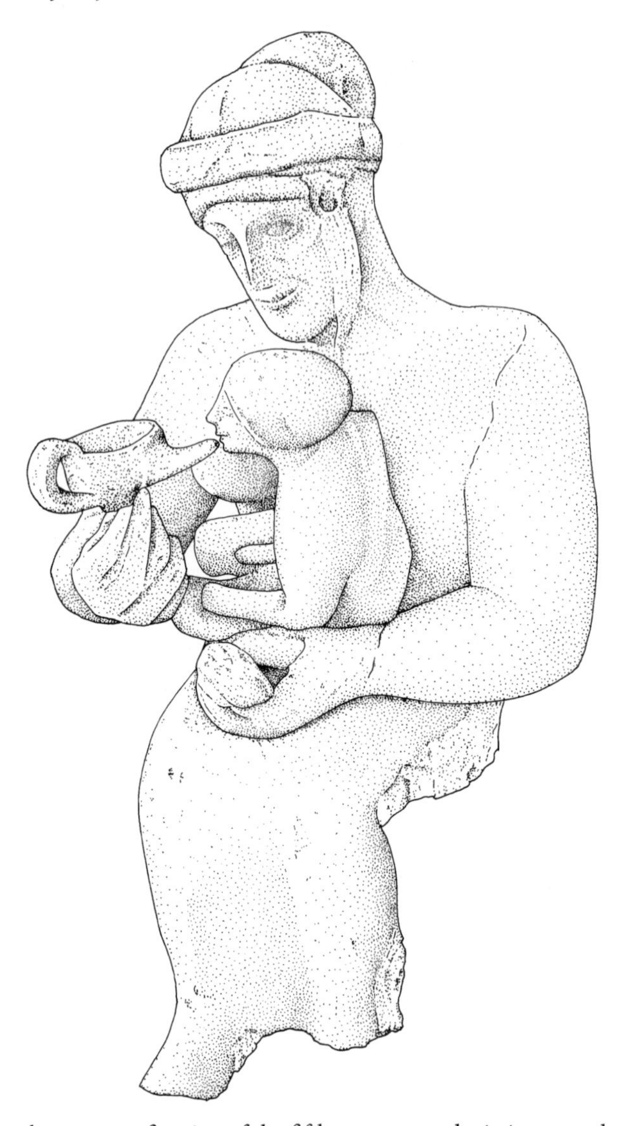

Fig. 2.4 Greek terracotta figurine of the fifth century BC, depicting a mother holding a spouted cup to the lips of a baby on her lap.
Drawing: Irene de Luis.

in the Athenian Kerameikos in the late sixth and fifth centuries. Stroszeck has suggested that these might have been used as a spoon or feeding tool for the neonates and young babies, but since the shells she illustrates are all of edible mussels, it may be that they are simply food offerings.[86] An infant burial at

[86] Stroszeck 2012, 71.

Himera, dating to the first quarter of the sixth century BC, contained the remains of the child, a small Corinthian *aryballos* in the shape of a ram, and 105 cowrie shells (genus *Cypraea*) that may have been picked up and curated because of their shiny, smooth, and colourful surface and also because of their symbolic value.[87] Cowrie shells are known also in the Near East from prehistoric periods onwards, where they are found in various contexts, including tombs of children and females.[88] These shells are suggestive of female genitalia, because of the long 'serrated' opening on the side, and, therefore, also may have been associated with fertility, birth, and perhaps rebirth.[89] For this reason, the cowrie shells from Himera might be seen as protective and prophylactic, but, because there is no evidence to suggest that these shells were worn on the infant's body, it is uncertain whether they acted as amulets in the usual sense. Of course, they certainly still could have had an apotropaic function. One that was pierced to be strung on a cord or strap was deposited in the fourth century BC with an infant only five to seven months of age at Castellet de Bernabé.[90] Marine shells are not found exclusively in Greece or regions influenced by Greek culture, however, as they have a very long pedigree in France, Spain, and Italy, reaching back to the Palaeolithic period.[91]

Houby-Nielsen suggests that grave goods in children's graves in Athens were carefully selected to relate to the age of the child.[92] According to her analysis, infant burials contained ceramic containers for food, those somewhat older were provided with toys, and yet older children were given items relating to their unattained adult gender roles. If this is the pattern in Athens, it is not necessarily reflected in practice elsewhere, especially when items relating to adult gender roles are concerned. It is not unusual at the rural Pantanello necropolis in the territory of Metaponto, from the first half of the sixth to the early third centuries BC, for example, to find girls who died young being provided in death with a *lebes gamikos*, a highly decorated vase possibly used in the ritual bathing of the bride before the wedding.[93] When they appear in the graves of juvenile girls, whether as miniature or normal-sized vessels, they can be interpreted as a gift in compensation for the non-fulfilment of marriage.[94] At Metaponto, a girl aged ten to fourteen years, and therefore of marriageable age, was deposited not only with two *lebetes gamikoi*, but also other ceramic vessels, a gilded necklace(?), three brooches, and two mirrors, all of which could represent wedding gifts and elements of her bridal costume.[95] But a newborn, a baby less than three months old, and one less than a year at

[87] Vassallo 2014, 284, fig. 30 (grave RA69).
[88] Golani 2014. See also Muriel and Playà 2008 for a survey of marine shells in child graves.
[89] Golani 2014, 75–6.
[90] Muriel and Playà 2008, 647, fig. 2.
[91] Pettitt 2011, 234–44.
[92] Houby-Nielsen 2000, 153–5.
[93] Carter 1998, 251 (tomb 88), 274 (tomb 98), 355 (tomb 330).
[94] Dillon 2002, 219–20.
[95] Carter 1998, 275 (tomb 95). Alternatively, they might have been elements of a funerary costume.

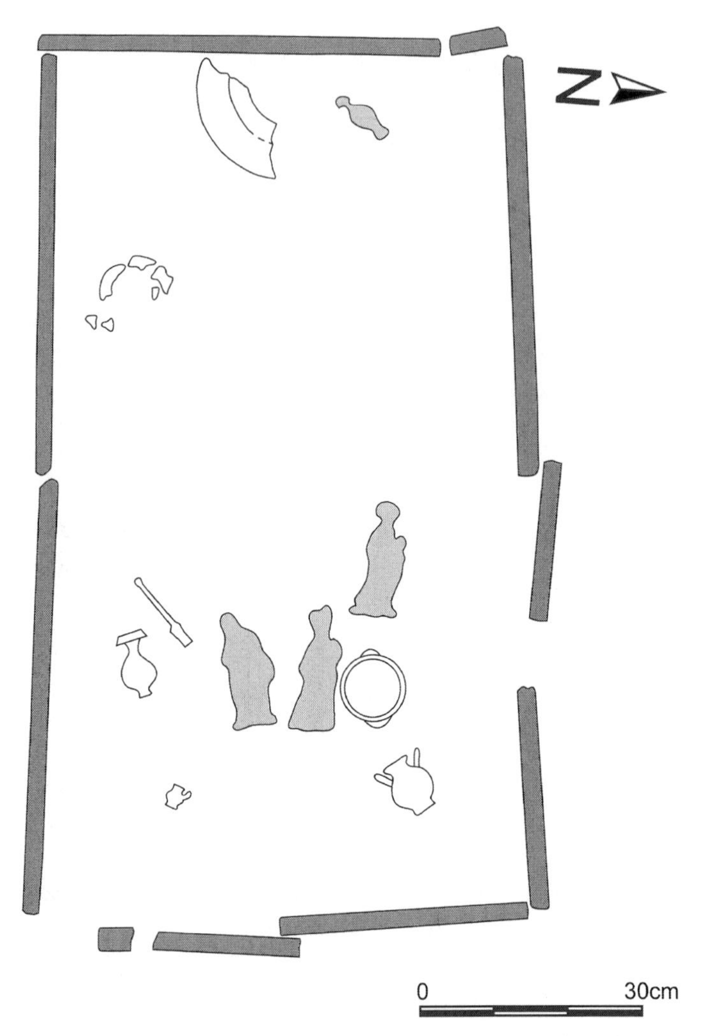

Fig. 2.5 Burial in a tile cist (grey) of a newborn (not shown) (tomb 192) at Metaponto, early third century BC, with four terracotta figurines (grey) and a miniature *lebes gamikos* (vessel on lower right).
Drawing: Irene de Luis.

Metaponto were also given both large and miniature *lebetes gamikoi* in the fifth, fourth, and early third centuries, suggesting that even at this tender age children might already have been invested with not only a social persona, but also a gendered one, even if premature death precluded its development into adulthood (Fig. 2.5).[96]

[96] Carter 1998, 358 (3rd cent. tomb 156), 373 (4th cent. tomb 337), 426 (5th cent. tomb 192).

Susan Langdon recognized that in Greece in the ninth and eighth centuries BC young girls from about the age of ten were buried with a gender-specific ensemble of goods which she termed "the maiden kit"; this comprised combinations of dolls, terracotta models of boots and chests, and wool baskets (*kalathoi*), all of which alluded to the role of the girl as a future wife and homemaker.[97] We might also call an assemblage of the late fourth century BC in the grave of a three-year-old in the cemetery of Touzla Giol at Abdera a 'maiden kit' of sorts.[98] It consisted of an articulated terracotta doll, several terracotta figurines of women (or goddesses?) and animals, perfume jars and flasks, twenty-one bone amulets or figurines only one to two centimetres in size once strung on a necklace, and gold, bronze, and terracotta jewellery.[99] As for the dolls, most recent work interprets them as objects symbolic of female sexual maturity and as representations of the ideal wife and mother, rather than as mere toys, and, as such, they may have had a votive connotation, especially because girls dedicated their dolls to goddesses such as Artemis, Demeter, and Aphrodite when they reached sexual maturity.[100] Thus, the dolls in the graves of pre-pubescent girls are symbolic of a premature death which precluded such a dedication in the sanctuary. The perfume flasks and combs represent objects relevant to feminine beauty of a more mature girl, and the rings and jewellery could be objects of bodily adornment associated with sexual maturity and even an important event such as a wedding. Once again, the female child was prepared for its future role as wife and mother; the accompanying grave goods represent this projected role and compensate for its non-achievement.

Gender-specific toys and games also are found in the graves of boys, and not only older boys. In the Pantanello and Saldone cemeteries at Metaponto, for example, not only was a child between the age of eight and twelve provided with three *astragaloi*, knucklebones, for a child's game, but also much younger individuals.[101] In fact, one baby less than a year old had seven *astragaloi*, as did another baby only three to six months old, many more than the oldest boy, even though infants that young would not yet have been engaged in such a game requiring dexterity and numerate skills.[102] In Greek art, children depicted playing knucklebones are always at least a few years old.[103] It has been proposed that knucklebones were symbolic of the appropriate life stage at which a child would play with toys; in a funerary context, they might represent the non-achievement of sexual maturity and marriage, a point in the life cycle

[97] Langdon 2007. [98] Papaikonomou 2008, 697–8, figs. 6–7.

[99] See also grave 3 at the Touzla Giol site for figurines, perfume flasks, jewellery, including finger rings, and a gold wreath: Kallintzi and Papaikonomou 2010, fig. 1.

[100] Reilly 1997; Merker 2000; Dillon 2002, 215; Papaikonomou 2008, 699–702.

[101] Carter 1998, 433–4, tomb 12 (8–12 years old); 3332, tomb 307 (7 years old).

[102] Carter 1998, 329 (tomb 263), 332 (tomb 307).

[103] For example, Carè 2012, 405, fig.1.

when a child's toys would have been laid aside or dedicated in a sanctuary to mark the change in status.[104] But *astragaloi* and other items may represent a kind of possible boy's kit relevant to a male child's progression in the life-course to adolescence and gymnasial education in preparation for the life of a citizen man.[105] This is well demonstrated by the inclusion of fifty-eight *astragaloi*, a bronze strigil (body oil scraper), and two aryballic *lekythoi* in the late fifth-century grave of a boy a few years old at Eleusis, the scraper and *lekythoi* representing a set of objects used in athletic activities in the gymnasium.[106] This particular grave also included one miniature wine jug, a *chous*, which was used at the Anthesteria, a festival marking the completion of a child's third year of life (see Fig. 2.11).[107] This may demonstrate, again, that future needs were projected in the selected grave goods given to infants. But objects such as *astragaloi* may have had other meanings as well, particularly when they appear in graves of older individuals. At Lokri Epizephyri in southern Italy, where *astragaloi* are particularly frequent finds in graves of the sixth to fourth centuries BC, not only children, but also adolescents and adults were sometimes buried with hundreds and even up to 1400 *astragaloi* arranged around the body. Carè suggests that these items may have had magical properties or acted as apotropaic talismans shielding the body from negative forces.[108]

Status would also have played a role in determining which infants were recipients of grave goods and how elaborate or extensive they were. At Eretria, for example, two infants between six and twelve months of age were buried together in the eighth century with rich grave goods, including one necklace of fifty glass beads and another of twenty-nine amber beads, and one of the babies had a gold diadem on its head.[109] The gold diadem suggests that there had been a *prothesis*, a presentation of the dead in the home as the first step in the funeral, for which there are parallels throughout the Greek world.[110] Clearly the family of these two children was wealthy and of elevated status, possibly being members of the social elite, who chose an ostentatious rite when faced with the loss of their offspring and heirs.

PREGNANCY AND CHILDBIRTH IN PRE-ROMAN ART

A population fundamentally needs to reproduce to survive, yet, in antiquity, the theme of pregnancy and childbirth was not necessarily a matter for public consumption. In the pre-Roman world, such matters were deemed largely to

[104] Carè 2012, 407. [105] Kallintzi and Papaikonomou 2010, 138.
[106] Kallintzi and Papaikonomou 2010, 138, fig. 9c (grave 17). [107] Hamilton 1992.
[108] Carè 2012, 410–11. [109] Blandin 2010, 52, fig. 6.
[110] Oakley 2004, 76–87, especially a *lekythos* depicting an adult woman on a funeral bed who wears a bridal diadem or crown, 80–1, fig. 48; Vlachou 2012, 364–6.

be domestic in nature and embedded in the female domain, just as, in contrast, political power, matters of state, and warfare, were aspects of masculinity and, therefore, visibly part of public life in literature and art.

The earliest depictions of pregnancy and reproduction do not appear in monumental and public art, but on objects of small format for personal use in a cultic context. Small clay plaques of the thirteenth century BC from Levantine sites such as Revadim Quarry, for example, represent a woman who reaches down with both hands to hold open her vagina whilst two babies appear in front of her chest. Ornan suggests that these might have been amulets to assist in the birthing process, interpreting the depicted babies as foetuses still in the womb and the pronounced pubic opening as heralding imminent birth.[111] Budin, on the other hand, claims that these are more likely to be potency figurines similar to those in Egypt depicting individual females typically naked and with emphasized sexual characteristics.[112] Whatever their true purpose, they are graphically related to human reproduction.

As for images of women in the actual process of giving birth, a few early depictions of this event survive from Cyprus, all of them in small format and of a private and religious nature. Two terracotta groups of the early fifth century BC portray a birthing woman assisted by a midwife, and one of them even has the baby emerging head first from the mother.[113] These, apparently, were found in a sanctuary of the Great Goddess, suggesting that they are private votive dedications in connection with a successful outcome of the wish for conception and childbirth. Also from Cyprus, from a sanctuary at Golgoi-Agios Photios, is a small limestone sculpture of the fourth century BC depicting a woman in childbirth who lies on a couch and is supported by an attendant behind her, while the midwife at the foot of the bed holds the newborn baby (Fig. 2.6).[114] Pregnancy and childbirth were very risky ventures, and women in the ancient world needed all the help they could get. It is not surprising, therefore, that divine help was sought (discussed in the final section of this chapter).

Visual depictions of women in childbirth began to appear in funerary reliefs on grave *stelae* and marble *lekythoi* in the fourth century BC, particularly in Athens, and they continued in the Hellenistic period in funerary paintings and reliefs from Demetrias-Pagasai in north-east Greece, Alexandria, and Rhodes. No such genre survives in Iron-Age Gaul or Spain or any of the other cultures around the Mediterranean basin. In all these scenes, the collapsed and seated parturient, dishevelled and exhausted from her ordeal in giving birth, or attempting to do so, is supported and helped by one or two other women; very occasionally, the husband is part of the scene

[111] Ornan 2007. [112] Budin 2011, 117–35, 165–9, fig. 16.
[113] Budin 2011, 227; Cohen 2011, 471–2, fig. 28.3.
[114] Vandervondelen 2002, 145, fig. 1; Budin 2011, 227; on the temple site, see Counts 2012.

Fig. 2.6 Limestone figurine of a woman in childbirth from Cyprus, fourth century BC. The Cesnola Collection, purchased by subscription, 1874–76. The Metropolitan Museum of Art, 74.51.2698.

Photo: The Metropolitan Museum of Art, New York (www.metmuseum.org).

(Fig. 2.7).[115] In those cases where the woman's torso is naked, a slight hint of a swollen belly can be seen. In the earliest of the series, a marble *lekythos* of *c.*370–*c.*360 BC commemorating Pheidestrate (her name is inscribed above her), the limp parturient is seated in the middle while another woman to her right supports her, and a third female figure to the left is shown in a pose of mourning.[116] More active, and alluding to the drama of a difficult birth, is the figure of Plangon on a marble *lekythos* of the 320s BC from Oropos.[117] She is contorted and flails a leg in the air while two women offer her assistance; her husband (Tolmides) stands dejectedly to one side with his head in his hands. There is no baby, either dead or alive, depicted in any of these images.

The pathos of the situation is heightened on the painted funerary *stele* of Hediste from Demetrias-Pagasai which presents a complex scene of a woman dying in childbirth in this genre.[118] The events that led to the death of Hediste

[115] Demand 1994, 122–40. [116] Demand 1994, 123, pl. 3.
[117] Demand 1994, 124, pl. 6; Oakley 2003, 186, fig. 28.
[118] Stewart and Gray 2000; Salowey 2012, 251–3, fig. 18.1.

Fig. 2.7 Funerary monument of a woman who may have died in childbirth, from Athens, *c.*330 BC. Carved, Pentelic marble: 84.5 cm h × 59.1 cm w × 14 cm d (33¼ × 23¼ × 5½ in.). Harvard Art Museums/Arthur M. Sackler Museum, Gift of Edward W. Forbes, 1905.8.

Photo: Imaging Department © President and Fellows of Harvard College.

in the early second century BC took place in her house, and here it is that Hediste lies on a bed with her husband at the foot of it gazing mournfully upon her. Two figures in the background might be house slaves, although the one holding a tiny infant wrapped in red cloth could be either the midwife who delivered the baby or a female relative. Hediste and her baby did not survive; the epitaph informs the reader that "it was not fated that she should cradle the infant in her arms", and that they have been "brought both to a single tomb".[119] Without such an explicit text on the other monuments in this group, we still might assume that all these images are straightforward and that the seated woman is the person who died in childbirth and is commemorated. But Christoph Clairmont suggests that the seated and distressed woman in these scenes may not always be the person commemorated by the monument.[120] He proposes this, in particular, for a *stele* of *c.*300 BC from Piraeus commemorating a woman named Malthake. Malthake is named as *chreste*, a term used for a slave or foreign resident (metic), and which, according to Clairmont, might be appropriate for a midwife. In this interpretation, Malthake would not be the seated woman, but the standing one helping her in her capacity as midwife. Clairmont's reading of the iconography has been challenged by, among others, Leslie Beaumont.[121] Beaumont sees no reason to view Malthake, whether metic or freed slave, as anyone other than the pregnant woman in labour, depicted iconographically in the same way as all other Athenian women in this life-threatening situation, nor can she imagine that Malthake, if she were a midwife, would want to be commemorated in the process of unsuccessfully delivering a baby. Success in the profession surely would be a source of pride and something worth remembering, and the iconography of the funerary relief of an Athenian midwife name Phanostrate, who is named a midwife (*maia*), and a doctor (*iatros*) in her epitaph, conveys this very well.[122] This relief does not show anyone in the throes of childbirth. A seated and a standing woman are depicted, either one of which could be Phanostrate, in the company of four children of various ages who symbolize the many babies she delivered successfully.[123]

There is occasional ambiguity in funerary depictions of the family, leading Nancy Demand to suggest that contemporary Greek viewers may well have read the scenes of death in childbirth with a degree of flexibility that we tend to overlook.[124] A fourth-century epigram supports this, as it refers to the image on a funerary monument of a woman who has died in childbirth: "Unhappy Mnasylla, why does it stand on your tomb, this picture of your daughter Neotima whom you lament, her whose life was taken from her by the pangs of labour? She lies in her dear mother's arms, as if a heavy cloud had gathered on her eyelids and, alas, not far away her father Aristoteles rests his head in his right hand. O most miserable pair, not even in death have you forgotten

[119] Arvanitopoulos 1928, 147–8.
[120] Clairmont 1993.
[121] Beaumont 2012, 46, fn. 6; see also Demand 1994, 133–4; Stewart and Gray 2012, 261–2, fn. 26.
[122] *Inscriptiones Graecae* (*IG*) II^2.6873.
[123] Demand 1994, 132–3, pl. 12.
[124] Demand 1994, 130–1.

your grief."[125] The described image sounds like the death in childbirth reliefs on the *stelae* discussed above, but the text indicates that the commemorated woman was not the one in childbirth, but her mother who had assisted at the birth. This ambiguity is also apparent in the late-fifth-century grave *stele* of Ampharete from Athens, because only the epitaph reveals that the depicted woman with a tiny baby on her lap is not the child's mother, but its grandmother, both of them now dead.[126]

Furthermore, the woman who died in childbirth is not always depicted in a pose relating to that event or even with an infant. The carved grave *stele* for Aline from the Greek island of Rheneia, for example, informs the reader that she was a pregnant Phoenician woman from Ashkelon in Israel who, for reasons unexplained, died and was buried in a grave "in a foreign land destined for her".[127] It is the text alone on this monument of the late second century BC that gives insight into the causes of death, as her so-called portrait simply shows her sitting on a chair with no baby in sight. Perhaps this was a monument taken from available stock in a sculptor's workshop on Rheneia, or it was a versatile image that could be used to commemorate any woman who died. If this is the case, the viewer would need to read into the scene the events recorded in the text, as they are not explicitly shown. Equally, a marble grave *stele* from Pella's east cemetery may have been a standard one portraying the death of a woman that was later altered to suit the circumstances.[128] In the relief, a seated woman on the right looks up to a standing woman on the left, the latter in a pose of mourning. These appear to have been the only figures in the scene, until a swaddled infant was later inserted in very low relief in the arm of the mourning woman.[129] If this reading of the relief is correct, the stone would have been carved with a stock image which can only have been altered in accordance with the wishes of the person who commissioned the monument, the commemorator of the woman who died in childbirth. Even then, it is unclear whether the woman who died in childbirth is the standing woman or the seated woman. The dead woman could be the seated one, and the standing woman is one of her relatives holding a surviving or dead baby; equally the standing woman might represent the one who died in childbirth.

In a controversial paper on the meaning of Attic grave *stelae*, Ursula Vedder proposes that the depictions of death in childbirth on women's monuments

[125] *Anthologia Palatina* 7, no. 730.

[126] Clairmont 1993, 1.660; Beaumont 2012, 98, fig. 3.36; S. Lewis 2002, 18.

[127] Couilloud 1974, 204–5, cat. no. 468; Salowey 2012, 258–9, fig. 18.3.

[128] Lilimpaki-Akamati 1998. For other funerary monuments on which infants and toddlers appear, see Kalaitzi 2010, 329–30.

[129] Lilimpaki-Akamati 1998, pls. 75, 78.

were related to the depictions of active warriors on the *stelae* of men, both *Frauentod* and *Kriegertod* being rare instances in which scenes of activity are represented in funerary commemoration.[130] For Vedder, Attic soldiers had a special status, as a death in battle (*Kriegertod*) was an heroic one, and she proposed that women dying in childbirth (*Frauentod*) also had a special status, citing the example of Sparta where fallen soldiers and women dying in childbirth had the right to be honoured with an inscribed funerary monument.[131] Demand dismissed this interpretation, concluding that there was nothing heroic about dying in childbirth, stressing instead that the passivity of the dying woman, who fulfilled her socially expected gender role as mother, contrasted with the ideal gendered behaviour of the man as an active soldier.[132] The patience and submission of women could not match the courage of the warrior, the former eliciting pity in death, the latter inspiring admiration and emulation.[133]

IMAGES OF INFANTS AND THE FAMILY IN LIFE AND DEATH

Heroic these women might not be, but on many Classical Attic grave reliefs they certainly appear virtuous in ways that made them "essential for the stability of the household, the maintenance of citizenship, and therefore for the continuity of the community as a whole".[134] Women on these stones are represented as dignified and solemn, interacting subtly with other women, men, children, and slaves. Of particular interest here are those grave *stelae* on which infants are depicted. The youngest infants, probably newborns or babies only months old, are usually swaddled, although some are shown naked (Fig. 2.8). Swaddled infants and very young babies can be held by a central female figure, who may be the mother, or by various other girls and women. The depiction of a single infant is the norm, but in very rare cases twins and even triplets can also appear.[135]

It is extremely rare that very young children were ever depicted unaccompanied by adults on Attic funerary reliefs, and only three such monuments survive, all dating to the second half of the fourth century BC.[136] These infants, all boys, are not newborns, but are already advanced in age, and possibly about a year or two old. In their semi-nudity, their seated pose, and the exposure of

130 Vedder 1988. 131 Vedder 1988, 189. 132 Demand 1994, 140.
133 Demand 1994, 129; similarly Stewart and Gray 2012, 263–4.
134 Burton 2003, 20. 135 Clairmont 1993, 2.819 (twins), 1.12 (triplets).
136 Clairmont 1993, 868, 868a, 869; Beaumont 2012, 61, fig. 3.13.

Fig. 2.8 Funerary monument of a woman who may have died in childbirth (seated), with a servant and the surviving swaddled infant (left), from Athens.
Photo: © The Trustees of the British Museum.

their genitals, they are strikingly similar to the so-called temple boys discussed in the final section of this chapter.

One of the simplest and most beautiful relief scenes in Attic funerary commemoration appears on a grave *stele* of *c.*420–*c.*410 BC in which a short-haired slave girl hands a wriggling baby girl in a thin tunic to its dignified mother seated on a chair.[137] In this case, the baby reaches out to its mother, and she to it, but the mother on other reliefs can appear completely lost in her own thoughts, showing no reaction when a slave holds up an infant to her.[138] The seated woman sometimes holds an infant on her lap, but more often it is one of the assisting female figures, slaves or other family members, who cradles the baby (Fig. 2.8).[139] Occasionally, a standing man and a seated woman clasp hands in the so-called *dexiosis* motif, taking leave of each other, and a standing female in the background holds an infant, presumably the couple's.[140]

In the course of the fourth century BC, the number of figures on these reliefs increased. The most complex is the monument depicting a woman named Bako who stands on the left and clasps hands with a seated woman, Aristonike, on her right.[141] A toddler (Sokrates) reaches up to Bako, while in the background a servant weeps, and on the far right another sad-looking servant holds a swaddled infant. Clairmont's interpretation sees Bako having already had a son (Sokrates), and then dying whilst giving birth to a second child. Oakley, however, identifies the seated woman, Aristonike, as Bako's mother.[142] Of course, either of these readings might be correct, as the imagery itself is ambiguous.

These reliefs, in the opinion of several scholars, communicate the death in childbirth of the woman (or one of the women) in the group, whereby the infant serves to emphasize the loss to society of a woman in childbearing age.[143] Others, such as Oakley, suggest that infants and children in such scenes more likely indicate an area of a woman's responsibilities in general.[144] Schulze has been the most dismissive of interpretations of these monuments as records of maternal death in childbirth, suggesting, and I think rightly, that infants, in reality, were depicted in these Attic grave *stelae* as an attribute of motherhood, just as jewellery boxes or mirrors held by the female deceased or her female attendants were attributes indicating the beauty and wealth of the dead woman.[145] In fact, the baby held or cradled by the deceased woman or other females could be substituted for any other household object to which status was attached, and any figure in the group, and especially the slaves, could be holding possessions of the deceased or an infant almost interchangeably. Thus, the multi-figural reliefs on Attic funerary monuments need to be read with some caution, keeping in mind that a whole family of multiple

[137] Clairmont 1993, cat. no. 2.652; Foley 2003, 133, fig. 35. [138] Clairmont 1993, 2.780a.
[139] Clairmont 1993, 2.640, 2.727; Clairmont 1993, 2.881b, 2.894, 2.909: assisting women holding the baby. See Oakley 2003, 234–7, on how it is sometimes hard to distinguish slaves from family members.
[140] Clairmont 1993, 3.866, 3.919, 3.932. On the motif, see Davies 1985.
[141] Clairmont 1993, 4.910. [142] Oakley 2003, 185, fig. 27.
[143] Vedder 1988; Demand 1994, 125; Grossman 2007, 312.
[144] Oakley 2003, 185. [145] Schulze 1998, 27.

individuals may be represented to highlight the central role that the household and motherhood played in the social value system of women in Classical Athens, rather than to commemorate women who died in childbirth.[146] As an east Greek funerary monument of *c.*380 BC illustrates, a swaddled infant and an overly large spindle and distaff in the portrait of a woman act as attributes portraying the ideal wife who not only was a mother, but also spun the wool for the family's clothes.[147] What is important in Attic monuments is that by the middle of the fifth century, children and even the youngest of the offspring are portrayed publicly as integral members of the family—the *oikos*—which formed a fundamental building block of Athenian society. As Beaumont notes, the representation of the infant identifies that the pictorial context is that of the *oikos*.[148]

Thirty-five Classical Attic grave *stelae* have depictions of swaddled infants and they are an important source of information about the wrapping and protection of the infant body in this period and region. It is clear that the swaddled babies in Attic grave reliefs are newborns, because children several months of age or in the toddler phase look noticeably older and they are depicted naked or semi-naked, making it clear that they are almost always boys. It is impossible to recognize the sex of the swaddled babies because their entire body is hidden under fabric. The Attic grave *stelae* also provide important comparative material for a study of swaddling in the Roman period in Italy and Gaul (see Chapter 4). There is no surviving Iron-Age evidence for swaddling in Gaul, apart from the Greek colony of Marseille, where the position of the limbs of some buried infants suggests that they had been swaddled, a practice in this region that may have been intrusive and Greek in origin.[149]

In Greek thought, a baby being wrapped in swaddling bands could "be moulded like wax while still soft" and its physical form manipulated.[150] Plato's comments here suggest that an infant could be kept in swaddling clothes for more than a year, but this is rather unlikely, as an active and developing child of a year or older would not tolerate the constriction imposed by swaddling. Soranus, writing as a doctor in Rome in the second century AD, advised a duration of no more than sixty days which is a much more reasonable period of time (see Chapter 3).[151]

Without the physical remains of swaddling surviving in funerary or domestic contexts, we know almost nothing about the fabrics or colour of wrappings for infants, although one of the *enchytrismos* infant burials from Himera contained a little bronze ring to which fragments of textile still adhered.[152]

[146] Schulze 1998, 30.
[147] Grossman 2001, 107–8, cat. no. 39.
[148] Beaumont 2012, 58.
[149] Dedet and Schwaller 2010, 278.
[150] Plato, *Laws* 7.789e.
[151] Soranus, *Gynaecology* 2.42.
[152] Vassallo 2014, 284, fig. 32.

Analysis of the fragments revealed it to be hemp, but it is hard to say if this had been used as a blanket or shroud, or some other item of clothing or cover. Given the dearth of textile remains, the painted grave *stele* of Hediste from Demetrias-Pagasai is particularly informative about the colour of baby wrappings, because the newborn here is enveloped in bright red cloth.[153] Of course, this could be a length of fabric not specifically made for the baby, but taken from another garment or cover and reused. In many cases, the infant on Classical grave reliefs is wrapped in what appears to be a cloak or blanket, leaving only the head free. The material is wrapped around the baby to encase it, sometimes very loosely, other times rather tightly, but swaddling bands or strips of cloth wrapped around it diagonally are rarely visible.[154] The baby usually, but not always, wears a bonnet on its head which can fit like a skull cap or be more conical and pointed.

The presence of swaddling bands on a baby in Attic funerary art is a good indication of the very young age of the child. Generally, the act of breastfeeding also reflects the tender age of the baby, before it had been weaned off mother's milk, but this particular activity is rarely depicted in Greek art. In fact, it has been suggested that there may have been a sort of taboo against depicting breastfeeding and the naked breast in Greek art, especially in Athens.[155] The only funerary monuments of the Classical and Hellenistic periods in Greece to depict a woman actually breastfeeding her baby are *stelae* from Thessaly in north-east Greece and the islands of Kalymnos and Cos in the eastern Aegean.[156] In each relief, the infant is depicted in a different fashion: on the late fifth-century monument from Larissa in Thessaly, the baby wears a long tunic (and looks considerably older than a newborn); on the mid-fourth-century monument from Kalymnos the baby is tightly swaddled; and on the *stele* of the second or first century from Kos the baby is simply naked.

Since the middle of the fifth century, images of infants in a family context and in an intimate setting also began to appear in Attic vase painting.[157] The very youngest infants, wrapped in swaddling bands, however, do not appear in this medium, with the exception of baby Zeus entirely wrapped up in fabric and being handed over by his mother Rhea to his murderous father Kronos; in reality, the baby was substituted with a stone which Kronos swallowed after being fooled by the swaddling bands.[158] A popular motif among depictions of mortal babies in vase painting is the mother–infant–slave group in which a female slave either hands over a naked baby to its mother or takes it

[153] Stewart and Gray 2000; Salowey 2012, 251–3, fig. 18.1.
[154] Clairmont 1993, 3.866.
[155] Bonfante 1997, 184–8; Bonfante 2013, 437.
[156] Batziou-Efstathiou 1981, 53–4, fig. 1; Bosnakis 2013.
[157] Oakley 2013, 156–67.
[158] Shapiro 2003, 85–6, 205, cat. no. 4. For swaddled infants in a cradle as terracotta figurines (rattles?), see Graepler 1997, 140, fig. 155, tomb 98 (Taranto, fifth century BC).

Fig. 2.9 Red-figure *pyxis* with a scene of childcare.
Photo: Manchester Museum, the University of Manchester.

from her.[159] A red-figure *pyxis*, a cylindrical, lidded box used primarily by women for cosmetics, trinkets or jewellery, is a particularly appropriate ceramic vessel for scenes pertinent to the feminine sphere, and it is on such a mid-fifth-century *pyxis* in the Manchester Museum that we see a mother on a chair with a naked baby boy on her lap (Fig. 2.9).[160] Such scenes are thematically related to similar ones in contemporary Attic funerary portraits, but there are more playful interactions and childish activities in the paintings which would not have been appropriate material for grave *stelae*. For example, a red-figure *pyxis* of *c.*470 BC in Athens is decorated entirely with scenes in women's chambers in which women spin wool and play with infants and toddlers.[161] One of the women, possibly a slave girl, carries a very young child on her shoulders, much like another slave girl on a mid-fifth-century white-ground *lekythos*, both of them engaged in amusing the child and keeping it occupied before it is returned to its mother.[162] And since the infants in vase paintings are all beyond the age of a few months, they are also represented as engaged in activities that are related to their physical development. This includes potty training, hardly a dignified theme for the more solemn and ideal family scenes in funerary reliefs.[163]

[159] For example, a red-figure hydria in the Sackler Museum, *c.*430 BC: S. Lewis 2002, 15, fig. 1.3; Neils and Oakley 2003, 221, 230–1, cat. no. 29. Another fine example is the red-figure hydria of *c.*430–*c.*420 BC in the British Museum on which a slave or nurse hands a baby over to his seated mother; a wool basket on the floor indicates that this takes place in the home, particularly in the women's quarters: Jenkins et al. 2015, 151, with fig.

[160] S. Lewis 2002, 172, figs. 2.26, 5.2.

[161] S. Lewis 2002, 81, fig. 2.25.

[162] S. Lewis 2002, 17, fig. 1.4; Oakley 2004, 42, fig. 14. See also Oakley 2004, 47, fig. 21 for a mid-fifth-century *lekythos* on which a woman hands over a toddler to a seated mother.

[163] Beaumont 2012, 58, figs. 3.11–12.

The other area in the Mediterranean in which images of mothers and infants, or infants on their own, appear is Italy. The mid-fifth-century limestone statue of a seated woman with a baby on her lap, the so-called Mater Matuta from Chianciano, originates from the Pedata necropolis at Chianciano near Chiusi. The statue, in reality, is not of Mater Matuta, an early Roman goddess with connections to fertility and children, but a container for the ashes of the deceased who is depicted as a mother for perpetuity.[164] In the context of Chiusian ash containers in the form of seated women, reclining couples, and jars with human heads, this figure fits well within the local funerary traditions, although the addition of an infant is innovative and thus somewhat unique.[165] The infant is quite large, certainly not a newborn, and seems to be wrapped in a cloak or blanket, rather than swaddled. The child does not suckle at its mother's breast, even though its head is close to the breast. A roughly contemporaneous limestone statue from the north necropolis of the Greek colony of Megara Hyblaea in Sicily depicts a seated female figure with twin babies on her lap; each of the children holds a breast with one hand and sucks on it to feed.[166] The children are wrapped in swaddling bands, but the bands on the upper body are loosened enough to allow both babies to get their arms out. Opinion has oscillated between it being a funerary statue and a votive statue of a mother goddess, but there is no compelling reason to interpret the figure as divine, especially since the statue was set up in a cemetery and not a sanctuary. Gillian Shepherd sensibly sees the statue as a projection of the significance of motherhood and female nurturing.[167]

INFANTS AND THE DIVINE IN THE GREEK WORLD

Any ephemeral rites, such as sacrifices and prayers, for the well-being of the infant are no longer recognizable in the archaeological record, but there is a fairly wide range of votive offerings which reflect parental appeals and thanks for divine protection. In Classical Athens, in the first days, weeks, and months of the infant's life, various social and religious ceremonies took place that introduced the child into the community; these also may have been practised elsewhere in Greece, but the evidence is less clear.[168] The first rite took place at the *amphidromia* ceremony on the fifth day after birth, when the child was officially included in the family and carried around the house or hearth. On the seventh day, the infant was introduced to others outside the immediate family, and on the tenth day (*dekate*) the baby was named. Once the child had developed a little

[164] Haynes 2000, 297–8, fig. 239; Bonfante 2013, 438, fig. 20.11.
[165] Cristofani 1975; Huntsman 2014.
[166] Shepherd 2012, 214, fig. 16.1.
[167] Shepherd 2012, 214, fig. 16.1.
[168] Hamilton 1992; Garland 2013.

Fig. 2.10 Votive relief to Artemis Lochia, depicting a post-partum scene with an exhausted mother and her infant held by a servant at the right. Fletcher Fund, 1924. The Metropolitan Museum of Art, 24.97.92.

Photo: The Metropolitan Museum of Art, New York (www.metmuseum.org).

more, it was introduced to the members of its father's *phratry* or kinfolk. In addition to textual information about these activities, various votive offerings provide us with images of ceremonies and cultic rites involving infants.

Obviously, the birth of a healthy baby was a matter for celebration, and thanks were due to the gods and goddesses to whom parents had looked for divine assistance. Two of those goddesses who assisted with childbirth were Eileithyia and Artemis Lochia, who may be the figures portrayed in the middle of a fragmentary marble votive relief of the fifth century in New York (Fig. 2.10).[169] At the right, an exhausted woman is slumped on a chair, apparently having just given birth, and to her right is a smaller female figure holding the newborn baby. These same two goddesses were worshipped in Chora on the island of Astypalaia, as inscriptions indicate.[170] It was Artemis to

[169] Demand 1994, 87–8, pl. 1. See also Demangel 1922; Pingiatoglou 1981, 87–90; Beaumont 2012, 46, fig. 3.2.

[170] Michalaki-Kollia 2010, 174–8.

whom women dedicated thank-offerings of their clothing after giving birth, and particularly interesting in this regard is a votive relief from Echinos in northern Greece. In this relief, three women enter the sanctuary of Artemis, one of whom extends her infant to the goddess to be blessed; in the background are various garments hung as if on a washing line.[171] At Athens and Brauron, where Artemis and Iphigenia, a subsidiary divinity, were revered, items listed in gift inventories include jewellery and worn clothing as thank-offerings for successful childbirth; the clothing of women who had died in childbirth, however, was dedicated to Iphigenia.[172]

As long as the child was being breastfed, or at least until it had been entirely weaned, it was under the protection also of a variety of female gods and figures who are referred to as *kourotrophoi*, child nurturers.[173] They are depicted in statues and figurines, in stone and, above all, in terracotta, as a seated, sometimes standing, female figure holding an infant.[174] Some of the oldest come from Cyprus, from the sixth century BC, where they are particularly popular.[175] A large pit in the sanctuary of Hera at the Greek colony of Paestum, dating to the fifth century BC, contained large numbers of terracotta figurines of the goddess(?) giving an infant the breast.[176]

A few surviving fragments of marble votive reliefs of the fourth century BC from the sanctuary of Asklepios on the Athenian acropolis have been connected by Olga Palagia to the dedication of an infant in the sanctuary.[177] One of them shows a scene in a sanctuary, which is indicated by a votive *pinax* or relief plaque on a pillar in the background, with various figures who may be Asklepios, god of healing, and his sons and daughters. This and the other two more fragmentary reliefs have in common the depiction of a baby with upraised hands in a basket in the foreground. In two instances, the baby is being picked up by an adult. In Greek mythology, Athena hid Erichthonios, a legendary early ruler of Athens, in a basket and entrusted it to the three daughters of Kekrops, another Athenian king. Hermes later found the baby in Apollo's cave on the slopes of the acropolis.[178] Palagia does not identify the baby in the reliefs as Erichthonios, but as a mortal child who has been dedicated by its parents in the sanctuary of Asklepios to protect its health or to heal it.[179] This may be the subject of another fragmentary early fourth-century votive relief from the Asklepieion in Piraeus in which an adult man stands next to an altar holding a partially clothed toddler in his arms and with

[171] Dillon 2002, 231–2: Neils 2003, 145, fig. 6; Dasen 2011, 303, fig. 18.5; Lee 2012, 334–6, fig. 2.8.

[172] Demand 1994, 89–90; Cleland 2005.

[173] Beaumont 2012, 64–7.

[174] Bonfante 1986 and 1997.

[175] Budin 2011, 227–9.

[176] Sestieri 1954, 15; Sestieri 1955, 14.

[177] Palagia 2006.

[178] Euripides, *Ion* 16–53. The baby Erichthonios appears on Attic red-figure vases: Shapiro 2003, 87–8, cat. no. 6, fig. 3.

[179] Palagia 2006, 608–9. In this sense, see also Beaumont 2012, 67.

a sacrificial bull beside him.[180] Ajootian suggests that the scene may portray the father's presentation of his child for admission to the *phratry* (and to Athenian citizenship) at the annual *Apatouria* celebration.[181] Considering that the relief comes from the Asklepieion, however, it is more likely that it may represent the sacrifice of a bull as a thank-offering for the healing of a child who had recovered from an illness.[182] In any case, divine sanction of, and assistance for, the infant would be the main theme here.

By the completion of its third year, the child was ready to be incorporated into the religious community during the festival of the *Anthesteria*. At this festival, and particularly from about 430 into the early fourth century BC, children were given small or miniature wine jugs, *choes*, to symbolize their first official participation in the religious community (Fig. 2.11).[183] These *choes* provide the largest surviving corpus in Greek art of depictions of toddlers and young children, both boys and girls, engaged in play and childish activities.[184] The children usually are naked, apart from the strings of amulets they wear around their neck or across their body, and they crawl on the ground, play with dogs, grasp after grapes dangled in front of them, or play with a wheel on a stick, among other things. A red-figure *chous* in the Bloomington University art museum, for example, depicts a young boy on his knees reaching for a ball; he wears a strap or string around his chest with an attached pouch which may contain apotropaic amulets.[185]

In place of the physical body of the infant being presented or blessed in a sanctuary, substitute images of infants and toddlers in various materials often were deposited in such locations by parents to ensure divine protection for their children. Primarily, terracotta was used for figures of seated children perhaps one or two years of age, and these are almost always boys.[186] They appear sometimes naked, sometimes partially draped, and sometimes dressed

[180] Dasen 2011, 295, fig. 18.1. [181] Ajootian 2006, 618–19, fig. 2.

[182] So also Lawton 2007, 45, fig. 2.2 and Beaumont 2012, 68, fig. 3.19. On the Apatouria and the presentation of boys in early childhood, and possibly again in adolescence, see Lambert 1993, 162–78.

[183] Van Hoorn 1951; Hamilton 1992; Beaumont 2012, 67–84.

[184] Because this is a specific Athenian festival for children of the relevant age whose entry into the religious community took place on this occasion, the Attic red-figure *choes* found at a burial site in the interior of Spain, Los Villares (Hoya Gonzalo, Albacete), raise questions about a possible exportation of such a religious rite to the western Mediterranean. The *choes*, however, are part of a total of 53 different black-figure and red-figure vases and are interpreted as part of complete sets of imported vessels exported to Spain, possibly to Ampurias, for sale and distribution in the indigenous market. Furthermore, the *choes* in this case are not associated with child burials, but with cremation burials of high status individuals of the later fifth century BC. See Chapa-Brunet 2008, 628–31, fig. 7.

[185] Carroll 1989, 155–6, cat. no. 144.

[186] A marble statuette of a seated girl, possibly two or three years old, comes from the sanctuary of Eleitheiyia at Agrai near Athens and dates to the last third of the fourth century BC: Beaumont 2003, 77, fig. 14; Bobou 2015, 132, cat. no. 20.

Fig. 2.11 Red-figure wine juglet (*chous*) of the late fifth century BC from Athens, with an infant playing whilst wearing a string of apotropaic amulets.
Photo: © The Trustees of the British Museum.

in a short tunic. In the archaeological literature, they are commonly referred to as 'temple boys'.[187] Those retrieved from the sanctuary of Demeter and Kore at Corinth, for example, also may wear a pointed cap and, occasionally, a string of amulets with an apotropaic function.[188]

The best known series of so-called temple boys in stone are those of the fifth to third centuries BC from various temple sites in Cyprus and at Sidon on the Phoenician coast (Fig. 2.12).[189] These are very ornately draped with strings of apotropaic amulets of various shapes.[190] Marble statues of seated boys and girls, all of very young age, were also fairly popular in the late fourth century BC in and around Athens, and in Eretria, on Paros and Crete, and have been

[187] Hadzisteliou-Price 1969.
[188] Merker 2000, 68–73, eg. *c.* nos. 236, 237, 238; Bookidis 2010, 6, 214–19, cat. nos. 88–102, pls. 96–100.
[189] Beer 1994; Caneva and Delli Pizzi 2014.
[190] Dasen 2003a, 282–3; Costanzo and Dubois 2014, 163–4, 170, figs. 8, 11. For a silver pendant in the shape of a pomegranate, found on the chest of an infant buried in the seventh century BC at Vitsa in northern Greece, see Dubois 2012, 339, fig. 11a.

Fig. 2.12 So-called 'temple boy' terracotta votive, from Cyprus. The Cesnola Collection, Purchased by subscription, 1874–76. The Metropolitan Museum of Art, 74.51.1449.
Photo: The Metropolitan Museum of Art, New York (www.metmuseum.org).

found there in sanctuaries of Artemis and Eleitheiyia, both goddesses connected with childbirth and childhood, as well as sanctuaries of Asklepios.[191] Most of them sit with one leg bent, the torso twisted and one arm and the head directed towards something approaching or seen to the child's left. The male toddlers are naked, or have a loosely draped himation over part of the lower limbs, or wear a little tunic; the girls, on the other hand, are clothed in a chiton. Although the temple boy figures in the Greek world do not have dedicatory inscriptions on them, similar bronze figures from Etruria do and these Etruscan examples are good comparanda. The inscription "to the god Tec Sanś as a gift" appears incised, for example, on the arm of a third- or early second-century bronze statuette of a seated boy wearing a bulla, bracelets, and anklets from Sanguineto near Lake Trasimeno.[192]

[191] Bobou 2015, 128–33, 137, 140, cat. nos. 10–14, 17, 19–20, 23, 37, 47.

[192] Haynes 2000, 362–3, fig. 285; MacIntosh Turfa 2006, 92, fig. 6.2. See also Pautasso 1994, 59–63, pls. 32–4, who compares these Etruscan bronzes with terracotta toddler statuettes of the second century BC from Vulci. Interestingly, of the five terracotta toddlers at Vulci, one is a girl

These statues may have been deposited directly on the ground or on some kind of pedestal, plinth, or backdrop when dedicated and displayed in sanctuaries. The back of a marble statue of a very young girl from the sanctuary of Eileithyia in the Agrai district outside Athens, for example, is treated very summarily, suggesting that it stood in front of something, perhaps a wall, and that the toddler was not meant to be seen from all angles or in the round.[193] But the figures also could have been mounted on a column, as indicated by the marble statue of a male toddler of the late fourth century in the sanctuary of Asklepios in Athens.[194]

Figures such as these were not deposited exclusively in sanctuaries. At least one of the so-called temple boys from Cyprus comes from a tomb, and terracotta examples are also attested as grave goods at Taranto and Corinth, leading Caneva and Delli Pizzi to suggest that a statue purchased by the parents for sanctuary use could become part of the funerary assemblage when the child died unexpectedly or that such statues may have been grave gifts from the outset to ensure divine protection of the child, even in death.[195] Perhaps the seated toddler, as it became a popular votive image in the Hellenistic period in Greece, did double duty to a certain extent in a funerary context. The precise same pose as many of the late fourth-century temple boys, seated and twisted towards and gesturing to the left, was used for the relief of a toddler on an Attic grave *stele* of the later fourth century, perhaps instilling something of the sacred in the child's portrait or alluding to divine protection of the child even after death.[196]

(wearing a *bulla*): Pautasso 1994, 61, cat. no. E 1, pls. 32a–b. Small bronze figurines of the baby Opheltes, a Nemean prince who died very young, have been found at Nemea where there was a shrine of the heroized Opheltes: Neils 2003, 141–2, fig. 3.

[193] Bobou 2015, 131, cat. no. 19.

[194] Beaumont 2012, 64, fig. 3.16. Another marble statue of a toddler from a sanctuary of Asklepios is the one found in a sanctuary of that deity in Lissos on Crete: Bobou 2015, 137, cat. no. 137.

[195] Graepler 1997, 242, fn. 333, fig. 258 (grave 191); Merker 2000; Caneva and Delli Pizzi 2014, 506.

[196] Beaumont 2012, 62, fig. 3.13.

3

Mother and Child

Pregnancy, Birth, and Health

FOETAL DEVELOPMENT IN THE WOMB

Ancient Greek and Roman medical texts reveal an awareness of the gradual development of the foetus in the mother's womb.[1] The Hippocratic treatises on gynaecology and embryology, the majority of which date to the fifth and fourth centuries BC and were influential on Roman medicine, vary in their focus, some, such as *On the Nature of the Child* dealing almost exclusively with the foetal, rather than the maternal body, and others, such as *On the Diseases of Women*, validating the woman's physical experiences.[2] In many ways, these medical texts perceive the mother and child as separate entities, with the two potentially set against each other. The mother could harm her foetus, either unintentionally with a "faulty womb", or intentionally through lack of care, but the foetus, too, could be the "protagonist of the story of childbirth" and affect the health of its mother.[3]

The period in the womb appears to have been viewed as a sort of life-course. The Hippocratic author of *The Eight Months' Child* divided gestation into periods of forty days, the first representing the period when the danger of miscarriage was greatest, and the last when the foetus gathered strength and was particularly active.[4] These periods, in part, also mapped onto the mother's changing body. After forty days of pregnancy, according to the second-century physician Soranus, mothers began craving so-called foods, such as charcoal or earth, which were to be avoided "because the foetus obtains food which is neither clean nor suitable".[5]

Pregnancy was calculated in lunar months, with the infant being born ideally in the tenth lunar month, the equivalent of nine gestational months. References

[1] Hanson 2008; Dasen 2013a. [2] Hong 2012. [3] Hong 2012, 80–1.
[4] Hippocrates, *The Eight Month Child* 4, 7, 9. [5] Soranus, *Gynaecology* 1.15.48.

to this ten-month period of pregnancy are frequent in medical texts.[6] Even in Roman poetry the mother's "ten long, tedious months of waiting" find mention.[7] Babies born before full term would have had little chance of surviving, and a quick and uneventful birth at full term was hoped for. This might be helped along with spells and magical devices such as inscribed amulets, known as quick-birthers. These amulets can give us some indication of the perception of the foetus when it was nearing or at full term. One such carnelian amulet of the third century AD, for example, bears the Greek inscription "onto your little feet", thereby directly addressing the foetus as if it were sentient enough at this point to be able to hear the command and to be born in response to it.[8] It is in this last phase when, according to the Hippocratic doctors, the mother's body could no longer supply enough nutrients for the baby, and the hungry foetus "tosses about and so ruptures the membranes" and is born.[9]

Roman personal correspondence suggests that the foetus and its mother required a suitable regimen of antenatal care. The miscarriage of Pliny the Younger's teenage wife, Calpurnia, in AD 107 is relevant in this context.[10] Pliny wrote to his wife's family to inform them of the tragedy, saying that because she was "young and inexperienced, she did not realize that she was pregnant, failed to take proper precautions, and did several things that were better left undone".[11] Pliny does not reveal what the "proper precautions" for a pregnant woman were, but we know from Soranus that a woman in this state should avoid vigorous exercise, lifting, pungent foods, and cold baths, among other things, in order to take proper care of the foetus and give it the best possible start in life.[12] The Hippocratic *On the Diseases of Women*, which focuses on female disorders and women's bodily experiences, also flags up the dangers of physical exertion, eating too little or too much, or eating something spicy or bitter, and excessive drink.[13] The same text says, not surprisingly, that if a pregnant woman were beaten, the embryo also might be aborted. According to Soranus, "women who transgress the rules harm the foetus", thereby weakening it, retarding its growth, and making it possible for the child to become misshapen and to possess "an ignoble soul".[14] For Soranus, a viable infant was one whose mother had spent her pregnancy in good health.

Pregnancy and parturition were potentially dangerous for both mother and child. A remarkable gold-leaf amulet of the third or fourth century AD found in 2007 in Oxfordshire sheds light on the concern for a pregnant mother's

[6] Hippocrates, *On the Fetal Nature* 1.18.
[7] Vergil, *Eclogues* 4.60–4.61.
[8] Hanson 2004; Hanson 2008, 105–6.
[9] Hippocrates, *The Nature of the Child* 30.4.
[10] Carlon 2009, 171–5; Shelton 2013, 125–7.
[11] Pliny, *Letters* 8.10, 8.11.
[12] Soranus, *Gynaecology* 1.14.46, 1.26.54–56.
[13] Hippocrates, *On the Diseases of Women* 1.25.
[14] Soranus, *Gynaecology* 1.47.

health.[15] This amulet, written in Greek, designed to be rolled up and worn in a cylindrical amulet case, is a charm for easy childbirth. It entreats the gods that "Fabia, whom Terentia her mother bore, being in full fitness and health, shall master the unborn child and bring it to birth". The length of Soranus's discussion in Book 4 of *Gynaecology* on difficult deliveries implies that midwives could expect to encounter complicated births routinely. The tragedy of such a death is made abundantly clear in Pliny the Younger's letter to Velius Cerealis.[16] He refers to two daughters of his friend Helvidius as "victims of their motherhood" because they died giving birth to baby girls. Pliny sympathized not only with the young women, but also with their surviving, now motherless, infants and with their widowed husbands. Cicero's daughter Tullia was also a victim of motherhood, as she died in 45 BC after giving birth at the age of thirty to her second son. The baby, Lentulus, born in February, probably did not survive long, as he is last mentioned in a letter by Cicero in March of the same year.[17] Juvenal, too, refers to "the perils of childbirth".[18] A miscarriage late in the pregnancy also could pose serious health risks to the mother, as it did for a woman who miscarried at five months, was seized with fever and delirium, and died seven days later.[19]

A variety of *in utero* abnormalities and disorders could cause the foetus to die. One such congenital disorder is *osteogenesis imperfecta*, also known as brittle bone disease, due to the typical bone fragility that results in frequent fractures. Some disorders, such as this, are recognizable in the skeletal record, at the Kellis 2 cemetery in the Dakhleh oasis in Roman Egypt, for example. The severely bowed limbs and barrel-shaped ribcage of a skeleton thirty-eight gestational weeks old at this site is one instance of such a child afflicted with the disease who died stillborn or very shortly after birth.[20]

The removal of the baby during birth could be difficult if it was not positioned correctly, and the force used to pull or twist the baby out of the pelvic outlet in those cases could result in fractures to the clavicle and arms, as indicated in several buried infants and young children at Kellis 2 cemetery.[21] Occasionally, the foetus died in the womb and needed to be extracted to save the mother's life. The horrific circumstances of this procedure known as an embryotomy are described in several medical sources.[22] In fact, the Hippocratic doctors wrote a whole treatise, *On the Extraction of the Dead*, on the subject, and *Of Female Diseases* also includes instructions for an embryotomy. If the foetus was dead, according to the latter treatise, it was to be pulled out of the womb by hand, but if this was not possible, the skull of the foetus was to be opened with a surgical knife and crushed, and the bones pulled out of the

[15] Tomlin 2008. [16] Pliny, *Letters* 4.21.
[17] Cicero, *To Atticus* 270. See also Treggiari 2007. [18] Juvenal, *Satires* 6.592.
[19] Hippocrates, *Epidemics* 2.2, case iii. [20] Cope and Dupras 2011.
[21] Dupras et al. 2015, 61–4. [22] Gourevitch 2004.

mother by hook or forceps.[23] Instructions are also given on the piecemeal dissection of the foetus, which entailed detaching its arms, opening its thorax, and crushing its ribs, avoiding its belly to avoid an eruption of the intestines. Another suggested treatment to expel the foetus was to turn the mother upside down and shake her, which cannot have been a pleasant experience for a distraught woman in these circumstances.[24] Soranus wrote that some midwife's chairs had an axle and windlass so that, if necessary, a dead foetus could be extracted by hooks and ropes.[25]

Archaeological evidence for this surgical procedure is rare, but there are a few indications of it in skeletal assemblages. In the late Roman cemetery at Poundbury Camp near Dorset, a nearly complete, but disarticulated, skeleton of a full-term (between thirty-eight and forty gestational weeks) infant was found buried in a wooden coffin, a standard burial container of the region.[26] Numerous cut-marks are present throughout the skeleton on torso, arms, and legs, and conform to Soranus's surgical instructions to dismember the baby and draw the body parts through the birth canal using a series of medical instruments. Elsewhere in Britain, at Yewden villa in Buckinghamshire, a nearly complete skeleton of a pre-term baby (thirty-five to thirty-seven weeks' gestation) exhibits five cut marks on a single femur, suggesting that this child might also have been removed surgically from its mother's womb.[27]

The mutual dangers facing mother and foetus are illustrated by a late Roman skeleton of a pregnant woman with the skeleton of her seven-month-old foetus still inside her, at Costebelle in southern France.[28] Palfi et al. suggest that the *periostitis* of the skull and other bones and the fusion of hand and feet bones of the foetus are pathological lesions resulting from infection transferred to it through the placenta, and they identify that infection as congenital syphilis.[29] While this is possible, other congenital infections cannot be ruled out.[30] More recently, this diagnosis has been questioned and it has been suggested that the character of the pathology is indicative of a *lithopedion* (stone baby), a calcium-encased foetus occurring in ectopic abdominal pregnancies when the foetus dies and is not reabsorbed by the maternal body.[31] In encasing the dead baby in calcium deposits, the mother's body defends itself against fatal infection from a decomposing corpse. There are modern cases of quite elderly women whose doctors have discovered a stone baby still in their bodies, causing excruciating pain up to fifty years after

[23] Hippocrates, *On the Diseases of Women* 1.36. For a discussion of caesarians and embryotomies, see Do Sameiro Barroso 2013.

[24] Hippocrates, *On Superfoetation*.

[25] Soranus, *Gynaecology* 2.2.3.

[26] Molleson and Cox 1988; Redfern 2010, 462–3, figs. 15–16; Redfern and Gowland 2012, 121–3, fig. 7.3.

[27] Mays et al. 2014.

[28] Palfi et al. 1992 and 1993.

[29] Palfi et al. 1993, 4–5.

[30] Mays 2002.

[31] M. Rose 1997b.

the foetus had died inside them.[32] The age of the mother at Costebelle is estimated at fifty, so she would have been too old to conceive. It is, therefore, worth considering whether the Costebelle foetus also could be a long-dead *lithopedion* that had lodged hidden in its mother for many years until she was older. In this scenario, the baby might have died in the womb, never having been extracted, and the resulting calcified foreign body and long-term complications ultimately killed the mother.

There was, of course, another way of losing a baby, namely abortion.[33] Not all women wanted the children they were carrying, for a variety of reasons. Women could induce labour by physical exertion, such as jumping, as did a female musician, according to Hippocrates.[34] Juvenal was particularly scathing about pampered, rich women who did not want to have their looks or lifestyle ruined by having children and who paid abortionists with powerful drugs to "murder mankind within the womb".[35] Although abortion was not illegal, Cicero condemned a woman from Miletus who had procured an abortion and robbed the father of his hopes of "his name of continuity, the family of support, the house of an heir, and the state of a prospective citizen".[36] How great a burden could rest on the shoulders of a future child!

CHILDBIRTH AND DEATH IN CHILDBIRTH

Brent Shaw's study of demographic data, primarily late Roman (Christian) funerary epitaphs, suggests that there was a clear birthing cycle of women in Rome and Roman Italy.[37] Based on the age at death and the death-date given in these funerary inscriptions, he calculated birth dates and distributed them by month for an annual cycle. Patterns emerged which show that the high points in births in Rome were in December and January and again in May and August; for Italy, in general, births peaked in February and March, and again from September to November. By combining this data with information on medieval and early modern Mediterranean seasonal infant mortality, Shaw demonstrates that infant deaths also peaked in December and January and from May to November. The co-relation between birth and death relates to the fact that the period immediately following birth is the most dangerous, and newborns are vulnerable to all kinds of diseases and infections. As Shaw puts it, "the months in which by far the heaviest infant mortality occurs will tend to

[32] Ede et al. 2011; Ramos-Andrade et al. 2014; Holdt Sommer 2016.
[33] Kapparis 2002.
[34] Hippocrates, *On the Fetal Nature* 1.2, *On the Origin of Man*.
[35] Juvenal, *Satires* 6.592.
[36] Cicero, *In Defence of Cluentius* 32.
[37] Shaw 2001b.

be the same months in which more infants are being born".[38] Although the data on which Shaw's results are based are somewhat indirect, seasonality of birth and death in the Roman context might well reflect patterns of reproductive activity in antiquity.

The process and involvement of third parties in the birthing process in the Roman world are known through medical descriptions and instructions and from a few pictorial depictions of delivery in Roman art. For normal labour, Soranus recommended the advance preparation of olive oil, warm water, sponges, pieces of wool, bandages to swaddle the newborn, a pillow on which to place the newborn, things for the parturient to smell, a midwife's stool or chair, two beds, and an appropriate room.[39] The seat of the midwife's stool should have a crescent-shaped cut-out of medium size, and below the seat the sides of the stool should be closed in, but the front and rear open. Furthermore, arms and a backrest should be present on the stool, so that the parturient can support herself whilst straining. Three female birth helpers on either side of and behind the parturient are recommended, the midwife positioning herself opposite and below her patient.

It is fortuitous that Scribonia Attice, clearly a midwife by trade, chose a scene from her working life to advertise her profession on a terracotta plaque fixed to the facade of her tomb (Tomb 100) of the mid-second century AD in the Isola Sacra cemetery at Portus (Fig. 3.1).[40] There are far fewer birthing assistants depicted here than Soranus recommended, but Soranus was writing for women of status who could afford a large staff, and this is not a scene of elite childbirth. Moreover, the number of active participants has been reduced to a minimum to fit the plaque format. Scribonia Attice sits opposite the woman giving birth, level with her lower body and reaching between her legs to extract the newborn. Only one assistant can be seen behind the birthing chair, and she has wrapped her arms around the woman to support her during delivery.

Another childbirth scene survives on a small ivory plaque of the first century AD from Pompeii, although this almost certainly depicts an episode from Greek mythology rather than illustrating a daily activity.[41] The relevant plaque is one of two relief-decorated end pieces of a papyrus-roll winder, each end piece being carved with scenes on mythology. One of these may depict the birth of Meleager. The parturient here, Althaia, appears to be sitting on a birthing stool, rather than a chair; she reaches back with her left arm to hold on to a birthing assistant, while she supports herself with her right hand on a staff or sceptre. The midwife squatting (or seated?) in front of the woman

[38] B. D. Shaw 2001b, 96. [39] Soranus, *Gynaecology* 2.2.2–3.

[40] Kampen 1981, 69–71, fig. 58.

[41] Kampen 1981, 70, fig. 60; S. E. Wood 2001b, esp. 32–6, figs. 1–4, in which she corrects her earlier interpretation of the pieces in S. E. Wood 2000, 84–6, fig. 5.4.

Fig. 3.1 Terracotta relief (cast) of a midwife delivering a baby, tomb 100, Isola Sacra cemetery at Portus.
Photo: Maureen Carroll.

appears to be pulling the baby out of its mother, or at least she holds something in her right hand that could either be the baby's head or perhaps a sponge. Behind the midwife is another assistant with arms held out as if to take the baby once it has been born.

Four reputedly authentic Roman stone reliefs with childbirth scenes have come to light recently.[42] Some doubt is thrown on their authenticity not only due to the lack of secure provenance but also because the figures and unusual nature of the activity in the reliefs look somewhat suspect. One panel depicts a naked woman squatting on a chair, assisted by four women, the head of the infant just beginning to appear in her opened vagina.[43] This may be a birthing chair with a cut-out on the seat, as Soranus describes it, but why she squats on the chair, rather than sitting on it, is odd. Two other panels now in the Wellcome Library in London depict a single female giving birth to a baby in

[42] Perkins 2012, 178–81, figs. 15–17. Coulon 2004a, 31–5, illustrates a very small number of stone reliefs or votives from Gaul which may depict the birth of a child, but they are so poorly executed and grotesque that it is difficult to be sure that this is the subject matter.

[43] Perkins 2012, 178.

the company of what must be a midwife.[44] Both parturients are completely naked, with their legs open and their vaginas on full display. On one of the plaques the baby is in the process of exiting the woman's body as she sits on a draped chair; on the other the baby has already been born and the midwife holds it while the mother reclines on what looks more like a couch. Both midwives on the Wellcome reliefs are naked from the waist up. Neither offers any of the kind of physical support recommended by Soranus or depicted in the Ostian and Pompeian reliefs discussed above. The fourth relief in the Science Museum in London (Blythe House) is supposedly from Ostia and was purchased in Rome in 1932 (Fig. 3.2).[45] The mother here lies completely on her back, with her arms above her head resting on a pillow; she looks completely relaxed and rather seductively posed! She is attended to by three other women, one of whom holds the baby she has given birth to on a tray

Fig. 3.2 Marble relief showing the aftermath of childbirth.
Photo: Science and Society Picture Library, London.

[44] Perkins 2012, 178, figs. 15–16.
[45] Perkins 2012, 178, fn. 145, fig. 17. The art collector was Mariano Rocchi from Perugia, according to Caroline Lawrence: http://the-history-girls.blogspot.co.uk/2012/02/historical-detectives-social-networking.html.

or a basin. A personal inspection of the relief in Blythe House failed to reveal any details which indicate clearly that this relief might be a modern forgery, but I am not the first person to think that all of them must be.[46] There are several problems in accepting the authenticity of the reliefs: their sale on the antiquities market; the explicit subject matter; the poses of the birthing women; and the similarity in the physical details of the midwives. But the most important factor is the lack of parallels in any childbirth scenes with a secure provenance and date.[47]

Even if a baby were delivered alive and well, there were still many dangers for the mother in the post-partum period. The Hippocratic doctors recorded numerous cases of painful and violent maternal deaths after childbirth. The wife of Dromeades, for example, delivered a healthy baby girl, but on the second day she became feverish and finally expired on the sixth day after nausea, discharges, delirium, and spasms.[48] Even a couple weeks after childbirth, new mothers were not out of danger. The wife of Philinus in Thasos gave birth to a daughter, but on the fourteenth day after delivery she suffered from pain, fever, sleeplessness, intestinal problems, and convulsions, dying on the twentieth day.[49] Pity the poor woman who after having delivered a child endured all manner of afflictions for eighty days before she perished.[50] These Hippocratic case studies of childbirth and post-partum mortality offer much detail, and they chart the entire period of illness.

Archaeological evidence for miscarriages, stillbirths, and the death of mother and baby in childbirth survives in the burial evidence at many Roman sites. At Ampurias in Spain, for example, a woman was buried with a newborn placed between her legs in what is likely to represent a case of death in childbirth; they lay together in two amphorae placed end to end.[51] In London, a woman between eighteen and twenty-five years of age was buried with a pre-term (twenty-eight weeks' gestation) infant placed at her right foot.[52] At Cambodunum (Kempten) in Germany, several infants and newborns were interred in the northern cemetery (Keckwiese), two of them with adult females. These have been interpreted as double burials of mother and infant and as cases of death in childbirth or as a result of associated

[46] Perkins 2012, 180, with bibliography. See also The History Girls website for a discussion of authenticity, although Lawrence comes to the conclusion that it might be genuinely of second-century date: http://the-history-girls.blogspot.co.uk/2012/02/historical-detectives-social-networking.html.

[47] There is also a fifth relief related to the aftermath of childbirth, a reclining woman breastfeeding a baby (Perkins 2012, 180, fig. 18). This relief also was bought on the art market in Rome in 1932, and I am sceptical about its authenticity as well, not least because it has similarities with another (genuine?) relief panel depicting Ino(?) breastfeeding the infant Dionysus that was walled into the Palazzo Cardelli: Matz 1969, 343–5, Beilage 106.1.

[48] Hippocrates, *Epidemics* 1.3, case i.

[49] Hippocrates, *Epidemics* 1.3, case v.

[50] Hippocrates, *Epidemics* 2.3, case i.

[51] Almagro 1955, 293, 298, figs. 266, 269.

[52] Mackinder 2000, 19–20, 42–3, figs. 20, 32.

complications.[53] Judging by the number of foetuses buried in the Kellis 2 cemetery, roughly 15 per cent of pregnancies did not reach full term, and the death of mother and infant due to complications at childbirth was not rare.[54] One woman in her twenties in Burial 513 at Kellis 2 seems to have died in or after labour (Fig. 3.3).[55] She was found with a late-term foetus positioned at the pelvic inlet and facing downwards, suggesting that the foetus might have been expelled after the woman's death, during the decomposition process. In this case of possible dystocic or obstructed birth, various factors, such as a large or abnormally positioned baby, a small pelvis, the mother's age at first

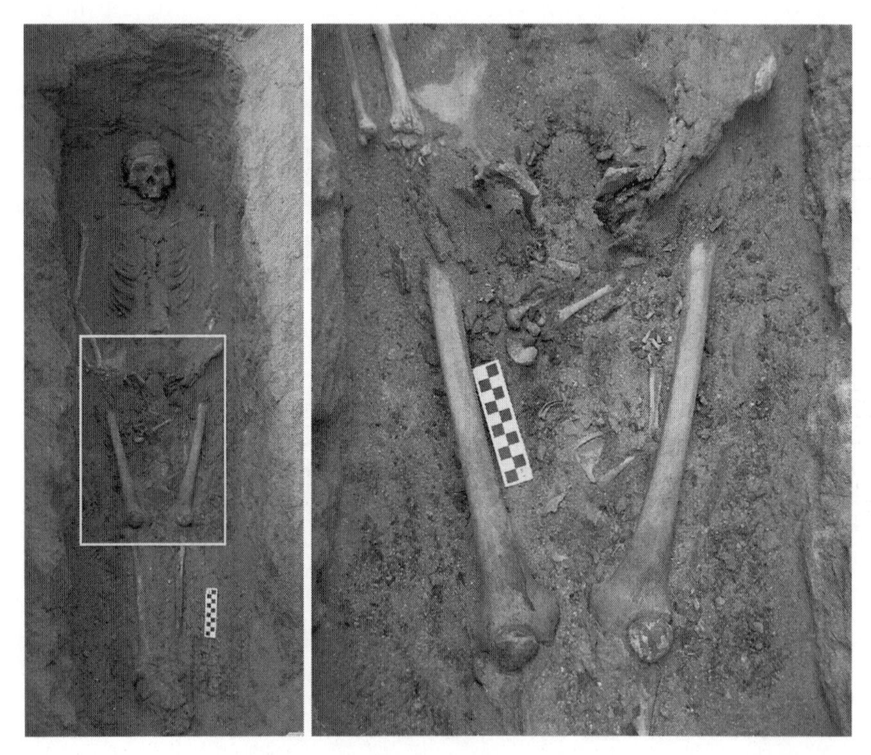

Fig. 3.3 Burial 513 in the Kellis 2 cemetery, Dakhleh Oasis, Egypt. The burial represents an adult female, about 20–25 years old, and an infant, estimated gestational age of 39 weeks, or right around birth, between the legs of the female.
Photo: courtesy of the Dakhleh Oasis Project Bioarchaeology Team.

[53] For example, Mackensen 1978a, 147, 242 (graves 153–4).
[54] Marlow 2001; Bowen 2002; Tocheri et al. 2005, 337, fig. 8; Cope and Dupras 2011. Foetuses and perinates make up one third of all juveniles at Kellis 2: Wheeler 2012, 228.
[55] Wheeler 2012, 228; Dupras et al. 2015, 59, fig. 3B.

pregnancy, or problems with the birth canal, could have contributed to the death of both mother and baby.

Outside a cemetery context, any kind of evidence for difficult pregnancies or concomitant death of mother and infant is extremely rare, but the sudden and catastrophic death of the inhabitants in the eruption of Vesuvius in AD 79 in Herculaneum and Pompeii has given us the skeletons of a number of women, unborn children, and infants which we can study.[56] One of the skeletons found in the ship sheds on the beach at Herculaneum, where people took refuge from the eruption, is that of a woman twenty to twenty-five years old (Erc 52) whose foetus (eight and a half to nine lunar months) was still inside her body.[57] In the same group, another young woman, only about sixteen years old (Erc 110), and pregnant for the first time, died with her pre-term baby (Erc 110bis) in her womb.[58] The pyroclastic flow that destroyed the Vesuvian cities also claimed the life of a young woman between the age of sixteen and eighteen and her unborn child, as she sought shelter with her family in the House of Julius Polybius in Pompeii.[59]

Indications of the death of mother and infant due to complications in labour or as a consequence of childbirth can also be found in epitaphs on Roman funerary monuments.[60] They can be very matter of fact and simply state that the woman died in childbirth (*obi(i)t in partu*), or was snatched away in childbirth, but they can give more details.[61] One, in particular, seems to blame the baby for the death of the mother, as if confirming Hippocratic embryological ideas on the opposition of the foetus and the mother: "The unstoppable Fury of the newborn infant took me, bitter, from my happy life with a fatal hemorrhage. I did not bring the child into the light by my labour pains, but it lies hidden in its mother's womb among the dead."[62] Another epitaph of a slave woman, Candida, from Salona in Dalmatia reveals that she was in labour for four whole days before she and her unborn child died; the inscription commissioned by her fellow slave husband says that labour had been tortuous (*cruciata*).[63] The inscription of a freedman's daughter in Rome reveals that the birth of twins resulted in her death at the age of twenty.[64] Women experiencing multiple births, such as twins, would have been at very high risk, but the infants were also in danger.[65] Rusticeia Matrona,

56 Capasso 2001; Bisel and Bisel 2002.

57 Capasso 2001, 470–4, figs. 632–54; Bisel and Bisel 2002, 465–7, fig. 378.

58 Capasso 2001, 779–82, figs. 1180–4; Bisel and Bisel 2002, 465.

59 Henneberg and Henneberg 2001, 82, figs. 1–2.

60 Gourevitch 1987; Laes 2011a, 50–6; Carroll 2014.

61 *AE* 1991.1076; *AE* 1994.1060; *CIL* XIV.2737.

62 Kaibel 1878, 218.

63 *CIL* III.2267.

64 *CIL* I.1215; Carroll 2006, 153.

65 For the burial of twins at Kellis 2 who did not survive birth, see Dupras et al. 2015, 59, fig. 3C.

a young woman of twenty-five from Mauretania in North Africa was given an epitaph that states: "The cause of my death was childbirth and malignant fate."[66] What actually went wrong during the birth is, of course, unknown, but as a selfless mother, she comforts her husband, telling him not to waste his tears on her and to take care of their son. Whether the son in question is the one who survived the birth, or this child is one born earlier, we cannot tell. In Rome, Veturia Grata was buried by her husband who chose to include the very detailed information in her epitaph that she died at the age of twenty-one, being eight months pregnant with her fourth child.[67] The three living children were still small, and now without a mother.

The young age of some women giving birth is apparent in various funerary inscriptions, their physical immaturity possibly having had an adverse effect on the likelihood of a healthy, normal birth.[68] Only one of the six infants that Veturia in Aquincum had carried in her life had survived; she was married at the age of eleven years and died sixteen years later, according to her epitaph.[69] If her multiple pregnancies had begun shortly after she married, it is little wonder that she lost so many babies. The epitaph of Aeturnia Zotica in Ankara states only that she was just fifteen and a half years old when she died sixteen days after having given birth to her first child.[70] Rhanis from Tusculum, not yet sixteen, perished in childbirth, her epitaph making it clear that the baby was still in her womb and the two were cremated together, "two burials in a single body, one pile of ashes for the remains of two".[71] Knowing that very young wives might well have serious difficulty in carrying and delivering babies, Soranus, in fact, advised a pregnancy termination "to prevent subsequent danger in parturition if the uterus is small and not capable of accommodating the complete development".[72] Although the pyroclastic flow from Vesuvius killed the sixteen-year-old girl in the ship sheds at Herculaneum and the baby in her womb (Erc 110 and Erc 110bis), Capasso speculated that she may anyway have died struggling to give birth to the baby because her immature pelvis might have been too narrow for the baby to emerge properly.[73] Sandra Wheeler attributes the high proportion of juveniles at Kellis 2 to the early age of first marriage for women (around fifteen years) and the need for women to maintain a high level of reproduction to sustain the population.[74] Having babies so young, and repeatedly, could have been deadly.

[66] *CIL* VIII.20288. [67] *CIL* VI.28753; Carroll 2006, 153.

[68] The topic of teenage pregnancies and the dangers to maternal health is of importance even today. See World Health Organization findings at http://www.who.int/maternal_child_adolescent/topics/maternal/adolescent_pregnancy/en/; http://www.who.int/mediacentre/factsheets/fs364/en/. See also Fraser et al. 1995.

[69] *CIL* III.3572. [70] *CIL* III.6759. [71] *CIL* XIV.2737.

[72] Soranus, *Gynaecology* 1.60. [73] Capasso 2001, 779–81, figs. 1180–3.

[74] Wheeler 2012, 228.

THE LIFE-COURSE: MILESTONES IN THE FIRST YEAR OF LIFE

The first year of life was punctuated and marked by various events and milestones of a physical, social, and legal nature. The infant's socialization began as soon as the umbilical cord was cut because it was finally physically independent of its mother. When it received its first bath, the baby was transformed from a part of the mother's womb to an individual at the beginning of its own life. Soranus did not favour cold baths or rinsing the infant in wine to remove blood and traces of afterbirth, but he recommended massaging a mixture of salt and honey, or olive oil and vegetable juice into the infant's skin and then rinsing off the emulsion with lukewarm water.[75] The next step was to swaddle the infant with bandages, first its individual limbs and then the whole body from the chest to the feet. Most people kept their babies swaddled for at least forty to sixty days, sometimes longer, before they were released from their constraints limb by limb over a period of several days.[76]

There were medical reasons for this; for one thing, the infant was contained and unable to twist or damage its joints, and, secondly, it could not put its fingers into its eyes and damage them. In Roman thought, however, swaddling also had an important socializing effect. Swaddling and bodily routines intensified the interaction between carer and infant and contributed towards the socialization of the growing child. The newborn was unwrapped from its swaddling constraints several times daily, especially when "it soils itself very much or is roughened by a rash".[77] Furthermore, the baby's body was straightened and kept firm through swaddling in infancy; an infant was thereby moulded into a person and its future as a well-formed adult given a good start for the further life-course.[78]

A major milestone in the infant's life was its naming day, the *dies lustricus*. In assuming the family name and acquiring a given name, the baby gained a social persona as part of the family. The naming day was celebrated by various rituals on the eighth day for girls, and on the ninth day for boys.[79] The period between birth and the *dies lustricus* was considered dangerous, and the seventh day, when the umbilical cord fell off, was especially so. Aristotle interpreted the timing of the name-giving as being related to the extreme vulnerability of newborns, claiming that "the majority of deaths occur before the child is a week old".[80]

The infant's embedded place in the family's past, present, and future becomes particularly clear when we look at the system of registering births.[81]

[75] Soranus, *Gynaecology* 2.8.12–13.
[76] Soranus, *Gynaecology* 19.42.
[77] Soranus, *Gynaecology* 2.16.30.
[78] Soranus, *Gynaecology* 2.15, 2.42.
[79] Plutarch, *Roman Questions* 102.
[80] Aristotle, *Historia Animalum* 587b.
[81] Sanders 1927; Schulz 1942 and 1943.

Since the time of Augustus, the birth of a legitimate infant in possession of Roman citizenship was registered in a declaration (*professio*) before magistrates, either at the *Aerarium Saturni* in Rome or at the *tabularium publicum* of the *praeses provinciae* in the provinces. This was to take place within thirty days of birth. The registration contained the names of the parents, occasionally also the name of the paternal grandfather, the sex and name of the child, date and place of birth, and the domicile of the parents. Thus, each infant had a very specific context that was familial, social, and civic. Births were publicly recorded on white boards (*tabula albi*) for everyone to see, but because these public notices were only temporary, births also were recorded in a codex or a papyrus roll that was kept in the official archives. Surviving texts on wax tablets of the second century AD indicate that births were recorded and exhibited monthly in Rome in the Forum of Augustus, and a copy of records was kept there.[82] The parents of illegitimate children were allowed to make a private statement of birth (*testatio*) before seven witnesses and to draw up a document on this declaration, as a sort of substitute for the *professio*. The witnesses were there to confirm the private declaration of birth by the father or mother and the veracity of the declaration. From the end of the second century, however, every Roman child, whether legitimate or illegitimate, had to be registered through the process of *professio*. These were, of course, official records, but happy families are also known to have incised or painted unofficial brief notices of birth on house walls, such as the one over the entrance to the House of the Priest Amandus at Pompeii announcing "*natus (est) Cornelius Sabinus*", Cornelius Sabinus has been born.[83]

Another milestone in the first year of life is represented by the commencement of weaning. The infant was breastfed for at least six months, when teething began and solid foods were introduced into the infant's diet. Those infants who received supplementary foods too soon after birth would have been adversely affected and susceptible to disease. Galen advised that infants should be given supplementary foods from the age of about seven months, while Soranus recommended an age of six months; full weaning should not occur until at least eighteen months or two years.[84] This was not a sudden dietary change for the baby; "one must stealthily and gradually take it off the breast and wean it by adding constantly to the amount of other food but diminishing the quantity of milk".[85] Supplementary foods included crumbs of bread softened with hydromel or milk, sweet wine, or honey wine, soup made from spelt, very moist porridge, and eggs.[86] This schedule for the weaning process was considered best practice, but it may not have been universal to all social groups everywhere in the empire, as studies of the human remains indicate.

[82] Sanders 1927. [83] *CIL* VI.8149; see also; *CIL* IV.294, *CIL* IV.3890; Kepartová 1984.
[84] Galen, *On Hygiene* 9.29, 10.31; Soranus, *Gynaecology* 2.46–48.
[85] Soranus, *Gynaecology* 2.47. [86] Soranus, *Gynaecology* 2.46.

The stable isotope analysis of carbon and nitrogen values from human bone is a useful method of reconstructing breastfeeding and weaning patterns in ancient populations, and such analysis has been undertaken on skeletal remains in various locations.[87] Nitrogen levels record the duration of breast-feeding, while carbon indicates the initiation of the weaning process. During pregnancy, a foetus derives all of its nutrients from its mother's diet, and its bodily tissues will have an equivalent nitrogen value to that of its mother. The infant becomes a consumer of its mother's tissues after birth, obtaining all of its protein from breast milk, so that its nitrogen values during breastfeeding are elevated above that of the mother and reach a peak. When weaning begins and breast milk is gradually replaced with supplementary foods, the nitrogen ratios of the infant decrease to a level similar to that of the adult female population. Carbon isotope analysis of the skeletons of infants at Kellis 2, for example, indicates that nitrogen enriched supplementary foods were introduced around six months of age, while the data show that breastfeeding continued for approximately the first three years of life.[88] Also, at Leptiminus in Tunisia, Roman babies began to be weaned before the age of two, with weaning completed by about three years of age.[89] In Roman London, the evidence suggests that cereal-based supplementary foods were introduced into the diet of infants around the age of six months, but they were not fully weaned until four years old.[90] At Isola Sacra (Portus) near Rome, however, infants were fully weaned by only two and a half years of age.[91]

Once the infant reached the age of one year, another change of status is alluded to by legal texts, and this pertains to the social norms of mourning according to the age of the deceased. From the age of one year, children were officially and publicly mourned if they died. According to Ulpian, "children younger than three are not formally mourned, but are mourned in marginal form; a child less than a year receives neither formal mourning nor marginal mourning".[92] The terms used are *lugetur* for formal mourning, and *sublugetur* for marginal mourning. *Lugetur* probably involved the abstinence from banquets and bathing, wearing black, purple, or white clothing, and cropping one's hair.[93] The meaning of *sublugetur* is obscure. The comments of the jurist Paulus include no direct statement on *sublugetur*, but by stating that children up to the age of three years should be mourned for one month for each year of their age at the time of death, he implies that a one-year-old child would be mourned for a month, but for children who had not yet lived a year there was no mourning period at all.[94] But, as Chapters 6–8 seek to demonstrate, such

[87] Dupras 2010. [88] Dupras et al. 2001. [89] Keenleyside et al. 2009.
[90] Powell et al. 2014. [91] Prowse et al. 2008, 306.
[92] *FIRA* 2.536. See also Plutarch, *Numa* 12.
[93] Plutarch, *Letter of Consolation to his Wife* 4, 6; Paulus, *Opinions* 1.21.14; Plutarch, *Roman Questions* 14, 26.
[94] Paulus, *Opinions* 1.21.13.

apparent regulations on mourning relate to the public sphere, not necessarily to sentiments expressed or activities conducted in private.

HEALTH AND DISEASE OF INFANTS: THE BIOARCHAEOLOGICAL EVIDENCE

The skeletal remains of children can reveal signs of disease episodes which affected the child from birth, but analysis of adult individuals can also provide evidence of poor health during childhood.[95] A particular cause of ill health and disease was poor nutrition. A mother's health has an impact on the growth and survival of the child while it is in the womb, but once the child is born its growth is affected, among other things, by a lack, insufficiency, or reduction of mother's milk, and by the introduction of supplementary foods. Periods of physiological postnatal stress can manifest themselves in the human skeleton in the formation of furrows or *hypoplasias* in tooth enamel (so-called Wilson bands) when the normal process of tooth growth stops. These dental *hypoplasias* provide a good indicator of health status during childhood when the enamel of the tooth crown is being formed, and they are often associated with weaning. In a skeletal sample of children under the age of one year in the Isola Sacra cemetery at Portus, these dental *hypoplasias* allowed Fitzgerald et al. to recognize two stress episodes or horizons, the first beginning at about two months and continuing to five months and a second between six and nine months, both of which reflect a less than optimal weaning diet.[96] A poor weaning diet might be rich in carbohydrates (for example barley, wheat, and corn), but such a diet provides only low amounts of iron and includes phosphorus and phytates which inhibit the intestinal absorption of iron, resulting in anaemia.[97] Anaemia also may be the result of diarrhoeal infections contracted when breast milk is replaced or partially replaced by other foods and animal milk. At Kellis 2, for example, a weaning diet of goat's milk may have contributed to nutritional deficiencies amongst infants because it would be lacking in folic acid.[98]

Almost 90 per cent of the individuals trapped in the House of Julius Polybius at Pompeii in the eruption of Vesuvius in AD 79 had experienced

[95] Redfern and Gowland 2012. The bones of premature and neonatal babies sometimes can *suggest* what the infant died of, but this is rare. A newborn who died around AD 300 in Augst, for example, may have died as the result of an infection contracted by the cutting of the umbilical cord, but the porous and pitted surface of the thigh bone can really only tell us that the baby likely had a bone marrow infection (osteomyelitis), not how that infection was caused. See Pfäffli 2013a, 39, cat. no. 23; Kramis and Trancik 2014, 14.

[96] Fitzgerald et al. 2006.

[97] Garnsey 1999, 47–8; Facchini et al. 2004, 130.

[98] Fairgrieve and Molto 2000, 328.

periods of acute illness or starvation for more than two weeks that had prevented the assimilation of calcium, as indicated by enamel *hypoplasias*. Torino and Fornaciari determined the point during childhood at which some of the adults had experienced stresses on their health.[99] Three of the adult males had been affected at one year and eight months, at one and a half and two and a half years, and at two and two and a half years respectively, whilst one of the children in the group had experienced acute illness at the age of one year and again at nine years of age. Weaning problems may have caused these episodes, but other childhood illnesses cannot be ruled out.

Other indicators of nutritional and physiological impairment in early growth appear in the human skull. The presence of porotic hyperostosis, a pathological condition affecting cranial bones and attested by localized areas of spongy, pitted, or porous bone tissue in the eye orbits (*cribra orbitalia*) and the cranial vault (*cribra crania*), is considered evidence that a past population suffered malnutrition and nutritional stress.[100] Parasitic infections and other hygiene problems can play a contributory role. Because hyperostotic lesions reflect chronic iron-deficiency anaemia and other disorders, *cribra orbitalia* has also been linked to weaning practices and the introduction of cereals.[101] Roman skeletal assemblages from a number of sites preserve evidence for lesions in the eye orbits or cranial vault and they have been used to draw conclusions on childhood nutrition and health in those populations. At Kellis 2, the high prevalence of porotic hyperostosis (70 per cent) indicates that chronic iron-deficiency anaemia was very common in the lives of infants and children.[102] At Lucus Feroniae near Rome, iron-deficiency anaemia in early childhood has been proposed as the causative agent of such hyperostotic lesions.[103] A lack of vitamin C and resultant scurvy clearly caused skeletal changes and severe *cribra orbitalia* in a child three to five years old buried in a large cemetery on the Via Collatina on the outskirts of Rome.[104] A study by Facchini et al. on human remains at Ravenna concludes that lesions in this population were due to acquired chronic anaemia caused by poor diet, worm infestation, and parasitic diseases.[105] Cranial pitting exhibited in the bones of adults at Urbino in north-east Italy is attributed to chronic environmental origins, either by diet deficiency, non-malarial parasites, lead toxicity, or by some other undetected environmental factor during childhood and early growth.[106]

Vitamin D is extremely important for growth, and deficiency in this vitamin could have further serious consequences. Vitamin D deficiency in an infant may already have begun whilst the baby was still in its mother's womb, as

[99] Torino and Fornaciari 2001.
[100] Walker et al. 2009.
[101] Fairgrieve and Molto 2000.
[102] Fairgrieve and Molto 2000.
[103] Salvadei et al. 2001.
[104] Minozzi et al. 2012, 278–9, figs. 13–14.
[105] Facchini et al. 2004.
[106] Paine et al. 2009.

pregnant and breastfeeding women are also at risk of vitamin D deficiency.[107] Galen flagged up "women, namely mothers" who remained indoors, not "exposing themselves to direct sunlight"; breast milk from these mothers would not provide sufficient levels of vitamin D to their babies.[108] And if a baby started to be weaned off mother's milk too early, the health of the baby would be compromised further from an early stage. The Roman practice of keeping a child covered in swaddling clothes for months might also have had a detrimental effect on the baby's health, as it would not be exposed to sunlight and, therefore, further prone to a deficiency in vitamin D.[109]

A frequent result of this vitamin deficiency in an infant is rickets, the baby's bones being un-mineralized and, therefore, lacking mechanical strength and becoming deformed when subject to bearing weight.[110] Bowing of the femurs is the visible sign of the disorder, as demonstrated in deformed leg bones of infants and young children from Roman Britain and Egypt.[111] Deformed arm and leg bones indicate active rickets while the baby was crawling and later when learning to walk, as demonstrated by a skeletal analysis of burials in the Isola Sacra cemetery at Portus.[112] Capasso noted that two of the babies present among the victims of Vesuvius at Herculaneum (E122 and E137) displayed an alteration of the femurs which he suggested might be the result of swaddling in the first few months of infancy, but perhaps rickets is an equally plausible diagnosis.[113] And a thirty-six-year-old woman (E103) in the same group at Herculaneum displayed evidence of rickets in childhood, with the period of stress in her life occurring between eighteen months and four years.[114]

Rickets was not fatal, however, and individuals could grow into adulthood with the visible reminders of what Soranus described as legs "twisted at the thighs".[115] Such a case of a woman between about twenty-seven and thirty-seven years of age with bowed femurs and tibias and stunted growth has been reported from Rome's Collatina necropolis.[116] This woman also displayed enamel *hypoplasias*, giving independent confirmation of poor health and afflictions already in early childhood. Despite the survivability of rickets, adult women with the disorder might not be able to carry a child or give birth successfully with the kind of deformities their bodies had, resulting in infant mortality further down the line.

Radiographs of long bones and *epitheses* can reveal another indicator of childhood health problems, namely lines or bands referred to as growth arrest lines or Harris lines.[117] Environmental stressors, nutritional and vitamin

[107] Dawodu and Wagner 2007. [108] Galen, *On Hygiene* 11.164.
[109] Rajakumar 2003; Choi et al. 2013.
[110] Ortner and Mays 1998; Redfern et al. 2013, 82–3.
[111] Redfern and Gowland 2012, 127, fig. 7.5. [112] C. Wood 2004.
[113] Capasso 2001. [114] Bisel and Bisel 2002, 472–3.
[115] Soranus, *Gynaecology* 2.43. [116] Minozzi et al. 2012, 277, fig. 11.
[117] H. A. Harris 1933.

deficiencies, and illness elicit periods of growth disruption in which cartilage cell division slows down or stops, while mineralization continues. Should the stressor be overcome, bone growth resumes, resulting in a line of increased mineral density. Harris lines, therefore, are useful indicators of developmental stress during the infant's life. Nevertheless, some argue that the formation of Harris lines might better be interpreted as a result of normal growth and growth spurts, rather than purely an outcome of nutritional or pathologic stress.[118] When Harris lines appear in combination with hyperostotic lesions, however, it is clear that health problems and deficiencies seriously affected a young population. At Carnuntum in Austria, for example, the bones of half the children buried in the cemetery south of the Roman civilian settlement, including foetuses and newborns, showed *cribra orbitalia* and *cribra cranii.*[119] Several newborns and infants exhibited both porous hyperostotic deposits and Harris lines on arms and leg bones (graves 92, 114, 135, 150, and 151).

It is evident from this brief survey of bioarchaeological evidence that infancy and earliest childhood were very high-risk periods of life. The danger of illness and disease may have been higher in some environments than others. The overcrowded city of Rome and its associated suburbs and harbours, in particular, seem to have been an unhealthy place to grow up. Discussing ailments in infants, especially rickets, Soranus explicitly names Rome as a place where this disorder was exceptionally common.[120] Skeletons from large cemeteries such as those on the Via Collatina indicate that over 80 per cent of the population had enamel *hypoplasia*, and almost 70 per cent of the population buried at Vallerano suffered from *cribra orbitalia.*[121] But in other areas outside Rome, such as Casal Bertone and Castellacio Europarco, enamel *hypoplasia* and *cribra orbitalia* were far less frequent, with orbital lesions evident in only 20 per cent of the population.[122] This may be accounted for by a more salubrious environment (more light, air, etc.), or it may be connected to the social status of the people living there who enjoyed a higher standard of living.

But cultural determinants may also have played a role in the health and wellbeing of the youngest children, and the physical mobility of Roman populations may have introduced new risks to indigenous populations. Lewis suggests that the common skeletal evidence for *cribra orbitalia*, anaemia, rickets, and/or scurvy in the children in the Poundbury cemetery at Durnovaria (Dorchester) might be an indication that the local population from the third to fifth centuries AD had adopted Mediterranean or Roman child-rearing practices that involved "a poor quality weaning diet, and swaddling,

[118] Papageorgopoulou et al. 2011. [119] Schweder and Winkler 2004.
[120] Soranus, *Gynaecology* 2.44.
[121] Via Collatina: Buccellato et al. 2003; Vallerano: Catalano et al. 2001, 135; Cucina et al. 2006.
[122] Killgrove 2010, 132–5.

leading to general malnutrition and inadequate exposure to sunlight".[123] At the same site, infantile cortical *hypertostosis* (or Caffey's disease), an inflammatory disorder causing bone changes, soft tissue swelling, and irritability, was thought to be present in a one-year-old buried in mausoleum R10.[124] If the infant had suffered from Caffey's disease, it is unlikely to have been the cause of death because the disorder usually rectifies itself within six to nine months after birth; it is lethal, however, if it presents in the prenatal period, i.e. when the foetus is in the mother's womb.[125] Farwell and Molleson detected a further fifty-six potential cases of infantile cortical hypertostosis at Poundbury, suggesting that there were many babies and children who must have been chronically ill for longer periods of time.[126] However, this diagnosis has been challenged by Lewis who has proposed *Thalassaemia major*, a genetic form of anaemia widely spread in the Mediterranean, as the cause of death of the infant in mausoleum R10 and of other infants.[127] In the Mediterranean itself, *Thalassaemia major* potentially has been detected in babies only months old buried under the floors of a possible slave barracks of the fifth century AD at Villa Magna outside Rome.[128] Since this is a genetic disease prevalent in the Mediterranean, its presence in infants at Durnovaria may be an indication that the parents of these children had migrated to Britain.[129]

DIVINE PROTECTION OF THE INFANT

The importance of female fertility to the survival of a family and its name, possibly of more concern to the elite than the middle and working classes, is hinted at in Pliny's letter to his wife's grandfather.[130] Although his wife miscarried, "evidence of her fertility" had been proven, and Pliny was sure that they would be granted children later on. In fact, they were not, and his wife's family were "robbed of a descendant".[131] If a woman did become pregnant, she had every reason to be anxious about the healthy development and survival of the infant. Furthermore, not everyone had access to professional medical care. In this context, the role of the divine world in providing protection for an infant and its mother is important and instructive. Surviving infancy, in general, in the Roman world was clearly fraught with a whole range of dangers and difficulties, as the preceding section demonstrates, and it is

[123] M. E. Lewis 2010, 414.
[124] Farwell and Molleson 1993, 151; M. E. Lewis and Gowland 2009.
[125] Wright et al. 2005.
[126] Farwell and Molleson 1993.
[127] M. E. Lewis 2012, 689. She proposed this on the basis of the radiographs of the bones and the lesions on the ribs.
[128] Cox 2016, 183–7.
[129] Redfern 2007, 189–91; M. E. Lewis 2012, 686, 691.
[130] Pliny, *Letters* 8.10.
[131] Carlon 2009, 157–74; Shelton 2013, 125–7.

no wonder that parents (and parents-to-be) asked the gods for help as often as they did.

Several deities were associated with motherhood and children. Since the sixth century BC, these had included Greek, Latin, or Etruscan gods, many of them syncretic versions of each other; Eileithyia, Leucothea, Juno Lucina, Hera-Uni, and Aphrodite-Turan (also Aphrodite-Iovia), for example, attested through votive dedications at sanctuary sites such as Gravisca and Pyrgi.[132] The goddess Mater Matuta also was connected with the rising of the sun and therefore helpful in bringing a newborn into the light of the world, her main temples situated in the Forum Boarium in Rome (S. Omobono) and at Satricum.[133]

Women's concerns regarding conception, pregnancy, and childbirth made them key participants in any cult that might have offered the blessings of reproductive health. Their role in supplication and the dedication of votive offerings to promote maternal health and safeguard family continuity is especially clear at Capua in Campania where approximately 160 stone statues of seated women holding or suckling swaddled infants were found in a sanctuary outside the eastern gate of the city.[134] These almost certainly represent inscribed votive gifts dedicated by local women in return for divinely granted favours, most likely conception and the birth of children. The statues are a visually powerful metaphor for motherhood through divine assistance and they illuminate the integration of women in religious life and their cult activities in matters of fertility from roughly the fifth to the early first centuries BC.[135]

[132] Comella 1978; Comella 1981; MacIntosh Turfa 2004, 362–3; Glinister 2006, 23; Fiorini 2014.

[133] Castagnoli 1979; Coarelli 1988, 205–44; Bouma 1996. For a discussion on the name and characteristics of Mater Matuta, see Bouma 1996, 250–62. By the first century BC, at the latest, she was conflated with Leucothea, a Greek goddess who protected children and seafarers: Cicero, *Tusculan Disputations* 1.12.28; Ovid, *Fasti* 6.545–546; Plutarch, *On Moral Virtue* 492D. In this regard, see also Coarelli 1988, 244–53; Bouma 1996, 251–2. For literary references to the temple of Mater Matuta in the Forum Boarium, see Plutarch, *Camillus* 5.1; Livy, *History of Rome* 24.47.15–16, 25.7.5–6. For the Mater Matuta temple at Satricum, see Livy, *History of Rome* 6.33.4–5, 28.11.2. Mater Matuta also may have had another temple in the northern part of Rome in the imperial period, as a funerary inscription commemorating a musician named Eucerus seems to locate his place of work at a temple of Mater Matuta that was not in the area of the Forum Boarium (*regio* VIII and IX), but in *regio VI*: Brunn 1996. Some temples that have been attributed to Mater Matuta, such as Temple D at Cosa, on the other hand, cannot be shown definitively to have belonged to this goddess, given the lack of substantive evidence: Lundeen 2006, 48. An inscribed votive *cippus* of third- or second-century date from Pesaro, a Roman colony, and votive inscriptions from Cora also attest to her veneration elsewhere in Italy: Pesaro: *CIL* I^2 379, *CIL* XI.6301; Harvey 2006. Cora: *CIL* X.6511 (a dedication to Mater Matuta of a statue of Jupiter) and *CIL* X.8416 (an unspecified gift to Mater Matuta). I am grateful to the British School at Rome for the award of the Hugh Last Fellowship in spring 2016 to study Mater Matuta and other so-called fertility cults in early Roman Italy; the publication of the results of that research project is forthcoming.

[134] Adriani 1939; Coarelli 1995; Rescigno 2009; Nava 2012, 27–34.

[135] These statues currently are the focus of a research project by the author. On women's votive activities in cults, see Schultz 2006, 95–120.

These tufa statues from Capua are unique, but throughout central Italy, in Etruria, Latium, and parts of Campania, votive gifts made of terracotta were dedicated frequently in sanctuaries to a variety of female and male gods from the fourth to the second centuries BC. Terracotta body parts in the form of heads, feet, hands, legs, eyes, ears, mouths, hearts, bladders, and intestines suggest that worshippers sought healing from the gods.[136] These votives enable us to infer the simple rituals of supplication and vow, and the dedication of a thank-offering after receiving divine help (or the belief that help had been received) for a broad range of health concerns.[137] Regularly mixed with these deposits of anatomical votives are male and female genitalia, especially penises and wombs, as well as swaddled babies, all of which are clearly connected with fertility and sexual and infant health, but they are difficult to assign to a particular deity when there is no accompanying epigraphic evidence. A rare snippet of information on the donor and the deity survives in the inscription of a female dedicant on two terracotta votive wombs from Vulci-Fontanile di Legnisina; the goddess named is Vei or Vea, the Etruscan equivalent of the Greek goddess Demeter.[138] Similar votive material associated with Mater Matuta is not abundant, and only at her temple at Satricum have terracotta swaddled infants and figurines of women and women with children been excavated.[139]

The terracotta swaddled infants, on average about fifty centimetres in length and, therefore, roughly life-size, illustrate the contemporary practice of swaddling and caring for very young infants (see Chapter 4; Figs. 1.1, 3.4).[140] As Graham has demonstrated, the baby votives are emblematic of one particular period in the life-course of an infant, the period in which it was swaddled, roughly forty to sixty days.[141] If a baby successfully survived the early weeks and months of life and it was ready to be unswaddled, "it would have been an appropriate time for parents to thank the divine community for the successful passage of the infant from non-being to human".[142] This is the moment when a votive swaddled infant would be given up as a suitable offering in fulfilment of the original vow. It is possible, also, that the swaddling bands may have been dedicated in a shrine once they were no longer needed, but they have not survived in the archaeological record.[143] But favours were not always granted

[136] Glinister 2006; Graham 2013.
[137] MacIntosh Turfa 2006, 91–2; Derks 2014, 59–63.
[138] Ricciardi 1992, 189, fig. 48.
[139] Bouma 1996, 291–2, fig. 19.
[140] Although a very small terracotta votive of an infant wrapped in swaddling bands survives from the sanctuary of Artemis Mounichia in Piraeus, the widespread Italic votive phenomenon of dedicating votives of swaddling infants is not paralleled in Classical Greece. See Beaumont 2012, 38, 50, figs. 2.6, 3.5; Lee 2015, 94, fig. 4.3.
[141] Graham 2014.
[142] Graham 2014, 40. Less convincing suggestions for swaddled infant votives include offerings in the hope of conception and birth and others in gratitude for the healing of an infant: de Cazanove 2008; Carroll 2011a, 114–15; Ehmig 2013, 120–1.
[143] Graham 2014, 41.

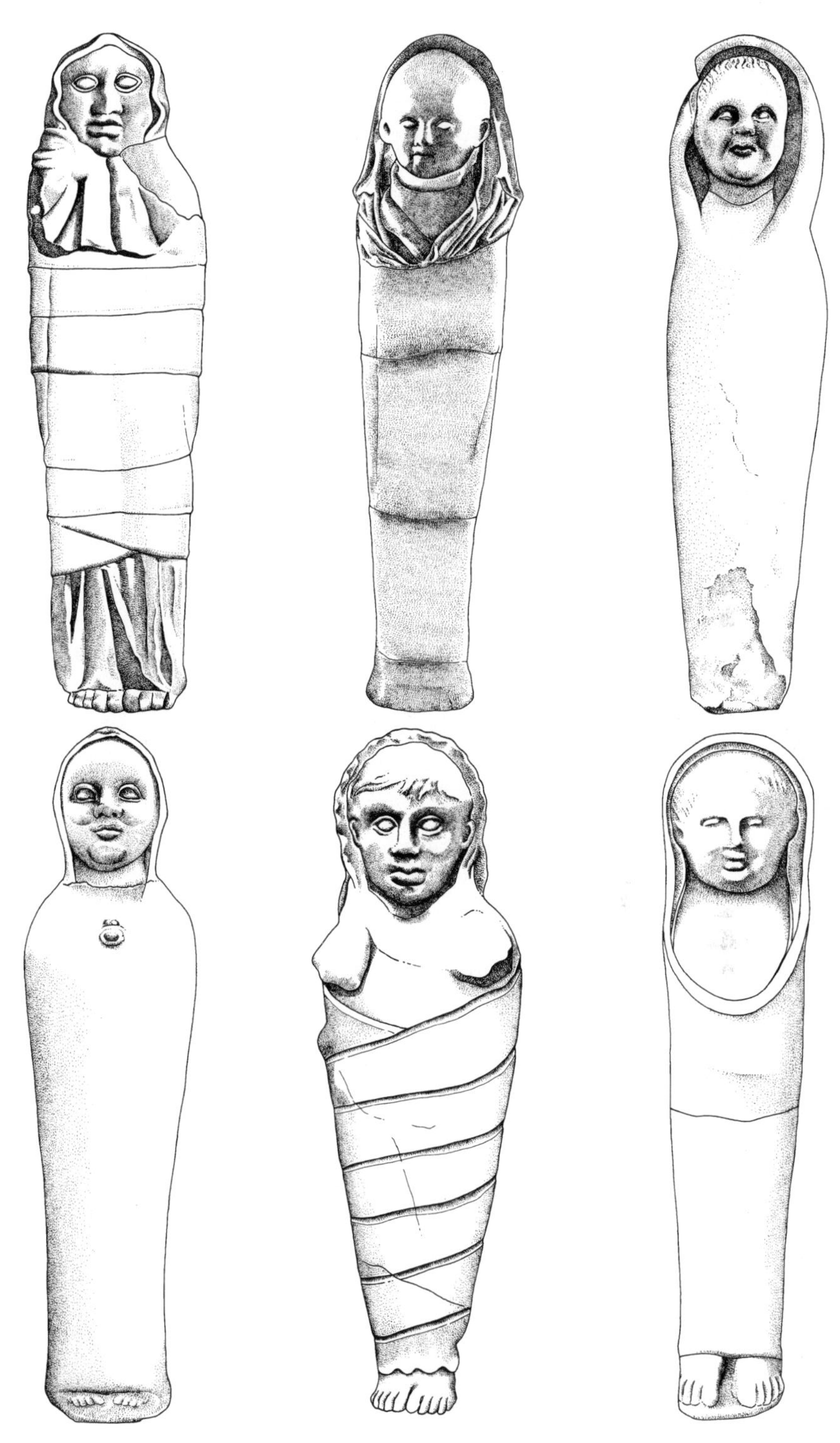

Fig. 3.4 Selection of terracotta votives of swaddled infants from sanctuaries in Italy.
Drawings: Jerneja Willmott.

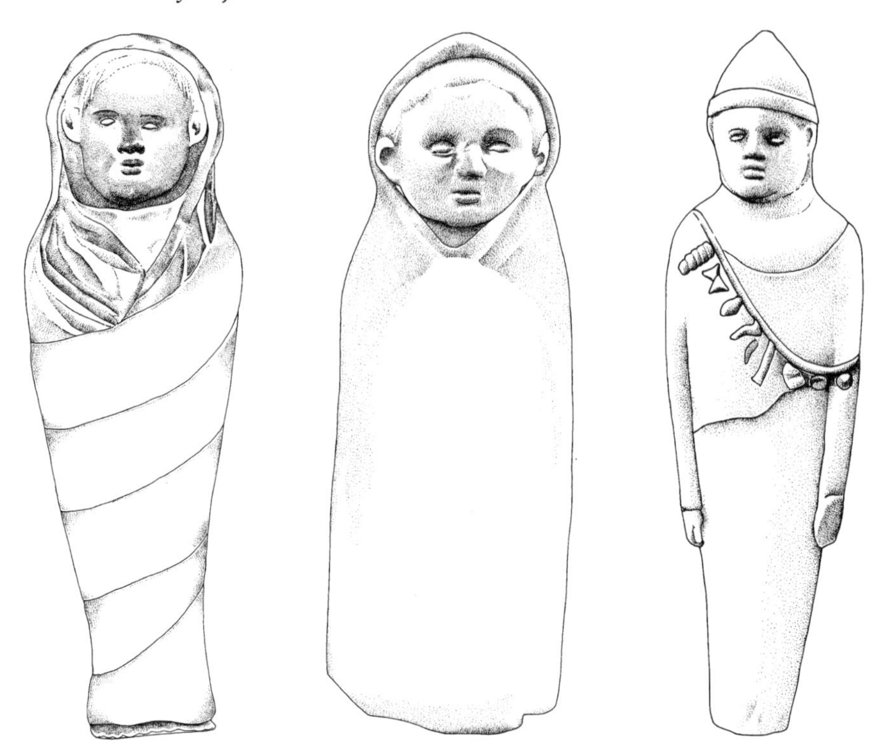

Fig. 3.4 Continued.

by the gods, as the sad epitaph of Orestilla from Sarno reveals. Her husband performed the duty of burying and commemorating his wife, "barely emerged from childbirth", and he did this "even though his prayers were not answered" (*contra votum*).[144] He clearly had sought divine assistance in vain for his wife and child in the hope that both would survive and be healthy.

The phenomenon of dedicating terracotta votives and swaddled infants in Italy had ended by the early first century BC, although it is not entirely clear why this happened. What is certain, however, is that Roman parents in the late Republic and in the imperial periods did not cease to be concerned about procreation, reproductive health, and the survival of their children, as the many stone votive offerings in the form of swaddled babies from the first three centuries AD in Roman Gaul demonstrate (Fig. 3.5).[145] These have been found in sanctuaries associated with springs and the sources of rivers in the Burgundy region (Sources de la Seine, Essarois) and elsewhere (Halatte) in Gaul. Like

[144] *CIL* X.1112. See also *CIL* V.1634 and *CIL* XI.6810 for infant death *contra votum*.
[145] Derks 2014.

Fig. 3.5 Selection of stone votives of swaddled infants from sanctuaries in Roman Gaul.
Drawings: Jerneja Willmott.

Graham, Derks sees the votive figurines of swaddled infants in Roman Gaul as dedications triggered by the reception of divine assistance for infants.[146] Derks argues convincingly that parents will have prayed to the gods before the birth of their baby for its health and survival, pledging a vow (*votum*) if their prayers were fulfilled. Once the infant was born, and it survived the first dangerous weeks, the milestone of the completion of the swaddling age was the point when an infant votive would be dedicated as a thank-offering.

Recent excavations by Olivier de Cazanove in the sanctuary of the Gallo-Roman god Apollo Moritasgus at Alesia (La Croix Saint-Charles) have helped to clarify the nature of the cult and the association of Moritasgus with healing, curing, and assisting with physical needs of worshippers.[147] The votive offerings include metal plaques depicting eyes (85 per cent), anatomical body parts, including a leg with a dedication to Apollo Moritasgus, as well as heads and breasts, and swaddled infants made of stone. Less than half a kilometre south-east of the sanctuary of Apollo Moritasgus at Alesia, limited investigations of a rock shelter by Abbot Joseph Joly uncovered the remains of a dozen infants, interpreting the site as a "*cimetière de bébés*", a baby cemetery.[148] But the skeletons were not just those of perinates, so Joly may have explored only part of a larger assemblage of burials.[149] Since then, Jaeggi has proposed a connection between the sanctuary of Apollo Moritasgus and this burial site.[150]

A connection between a sanctuary housing cults associated with healing and a nearby cemetery with infant burials has also been proposed for another Gallic site, that of des Bolards (Nuits-Saint-Georges) in Burgundy. An assemblage of votive offerings, including plaques of eyes and breasts, female figurines, and swaddled infants, was found in a sanctuary, possibly of Mars Segomo and Venus(?), in the settlement (*vicus*).[151] About 120 infant burials found in the necropolis just down the road, and belonging to the settlement, have been flagged up as an unusually large number of very young children, although the cemetery was in use for at least a century and this does not, therefore, represent a significant number of dead infants per year.[152] They have been interpreted as ailing infants whose parents had sought divine assistance and healing at the sanctuary, but who nonetheless died and were buried, apparently, within the aura of nearby divinity. This explanation is rather anachronistic, however, and seems, rather, to reflect medieval Christian burial ideas whereby only infants who had been baptized had a claim on Christian burial in a cemetery or churchyard.[153] And this is not how Roman religion worked. If parents had vowed to give the gods a votive gift in return for the health of

[146] Derks 2014. [147] De Cazanove 2013. [148] Joly 1951 and 1954.
[149] Jaeggi 2012a; Gadacz 2013. [150] Jaeggi 2012b, 50.
[151] Pommeret 2001; Maza and Montandon 2011.
[152] Planson et al. 1982, 170–6; Laubenheimer 2004, 298, figs. 1–2.
[153] Baills-Talbi and Dasen 2008, 610.

the infant, but the child died, the gods had not granted the favour and the parents were not obliged contractually to pay this *votum*.[154] And it seems unlikely to me that parents would want to bury their infants in the proximity of those same gods who had failed their infants in the first place. Furthermore, the cemetery at des Bolards contains almost the same number (109) of adult cremations and inhumations, and is therefore neither a cemetery reserved for infants, nor does it differ significantly from any other extramural burial grounds where different age groups are represented.

In the Roman imperial period, expressions of thanks and the fulfilment of vows were recorded in a permanent medium, in stone, and with inscriptions commemorating the event and the dedicants involved.[155] *Pro salute*—for the health/welfare of (name of individual)—becomes a standard phrase in the imperial period, whether in the context of vow fulfilment inscribed solely as text on an altar or statue base, or within the textual dedication on a figural votive relief, although, as Celia Schultz points out, late Republican votive dedications already express the sentiment "on behalf of" named individuals, including children.[156] Numisia Afrodite in Rome, for example, set up a votive dedication to Hercules on behalf of the health of her son and her family (*pro salute fili maei et meorum*).[157]

Pro salute as a formula appears also in the context of fertility and thank-offerings in the provinces in the Roman imperial period. A unique group of votive reliefs of the late second and third centuries AD from Poetovio in Pannonia (modern Ptuj in Slovenia) is indicative of regional variety in the depiction of mortal worship and divine sanction (Fig. 3.6). Forty votive reliefs dedicated to the *Nutrices Augustae* (noble nurses) have been found in three sanctuaries in the Roman colony.[158] Several of the inscription fragments refer to the stone dedication specifically as an *ex voto* and state that they were given *votum solvit libens merito*, willingly and deservedly in fulfilment of the vow. These female deities associated with childbirth and child health are usually depicted on the votive reliefs as a single figure, but they can appear as a pair of figures. The goddesses in the reliefs are shown breastfeeding a swaddled or naked baby, while cult servants or worshippers bring baskets of offerings and mothers with babies or young children approach the goddess. These mothers sometimes hold up their babies and present them in supplication to

[154] Derks 2014. [155] Schultz 2006, 100–2.

[156] Schultz 2006, 104. The search for divine protection certainly continued throughout childhood, as a second-century votive altar from the temple precinct of Apollo in the Grienmatt area of Augst shows: Pfäffli 2013a, 52–3, cat. no. 50; Pfäffli 2013b, 72. Although the age of Nobilianus is not stated in this inscription, his health and welfare (*pro saluti*) was the blessing that Maria Paterna, his mother, requested from Apollo for her son. The thank-offering attests not only to the request, but also to the granting of the favour to the boy and the mother's gratitude and duty in setting up the altar to commemorate the event.

[157] *CIL* VI.286; Schultz 2006 104. [158] Wigand 1915; Šašel Kos 1999.

Fig. 3.6 Votive relief to the *Nutrices Augustae* from Poetovio/Ptuj. Ptuj–Ormož Regional Museum, RL 973.
Photo: Boris Farič, Ptuj–Ormož Regional Museum.

the goddess, eternalizing the event and acting as a thank-offering.[159] One mother holds a swaddled infant whilst another, seemingly ahead of her in the queue, presents her naked toddler to the *Nutrices* for blessing.[160] The reliefs set up in the sanctuaries furthermore acted as a perpetual request and sign of gratitude for the continued welfare of the children.

Both mother and father are named in the inscriptions as dedicators of these votive reliefs; fathers or mothers alone, however, can also make the offerings in fulfilment of a vow. Aurelius Servandus and his wife Ulpia Secundina record in the third century that with their votive they are willingly fulfilling their vow on behalf of their two children, Secundinus and Servatus.[161] Presumably the two boys named in the inscription are the naked infant being suckled by the

[159] For example, Šašel Kos 1999, 162–3, fig. 10 (no. 14); 171, fig. 16 (no. 30); 172, fig. 18 (no. 32).
[160] Šašel Kos 1999, 176, fig. 23 (no. 37).
[161] *AE* 1986, 565; Šašel Kos 1999, 173, fig. 19 (no. 33).

goddess and the toddler held up by a worshipper (Ulpia Secundina herself?), and thrust at the *Nutrix*. On another relief of the late second century, Vitalis and his wife Vintumila fulfil their vow in regard to their daughter Maximilla.[162] In this image, Vintumila, holding her young daughter Maximilla by the hand, sacrifices between two seated goddesses with swaddled infants on their laps. In other dedications, parents like Successius Maximianus and Malia Verina thank the goddess for the health or well-being of their children (*pro salute*), whilst a cult servant leads the couple's young daughter, Successia Vera, into the sanctuary by the hand.[163]

The dedicators of the *Nutrices Augustae* votive reliefs from Poetovio went to some expense to make their offerings, in that images and texts were carved on imported marble, often in a very accomplished fashion. Votive offerings, such as these multi-figure reliefs with texts, had a public character and they could function as objects of competition and prestige, used to perpetuate social esteem.[164] The status of some individuals is sometimes explicitly stated, and they include members of Poetovio's highest elite, such as T. Cassius Verinus, who was a *decurio*, *praefectus fabrum* and *praefectus pro duumvir*, Aelius Secundinus, another *decurio*, and L. Fuscinius Exsuperatus, a freedman magistrate (*Augustalis*) (Fig. 3.6).[165]

Unnamed mother goddesses are represented also on votive reliefs in Gaul and Britain.[166] These goddesses often appear as a triad of women holding various objects. A particularly fine relief from Bibracte depicts one goddess holding a bowl and sponge for the infant's first bath, one rolling out a length of swaddling cloth, and one holding an infant already swaddled in this cloth (Fig. 3.7).[167] The connection between the veneration of mother goddesses and medical care is particularly clear in the case of a relief dedication to the *Matres Augustae* of the first or second century AD from Lyon, as this votive dedication was a gift to the august mothers by Phlegon, a doctor (*medicus*).[168] Perhaps Phlegon was fulfilling a vow he had made to the goddesses in return for successfully healing or delivering children. A popular motif in objects of smaller format in terracotta is the duo of mother and infant, although it is not always clear whether these female figures are meant to be goddesses or mortal mothers. In Gaul, female figures seated in a high-backed wicker chair with one or two babies being breastfed are consistently referred to in French

[162] *AE* 1986, 564; Šašel Kos 1999, 174, fig. 21 (no. 35).

[163] Wigand 1915, 192–3, cat. no. 2, fig. 98; Šašel Kos 1999, 166–7, fig. 11 (no. 25).

[164] Derks 1998, 216–17.

[165] T. Cassius Verinus: *AE* 1986, no. 568; Šašel Kos 1999, 169, fig. 14 (no. 28); Aelius Secundinus: *CIL* III.4052; Wigand 1915, 208, cat. no. 11, fig. 115; Šašel Kos 1999, 170, fig. 15 (no. 29); L. Fuscinius Exsuperatus: *AE* 1986, no. 579; Šašel Kos 1999, 171, fig. 16 (no. 30).

[166] Coulon 2004a, 174–7, figs. on pp. 174 and 175.

[167] Carroll 2012b, 138, fig. 1.

[168] *CIL* XIII.1762; Rémy 1984, 135–6, no. 16, fig. 13.

Fig. 3.7 A votive relief of three mother or nursing goddesses with a swaddled infant, from Bibracte.
Drawing: Jerneja Willmott.

scholarship as *déeses mères*, mother goddesses (Fig. 3.8). These Gallic terracotta figurines are found in sanctuaries and sacred deposits, as well as in domestic contexts, but they also form part of the burial assemblages of infants and children in the second and third centuries, perhaps as protectors of the very young in the afterlife.[169]

The dedication of a thank-offering in any material is an acknowledgement of the fulfilment of a vow, whether or not it was inscribed. At the heart of any of these *ex votos* is the belief in the efficacy of divine assistance in matters of conception, pregnancy, and maternal and infant health. They express admirably the concerted effort made by parents to further ensure the healthy continuity of their family.

[169] Schauerte 1985, 329–35, cat. nos. 890–948, pls. 106–12; Dasen 1997; Talvas 2007, 165, 178–9, 185, 191.

Fig. 3.8 Pipe clay figurine of a nursing goddess with two infants, from Drapers' Gardens, London.

Photo: Pre-Construct Archaeology.

4

The Material Culture of Infancy

FEEDING BOTTLES

Many of the surviving artefacts of infant material culture relate to the care and protection of the child. Perhaps the most fundamental task in raising a healthy infant was feeding, not only in the days, weeks, and months following birth, but also during the weaning period when supplementary foods were introduced to the child's diet. Soranus recommended weaning foods such as bread softened with milk, wine, or honey, or spelt soup or an uncooked egg (for sipping).[1] He warned against giving the baby milk during such a meal, as, in his opinion, the mixture would be hard to digest. But he acknowledged that the baby might well be thirsty, so he recommended giving water or a little watery wine "through artificial nipples".[2] These artificial nipples will have been attached to some kind of vessel containing the suggested liquids. The sixth-century Latin paraphrased version of Soranus by Muscio (or Mustio) refers to such items as "glass vessels in the shape of a breast and bored through, which country folk call 'ubuppa' or 'titina'", although this terminology is not used in Soranus's original Greek text.[3] Perhaps by the sixth century AD, feeding vessels were made only of glass.

But there must have been a need for feeding vessels when the infant was younger than six months or before weaning could begin, especially because some mothers might have been unable to produce milk or perhaps were too ill to breastfeed. If a wet nurse were too costly or unavailable, artificial nipples might have been the only recourse. If "a woman well able to provide milk is not at hand", the infant was to be given boiled honey or honey mixed with goat's milk, possibly administered through artificial nipples.[4]

The question is whether we can identify vessels with artificial nipples in the archaeological record. Hundreds of small spouted vessels made of ceramic or glass—sometimes referred to as a *guttus* or *askos*—have been found in settlements, and particularly in the graves of infants and children, which might

[1] Soranus, *Gynaecology* 2.46. [2] Soranus, *Gynaecology* 2.46.
[3] Fischer 1987; Adams 2007, 539–40. [4] Soranus, *Gynaecology* 2.17.

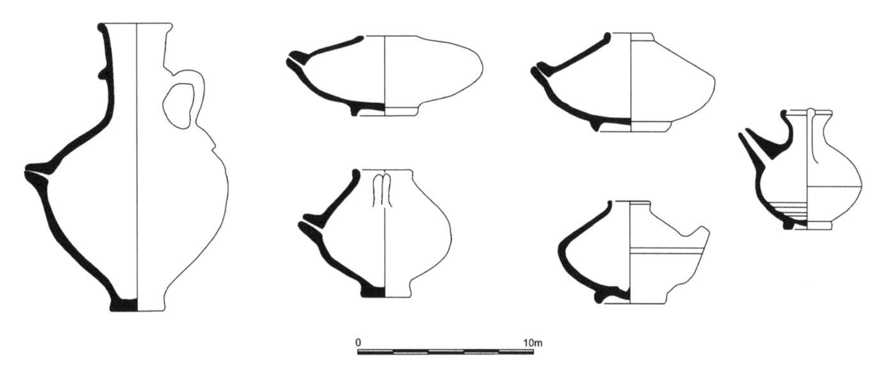

Fig. 4.1 Various forms of ceramic feeding bottles from Roman Gaul.
Drawing: Irene de Luis.

qualify as feeding bottles. Both Greek and Roman spouted vessels have been interpreted in various ways: as infant feeding bottles, as vessels for refilling lamps with oil, or for dosing small quantities of perfume, but, as we have seen in Chapter 2, a Greek terracotta figurine of the fifth century BC illustrates the use and purpose of these bottles as baby feeders (see Fig. 2.4).[5] In Roman Gaul, over 300 examples are known, in the main dating to the first to third centuries AD, of which 179 are from secure funerary contexts.[6] Residue analysis has been conducted on spouted ceramic vessels from Nijmegen, Aachen, and Cologne, and although it suggests milk may well have been the contents, it did not clarify whether the milk was human or animal.[7]

The ceramic vessels generally are round or ovoid with a large opening in the upper part, and many, but not all of them have a handle (Fig. 4.1). Some have a short or a longer neck, and others no neck at all. Vessels of this type are made of rather coarse unglazed pottery, of finer slipped ceramics, or even glossy red *terra sigillata*.[8] One very specific group of feeding bottles of the first century AD of a rather different shape is known from several examples in Pompeii and other Vesuvian sites. These vessels are quite low with a noticeably long spout and a circular ring handle on one side. They also have relief decoration on the top, but by far the most relevant to and indicative of their function is the depiction of a woman feeding an infant on one of them.[9] Feeding bottles of glass are also fairly common, and they are generally taller, with a cylindrical neck and a spherical body. All ceramic and glass vessels have something in common: a spout on the side. The end of the spout on many of the excavated ceramic and glass vessels is rough or sharp, and it is hard to imagine it in the

[5] Gourevitch and Chamay 1992; Beaumont 2012, 55, fig. 3.8; Dubois 2013, 66.
[6] Rouquet and Loridant 2000. [7] Huttmann et al. 1989.
[8] Alfonso and Blaizot 2004, 226–8, figs. 138–9 (Champ Madame, Beaumont, grave SP 7).
[9] Gourevitch and Chamay 1992, 8, pl. 19.4; Rouquet 2003, 169, fig. 10.

tender mouth of an infant. But a small rag or piece of cloth could have been tied over the spout through which infants could suck liquids. Leather teats or nipples are also possible; they are, at least, known much later, in the nineteenth century.[10]

Natalie Rouquet has recently proposed that the vessels might have been used as breast pumps (*tire-lait*), drawing parallels to nineteenth-century glass breast pumps with long tubular spouts.[11] She interprets the presence of these spouted bottles in graves as a mother's last feeding for her dead child. An experiment was conducted with the collaboration of a woman with children of her own. The larger opening at the top of the vessel was positioned over the woman's nipple, and the tubular spout placed in her mouth so that she could draw the milk out of her breast. According to Rouquet, the woman did not find this particularly difficult; however, the photo and the reconstruction drawing make the procedure look rather uncomfortable. This suggested use of these vessels is not convincing. There is no compelling reason why breast milk could not be hand expressed and collected in a glass or cup and filled into this spouted vessel, rather than having to suction it from the breast. This would not require such contortions.

A brief survey of the ages of children with whom the feeding vessels were buried may help to clarify at which stage in infancy they could be used. They are found in the burials of newborns, as at Portorecanati and Chantambre, as well as in the graves of infants anywhere between three and nine months of age, as at Avenches and Payerne.[12] In the twenty-eight burials of infants under the age of six months at Beaumont Champ Madame, 8.5 per cent of the ceramic assemblage is made up of feeding bottles.[13] One of the babies (in grave 40) had not just one, but two of them. But older children between one and two years of age were also buried with them, as at Rottweil.[14] A feeding bottle was found in the grave of a child of possible weaning age at Iasos in western Asia Minor, but none of the perinatal infants in this cemetery of the late first century BC to the middle of the first century AD had been buried with one.[15] An interesting find is the used feeding bottle in the grave of a very young infant at Tavant, indicating that it had probably belonged to the baby in life.[16] It appears, then, that these spouted bottles could have been used throughout the period following birth and into the weaning phase.

[10] Obladen 2014. [11] Rouquet 2003.

[12] Mercando et al. 1974, 252–4,439, figs. 112, 140–1, 144 (Portorecanati); Girard 1997, 218 (grave 241) (Chantambre); Castella 1987, 84–6, 110, figs. 84–8 (Avenches); Castella and Blanc 2007, 336, fig. 11 (Payerne).

[13] Alfonso and Blaizot 2004.

[14] Fecher and Burger-Heinrich 2010, 99–100, pl. 105 (tomb 223).

[15] Baldoni 2013, 303, fig. 15 (tomb 14).

[16] Riquier and Salé 2006, 47–9, figs. 52–5 (grave 15).

It has been pointed out that these vessels are also found in adult graves of the Roman period and they cannot, therefore, have been infant feeding bottles.[17] But a consideration of more recent parallels is useful here, because, as late as the twentieth century, spouted feeding bottles, called teapot or invalid feeders, were used in the nursing of adults too ill to feed themselves.[18] These vessels are virtually identical with those for infant use.

CLOTHING

In addition to the need for food, Roman infants required protection through clothing and textile coverings. To gain insight into what they wore, we can examine a relatively broad array of artefacts and images. These range from actual remains of blankets and articles of clothing, to impressions of textiles in plaster in some infant burials, and depictions of swaddling bands on infant bodies in terracotta and stone. Furthermore, we have a very detailed Roman description of the types of textiles chosen for swaddling babies and the wrapping techniques best suited for the infant's comfort, and it is useful to consult this medical text first.

According to Soranus, it was the midwife who was entrusted with the swaddling and bodily care of the infant, but, of course, many mothers would also have performed this task in the period after birth.[19] His directions in Book 2 are detailed and they indicate that the delicate body of a newborn was to be handled with utmost care and attention. One "must take soft woollen bandages which are clean and not too worn out, some of them three fingers in breadth, others four fingers. 'Woollen', because of the smoothness of the material and because linen ones shrink from the sweat; 'soft', so as not to cause bruises when covering the body which is still delicate; 'clean', so that they may be light and not heavy, nor of evil smell, nor irritate the surface by containing natron; and 'not too worn out': for whereas new ones are heavy, worn out ones are too cold, and sometimes rough as well and very easily torn. They must have neither hems nor selvages, otherwise they cut or compress unevenly." Legs and arms were wrapped separately, covering the hands and the feet to the tips of the toes. The arms were to be laid along the sides of the infant and the feet against one another, and, with a broad bandage, one "should wrap up the whole infant circularly from the thorax to the feet"; the baby's head "should be covered by bandaging it circularly with a soft clean cloth or piece of wool". For the comfort of the baby, and to avoid sores, a piece of wool was inserted between the ankles and knees and at the elbows. There

[17] Castella 1999, 91. [18] Dubois 2013, 67. [19] Soranus, *Gynaecology* 2.14.

are some variations on this, but in any event, the infant is completely wrapped up in its swaddling bands.

The newborn was to be bathed and cleansed up to three times a day; Soranus's recommendation that it be limited to once a day seems unhygienic and extremely inadequate.[20] The swaddling clothes were removed for this procedure, and the baby's body rubbed with lukewarm olive oil and then washed with warm water. Once wiped dry, the infant was to be massaged bit by bit and its joints moved and exercised. Following this, the baby was rubbed down with olive oil before being wrapped up again. A suggested alternative to simple olive oil as a moisturizer was Etruscan wax melted with olive oil, to soften, warm, nourish, and whiten the skin.[21] The daily routines of swaddling, unswaddling, cleansing, massaging, moisturizing, and re-swaddling, would have been work-intensive, ensuring close, intimate contact between infant and carer.

While the swaddling bands were protection for the sensitive infant body, they were also meant to shape the body and to establish the groundwork for an aesthetically pleasing and morally upright individual in adolescence and adulthood. "The swaddling clothes", according to Soranus, "serve to give firmness and an undistorted figure"; they should be loosened "when the body has already become reasonably firm and when there is no longer fear of any of its parts being distorted".[22] Not to swaddle, according to the Hippocratic treatise *On Airs, Waters and Localities*, would doom a child to grow up ugly; according to this text, the most negative example of such apparent neglect were the Scythians on the Black Sea who "grow up flabby and stout" because they were not wrapped in swaddling clothes in infancy.[23] We learn also in the same Hippocratic text that infants in Egypt were not swaddled, although no comment on their physical appearance later in adulthood is made.

Modern medical studies have suggested that swaddling promotes more sustained sleep and reduces the frequency of spontaneous awakenings, and that it can have a beneficial effect on excessively crying infants less than eight weeks of age.[24] But the possible detrimental effects of swaddling on the infant's joints, leading to hip dysplasia, have also been highlighted, although this can be alleviated by wrapping the infant less tightly and allowing more room to move.[25] Very recently, a medical study concluded that swaddled infants may be at increased risk of sudden infant death syndrome (SIDS) unless they lie on their backs.[26] Swaddled babies six months or older are also more likely to roll over on their stomach and be at risk of SIDS, and the study recommends that consideration should be given to an age after which swaddling should be discouraged. It is

[20] Soranus, *Gynaecology* 2.30.
[21] Soranus, *Gynaecology* 2.16.35.
[22] Soranus, *Gynaecology* 2.42.
[23] Hippocrates, *On Airs, Waters and Localities* 20.
[24] Gerard et al. 2002; Franco et al. 2005; Van Sleuwen et al. 2006.
[25] Kutlu et al. 1992; Mafart et al. 2007; Clarke 2014.
[26] Pease et al. 2016.

uncertain whether Roman parents or doctors were aware of such consequences of swaddling, but they would have appreciated how the practice induced a more restful and calmer sleep for the child (and presumably themselves).

The techniques of wrapping the infant in swaddling bands can be most clearly read from Italian votive terracottas of the fourth to second centuries BC as well as from Gallic stone votives of the second and third centuries AD (see Figs. 1.1, 3.4a–b, 3.5). These often life-size figures, introduced in Chapter 3, are wrapped in rather different ways, and we can contrast them with the infants on Attic grave *stelae* who are wrapped in what looks like a blanket cocoon (see Fig. 2.8).[27] The swaddling bands on early Roman children in Italy are usually wrapped diagonally around the baby's whole body, although sometimes they are placed horizontally (see Fig. 1.1). The head is also enclosed in a cap-like cloth or little hood. Rarely do the infant's feet or toes peek out below. In all cases, the encasing swaddling bands lie flat, and look compact and expertly bound. On those votives on which the swaddling bands stop just above the ankles, we can see that the infant wears a tunic underneath them.

The infant held in the arms of its heavily draped mother, the so-called *kourotrophos Maffei*, from Volterra is swaddled in a way that conforms precisely to the wrapping techniques exhibited in the contemporary votive terracottas (Fig. 4.2).[28] This marble statue from the first half of the third century BC, almost certainly a funerary statue, has an Etruscan inscription carved on the arm of the woman holding the baby which reads: "I (am) the image of Larthia Zan. Velchine Se(thra) gave me", indicating that one woman, Velchine Sethra, commemorated the other, the depicted Larthia Zan. By adding the infant, swaddled in the typical contemporary manner, Larthia Zan is highlighted "in her social role as a mother".[29] The Volterra baby is entirely enveloped in horizontally wrapped swaddling bands and its head is also wrapped; only its face is uncovered.

The Gallic infants also wear a full-length shirt or tunic or occasionally a hooded wrap, but they often are bound on top of this with coarse ropes, rather than swaddling bands (see Figs. 3.5a–d).[30] The whole arrangement looks remarkably coarse and uncomfortable! The ropes can be tied horizontally across the body, or diagonally, or crossed over the body, or a combination of all three. The same tunic and rope combination can be seen on Gallo-Roman funerary monuments depicting a single swaddled infant, such as that from Chauvigny.[31] Some Gallic votive statuettes and figurines made of stone or bronze depict a ring

[27] Baggieri and Rinaldi Veloccia 1996; De Cazanove 2008; Derks 2014; Graham 2014.

[28] Bianchi Bandinelli and Bianchi Bandinelli 1968; Bonfante 1997, 179; Haynes 2000, 357, fig. 279.

[29] Haynes 2000, 357. For the interpretation of the statue as a votive gift, see Fiumi 1976, 29–31, fig. 19; Bonfante 2006, 20.

[30] Coulon 2003; Derks 2014, 56–7, fig. 4.

[31] Coulon 2004a, 46 (with fig.); Deyts 2004, 236, fig. 9.

Fig. 4.2 Marble funerary statue of a woman and her swaddled infant, the so-called *kourotrophos Maffei*, from Volterra.
Drawing: Irene de Luis.

at chest level through which the ropes are pulled and by which they are held in place.[32] Gérard Coulon suggests that the ring might have assisted the carer in lifting the infant up and out of its cradle.[33]

[32] De Cazanove 2013, 11.
[33] Coulon 2004b, 8. Several rings are illustrated in Gourevitch et al. 2003, 202–3, cat. nos. 91–4.

It is possible that parents dedicated the swaddling bands of their newly liberated baby in a sanctuary, although neither in Roman Italy, nor in Roman Gaul, have textiles of this kind survived. Nevertheless, sometimes votive objects left in temple complexes may point to rituals and events celebrated by families throughout the early life-course of a child. An interesting site in this regard is the Roman sanctuary of the second and third centuries AD outside Augst (Flühweghalde) which appears to have been the site of a cult with fertility and family connections. The shattered remains of an under-life-size limestone statue of a goddess wearing a murate crown and holding a cornucopia were found next to a votive pit.[34] Beside the lower left leg of the statue, a small adjoined relief panel depicts worshippers, five women and a child, who are seeking assistance from her. An iron ring found in the precinct of this temple might be the remains of the swaddling clothes of a baby dedicated in celebration of that successfully completed phase of its life, but this remains speculation.[35] Furthermore, a glass feeding bottle was found here which might have been deposited as a thank-offering to mark the successful negotiation of the weaning process.[36]

Indirect evidence of swaddling survives in some infant burials. Lying at the bottom of the grave of an infant buried in a wooden coffin at Argenton, an iron ring was found at approximately the chest level of the baby, which may have held the constricting ropes or swaddling bands of the infant when it was interred, mirroring the combination of ropes and a ring on Gallic votives and funerary reliefs (Fig. 4.3).[37] The bronze ring found at waist height of the infant in grave 11 at Alesia, and another in an infant's sarcophagus of the late first or early second century at Tavant, found near the cervical vertebrae, may also have been associated with swaddling and holding the bands together.[38] In the necropolis at Tavaux in the Jura Mountains, small bronze rings found in infant graves have something to do with fixing swaddling bands on the body, but Barbet et al. could not be certain that they functioned in this way.[39] Furthermore, the positioning of the limbs of infant skeletons might be evidence for the child having been buried in swaddling bands. According to Henri Duday, who examined the skeletons of babies buried under the floor of a pottery workshop at Sallèles d'Aude, one of the thirteen infants there was probably interred in this way, as its arms and legs were in an extended position.[40]

Soranus recommended covering a baby's head by bandaging it with cloth, and indirect evidence for this survives in a late Roman burial in Paris

[34] Bossert-Radtke 1992, 17–23, cat. no. 1, pls. 2–4.
[35] Pfäffli 2013a, 34, cat. no. 19.
[36] Pfäffli 2013a, 35, cat. no. 20, fig. 12; Pfäffli 2013b, 72.
[37] Allain et al. 1992, 95, fig. 27 (tomb 85); Dasen 2003a, 202–3.
[38] Riquier and Salé 2006, 47–9, figs. 52–5 (grave 15); Jaeggi 2012a, 231, 235–6, fig.15; Jaeggi 2013, 55–6.
[39] Barbet et al. 2014, 89, 205–7 (graves Se11, Se18, Se20).
[40] Duday 2009, 63–9.

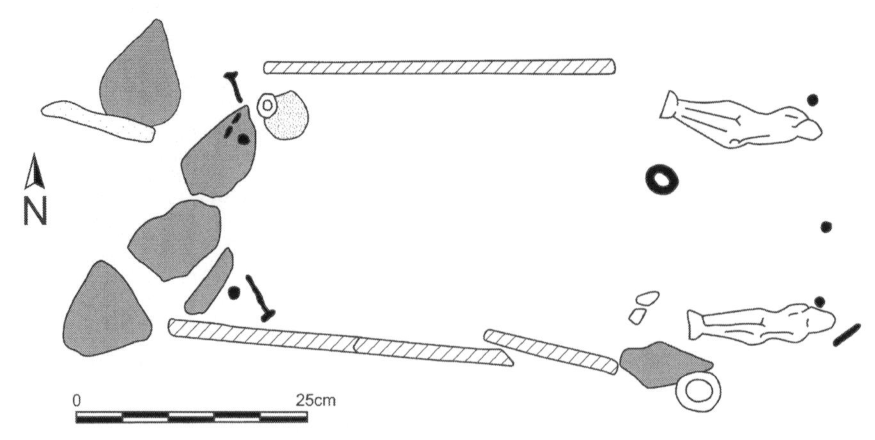

Fig. 4.3 Infant burial (tomb 25) in a wooden coffin, to which the nails attest, inside upright tiles (cross-hatched), Argenton. In the grave were an iron ring and Venus figurines.
Drawing: Irene de Luis.

(see Fig. 5.15). When the baby died, a plaster mould was made of its face, the hardening plaster preserving the imprint of the infant's face and the textiles wrapped around the face and under the chin, as Soranus suggested.[41] From the plaster mould a positive cast would have been taken as a basis on which a portrait in another material such as stone or bronze could be fashioned. The mould was then placed with the infant in the grave, only to be rediscovered in the nineteenth century by excavators. A terracotta figurine from Reims shows more clearly how this baby's head might have been wrapped (Fig. 4.4).

Soranus advised dressing the infant in a "simple little shirt" if its skin was irritated by swaddling bands.[42] Once the swaddling period had passed, all children graduated to simple tunics when they were roughly anywhere from the age of about three months. Funerary portraits depict such clothing. The garment is worn by a baby girl of six months who was commemorated by her mother Telesphoris in Mainz and by Ursio from Fermo who died at one year, seven months, and ten days (Fig. 4.5).[43] The marble sarcophagus of M. Cornelius Statius from Ostia, a so-called biographical sarcophagus, is decorated with relief scenes of the boy at various stages of his short life, and in each of these stages he wears clothing appropriate to his age (Fig. 4.6).[44] When being suckled by his mother, he wears a very short shirt or tunic that just covers his buttocks, but his torso seems to be bound still in swaddling bands, perhaps as some kind of

[41] Dasen 2010, 131–3, figs. 5, 8a–b; Carroll 2011b, 68–9, fig. 4.2.
[42] Soranus, *Gynaecology* 2.42.
[43] *CIL* XIII.7113; Selzer 1988, 127; Boppert 1992, 120–2, cat. no. 88, pl. 54; Carroll 2006, 169, 198, fig. 56; Mander 2013, 29–30, cat. no. 453, fig. 13.
[44] Amedick 1991, 140, cat. no. 114.4, pl. 53; George 2000, 192, fig. 2; Rawson 2003a, 106, fig. 2.2.

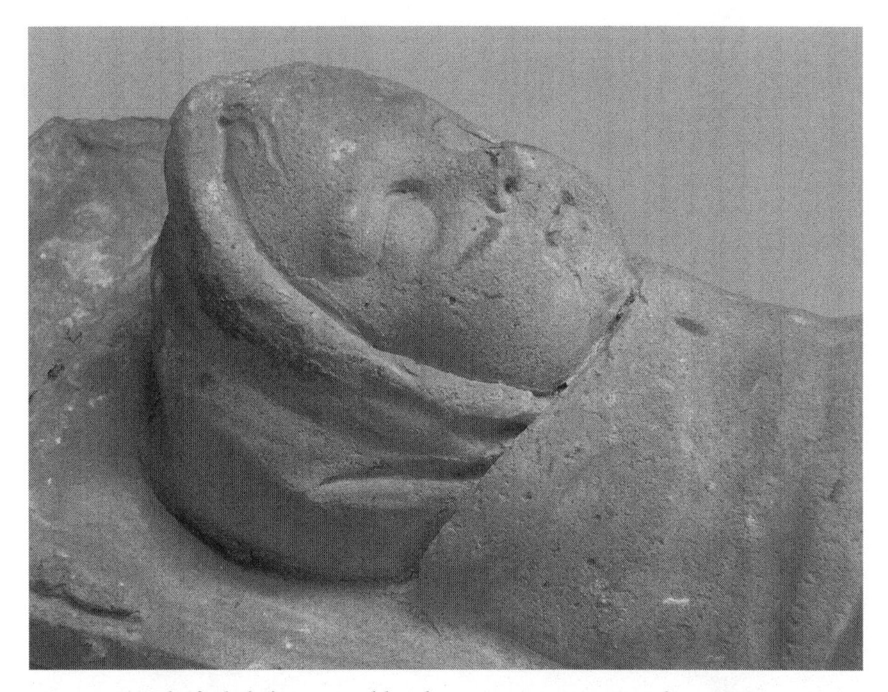

Fig. 4.4 Detail of a baby's wrapped head on a terracotta votive, from Reims.
Photo: https://commons.wikimedia.org/wiki/File:Bébé_Ex-voto_gallo-romain_Musée_Saint-Remi_120208.jpg.

support.[45] As a toddler of one or two years of age on his father's shoulder he wears a longer, sleeved tunic that covers his knees. As a boy of a few years, over the tunic he wears the *toga praetexta*, the garment worn by freeborn citizen boys until the age of fourteen.

Shirts or tunics of very young infants are rare as textile finds in the archaeological record.[46] But the simple tunic was worn also by older boys, and for these there is more physical evidence. At Bourges, a child between two and three years of age was buried in the third century AD in a simple, knee-length woollen tunic with sleeves.[47] This garment is the most common one shown in depictions of boys of various ages on Gallo-Roman tombstones. Clothing accessories, in particular *fibulae* or brooches, are found in burials of infants, in Gaul at Kempten and Alesia, and in Italy in Nave.[48] It is unknown how they were used and with which garments, but they could perhaps have been used to hold swaddling bands or a little cloak in place, depending on the age of the baby.

[45] Backe 2015, 60, refers to this as a kind of girdle or support belt.

[46] Fluck and Finneiser 2009: 16–18, cat. no. 3; Gallazzi and Hadji-Minaglou 2012, 395–6, figs. 8–9.

[47] Roche-Bernard 1993, 8–9; Coulon 2004a, 122–3, 165–6.

[48] Kempten: Mackensen 1978a, graves 54, 116, 174, 212, 230, 247; Alesia: Jaeggi 2013, 55; Nave: Passi Pitcher 1987, 34 (tomb 48).

Fig. 4.5 Funerary monument of a six-month-old girl, daughter of Telesphoris, from Mainz. Landesmuseum Mainz, Inv.-Nr. S 995.

Photo: Ortolf Harl, *ubi erat lupa*, with permission of the Landesmuseum Mainz.

Fig. 4.6 Marble sarcophagus of the child M. Cornelius Statius from Ostia, with scenes of early childhood in the family.
Drawing: Jerneja Willmott.

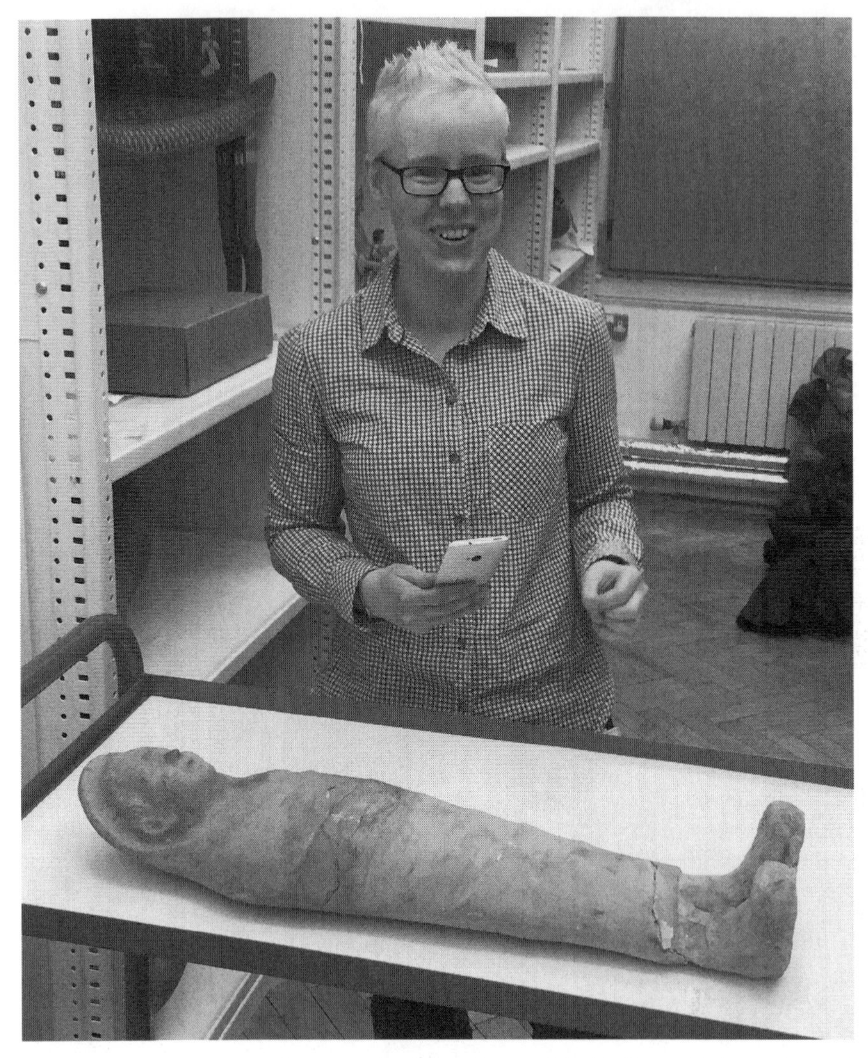

Fig. 4.7 Votive terracotta figure in the form of a swaddled infant with large feet and shoes, from Italy.
Photo: Emma-Jayne Graham.

At some point, children would need footwear, but shoes or booties could be worn even before the child could walk, as they are today. A terracotta votive infant from Italy, for example, is shod with a pair of rather large boots, despite the fact that the rest of his body is wrapped in swaddling bands, indicating a very young age of only a couple months (Fig. 4.7).[49] In the Roman cemetery

[49] To my knowledge, this votive is unpublished. But see https://thevotivesproject.org/2015/06/08/blythe-house/.

at Marseille, a one-year-old was buried with shoes placed near his abdomen, of which only tiny nails have survived.[50] Shoe nails also survive in grave 77 at Rottweil, that of an infant between nine and fifteen months of age, and in another (grave 223) at the same site belonging to a child less than two years old.[51] Unfortunately, we have no sure way of knowing what these little hobnailed shoes looked like when they were intact, but depictions of children who are at least two or three years old often wear little boots that come up to just above the ankles. Perhaps this is what was deposited in these graves.

CRIBS, CRADLES, AND BLANKETS

A baby's paraphernalia also included cribs, cradles, blankets, and coverlets. Soranus recommended bedding the infant on a pillow, mattress, or soft hay, with a hollow in the centre to prevent the baby rolling out and being hurt.[52] Even a trough could be made up as a bed, but it was important to air and change the bedding often and to improve the smell of the bedding by laying sweet bay or myrtle leaves under it. Coverlets should be thicker and thinner, depending on the weather and the baby's needs.

The only surviving cradle in the Roman world is one excavated in the house of M. Pilius Primigenius Granianus at Herculaneum.[53] It is made of oak, carbonized in the eruption of Vesuvius in AD 79, and has a slatted bottom and curved runners to enable the baby to be rocked. According to the excavation notebooks, the remains of an infant, as well as charred leaves and bits of textile, presumably from a little mattress, were found within it.[54]

The movement of the cradle was soothing for a baby, and when not rocked in its small bed, the baby would be rocked by its mother, nurse, or another carer. The Roman poet and satirist Persius refers to a grandmother or aunt lifting a little boy from its cradle and then rocking him in her arms.[55] Soranus advises gently rocking the crib or suspending the cradle or "balancing it upon diagonally opposed stones", but not before the baby had digested its food to avoid stomach upset.[56] Soranus also advises that when it is a bit older the infant should be rocked in a litter, and when four months old "the wet nurse should hold it in her arms and walk about" or the child should "be rocked in a carriage drawn by animals".[57]

A baby in a cradle, tucked up under a blanket or coverlet, is an occasional motif in Gallo-Roman votive figurines and funerary art. The infant in a cradle

[50] Moliner et al. 2003, 363–4, pl. 56 (tomb 444).

[51] Fecher and Burger-Heinrich 2010, 55, 409, fig. 54 (grave 77); 259, 435 (grave 223).

[52] Soranus, *Gynaecology* 2.16.

[53] Mols 2002, 230; Mols 2007–8, 149, fig. 9.

[54] A photograph in Deiss 1993, 55, shows a scattering of burnt bones on the bottom of the crib.

[55] Juvenal, *Satires* 2.

[56] Soranus, *Gynaecology* 2.40.

[57] Soranus, *Gynaecology* 2.40.

Fig. 4.8 Stone votive figurine of a swaddled infant in a cradle, from the sanctuary of Mars Segomo at Nuits-Saint-Georges.
Drawing: Jerneja Willmott.

on a stone votive from the sanctuary of Mars Segomo at Nuits-Saint-Georges in Burgundy is wrapped tightly in his cradle with his head on a pillow, his body covered with a blanket, and a dog at his feet (Fig. 4.8).[58] Presumably there is a mattress too, but this is not visible. The baby is firmly tied into his cradle by ropes that are woven through hooks on the sides of the cradle and cross diagonally over the blanket. The bottom of the cradle is curved, suggesting that it could be rocked. A particularly fine rendering of a swaddled infant in a cradle decorates one of the sides of a funerary monument of the third century AD in Cologne.[59] This gravestone, commemorating the wet nurse Severina, shows the tightly wrapped infant looking up from its cradle as the wet nurse attends to it (Fig. 4.9). Although the cradle does not seem to have any rockers on the bottom, the positioning of Severina's hands suggest that she is rocking the cradle to ease the infant into sleep or comfort him. There is no way of knowing whether all these cradles were made of wood or perhaps wicker.

A swaddled infant in a cradle is a motif in small-scale terracotta figurines as well. An infant on a terracotta votive from Reims is laid in its swaddling clothes directly in the cradle without any fasteners holding it in (Figs. 4.4 and 4.10).[60] Two almost identical figurines 7 centimetres and 8.3 centimetres in length, respectively, show a baby wearing swaddling clothes and a bonnet, lying on its

[58] Planson et al. 1982, 176, fig. 37; Coulon 2004a, 49–50; Deyts 2004, 227–35; Carroll 2012b, 138, fig. 4; Barbet et al. 2014, 205, fig. 213.
[59] Galsterer and Galsterer 1975, cat. no. 331, pl. 73; Carroll 2001, 59, colour pl. 7; Mander 2013, 139–41, cat. no. 415, figs. 122–4.
[60] Coulon 2004a, 49, fig. p. 47.

Fig. 4.9 Funerary relief of Severina, a wet-nurse, breastfeeding and rocking a baby in its cradle.

Photo: Anja Wegner, © Rheinisches Bildarchiv Köln.

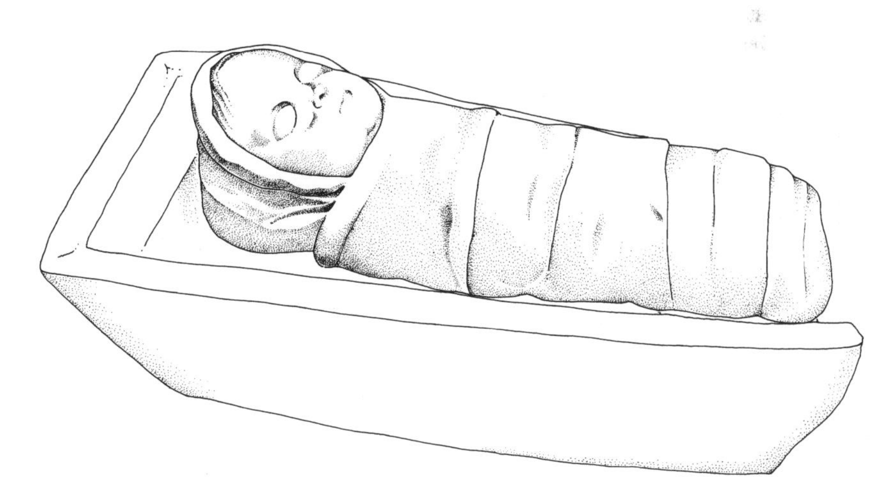

Fig. 4.10 Terracotta votive of a baby in a cradle, from Reims.

Drawing: Jerneja Willmott.

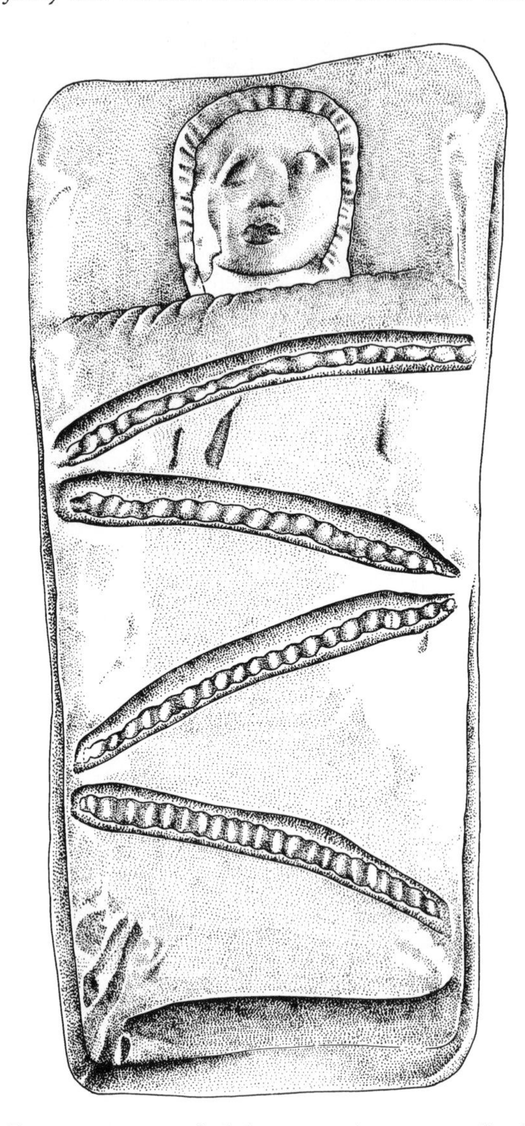

Fig. 4.11 Terracotta votive of a baby strapped into its cradle, from Trier.
Drawing: Jerneja Willmott.

back with its head resting on a plump pillow. One of these babies lies with his pet dog in the cradle.[61] An even smaller figurine only 5.7 centimetres long comes from Trier.[62] It shows less detail, but the baby lies on its back under a blanket, its head on a pillow, and it is held in place in its cradle by ropes or bands on top of the blanket which are depicted as incised zigzag lines (Fig. 4.11).

[61] Rouvier Jeanlin 1972, cat. nos. 598–9.

[62] Schauerte 1985, 297–8, cat. no. 787, pls. 94.2–3.

In very rare cases, blankets and coverlets survive as textile remains in burial assemblages (see Chapter 7). It would be a reasonable assumption that these had been used by the child in life and that they were used for a last time to wrap or cover the infant in death. These include the woollen wrappings dyed with madder and indigo in the burial of an infant about ten or eleven months old in a lead sarcophagus at Arrington Bridge in Cambridgeshire.[63] The environment within a lead sarcophagus of the third century AD in Holborough in Kent contributed to the preservation of another coverlet, one of patterned silk damask, probably from a Syrian workshop.[64] This costly and exotic fabric accompanied a one-year-old child. Surviving textiles in Roman Switzerland include a newborn buried in a woollen blanket in Tasgetium (modern Eschenz).[65] The infant was also interred with a small bouquet of flowers.

APOTROPAIC JEWELLERY

Very young children at the beginning of life were exposed to all manner of dangers or *invidia*, as Macrobius calls them.[66] Their lives were particularly precarious. No doubt medical care would be sought if a child fell ill, but it was not always available, nor was it necessarily on time or of any use. In general, Roman parents attempted to pre-empt and ward off health problems by giving pieces of apotropaic jewellery to babies and young children, to be worn on the body. This might be given on particular occasions, such as birthdays. In Plautus's play *Epidicus*, Epidicus asks the young girl Telestis: "Don't you remember my bringing you a gold *lunula* on your birthday, and a little gold ring for your finger?"[67] And in another of his plays (*Rudens*), a female character, Palaestra, stolen from her parents by pirates at the age of three, had been given a golden *bulla* at her birth.[68] A *bulla*, a disc-shaped locket acting as a protective device with curative powers against *invidia* is sometimes represented in Italic terracotta votives hanging from the neck of a swaddled infant, indicating that this could indeed be a gift from birth (see Fig. 3.4a, bottom left).[69] Amuletic jewellery was thought not only to give the baby protection, but also to entertain and distract the child as the individual pieces on necklaces and bracelets moved, made noises, and reflected light. The

[63] Taylor 1993, 203–4. [64] Wild 1965; Wild 1970, 52.

[65] Pfäffli 2013b, 73; Kramis and Trancik 2014, 11.

[66] Macrobius, *Saturnalia* 1.6.9. Translated as 'evil eye' by J. Henderson (*Macrobius*, Loeb 2011). For amulets in general, see Dasen 2003a and Dasen 2003b.

[67] Plautus, *Epidicus* 639–40. [68] Plautus, *Rudens* 1171.

[69] Warden 1983. Several examples of terracotta swaddled infants wearing a *bulla* are known at Vulci: Pautasso 1994, 41–4, pls. 21–5; de Cazanove 2013, 8–9. These are not all boy babies, as a terracotta infant with earrings from Vulci must be a girl: Pautasso 1994, 44, cat. no. CXX, pl. 25c.

swaddled infant votives from Paestum show necklaces of amulets worn diagonally across the chest and tucked under an arm (see Fig. 3.4b, right).[70]

Funerary finds confirm that infants could be protected against threats to their health right from birth. Fortuitously, the material on which amulets were strung occasionally survives, for example at Vindonissa and Marseille where a cord of linen and flax and a length of iron wire were used, respectively.[71] At Gubbio (tomb 220) and Kempten (grave 395), a silver denarius, pierced to be threaded onto a necklace, and a silver lunula pendant were found in graves of newborns.[72] In the Roman cemetery of Sainte-Barbe at Marseille, two perinatal infants were buried with various amulets. One (tomb 308) had three glass beads, a pierced coin, and a phallic amulet of amber; the other (tomb 527) had a pierced coin and a bead.[73] Green glass paste beads on a necklace were worn by a newborn at Salo.[74]

Numerous amulets, as well as necklaces and bracelets still strung with pendants, are known not just in the burials of newborns, but also in the graves of infants at all stages of their first year of life in Italy, France, Switzerland, Germany, and Britain, and they provide us with information on a wide variety of materials, colours, shapes, and properties. The most common amulets or pendants were glass beads; amber pendants in various shapes; small phalluses in glass, metal, or amber; bone pendants in various shapes; bronze bells; pierced coins; pierced animal teeth; and fragments of silver. Less common materials include jet, and this appears in some quantity in late Roman Britain.[75]

There seems to have been no relationship between the age of the child and the number or type of amulet given to it, and it is not necessarily the case that new and additional amulets, pendants, and other talismans were given to a child every year on its birthday or the anniversary of its *dies lustricus*. The thirty-two objects making up the necklace belonging to the child in grave 93-100 at Vindonissa, for example, cannot represent the accumulation of amulets over several birthdays or name days, because the child was only one year old when it died shortly after the middle of the first century AD.[76] The objects include twelve faience melon beads, seventeen blue glass beads, a bronze

[70] Ammerman 1993, 330–5, cat. nos. 2785–808, pls. 79–90, also especially 330, cat. no. U, pl. 90. The Cypriot limestone statuettes of toddlers and young boys, so-called temple boys, discussed in Chapter 2, are also regularly draped in long necklaces with amulets of all shapes, usually worn diagonally across the body, but also hung around the neck: Costanzo and Dubois 2014, 163–4, fig. 8.

[71] Vindonissa: Hintermann 2000, 129, 131, fig. 155 (grave 93-127, an adult woman); 128–32, 262–3, figs. 158–9, pl. 20 (grave 93-38, a child three to six years of age); Marseille: Moliner et al. 2003, 172, 380, fig. 126, pl. 61 (tomb 534, a two-year-old child). For a wire bracelet still strung with beads, see the cremation burial of an infant (burial no. 10) outside the Porta Nocera at Pompeii: Van Andringa et al. 2013, 353, fig. 238.

[72] Gubbio: Cipollone 2002, 283–94, figs. 281b–c; Kempten: Mackensen 1978a, 153, 310, grave 395.

[73] Moliner et al. 2003, 334, pls. 44, 81.2 (tomb 308); 379 (tomb 527).

[74] Massa 1997, 81, pl. 16.1 (tomb 135).

[75] Crummy 2010 gives a good overview of jet amulets, as well as a whole range of others.

[76] Hintermann 2000, 275–6, 386, pl. 46 (grave 93-100). There were 53 objects in the grave.

phallic amulet, a little bronze bell, and a bronze filigree object once strung on a necklace. But this considerable assemblage of amulets might reflect the poor health or periods of stress through which the infant lived, the parents perhaps attempting in vain to give the child as much protection as possible to counteract ills.

Several children who reached the important milestone of their first birthday had exceptionally rich amuletic jewellery assemblages in their graves. A spectacular necklace of seventeen faience, amber, shell, and bone amulets was recovered from the second-century burial of a one-year-old infant (possibly a girl) in the cemetery at Castel Malnome outside Ostia (Fig. 4.12).[77] The faience amulet is in the shape of the Egyptian god Bes who was a household protector and associated with childbirth.[78] The amber pieces take the form of a phallus, a hare, a possible dove, and a spindle whorl, the latter referring to the future role of mother and homemaker. Particularly interesting also are a boar's tooth and a human tooth, both pierced to be worn on the necklace. Given that this cemetery appears to have been the last resting place of a working population associated with the salt pans near Rome's harbour, and because of the otherwise sparsely furnished graves here, the wealth invested in this infant stands out noticeably.[79] A one-year-old child buried in the first half of the second century at Marseille (tomb 169) had an extensive set of amulets that included eight glass beads, a bronze phallic amulet, two pierced dog teeth, and various pierced bone gaming tokens in the shape of a tabula ansata and fish, as well as a phallic amulet of amber (Fig. 4.13).[80] An infant of the same age in the cemetery at 78 Avenue de Jean Jaurès in Nîmes was given a necklace of amulets, consisting of three pierced bovid teeth, four glass beads, three amber pendants shaped like a rabbit, a fish, and a canine tooth, and a rectangular bone gaming token drilled for suspension from the necklace.[81]

Children as old as five or six years still wore apotropaic jewellery as protection. Red glass paste beads made up a necklace of a young child one to two years of age at Urbino.[82] A six-year-old child in the Clos au Duc necropolis at Évreux in Normandy was cremated in the first century AD with the clothes and bodily adornment he wore in life, including a necklace or bracelet strung with four glass paste beads and one millefiori bead.[83] That necklace appears rather modest in comparison to the one wrapped several times around the neck of a child of five or six years in the late third or early fourth century at Draria-el-Achour in Algeria; on this necklace were threaded 453 blue, yellow, and green glass beads.[84] It may be that these coloured glass beads, due to their similarity to

[77] Cianfriglia and De Cristofaro 2013.
[78] Dasen, 1993, 70–5; Costanzo and Dubois 2014, 161, fig. 7.
[79] Cianfriglia et al. 2013.
[80] Moliner et al. 2003, 172, 309, pls. 31, 80.1, 80.2 (tomb 169).
[81] Bel 2012, 204, fig. 14.
[82] Mercando et al. 1982, 212, fig. 77.
[83] Pluton et al. 2008, 216–17, fig. 10 (grave 176).
[84] De Larminat 2012b, 507.

Fig. 4.12 Amulets of amber, bone, glass, and animal and human teeth from a necklace found in the burial of a one-year-old at Castel Malnome near Rome's harbour at Portus.

Photo: courtesy of Alessio De Cristofaro

gemstones, were thought to have had some medicinal and amuletic properties; equally, different colours may have had different apotropaic roles.

One particular type of talisman appears to have been current only in Roman Gaul: the deer antler disk (Fig. 4.14). These disks are known from archaeological excavations of towns, forts, farms, and sanctuaries in France, Switzerland,

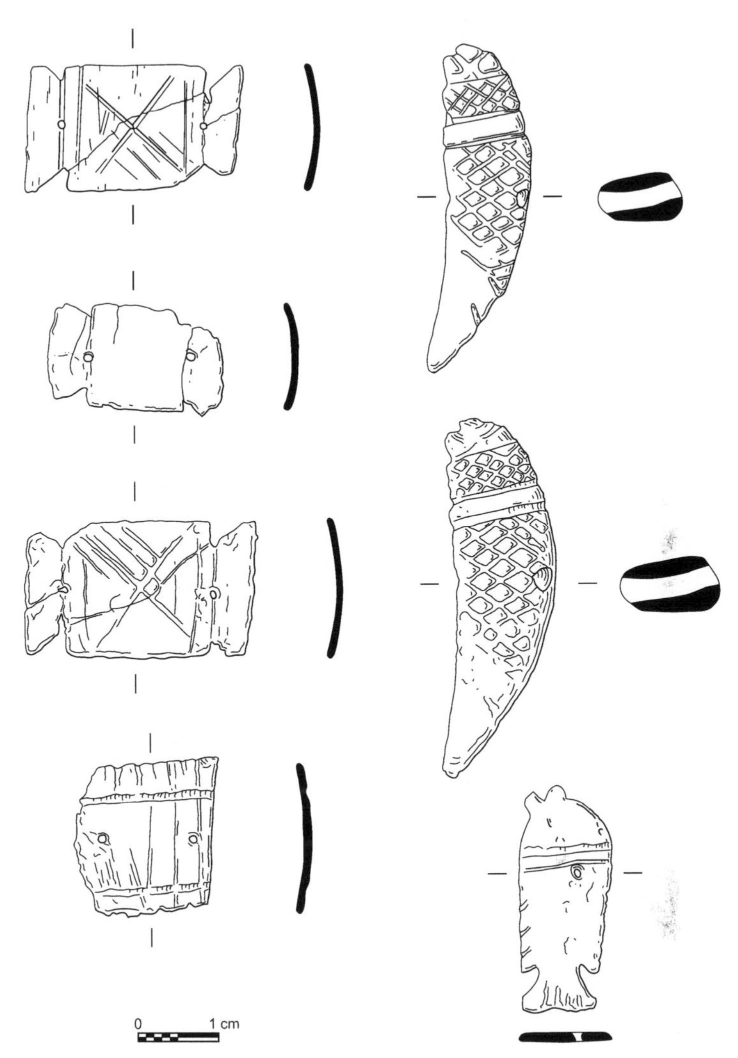

Fig. 4.13 Amulets of bone (left and lower right) and pierced dog teeth (right), from a burial (tomb 169) of a one-year-old at Marseille.
Drawing: Irene de Luis.

Germany, and the Netherlands, the earliest of them appearing already in the fifth century BC in Switzerland and in a pre-Roman tumulus in the Saône-et-Loire region of France.[85] At the rural estate at Beaumont Champ Madame, one or two antler disks have been found in the graves of infants under six months of age.[86] Several Gallo-Roman funerary monuments and votive statuettes illustrate young

[85] Alonso 2006, 211.
[86] Alfonso and Blaizot 2004, 215–19, figs. 128–9; 228–32, figs. 140–1 (graves SP2, SP8).

Fig. 4.14 Antler disk amulets from Augst.
Photos: Susanne Schenker; Augusta Raurica.

children wearing the disks and they shed light on how they were worn.[87] The disks were positioned in the middle of the chest or the back, and two criss-crossing bands passed through them and encircled the torso of the child. This would only be possible with those disks with four holes in them. Other amulets, however, have only one or two, so these must have been sewn onto clothing or simply suspended from a string or cord. In a child's grave at Wederath-Belginum, for example, the antler disk was still attached to an iron ring from which it had been hung, perhaps on a necklace.[88] The antler disk amulet, therefore, warded off evils from the front and the back by being worn visibly over the child's clothing.

Most of the disks are plain, as they are in an assemblage of fifteen disks from Alesia, but simple carvings, such as concentric circles, and more elaborate motifs are also attested.[89] One of the antler disks found in a sanctuary at the source of the Seine is pierced by four holes to fix straps to it, and it has the head of a child carved in the centre.[90] Other disks, particularly from Germany and Switzerland, have a carving of a phallus in the middle.[91]

The symbolism of antler disks is fairly clear. The red deer (*cervus elaphus*) was one of the largest forest-dwelling mammals in Europe, and still is today. Only the males have antlers which are shed annually in the spring and are replaced by new growth, taking about four months to develop. Some antlers also are broken off in mortal combat between competing stags. The material of the disks, therefore, is symbolic of strength, virility, and rebirth, following the moulting and rutting cycle of the powerful animal from which it came, all properties that made these talismans desirable for supernatural defence. The antler disks are possibly also associated with the antler-headed Celtic god Cernunnos, an indigenous god of nature and fruitfulness who was venerated throughout Gaul, northern (Celtic) Italy and Celt-Iberian Spain.[92] At the sanctuary at des Bolards, where parents may have sought divine protection for their living offspring, Cernunnos appears in a divine triad with a female goddess (Fortuna?) and a *genius loci* on a second-century stone votive relief.[93]

But what were the perceived apotropaic qualities of the other talismans? Baltic amber, for example, because of its sun-like colour, lustre, and origins from the margins of the known world, was exotic and mysterious. According to Pliny the Elder, the "female peasantry" north of the Po wore "pieces of amber as necklaces, chiefly as adornment, but also because of its medicinal properties. Amber, indeed, is supposed to be a prophylactic against tonsillitis and other affections of the pharynx."[94] He also states that "it is of benefit to

[87] Coulon 2004a, 139–41, 158, figs. on pp. 140–1, 158. Child burials at Kempten show that antler disks were worn by children who may have been several years old: Mackensen 1978a, 119–20, 253, pl. 75.8 (grave 195); 275, pl. 107.16 (grave 268).

[88] Haffner 1971, 69, pl. 126.3 (grave 314).

[89] Alonso 2006 and 2008.

[90] Hatt et al. 1954, 59–66, fig. 16; Alonso 2006, fig. 12.

[91] Hatt et al. 1954, 59–66, fig. 15; Alonso 2006, 214; Pfäffli 2013a, 43, cat. no. 29.

[92] Green 1992, 227–8; Alonso 2006, 213.

[93] Deyts 2001, 132–3, figs. 8–10.

[94] Pliny, *Natural History* 37.11.3.

Fig. 4.15 Blue glass phallic amulet from an infant burial (F38) at Vagnari.
Photo: Alastair Small.

babies when it is attached to them as an amulet". Diodorus Siculus wrote that amber was "commonly used in connection with the mourning attending the death of the young".[95] Jet was supposed to cure toothache and could alleviate scrofula, a form of tuberculosis, when mixed with wax.[96] Various shapes had apotropaic meaning too, for example the phallus, attested in amber, bronze, and bone, as it was thought to bring prosperity and good fortune. This is the case clearly even for infants, as the inclusion of a blue glass paste phallic amulet in the burial of a child under twelve months in the cemetery of the Roman imperial estate at Vagnari in Puglia demonstrates (Fig. 4.15).[97]

Animal teeth also were deemed effective talismans. The popularity of pierced animal teeth might be related to the qualities of the creature from which they were taken. The remarkable lion tooth set in gold and pierced with a bronze ring for suspension as an amulet in Roman Augst probably would have afforded the ancient wearer particularly impressive protection (Fig. 4.16, top left).[98] Other

[95] Diodorus Siculus 5.23. [96] Pliny, *Natural History* 36.141–142.

[97] Small and Small 2007, 174–6, figs. 22–3, burial F38. For similar blue glass phalluses as amulets, from the suburbs of Rome (Rebibbia), see Angeli and Quarante 2006, 262, cat. no. II.335, with fig. Burial 10 outside the Porta Nocera at Pompeii, an infant of about six months, had a small phallus amulet of bone, pierced to be worn on a necklace: Van Andringa et al. 2013, 363, fig. 238.

[98] Pfäffli 2013a, 44, cat. no. 30; see also cat. no. 31, another lion tooth.

Fig. 4.16 Pierced animal teeth amulets from Augst. The top two are lions' teeth (one with a gold cap); bottom left, a bear's tooth; bottom right, a boar's tusk.

Photos: Susanne Schenker; Augusta Raurica.

Fig. 4.17 Jet bear amulet from an infant burial of the fourth century AD, Abbey Field, Colchester.

Photo: © Colchester Archaeological Trust.

pierced teeth of wild animals, such as bears, boars, and possible wolves and foxes, are known at various sites (Fig 4.16).[99] A rich assemblage of finds in the burial of an infant between one and four and a half months at the rural site of Rec de Ligno à Valros near Béziers included a pierced beaver tooth.[100] All these animals could have been viewed as fierce guardians. Bears, for example, may have been associated with Artemis and Gallic bear goddesses, representing an animal who may have been a protector of children. Tiny jet bear amulets have been found in infant graves in Britain; two of them only eleven and fourteen millimetres long were strung together with glass and jet beads on a bracelet worn by an infant in a fourth-century grave at Colchester, Abbey Field (Fig. 4.17).[101]

The teeth of domestic animals are also encountered as talismans. Pliny claimed that a black dog's tooth could be used to reduce fever, and that a wolf's tooth helped to lessen teething problems and nightmares in a child.[102] Pierced dog teeth could reflect chthonic connections or symbolize the protection the faithful family pet provided. Dog teeth are linked thematically with the burial of dogs with infants and babies, as attested by canine bones and skulls and whole dog skeletons at Argenton, Kempten, and Pâtural near

[99] Crummy 2010, 52–3; Pfäffli 2013a, 44–5, cat. nos. 32–4.

[100] Bel 2012, 199, 202, fig. 11. Amulets also included a pierced pig tooth, a gold phallic amulet, a glass bead, a bone phallic amulet, and a bone lunula amulet.

[101] Crummy 2010, 38–9, fig. 1 (feature 25).

[102] Pliny, *Natural History* 28.257, 30.98.

Clermont-Ferrand.[103] Interestingly, some bone and amber pendants at Nîmes, Marseille, and Augst were carved to look like canine teeth (see Fig. 4.13).[104] Even human teeth, for reasons unknown, could be pierced for use as amulets, as at Castel Malnome (see Fig. 4.12).

PETS AND TOYS

Children are often depicted with pets in Roman funerary art, especially those children who are already a few years old. These include dogs, birds, and turtles, although dogs and birds appear to have been the most popular.[105] The influence of animals, and especially pets, on children's social, cognitive, and emotional development is also a research focus of modern scholars of child development.[106] These studies show that children often develop strong ties to their pets, helping them to develop empathy for others, to learn about nurture, and to understand biological constructs. Pets also may have had a genuine role in socializing the child in the Roman period, as Keith Bradley suggested through an analysis of textual sources and visual depictions.[107] One of these texts is particularly charming because it contains the pet-keeping memories of an elderly author. Marcus Cornelius Fronto wrote of his little grandson's love for "chicks, pigeons and sparrows", revealing that he also "was enthralled by these birds" from his own earliest childhood (*prima infantia*).[108] Pets of various kinds are also depicted in Roman funerary art, and these could be genuine portrayals of real pets, but they may also have been a device used to allude to a privileged childhood, whether real or projected. Ursio in Fermo, one year and eight months old, pets a dog who trustingly rests his head in the boy's lap.[109] This could be a pampered, wealthy child, but Ursio, in fact, was a slave, as the inscription reveals, so the accompaniment of the boy with a pet dog might be aspirational or meant symbolically to elevate his status.

At what age might children actually have been given pets? Young Sextus Rufius Achilleus in Rome, only seven months and nine days old, is depicted with a cock and a tortoise, whether real or of symbolic significance (see Fig. 8.1).[110] The marble statue of a little boy about the age of one shows him

[103] Argenton: Allain et al. 1992, 95 (tombs 82–3); Kempten: Faber 1998, 155–8, 229–30 (graves 413 and 414); Pâtural: Foucras 2014. See dogs in well in Hellenistic Athens.

[104] Nîmes: Bel 2012, 202, 204, fig. 14; Marseille: Moliner et al. 2003, 173, 309, pl. 80 (tomb 169); Augst: Pfäffli 2013a, 45, cat. no. 36.

[105] Mander 2013.

[106] Myers 1998; Deloache et al. 2011; Endenberg and van Lith 2011.

[107] Bradley 1998.

[108] Cicero, *Letters to his Friends* 1.12.

[109] *CIL* IX.5416; Mander 2013, 38, cat. no. 186, fig. 22.

[110] *CIL* VI.25572; Carroll 2011a, 112, fig. 8; Mander 2013, 57, cat. no. 94.

sitting on the ground, holding a puppy in one arm and pressing the puppy's face affectionately to his own.[111] This late Hadrianic image, probably originally part of a decorative programme from a Roman tomb near Sta. Maria Maggiore in Rome, depicts a child who was well-fed and cared for, as the rolls of fat indicate, and the pet dog might be understood as a companion his parents could afford to provide for their son. But family pets might have played a role in an infant's life at an even earlier stage. The image of a swaddled infant in a cradle with the family dog curled up at its feet (depicted in a stone votive discussed earlier in this chapter), creates an atmosphere of domestic intimacy; here the baby can only be two or three months old (see Fig. 4.8).[112] This is repeated in a Gallo-Roman terracotta votive of a baby in its cradle in which a dog is stretched out next to the infant, its head touching that of the baby.[113] For such images to be effective, they would have had to reflect something familiar, and, of course, in a family with several children of various ages, a family pet would have been something even the youngest could relate to and share with the others.

Infants had other things to play with as well, and some toys can be attributed specifically to babies. Rattles (*crepitacilis*) belong in this category. They have the ability to distract and entertain a baby through the noise they make, but Lucretius suggests that they also had a soothing effect.[114] Rattles may also have had an apotropaic nature, their sound warding off harmful spirits. The (rare) depiction of rattles in funerary art is limited to very young children. The six-month-old baby daughter of Telesphoris in Mainz sits as a pudgy baby and wields a round rattle with a long handle in one hand (see Fig. 4.5).[115] A quick drawing etched into the wet plaster in the Apronius catacomb in the third century AD also portrays an infant in a cradle who brandishes a long-handled rattle with an ovoid head.[116]

A number of rattles survive in various materials around the empire, although they are not very common in the archaeological record. A terracotta rattle filled with clay pellets from Autun has a handle and a round head with incised concentric lines.[117] Another with two small clay pellets inside from a cemetery at Évreux has painted white dots on the head.[118] Terracotta rattles in the

[111] Fittschen and Zanker 2014, 23–4, cat. no. 25, pls. 34–5

[112] Deyts 2004, 234–5, fig. 8; Carroll 2012b, 138, fig. 4.

[113] Rouvier-Jeanlin 1972, 245, cat. no. 599; Coulon 2004a, 50, with fig. See also the terracotta figurines of this type from Autun and Lyon: Deyts 2004, 234, figs. 6–7.

[114] Lucretius, *Nature of Things* 5.228.

[115] Carroll 2006, 170–1, figs. 56–7; Mander 2013, 29–30, cat. nos. 452, 453, figs. 13–14; *CIL* XIII.7114 and 7113.

[116] Fittà 1998, 51, fig. 72.

[117] Gourevitch et al. 2003, 208, cat. no. 115; Pluton et al. 2008, 216, fig. 8. Also Augst, Pfäffli 2013a, 121, cat. no. 131, with rows of incised lines. Coulon 2004a, 76–9, has a selection of rattles from Gaul.

[118] Pluton et al. 2008, 216, fig. 8 (grave 192).

shape of a bird are known from children's graves at Wederath-Belginum in Germany.[119] And bird whistles made of white pipe clay from sites in Roman Gaul, with a hole on the top of the head and another on the back to allow air to be blown through them to produce a sound, are delightful children's playthings, although these are less likely to be the toy of a baby than one for an older child. Nevertheless, an adult making the appropriate 'bird noises' with one of these would certainly have entertained an infant.[120] Other animal-shaped rattles include a piglet just ten centimetres long studded with multi-coloured glass beads from the second-century grave of a child at Settecamini who might have been about a year old.[121] Piglets may have been particularly appropriate thematically for babies, as they were associated with Demeter, rebirth, and rejuvenation, and were offered for sacrifice at rituals intended to protect children in life and death (Fig. 4.18).

Roman rattles made of metal and of perishable materials also survive. A silver rattle is known from Lyon.[122] An unusual object from Verulamium has been interpreted as a possible rattle.[123] It consists of a hollow iron rod on which are set hexagonal beads of shale and bone, the noise and alternating colours perhaps appealing particularly to an active infant mind. A collection of amuletic jewellery, consisting of glass paste beads, a bronze bell, four coins, an iron ring, and two pierced boar's tusks, was found strung on a metal ring in a child's grave in Rouen; these objects could have done double duty, as apotropaic amulets and as a rattle that would have made noises when shaken.[124] Only the hot, dry climate of Egypt allowed the survival of a wicker or linen rattle, possibly of late Roman date.[125]

We are on less firm ground regarding toys specifically for babies when we come to objects such as gaming pieces, dice, dolls, and figurines. Eight gaming pieces and two dice were found in a tomb of a child one to two years old at Urbino, but would a child this young really have been able to play with them?[126] We can ask the same question about a bone die buried with an infant six to eighteen months old in the Porta Palio necropolis at Verona.[127] Perhaps such gaming pieces symbolically reflected future childhood games which had been interrupted by death. The mid-first century AD statue of a

[119] Haffner 1974, 17, pl. 225.5 (grave 528); Cordie-Hackenberg and Haffner 1991, 114–15, pl. 488.4 (grave 1787); Cordie-Hackenberg and Haffner 1997, pl. 702.9 (grave 1787).

[120] Rouvier-Jeanlin 1995, 78–9, pl. 2.4; Fecher and Burger-Heinrich 2010, 53, 142, 460, fig. 45, pls. 153–4 (Rottweil, grave 384).

[121] Messineo 1991–2, 19–32, figs. 1, 6; Ceci 2006, 265, cat. no. II.339, with fig. Two similar glass-studded piglets (boars?) come from an inhumation burial (grave 4) of a four-year-old, dating to the late first century AD: Musco 2006a, 323, cat. nos. II.544–5 with figs.

[122] Fittà 1998, 51, fig. 69.

[123] Crummy 2010, 66–7.

[124] Pfäffli 2013a, 40, fig.14.

[125] Fluck and Finneiser 2009, 54, cat. no. 22; Harlow 2013, 327–8, fig. 16.5.

[126] Mercando et al. 1982, 135–42, figs. 23, 25 (tomb 13).

[127] Cavalieri Manasse and Bola 1998, grave 114.

Fig. 4.18 Terracotta rattle with glass inserts in the form of a piglet. Gift of J. Pierpont Morgan, 1917. The Metropolitan Museum of Art, 17.194.1893.
Photo: The Metropolitan Museum of Art, New York (www.metmuseum.org).

pudgy baby boy about a year old or slightly younger from a tomb complex on the Via Latina in Rome depicts the boy engaged in an activity for which he would have been too young, namely playing knucklebones.[128] The game, with variations, involved throwing knucklebones into the air and catching them on the back of the hand, and involved speed, dexterity, and numeracy. With his right hand this little boy appears to be throwing up a knucklebone, whilst his left hand is held over another one lying on the ground. Perhaps this statue is meant to be endearing, to show a baby's somewhat clumsy attempt to play a game for which he as yet had no skill, but for which an appetite had already been piqued.

Roman girls played with dolls of which jointed or articulated ivory and pipe-clay examples are best known because they are fairly large and elaborate and almost certainly represented something costly. In her influential paper on gender and dolls, Dolansky demonstrates that Roman dolls may have

[128] Fittschen and Zanker 2014, 21–2, cat. no. 23, pl. 32.

encouraged girls "to contemplate being wives and mothers and engage in role-playing activities to that end", but they also represented an ideal of upper-class, adult femininity, especially when the dolls were coiffed in emulation of an empress.[129] Some of the dolls are even adorned with gold jewellery, such as bracelets and a necklace, and they probably would have been dressed with miniature clothes, although the textiles do not survive. They are securely associated with young or pubescent girls, both in the burial record and in primary texts, and it is very unlikely that any child played with dolls of this kind before her first birthday.[130] According to Persius, pubescent girls dedicated their dolls to Venus when they reached womanhood, and again when they gave birth to their first child.[131] The young girl reclining on the lid of a marble sarcophagus of the first half of the second century from Rome, now in Malibu, shown with two dolls of the articulated type at her feet, is clearly in her early teens or a bit younger.[132] The individual (almost certainly a girl, although the skeletal remains were badly damaged) who was buried with an articulated ivory doll of early fourth-century AD date at Yverdon-les-Bains in Switzerland was also almost certainly a teenager, about fourteen or fifteen years of age.[133] Girls also played with marionettes or small figures in masculine form. Claudia Victoria in Lyon, for example, who died in the late first or early second century AD at the age of ten years, one month and eleven days, was buried with a pipe-clay marionette representing a Roman soldier with a decorated breastplate, of which only fragments survive.[134]

Although there is no physical evidence to connect dolls made of soft materials directly to infants, they would have been popular with very young children, easier to handle, and kinder to the tender skin of a baby. They do not survive anywhere but in Roman and late Roman Egypt, but there is no real reason to think that they did not exist elsewhere. Rag dolls in many shapes and sizes survive from Karanis, Oxyrhynchus, and Hawara, but usually in

[129] Dolansky 2012, 286–8. Much simpler and smaller bone dolls, without articulated limbs, were also fairly common, but probably not so expensive: Giovannini 2006, 331–3, figs. 5–7; Rustico 2013, 251, fig. 7.

[130] The pipe-clay jointed doll from a grave in Heidelberg belonged potentially to a girl between four and six years of age (Hensen and Ludwig 2005, 378, fig. 504). Two ivory dolls were buried with a child between the age of six and nine years in a marble sarcophagus (sarcophagus D) of the mid-third century AD in a family hypogeum on Via di Tor Cervara in Rome: Musco 2006c, 292–3, cat. no. II.402. On the burials of girls, some with dolls, see Harlow 2012.

[131] Persius, *Satire* 2.69, *Satire* 6.274. See Athenaeus, *Deipnosophists* 9.410e, on the oath taken to Aphrodite and on the gift of doll/doll clothes or a hair net to Diana, etc.

[132] Koch 1988, 11–13; Wrede 1990.

[133] Rossi 1993.

[134] Fittà 1998, 86, fig. 155. Perhaps this was one of the clay marionettes that Macrobius (*Saturnalia* 1.11.1) refers to as things played with by infants during the Sigillaria, the festival following Saturnalia in December. For another terracotta marionette of a masculine figure, see Rustico 2013, 248, fig. 4.2.

domestic, rather than funerary contexts.[135] An exception is the linen doll stuffed with rushes that was found in a child's grave of Constantinian date at Hawara; the doll had its own wardrobe of linen and woollen garments, so the child would have been able to dress and undress her doll, perhaps in preparation for her projected role as a mother.[136] Perhaps the richest cloth doll known from Roman Egypt, with unknown provenance, is an adult female doll of the second century AD who not only has real human hair, but also gold earrings and a leather neck-ring, and bracelets and anklets covered in gold leaf (Fig. 4.19).[137]

Figurines found at Karanis generally are of small format, on average only 7.5 centimetres long, made rather roughly of recycled wool textile or papyrus strips bound together and sometimes wrapped around a wooden stick frame; also small wooden dolls survive here.[138] Because of the very small size of the Karanis figurines, Johnson suggests that they might have been amulets that were used to protect children, but this remains speculative.[139] The cloth dolls from Hawara of the first to fourth centuries AD, on the other hand, are larger, ranging from 13 to 25.5 centimetres, and they clearly are meant to represent post-pubescent girls or women, as their breasts are moulded and have embroidered or painted red nipples, or the breasts are accentuated by cloth bands.[140]

These dolls, whether of ivory, bone, or cloth, generally represent a more mature female. But an interesting find from a Roman house at Ouveillan near Narbonne in southern Gaul suggests that perhaps articulated babies also were part of the doll repertoire.[141] The baby, made of terracotta and painted pink, with blue eyes, is clearly very young, as its large, round head and pudgy proportions indicate (Fig. 4.20). Although only the torso and head survive to a height of 6.8 centimetres, another similar terracotta found at Salces in the eastern Pyrenees still had its articulated legs, so it is clear that these very few terracotta baby dolls, of which several have been found in southern France, were moveable and flexible.[142] Even though it is perhaps unlikely that a child of a year or less would have played with these dolls, they, perhaps more than any of the adolescent or teen dolls discussed above, would have stimulated a young girl's interest in babies and caring for them as a future mother.

My final category of material culture associated with very young children constitutes figurines of terracotta and wood. Several pipe-clay figurines have been found in the graves of newborns at Argenton. The cremated newborn in grave 74 here was buried in the second half of the second century in a terra

[135] van Minnen 1994, 233, 247–8; Janssen 1996; Johnson 2003, 58; Dasen 2012, 20, fig. 10; Dolansky 2012, 265–6, 270, figs. 4–6.

[136] Dolansky 2012, 266, fig. 5. See Shumka 1993, 168–9, on games of simulated maternity.

[137] Fluck and Finneiser 2009, 46–7, cat. no. 18, fig. 7.

[138] Johnson 2003.

[139] Johnson 2003, 61.

[140] Dolansky 2012, 266–7.

[141] Bouisset 1969.

[142] Bouisset 1977, 91–3. Coulon 2004a, 99, mentions a group of six dolls in total, and expresses regret that so few of the dolls have been published.

Fig. 4.19 Textile doll from Egypt with human hair and gold jewellery, second century AD.
Photo: Sandra Steiß, Staatliche Museen zu Berlin–Ägyptisches Museum und Papyrussammlung, Inv.-Nr. ÄM 17954.

sigillata bowl with six pipe-clay figurines arranged in a circle in the earth above the vessel.[143] These comprise three Venus figurines, one of a mother goddess suckling twins, and two horses. The pipe-clay figurines of a seated woman breastfeeding a baby or two infants simultaneously, so-called *déeses mères*,

[143] Allain et al. 1992, 52–3, 170, figs. 36, 64.

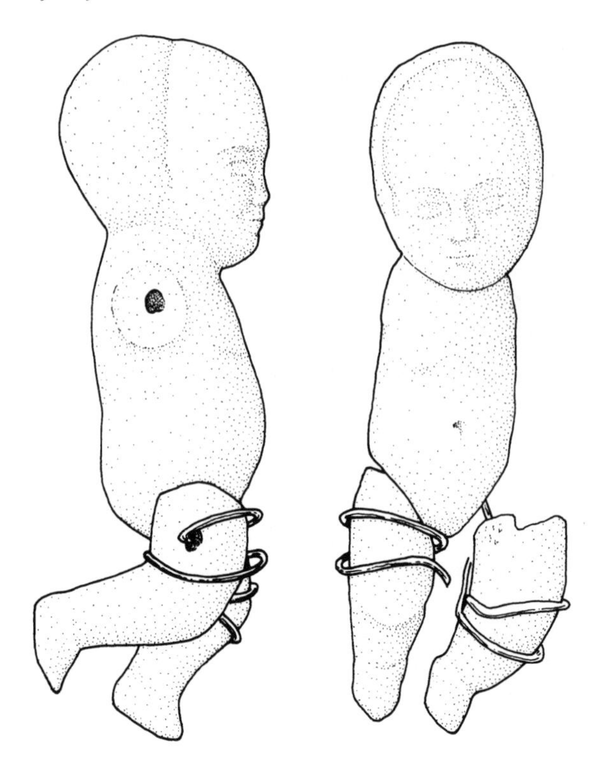

Fig. 4.20 Terracotta baby doll with moveable arms and legs (held with wire), from Ouveillan.
Drawing: Irene de Luis.

were particularly popular in Gaul, where they are found not only in child graves, but also in settlement assemblages (see Fig. 3.8).[144] Venus figurines were also found in the second-century grave of a newborn in grave 85 at Argenton, where they were placed on either side of the infant's head (see Fig. 4.3).[145] An iron ring was also found with the child that may have been used to hold together the swaddling bands. Elsewhere in Gaul, in the south necropolis of Paris, on the Boulevard Port-Royal, the very young child in tomb A50 was buried in the second century with a figurine of a mother goddess and a duck in a basin with suspension holes.[146]

[144] Schauerte 1985, 320–36, cat. nos. 890–948, pls. 106–12; Pfäffli 2013a, 71–2, 89, 101, cat. nos. 67–70, 85, 99–100.

[145] Allain et al. 1992, 95, fig. 27. The infant in tomb 47 at Argenton was buried with a figurine of a female bust: Allain et al. 1992, 92–3. For more Venus figurines from graves, see Pfäffli 2013a, 73–4, cat. nos. 71–5.

[146] Talvas 2007, 400–3, cat. nos. 75.1, 75.2.

The relevance to infants of Venus and nursing mothers is obvious. Both of them stand for fertility and protection, in life, and, apparently, also in death. But did such figurines also function as toys while the child was alive? Terracotta and pipe-clay figurines of animals, whether horses, birds, ducks, rams, and others, might seem more likely playthings for a child, especially when they are fitted with wheels on the bottom to allow them to be rolled around.[147] Wheeled wooden horses survive in Roman Egypt, but not, unfortunately in damper climates, and they are never interpreted as anything other than toys.[148] Figurines of this sort also in lead are known, but their purpose is not entirely clear. A small lead chariot with a charioteer in it found in a child's grave in a columbarium on Via Taranto in Rome may have been a toy, or perhaps was a grave gift symbolic of the journey through life and into the afterlife.[149]

Wheeled animals and other figurines of terracotta are known from domestic contexts in the European provinces, but they are also common in children's graves.[150] A child between ten and fourteen years of age at Rottweil, for example, was cremated in the late first century AD with nine pipe-clay figurines of cocks, doves, dogs, and a goddess, possibly Hebe.[151] It is impossible to determine whether these had been his toys during life, or whether they were purchased especially to include in the burial assemblage to keep the child occupied even in death.

[147] Rouvier-Jeanlin 1995, 78, pls. 1.1–2; Fittà 1998, 72–6, figs. 126–8; Coulon 2004a, 108–9, with figs.; Fluck and Finneiser 2009, 7–8, fig. 3; 52–3, cat. no. 21, with fig.

[148] Willfong 2012, 223–43, toy horses 237–8, figs. 14.15–16.

[149] Bolla 2013, 13–14, fig. 31.

[150] Talvas 2007, 269–71 (domestic context); Talvas 2007, 271–3 (graves); see also Augst, Pfäffli 2013a, 111–13, cat. nos. 113–21.

[151] Fecher and Burger-Heinrich 2010, 53, fig. 45, pls. 153–4 (grave 384).

5

Picturing Infants and Families in Roman Art

IMPERIAL AND IDEOLOGICAL IMAGES OF ROMAN INFANTS AND FAMILIES

Children are absent from Roman state art before the late first century BC, but given Augustus' ideological and social emphasis on marriage, children, and family life, it is not surprising that children were politicized and depicted on public monuments and works of art in this period. Infants (in this case mythological or allegorical) first appear on the Ara Pacis, the highly ornate altar commemorating the triumphs of Augustus in Gaul and Spain in 13 BC and dedicated in 9 BC on the Campus Martius outside the walls of Rome.[1]

There are two pairs of infants in the reliefs, one on the east side of the altar and the other on the west side. The two on the east side are naked and enveloped in baby fat, and they are seated on the lap of a voluptuous female figure who has been interpreted variously as Terra Mater, Italia, Venus, and *Pax Augusta* (Augustan Peace), the latter personification appearing to me the most convincing (Fig. 5.1).[2] One baby reaches for her breast, whilst the other brandishes a fruit that it has picked up from the woman's lap. The maternal–infant link is portrayed in a strong fashion to convey the idea of fertility and prosperity, *Pax Augusta* representing a *kourotrophos* nurturing the children of Roman Italy.[3] This group is flanked by two Horae, goddesses who bring prosperity through the seasons, and the foreground and background of the scene are occupied by various plants and animals also alluding to fecundity.

The other pair of infants on the west side of the altar are part of a scene connected with the origins of Rome itself, the discovery of Romulus and

[1] On the depiction of children in Augustan art, see Rawson 1997, 212–17.

[2] Strong 1937 (Terra Mater); Galinsky 1966 (Venus); De Grummond 1990 (Pax). Toynbee 1954, 80–1, pl. 13, interpreted the figure as Tellus Italia. Kleiner 1992, 96, fig. 80, also called her Tellus or Italia. See also Rossini 2006, 36–45 (interpreted as Tellus), with good photos.

[3] De Grummond 1990, 668.

Fig. 5.1 Relief from the east side of the Ara Pacis depicting *Pax Augusta*(?) with two babies.

Photo: Alessandro Vasari, Museo dell'Ara Pacis, Roma–Archivio Fotografico dei Musei Capitolini © Roma, Sovrintendenza Capitolina ai Beni Culturali–Musei Capitolini.

Remus by Faustulus, the shepherd, with Mars, as the father of the children, looking on.[4] Unfortunately, the panel is very fragmentary, although the torsos of Faustulus and Mars have survived, as have fragments of the scenery that indicate the outdoor location of the discovery, the Lupercal cave on the Palatine. Based on other depictions of Romulus and Remus suckled by the she-wolf, such as that on a Julio-Claudian relief in the Sebasteion at Aphrodisias, it is certain that the twins occupied the centre of the Ara Pacis panel.[5] On the fragmentary Aphrodisian relief, the twins are shown as fat, naked babies, and they will have been depicted this way on the Ara Pacis as well.

It is significant that one of the iconic images of Rome is a pair of infants, wronged, helpless, and half wild, but destined to establish a city which would come to rule an empire. The image was a recurring one for centuries after the dedication of the Ara Pacis. A statue of Hadrian, for example, known in

[4] Rossini 2006, 34–5, with fig.

[5] A. M. Smith 2013, 261–2, cat. no. D42, fig. 204, pl. 151.

several copies in Athens, Olympia, and Istanbul, utilizes the motif of the twins and the she-wolf as an image on the emperor's breastplate.[6] Romulus and Remus, with their four-legged nurse, were popular in art during the reign of Antoninus Pius. On one side of the relief-decorated base of the now lost column marking the site of this emperor's funeral pyre on the Campus Martius in Rome in AD 161, the goddess Roma sits and rests her arm on a shield, the central image of which consists of Romulus and Remus sucking milk from the swollen teats of the she-wolf.[7] Antoninus Pius also issued several coin types with mythological themes to mark the nine-hundredth anniversary of the founding of the city, and one of the chosen motifs shows the twins and the she-wolf.[8] Even though the images are of necessity small, it is easy to recognize two naked babies reaching up for the teats of the *lupa*.

The baby twins appear also on votive dedications by private individuals in Rome and its environs. On a marble votive altar set up by T. Claudius Faventinus in the late second century AD in Rome, for example, various scenes depict Mars and Venus and the Trojan War as part of the foundation myths of Rome, with one side of the altar dedicated entirely to the story of the exposure and rescue of Romulus and Remus. In the top register, their mother, Rhea Silvia, princess of Alba Longa, is seduced by Mars.[9] In the register below that, a female figure holds the twins as the product of this union on her lap. This figure is either Rhea Silvia herself or a wet-nurse (*nutrix*), but the latter is more likely as she has a kerchief on her head which most (servile) wet-nurses in Roman art wear. Having been taken away from their mother and set adrift on the Tiber in the third register, the twins reappear at the bottom of the altar's reliefs as babies being suckled by the she-wolf (Fig. 5.2). Elsewhere, in Ostia, a marble altar dedicated in the early second century to Mars and Venus, and found in a small shrine in the Piazzale delle Corporazioni, is adorned on one whole side with the discovery by the shepherds of the twins and the she-wolf in the Lupercal cave.[10] The naked infants tug on the teats of the wolf, and the baby fat on them suggests that they had been well nourished.

The twins and their four-legged nurse are a motif featured in reliefs on public monuments of different periods and from wildly different places throughout the empire. The trio appears on a relief panel adorning one of the engaged pilasters flanking the entrance to the Roman amphitheatre of the later first century AD at Nîmes in Gaul.[11] Although less accomplished, an early third-century marble relief from Avenches in Switzerland, possibly from an honorific monument, depicts two similarly fat babies pulling on and

[6] Kleiner 1992, 241, fig. 205; Opper 2008, 66–7, figs. 49, 52; Rissanen 2014, 340–1, fig. 6.

[7] Kleiner 1992, 285, fig. 253.

[8] *Roman Imperial Coinage* (*RIC*) 95, *RIC* 648.

[9] *CIL* VI.31098; Andreae et al. 1998, cat. no. 87a, pls. 240–9.

[10] *CIL* XIV.51; Weigel 1992, 292–6. The altar was rededicated in AD 124 to Silvanus.

[11] Teyssier 2014, 183–5, with fig. For an overview of the *lupa* on provincial monuments, see Rissanen 2014.

Fig. 5.2 Relief on the altar of T. Claudius Faventinus, Rome, depicting the twins Romulus and Remus and the she-wolf, late second century AD.
Drawing: Irene de Luis.

massaging the teats of the she-wolf.[12] The trio were relatively popular also in funerary art. In the second half of the first century AD, they appear on marble funerary altars in Rome, shown below a lush garland carved in the middle of the relief.[13] The same motif is employed on a funerary monument of the early second century from Pecs on the Danube.[14] Although the top of the *stele* is missing, the inscription indicates that it was dedicated by a mother to her daughter, so the image of nurturing is appropriate in this sense. Below the inscription are the twins and the she-wolf between two trees in low relief. A relief of the suckling twins is also a feature of two grave *stelae* from Sopron in Pannonia. One of them commemorates the Pannonian woman Litugena, her son, and her house-born slave girl; the other remembers a thirty-five-year-old auxiliary soldier from Siscia.[15] Reliefs on the basalt lintel from a possible funerary monument from Fiq in Syria also portray a somewhat stylized version of the she-wolf suckling the twins.[16] On all the reliefs from Rome, Italy, and the provinces in east and west, the she-wolf turns her head back to nuzzle the twins, licking them gently with her tongue.

[12] Bossert 1998, 89–92, cat. no. 43, pls. 35–6. The relief may, however, have adorned a funerary monument.

[13] Boschung 1987a, 97, cat. no. 651, pl. 17; 97, cat. no. 652, pl. 17 (*CIL* VI.20201, *CIL* VI.1968).

[14] *CIL* III.03311; *CIL* III.10292; *Die römischen Inscriften Ungarns* (*RIU*) 4 no. 990.

[15] *CIL* III.13441; *AE* 2001, 1641; *RIU* 1 no. 282; Kovács, 2005, no. 42.

[16] Weber 2006, 70, cat. no. 52, pl. 38.

Of course, real, not mythical, children were of great importance for the imperial family, both as heirs and for marriage alliances that reinforced imperial power. The birth of imperial children and the achievement of milestones in their lives were of dynastic significance, and images of such events could be utilized to good effect as propaganda.[17] This is particularly so with objects of small format, such as coins, decorative military accessories, and jewellery. Tiberius minted coins commemorating the birth of twin sons to Drusus Caesar and his wife Livia Drusilla (Livilla) in AD 22, thereby promoting dynastic ambitions of the imperial family.[18] These boys, Tiberius Gemellus and Germanicus Gemellus, were born in AD 19, so neither of them was an infant when they were portrayed as portrait busts in crossed cornucopias on the reverse of the coins. Neither was the young son of Domitian and Domitia a baby when he died at the age of three in AD 83 and was deified, although he looks more like a baby than a three-year-old on the reverse side of a denarius (Fig. 5.3).[19] This coin commemorating the boy's deification

Fig. 5.3 Gold coin of Domitian and Domitia, the reverse depicting their son who was deified on his death in AD 83.
Photo: © The Trustees of the British Museum.

[17] Haensch 2013. [18] Rawson 1997, 217, fig. 9.6. [19] *RIC* 209a, *RIC* 153.

depicts him naked on a globe surrounded by seven stars representing the constellation of Ursa Major.

General fecundity and the continuation of the imperial line seem to be the underlying theme of a series of coins of Marcus Aurelius for his wife Faustina the Younger. This empress had thirteen children, seven of whom died young, and she is shown either as *Fecunditas* with two babies and two older children, or as Venus Genetrix with one baby, or as a harbinger of *temporum felicitas*, happy times, with a group of babies and children (Fig. 5.4).[20] The symbolic merging of Faustina with Juno Lucina, a goddess associated with childbirth, is clear on the reverse of a coin on which Juno Lucina/Faustina is shown flanked by two young girls and with an infant in her arm.[21] In the same family, Lucilla, wife of Lucius Verus, had three children who, on her coins, are

Fig. 5.4 Coin of the empress Faustina the Younger, with children.
Photo: © The Trustees of the British Museum.

[20] Venus Genetrix: *RIC* 1386b; *Fecunditas*: *RIC* 676, *RIC* 677, *RIC* 1636; *felix temporum*: *RIC* 719, *RIC* 1674.

[21] *RIC* 1650.

seen as an infant in her lap and one or two older children at her side; she, too, is portrayed as *Fecunditas* or is associated with Juno Lucina.[22]

Whilst these coins utilize the imagery of children in dynastic claims, another coin series of Antoninus Pius drew attention to this emperor's charitable work providing for the poor orphaned girls of the city of Rome in memory of his wife Faustina the Elder. The Girls of Faustina, *Puellae Faustinianae*, was a charity established after her death in AD 141. The figures on the coin reverse are Antoninus and Faustina who bestow largesse on girls.[23] These girls, as children or adolescents, are led by adult men and women to the imperial couple; the infants among them are held up towards the emperor and empress. A couple of decades later, reliefs show a procession of girls approaching Faustina and her successor Lucilla, who continued the charitable scheme, but all the girls are adolescents and there are no infants in the scene.[24]

Dynastic succession in the imperial family is highlighted not only in Roman coinage, but also in a group of glass *phalerae* given to soldiers and officers as military decorations.[25] These mould-made disks were produced in the Julio-Claudian period and depict a portrait of an adult of the imperial family and busts of several children, usually three in number, the adult variously being interpreted as Drusus, Germanicus, or Claudius (Fig. 5.5). These *phalerae* are distributed widely in Germany, Austria, Dalmatia, and Britain. The children are very young, although it is difficult to know exactly what age they are; nevertheless, they appear to be perhaps a year old or a bit more. A disk from Ptuj, now in Vienna, depicts three infants, rather than just young children, the three faces looking particularly baby-like with chubby cheeks.[26]

Whereas the *phalerae* were given as gifts to individuals and groups outside the imperial family, cameos with relief decoration may be seen as jewellery or gifts exchanged within the emperor's family and entourage. A cameo, now in Berlin, depicting the offspring of the imperial family appears relevant here. This is a portrait of Livia Drusilla (Livilla) with her twin boys, Tiberius Gemellus and Germanicus Gemellus.[27] Both boys, born in AD 19, appear as miniscule figures in front of their mother's chest. It is difficult to recognize very much, but they seem to be infants, possibly naked, holding an object that might be a rattle. Their mother is depicted as Ceres, goddess of fertility, thus underscoring the main message of procreation and the continuation of the imperial line.

[22] *Fecunditas*: *RIC* 1736; Juno Lucina: *RIC* 770.

[23] *RIC* III 397–9; Rawson 1997, 225, fig. 9.10; Uzzi 2005, 46, fig. 11. See Hemelrijk 2015, 150–1, on this benefaction.

[24] Rawson 1997, 225, fig. 9.11; Uzzi 2005, 45–6, fig. 10.

[25] Boschung 1987b; Buljević 2013, 292–3, fig. 2.

[26] Boschung 1987b, 249–50, cat. no. 35, fig. 84. See also similar *phalerae* in Boschung 1987b, 249–50, cat. no. 36, fig. 85 (from Speyer) and 252, cat. no. 37, fig. 85 (from Colchester). According to Boschung, these *phalerae* depict Claudius and his children.

[27] Megow 1987, 295–6, cat. no. D22, pl. 12.7.

Fig. 5.5 Blue glass *phalera* with an imperial prince and his infant children.
Photo: © The Trustees of the British Museum.

BARBARIAN PARENTS AND INFANTS

The previous section began with a discussion of the Ara Pacis as a state monument on which mythological Roman children appear. Several other mortal Roman children appear on the north and south sides of the Ara Pacis in the procession scenes of Augustus and his family accompanied by Roman officials. Some of the children, but not all, are Roman. The Roman children range from a toddler (a boy) of perhaps three years to boys and girls between the ages of perhaps four and ten.[28] They are clothed in Roman dress, the boys in tunic and *toga praetexta* with a *bulla* and the girls also in a tunic and *toga praetexta*.[29] These children behave in a dignified way within this circle of adults. There are also two little boys in non-Roman dress who may be the children of Gallic chieftains and eastern royalty.[30] They most likely represent foreign children raised in Rome at the court of Augustus, a

[28] Uzzi 2005, 143–6. [29] Gabelmann 1985. [30] Uzzi 2005, 146–55.

custom reflected in the emperor's own memoirs.[31] Suetonius, too, says of Augustus that "he reared and educated the children of very many kings along with his own".[32] The older long-haired foreign child, perhaps seven or eight years old and wearing a diadem, may be a prince from the kingdom of Commagene in Anatolia, as Rose argues.[33] This boy wears a short tunic with his legs exposed, a tunic that has slipped on one side to reveal part of his shoulder. The youngest of the two boys on the north wall, a curly-haired toddler perhaps about two years old, turns away from the viewer, revealing plump legs and buttocks barely covered by his short little tunic; he looks up and lifts his arms to the nearest adult to his right (Fig. 5.6). His *torques*, or neck-ring, suggests a Gallic origin and a high-status identity, and he may be the son of a Gallic chieftain.[34] These elite children express the worldwide range of the Augustan peace and the recognition of Roman authority amongst subject, client, and foreign peoples. At the same time, however, as Jeannine Uzzi demonstrates, the poses of both the boys, their attire and the exposure of parts of their bodies, as well as their lack of interaction with the Roman adults in the group underscore their character as figures of submission and subordination.[35]

The Gallic toddler on the Ara Pacis is very similar to two toddlers with long locks and short tunics on one of the two silver cups of Augustan date from Boscoreale (BR I).[36] In the scenes on the cup, each toddler is led by his bearded and trouser-clad father to Augustus; a third slightly hidden boy sits on the shoulders of his father to get a good view. The clothing of the adult barbarians and the children, as well as bodily adornment such as *torques*, suggest that these are Gauls. Ann Kuttner has interpreted this scene as the aftermath of Augustan military campaigns in northern Europe, with barbarians presenting their children to Augustus.[37] In this interpretation, the children are "being transferred to the authority of Rome and Augustus to be brought up in honor under the emperor's *aegis*, perhaps even at the imperial court, as future Romanized leaders of their people".[38] The close relationship between the cup imagery and that of the Ara Pacis is evident, although it is unclear whether the cup scenes and the altar reliefs are derived from a large-scale monumental prototype rather than a common repertoire of images.

The motif of the transfer, or submission, of foreign children to the protection of Augustus recurs on Roman gold coins of 8/7 BC from the imperial mint in Lyon. On the reverse of these coins, a bearded barbarian holds up a naked

[31] *Res Gestae* 32; Rose 1990. [32] Suetonius, *Augustus* 48.
[33] C. B. Rose 1990, 455–9, figs. 2–3; Kuttner 1995, 104; Uzzi 2005, 146–51, fig. 60.
[34] Rose 1990, 459–61, figs. 5–6; Uzzi 2005, 151–3, fig. 61. [35] Uzzi 2005, 154–5.
[36] Kuttner 1995, 95–6, 99–100, pls. 4–5, 20, 22. [37] Kuttner 1995, 99–100.
[38] Kuttner 1995, 100.

Fig. 5.6 Barbarian (Gallic?) child on the Ara Pacis.

Photo: Alessandro Vasari, Museo dell'Ara Pacis, Roma–Archivio Fotografico dei Musei Capitolini © Roma, Sovrintendenza Capitolina ai Beni Culturali–Musei Capitolini.

toddler to the togate emperor (Fig. 5.7).[39] The message of Augustan peace and the existence of a world family is common to the Ara Pacis, the Boscoreale cup, and these gold coins, but the viewers of this message differed. Whilst the Ara Pacis would have been seen by and had an impact on the people of the city

[39] Kuttner 1995, 108; Uzzi 2005, 88, fig. 30.

Fig. 5.7 Coin with the motif of a barbarian father handing over his toddler to the emperor Augustus.
Photo: © The Trustees of the British Museum.

of Rome, the silver cup would have been enjoyed by its elite owner and was curated for his descendants (and their guests?) in Campania. The gold Lugdunum coins had a wider circulation in Gaul and Germany, if not amongst the civilian population, then certainly with the Roman armies on the Rhine and the settlements in the hinterland.

None of these barbarian children is a tiny baby; all are at least able to walk or are learning to do so. Babies and swaddled infants appear only in scenes of conflict between Romans and barbarians, and there they are closely associated only with their mothers, not with their fathers or male guardians. An early example of a conquered barbarian woman with an infant takes centre stage in the bottom range of images on the large cameo known as the Grand Camée de France.[40] The cameo's imagery celebrates the continuity and dynastic legitimacy of the Julio-Claudian imperial family, and dates probably to the AD 20s. Several dejected men and women in ethnic clothing are gathered together as captives,

[40] Megow 1987, 202–4, cat. no. A85, pl. 33.5; Zwierlein-Diehl 2007, 160–6.

and there is only one child among them. The central woman sitting on the ground holds a naked and corpulent baby very tightly in her arms while the baby stretches out an arm to its mother, placing its hand on her shoulder. This image of a helpless baby and its defeated mother on whom it depends for survival heightens the pathos of the situation. There is no willingness on the part of this child to be taken into the custody of the emperor, and no suggestion that the child's future would be anything but that of a Roman captive. As Kampen argues, the dynastic success of the Romans, in this case the Julio-Claudians, is played out against the defeat and capitulation of non-Roman people.[41]

The most extensive group of depictions of non-Roman families and children in Roman art was created in the reign of Trajan. The first of these appears on the *Tropaeum Traiani*, a monument erected at Adamklissi in Romania to celebrate Trajan's victory over the Dacians in the Battle of Tapae in AD 102.[42] This circular structure has fifty-four relief-decorated metopes around the base, most of them depicting battle scenes. Three children appear on the metopes, shown running away from a Roman soldier (Metope 35), being transported in a cart with Dacian men (Metope 9), and slumped dead on a rock (Metope 40). The only infant on the whole monument is depicted in Metope 54.[43] In this relief we see two standing Dacian women facing the viewer, the woman on the right holding a naked infant in the crook of her right arm, shielding the baby by tucking it into her cloak. All three of them are captives who have submitted to the power of Rome. Thus, at Adamklissi, there is a difference between infants and older children and the people with whom they are associated. The former are tied to their mothers as part of a maternal unit, the latter are associated with men and battle.

If Roman sculptors were practicing depicting Dacian men, women, children, and families on the *Tropaeum Traiani*, by AD 113 they had developed a full programme for the portrayal of barbarian families in various situations in the reliefs on the column of Trajan in Rome.[44] Dacians and Romans are clearly distinguishable in the reliefs by their very specific and detailed clothing and gestures. The story told by the column's reliefs can be divided into two sections: the first Dacian war (AD 101–2) and the second Dacian war (AD 105–6). One of the pivotal scenes for a discussion of barbarian families is scene 91 from the second Dacian war in which various groups sacrifice in the presence of Trajan.[45] Immediately to the right of the emperor are six men with three boys about five or six years old, all of them wearing the toga and, therefore, all Romans. Further to the right is another group of ten people in Dacian costume, including three men, four women, two young children, and a

[41] Kampen 2009, 61. [42] Florescu 1965. [43] Uzzi 2005, 128, fig. 51.

[44] Cichorius 1896; Lepper and Frere 1988; Coarelli 1999.

[45] Cichorius 1896, pl. 66; Lepper and Frere 1988, pl. 66; Coarelli 1999, 150–2, pls. 106–8; Kampen 2009, 52–3, fig. 12.

toddler. Elsewhere, in scene 30, five women, without their men, are herded together by the Romans to board a ship.[46] They take four children with them, including a toddler and what appears to be a baby; the latter is held by a woman whom we see from the back. Only the baby's head is visible. The woman with the toddler holds it up and away from her body and slightly above her head, as if showing it to a soldier or Trajan and asking for clemency.[47] None of the women or children is mistreated or even touched by Roman soldiers here, creating the impression that these enemies received gentle treatment, rather than the more likely physical violence.[48]

Uzzi claimed that depictions of non-Roman families show only the mother–child unit and that "in official imperial art, to be a Roman child is to have a father; to be a non-Roman child is to have a mother".[49] In reality, however, Dacian men take an active part in caring for and protecting their children in several scenes on Trajan's column. In scene 39, Dacian men, women, and children gather outside a Roman fort.[50] One man on his own carries a toddler on his shoulders, and another man in front of him does the same. The woman standing next to the latter touches the child; they are clearly the parents, and this is a family unit. In front of these two is a woman on her own who clutches a tiny baby to her breast. A father carries a toddler on his shoulders again in scene 76, whilst a second father flees, pulling what appears to be a reluctant older boy along with him (Fig. 5.8).[51] In this group of Dacians, three women accompany five further children, two of whom are naked babies in their arms. The most remarkable mother and infant on the column is portrayed in this scene: a woman balances a trough on her head in which a tightly swaddled infant lies. There is no evidence that the Dacians actually swaddled their babies, but the Roman sculptor clearly imagined it and drew on the repertoire of images in Roman art and his own experience of child care in Rome and Roman Italy.

The three infants in scenes 30, 39, and 76, therefore, are the only babies on the column who are clearly and recognizably under the age of one. They can be distinguished from older toddlers through their size, but also by the fact that toddlers are always clothed, whereas infants are either naked or swaddled. Both fathers and mothers protect the toddlers, but only mothers take care of the babies, almost certainly because of the reliability of the infants on what only their mothers could give them, namely mother's milk.

[46] Cichorius 1896, pl. 22; Miclea 1971, 54–6 (with plates); Lepper and Frere 1988, pl. 22; Coarelli 1999, 84–5, pls. 40–1; Kampen 2009, 47–8, fig. 14.

[47] Currie 1996, 159–69, fig. 18. [48] Kampen 2009, 48. [49] Uzzi 2005, 64.

[50] Cichorius 1896, pl. 39; Lepper and Frere 1988, pls. 29–30; Coarelli 1999, 84–5, pls. 40–1; Kampen 2009, 49–50, fig. 15.

[51] Cichorius 1896, pl. 56; Miclea 1971, 110 (with plate); Lepper and Frere 1988, pl. 56; Coarelli 1999, 133, pl. 89; Kampen 2009, 51–2, fig. 13. Kampen identified the swaddled baby in a trough on the woman's head as a "bundle", but that is incorrect.

Fig. 5.8 Scene 76 on Trajan's column, Rome, with conquered Dacian fathers, mothers, and children being rounded up.

Photo: K. Anger, Neg. D-DAI-ROM 89.749, Deutsches Archäologisches Institut, Rome.

Roman and non-Roman families appear again in the reign of Trajan in the reliefs on the arch at Benevento, built between AD 114 and 117 to commemorate the completion of the Via Appia from Rome to Benevento.[52] The two internal sides within the arch are decorated with reliefs, one of which depicts the institution of the *alimentaria* and the distribution of largesse by Trajan to the poor boys and girls of Italian cities. Fathers carrying children, a boy and a girl, on their shoulders come out to greet him, as do the cities of Italy, portrayed as women wearing mural crowns.[53] One of them holds a little girl in her arms. On the ground, one little boy stands anticipating his hand-out, whilst another turns away having already received his. The women are not real mothers, but the fathers appear to be, as they are dressed in simple tunics and, therefore, probably are working men who benefited by Trajan's largesse to their children. As Kampen notes, the placement of children on their fathers' shoulders mirrors the same poses of Dacian men and their toddlers on Trajan's column, suggesting that "this kind of paternal pose is only for men of relatively low status".[54] In the long frieze under the attic of the arch, both

[52] Currie 1996, 162–73; Ferris 2003, 60–2.
[53] Rotili 1972, pls. 66–70; Currie 1996, 168–70, fig. 22; Uzzi 2005, 41–4, fig. 9.
[54] Kampen 2009, 58.

mortal men and women are depicted; these are non-Roman captives paraded in a Roman triumph over Dacia.[55] Two Dacian children, already a few years old, cling to their mothers, whilst one mother carries a swaddled infant in her arms. As on the column of Trajan, the Roman sculptor imagined Dacian mothers to have swaddled their babies in the Roman fashion.

The imagery on the column of Marcus Aurelius, erected to commemorate the emperor's triumph over the Marcomanni, Quadi, and Sarmatians in AD 176, depicts more brutal and gruesome acts of violence in the battlefield and against the indigenous population than anything the reliefs on the column of Trajan has to offer.[56] Men, women, and children being injured, abducted, and killed occur in various scenes, but there is only one in which a woman has an infant. In scene 104/105, two women in the foreground, one with a child, are being pushed and scattered by Roman soldiers; in the background are five other women, one with a young boy, another holding a baby whose torso is naked and who holds out both arms to the woman next to his mother(?).[57] This is clearly a group of women and children being rounded up to be killed or sold into slavery, reassuring a Roman audience that "Roman victory would extend into the next generation".[58] As Zanker concludes, the violent images of the captivity and enslavement of women and children—the next generation—on the column are a visual sign of the destruction of the last traces of social unity amongst a non-Roman population.[59]

BIOGRAPHICAL SARCOPHAGI AND VIGNETTES OF ROMAN FAMILY LIFE

Although images of infants in a funerary context are discussed in Chapter 8, here I would like to deal with those portrayals that appear specifically on marble sarcophagi from the early second century AD, even though they are funerary, because the themes of family life and the socialization of the child on them make them relevant to the subject of this chapter.[60] The reliefs on these so-called biographical sarcophagi allow us to trace the transformation of a baby from fruit of the womb to child and person. Sarcophagi with this thematic decoration sometimes were manufactured specifically for children, but family life vignettes also decorated burial containers for adults. The

[55] Currie 1996, 171–3, fig. 24b; Uzzi 2005, 112–14, fig. 44.
[56] Ferris 2000, 86–98; Dillon 2006.
[57] Uzzi 2005, 131–2, fig. 54; Dillon 2006, 257–8, fig. 79; Kampen 2009, 62, fig. 22.
[58] Dillon 2006, 262. [59] Zanker 2000, 173.
[60] On the socialization of Roman children, see McWilliam 2013. For a good overview of family life and infant care scenes on biographical sarcophagi, see George 2000.

magnificent marble sarcophagus from Rome-Portonaccio of the late second century, for example, commemorates the lives of a successful general and his wife.[61] Complex and intricate battle scenes decorate this container, but the lid is reserved for selected moments in the life of the high-status couple, starting with a distinct group of an infant, its mother, and its nurse, and continuing with the adults fulfilling social expectations, he as husband and high-ranking soldier and she as wife and mother (Fig. 5.9).

An exquisite example of a sarcophagus manufactured for a child whose life was cut short in the mid-second century comes from Ostia, and it belonged to M. Cornelius Statius, as the inscription on the lower edge reveals.[62] At the left end of the main panel, the infant and his mother breastfeeding him are an intimate duo, with the father only looking on but not actively participating

Fig. 5.9 Reliefs on the lid of the marble sarcophagus from Portonaccio, Rome, depicting a baby reaching up to its nurse while the mother (left) looks on.

Photo: Maureen Carroll, with permission of the Ministero dei beni e delle attività culturali e del turismo—Soprintendenza Speciale per il Colosseo, il Museo Nazionale Romano e l'Area archeologica di Roma.

[61] Giuliano 1985, 177–88, cat. no. IV.4; Amedick 1991, 66, cat. no. 179, pl. 62.7.

[62] Amedick 1991, 64, cat. no. 114, pls. 52, 53.4; Huskinson 1996, 11, cat. no. I.23, pl. 2.1; Rawson 2003a, 106, fig. 2.2; Carroll 2012b, 141, fig. 5.

in something obviously outside his remit and physical possibilities (see Fig. 4.6).[63] But by the time the boy is older, the father has assumed the primary role in his son's life. As a toddler, he is shown in his father's arms; a little older, perhaps three or four years old, he plays in a goat-drawn wagon, and at the age of about seven, the end of *infantia*, the little toga-clad boy is taught rhetoric by his father, rehearsing for a life of public oratory as an adult. The story of the boy's life ends here.

More common are the biographical sarcophagi that begin their overview of the life stages of the deceased with the immediate aftermath of birth. The standard initial scene is the infant's first bath. The first bath is always administered in these scenes by the *nutrix*, a woman, either slave or free, in the employ of the family.[64] The nurse is recognizable by her age, her kerchief-like head covering, and the tunic that often slips off her shoulder. The infant is bathed in a basin, and sometimes another female servant stands behind with a towel or cloth to dry the child. On a large marble sarcophagus from Rome, now in rather worn condition, one woman washes a plump baby in a large basin, while another pours water into it from a jug (Fig. 5.10).[65] Once cleansed, the baby is presented to its mother who sits nearby and watches the proceedings. The mother looks somewhat aloof, and in many of these scenes the infant seems more eager to return to the arms of its nurse than be handed over to its mother. In other cases, however, the baby looks at and stretches it arms towards its mother, waiting to be picked up and cradled.[66]

Another postpartum task is the breastfeeding of the baby, although images of this activity are rare and known only on four surviving burial containers. The mother of M. Cornelius Statius (see Fig. 4.6) performs this task, as does the mother on a late second-century sarcophagus from Tivoli, now walled into the villa Doria Pamphilj in Rome.[67] But on another sarcophagus and a decorated ash chest in the Vatican, both dating to the third century, a wet-nurse is shown in this role (Fig. 5.11).[68] On the ash chest, while the nurse feeds the infant, an imposing female figure with her *palla*, or cloak, covering her head approaches with arms outstretched, almost certainly the mother who has come to retrieve her now sated baby.

[63] For an earlier Etruscan scene on a terracotta ash chest of the first half of the second century BC from Chiusi of the close-knit mother–baby duo, from whom the husband, a *haruspex*, takes leave, see Haynes 2000, 342, fig. 269.

[64] For example, a sarcophagus in the Museo Torlonia, Rome: Huskinson 1996, 11, cat. no. I.31, pl. 3.1. See also Amedick 1991, 62, cat. no. 2, pls. 53.2–3, from Agrigento. On the role and status of wet-nurses, see Sparreboom 2014.

[65] Giuliano 1985, 472–6, cat. no. IX.3; Amedick 1991, 62, cat. no. 178, pl. 60.1.

[66] Amedick 1991, 60, 64, cat. no. 198, pls. 54.1, 55.3–4.

[67] Amedick 1991, 64, cat. no. 236, pl. 55.2; Carroll 2014, 165, fig. 4.

[68] Sarcophagus: Andreae et al. 1995, cat. no. 424Ka, pl. 831; Amedick 1991, 63, cat. no. 273, pl. 64.1; ash chest: Andreae et al. 1995, cat. no. II69c, pl. 917; Uncini 1995, pl. 917; Carroll 2012a, 47, fig. 4.3.

Fig. 5.10 Reliefs on the lid of a marble sarcophagus from Rome showing the newborn's first bath administered by servants while the mother (left) looks on.
Photo: Maureen Carroll, with permission of the Ministero dei beni e delle attività culturali e del turismo—Soprintendenza Speciale per il Colosseo, il Museo Nazionale Romano e l'Area archeologica di Roma.

The care of the newborn infant, then, was consistently the province of women, but the women involved were not limited to the baby's mother. Elite Roman mothers may have routinely entrusted the feeding of their infants to a *nutrix*, although it cannot be demonstrated that all upper-class women did so, or that employing a nurse meant that mothers were not attached to their children. There is an inherent conflict between the Roman social image of the nursing mother as the maternal ideal and the reality of the families of the propertied classes who delegated the most basic childcare tasks to others, simply because they could afford to.[69] Given that many of the commissioners of figural sarcophagi, apart from the very large and elaborate ones like the Portonaccio sarcophagus, probably were not the socially elite, but members of the middle and freedman classes, it may be that they used these reliefs to allude to and emulate the world of wealth and privilege as they imagined it. As Natalie Kampen pointed out, these sarcophagus scenes reveal the social ideals of a particular stratum of prosperous buyers, but the true feelings about family

[69] George 2000, 199–202.

Fig. 5.11 A wet-nurse breastfeeds a baby while the mother approaches from right, depicted in a relief on a marble ash chest.
Drawing: Jerneja Willmott.

are far from clear.[70] In reality, most mothers outside elevated social circles will have breastfed and cared for their infants themselves.

The premature death of a child is an occasional central scene on biographical sarcophagi. The children shown on their death beds, however, are never babies; rather, they are older children who had been the focus of the family's investment and aspirations for at least a few years. A marble sarcophagus from Agrigento is decorated on each of the short sides with the image of the baby's first bath, on the one hand, and the young boy driving a goat-drawn carriage, on the other.[71] On the long side, the same child, a boy of perhaps ten years of age, lies dead, wrapped in a shroud. Other members of the *familia* include, first and foremost, the mother and father, each seated and veiled in mourning at either end of the death bed, a little toddler and another child in a tunic, perhaps siblings, and a nurse, teachers, and servants. Like the literature that portrays and advises a stoic and aristocratic attitude towards the loss of

[70] Kampen 2009, 17–18.
[71] Amedick 1991, 62, cat. no. 2, pls. 53.1–3; Carroll 2012b, 136, fig. 1.

children, the idealized parents in the deathbed scene are contrasted in their composed and noble demeanour with individuals of servile status such as slaves and child-minders who communicate their distress through bodily poses and gestures.[72]

The brief and transient life of a child is portrayed allegorically on a child's sarcophagus of the early second century from Rome, without death or the dead child itself being portrayed.[73] Again, the parents assume different roles according to the age of the child. On the left, mother and father travel in a carriage with their infant son, held as a swaddled baby by his mother, and on the right, the same couple travel in another carriage with their son who is now a toddler sitting on the lap of his father (Fig. 5.12). A winged putto flying above this wagon indicates that the child's life has come to an end. The relief scenes between the two ends of the story show that the boy has learned to walk with a baby walker and play as a pudgy toddler. Thus, life is portrayed as a short journey, from infancy in swaddling clothes to early childhood and a premature death.

Fig. 5.12 A swaddled infant held by its mother in a carriage (left) and later, as a toddler, held by its father in another carriage (right), on a child's sarcophagus in Rome.

Photo: Maureen Carroll, with permission of the Ministero dei beni e delle attività culturali e del turismo—Soprintendenza Speciale per il Colosseo, il Museo Nazionale Romano e l'Area archeologica di Roma.

[72] George 2000, 203–5.

[73] Giuliano 1981, 73–5, cat. no. 55; Amedick 1991, 64, cat. no. 190, pl. 45; Huskinson 1996, 10–11, cat. no. I.29, pl. 1.3; Rawson 2003a, 130, fig. 3.1.

Childcare tasks and related activities are depicted sometimes also in conjunction with Graeco-Roman gods. Dionysos is most often portrayed in his early life in scenes that are intended to be viewed as vignettes of his family life. In them, the chubby baby Dionysos is tended to by child-carers who are no ordinary mortals. In Graeco-Roman mythology, the young god was born in Asia Minor and raised by nymphs and satyrs, and in Roman art it is they who look after him. The figural relief on the Neronian funerary altar of Passiena Prima from the Santa Rosa area of the Vatican necropolis, for example, shows a naked baby Dionysos bouncing on the left leg of a seated satyr while a maenad looks on.[74] The satyr holds up a large bunch of grapes to which Dionysos holds out his arms greedily. On a marble sarcophagus of the mid-second century AD from Rome, now in Baltimore, even a panther cub looks on as part of the entourage of nymphs, satyrs, and creatures.[75] The sarcophagus is little more than 1.50 metres long and was probably especially manufactured for a child.

The triad of nymphs and the baby Dionysos, one nymph holding the baby on her lap, the other pouring water into his bath basin, is a motif that recurs in very similar fashion on three surviving marble sarcophagi now in Rome, Woburn Abbey, and Munich.[76] But the three figures on the sarcophagi in the Museo Nazionale in Rome (from Nepi) and in Woburn Abbey are so close in pose and gesture, that they must come from a pattern book or a common source used by the sculptors of both burial containers (Fig. 5.13). Even though the left arm and the right leg of the baby are restored on the Nepi sarcophagus, the unrestored baby on the panel in Woburn Abbey indicates that they are correctly done. Both babies squirm and kick in a charming and realistic manner, and both are well-fed and fat.

In Asia Minor, the themes of the bath and the education of the infant Dionysos appear to have had special resonance in non-funerary public art, probably because Lydia and Phrygia were areas in which his cult may have had its origins.[77] The Attalid kings of Pergamon even claimed Dionysos as their ancestor. The earliest portrayal in public art of Dionysos as a baby held by a nymph is on a panel at the Julio-Claudian Sebasteion in Aphrodisias.[78] The bath of the infant was absent in the reliefs of this period, but, by the second century AD, the motif of the first bath by the nymphs was fully developed, and

[74] Liverani and Spinola 2010, 240–1, figs. 80 and 82.

[75] Matz 1969, 350–1, cat. no. 199, pl. 211.1; Huskinson 1996, 33, cat. no. 3.12.

[76] Matz 1969, 351–3, cat. no. 200, pl. 215.1; Bowersock 2011, 4, fig. 5 (Rome); Matz 1969, 354–7, cat. no. 202, pl. 212.2 (Woburn Abbey); Matz 1969, 351–3, cat. no. 200, pl. 215.1; Bowersock 2011, 4, fig. 5 (Munich).

[77] Otto 1965, 59–64.

[78] R. Smith 1987, 97; R. Smith 2013, 225–6, cat. no. D20, fig. 181, pl. 123. Dionysos as a small child appears again in 265–7, cat. no. D44, fig. 206, pls. 154–5. Smith describes him as "swaddled" (p. 265), but, as he is already older, he is not; rather, he is draped in a mantle.

Fig. 5.13 The first bath of baby Dionysos in the reliefs of a marble sarcophagus from Nepi in Rome.

Photo: Maureen Carroll, with permission of the Sovrintendenza Capitolina ai Beni Culturali—Archivio Fotografico dei Musei Capitolini.

it appears on reliefs at the theatres at Perge in Pamphylia and Nysa in Caria.[79] In the bath scenes at both theatres, one nymph holds the infant and is about to plunge him into a large basin, while a second nymph pours water from a jug into the basin. At Perge, a third nymph stands by with a large towel in which to envelop Dionysos when he is lifted from the bath.[80] The cycle of the education of the infant Dionysos continues in other relief panels at Nysa, including the transfer of a particularly plump baby by Hermes to a nymph.[81]

PORTRAITS AND STATUES OF INFANTS

Portraits of loved ones were objects of remembrance that could be gazed upon, talked to, and touched. According to Suetonius, for example, Augustus had a statue in his bedroom of one of the children of Germanicus and Agrippina

[79] Bowersock 2011. [80] Nollé 2003, 639, fig. 12c. [81] Nollé 2003, 638–9, fig. 8b.

who had died young. The emperor "used to kiss it fondly whenever he entered" the room.[82] In cases of extreme parental grief and loss, multiple copies of a child's portrait could be produced. This, apparently, was the case on the death of the teenage son of M. Aquilius Regulus in the latter part of the first century AD According to Pliny the Younger, dozens of portraits and statues were made "in paint, wax, bronze, silver, gold, ivory, and marble" throughout Rome.[83] In the grieving father's mind, this proliferation of images would have compensated for a public career and honours that the boy had not lived long enough to achieve.

Numerous marble portrait busts of children are known in the Roman Empire, especially in Italy. Particularly individual and of high quality are a marble portrait of the second half of the second century of a young boy (maybe three years old) of African heritage in the Getty Museum, and a marble portrait of the early second century of a slave boy named Martialis in the same museum, who, according to the inscription, lived only two years, ten months, and eight days.[84] It is sometimes very difficult to determine whether a surviving bust or head of a child depicts someone only a year old or already a bit older, and it is also not always certain whether such pieces represent real children or mythological subjects. A variety of such pieces in the Vatican, for example, are alternately referred to as a *bimbo* or *putto* or *amorino*, without any real justification for the identification.[85] Roman marble copies of Greek originals with mythological subjects, such as the infant Hercules killing the snakes sent by the goddess Hera, might simply represent Hercules, but they might also be altered to allude to a specific child, as in the case of a Severan marble statue of a snake-killing boy whose face is a lightly stylized portrait.[86] Statues and portraits of children only months old or a year at the most, in contrast, are very rare. For Fittschen and Zanker, the reason for this is simple: the loss of a child was more painful to the parents when it had already lived a few years and, therefore, older children are commemorated more frequently.[87] Whether the situation is quite that simple may be debated.

A child's portrait may have been set up in domestic contexts, as the anecdote about Augustus suggests, but a secured provenance of several statues

[82] Suetonius, *Gaius* 7. [83] Pliny, *Letters* 4.7.

[84] African boy: Frel 1981, 87, 129, cat. no. 69, with fig. Martialis: Rawson 1997, 205–38, p. 227, fig. 9.12; Backe-Dahmen 2006, 97, 102, 178–9, cat. no. F40, pl. 42d. Possible slave children of a very young age might also be recognized in marble portaits in Rome by their long hair, according to Fittschen and Zanker 2014: 25–6, cat. no. 25b, pl. 37; 42–5, cat. no. 41, pl. 60. These are interpreted as *delicia*, 'pets' or 'favourites' of the master.

[85] Kaschnitz-Weinberg 1936–7: *bimbo*: 169, cat. no. 368, pl. 71; *putto*: 166, cat. no. 356, pl. 70; *amorino*: 163, cat. no. 351, pl. 68.

[86] Fittschen and Zanker 2014, 30–1, cat. no. 29, pls. 43–6. They suggest this may have been a grave statue, the equation with Hercules expressing the hope for a better life in the beyond. The child is certainly older than eight months, the age at which Hercules performed this feat.

[87] Fittschen and Zanker 2014, 14.

of very young children in Rome demonstrates that such images were clearly also part of funerary assemblages in tombs. These include portraits of a boy about a year old and of an older boy from a tomb complex on the Via Latina in Rome.[88] A case also can be made for a tomb as the provenance of a seated portrait statue of a chubby infant holding a puppy in Rome, the imagery shedding light again on the very young age at which a child might have a family pet (see Chapter 4).[89] Infants were not only depicted as statues, but also in abbreviated form as busts, and even herms. I flag up here a particularly high quality marble portrait head in the Metropolitan Museum in New York which may also have stood in a niche in a built tomb in Rome (Fig. 5.14).[90] The large head, soft and chubby cheeks, and large eyes, suggest that this little boy was only months old, clearly a very beloved baby. Two other marble portrait busts of children perhaps a year or so old from Rome, now in the Museo Nazionale Romano and the Ny Carlsberg Glyptotek in Copenhagen, also depict a physiognomy that is entirely consistent with a very young age.[91] They date to the mid-first century and the mid-third century AD respectively. Neither of the portraits is a generic child portrait; instead, each infant can be recognized as an individual child and is as realistic as one could expect it to be. The head of an infant on a herm of the first half of the second century in the Vatican is, on the other hand, somewhat stylized, but the filet on the child's head with ribbon-like ends fluttering down on either side of the face and the twisted ring around the child's neck suggest a more personalized and specific identity. According to Kaschnitz-Weinberg, these items of bodily adornment are of religious significance and they refer to a sacred rite in which the child had participated.[92] For him, the portrait herm is indubitably of a dead child and, therefore, a funerary portrait.

Realistic Roman portraits might have been based on death masks, as several surviving artefacts suggest. The original plaster moulds of the faces of various family members, including two children and an adult male, survived in the second-century tomb of the freedman C. Valerius Herma under St Peter's cathedral in Rome.[93] According to the inscriptions in the mausoleum, the family had a twelve-year-old daughter and a four-year-old

[88] Fittschen and Zanker 2014, 21–3, 35–6, cat. nos. 23–4, pls. 32–3, 49–50. Fittschen and Zanker doubted the existence of child portraits in a domestic context.

[89] Fittschen and Zanker 2014, 23–4, cat. no. 25, pls. 34–5.

[90] Zanker 2016, 134–6, cat. no. 43.

[91] Backe-Dahmen 2006, 174, cat. no. F27, pl. 37; 199, cat. no. F96, pl. 88c. A third baby portrait in a German private collection was considered by Backe-Dahmen (175, cat. no. F29, pl. 38) to be of the first century AD, but Fittschen and Zanker 2014, 14, reject this date, attributing it instead to the nineteenth century. See also a second-century portrait head of a baby probably younger than one year in the Vatican which was once inserted into a bust(?): Kaschnitz-Weinberg 1936–7, 170, cat. no. 373, pl. 71. He flags up the skilled characterization of "prima infanzia".

[92] Kaschnitz-Weinberg 1937, 171, cat. no. 377, pl. 71.

[93] Drerup 1980.

Fig. 5.14 Marble portrait of a very young Roman infant. Rogers Fund, 1912. The Metropolitan Museum of Art, 12.232.1.

Photo: The Metropolitan Museum of Art, New York (www.metmuseum.org).

son, and it is almost certainly their faces preserved in plaster moulds found by the tomb's excavators.[94] Modern plaster positives made of these moulds

[94] Drerup 1980, 85–7, pls. 34.1–2, 36, 37.1; Dasen 2010, 129–33, figs. 5.5(a)–(b), 5.6(a)–(b). Liverani and Spinola (2010, 101, figs. 58–9) propose that one of the masks shows the face of a child "not even one year old", but the child looks older than that to me.

Fig. 5.15 Plaster mould of the face of a baby, Paris, Musée Carnavalet.
Photo: © Rémi Briant/Musée Carnavalet/Roger-Viollet.

reveal the childish features and very long eyelashes of both children. The plaster negatives were left in the family's mausoleum after the burial of the children.

An even more remarkable mould of a face was taken from an infant in the Roman city of *Lutetia*, modern Paris, in the third century AD (Fig. 5.15).[95] The rounded head and pudgy cheeks clearly indicate that this infant was only weeks or months old, and the mould is a poignant reminder of the investment made in the memory of a beloved child whose death came far too early. The negative cast of this baby's face was laid in the grave with the child, only to be found centuries later when the site was excavated in the nineteenth century.

Before moulds like these were buried forever, wax or plaster positives could have been made from them. These casts either were the desired end product or they could have served as models from which to create portraits in more permanent and expensive materials such as stone or bronze, if financial resources allowed it. A plaster three-dimensional portrait head of another boy in the mausoleum of the Valerii under St Peter's basilica still has traces of gilt on it, suggesting that, in this case, plaster, as a cheaper material, was altered to appear costlier than it really was and to give the portrait the appearance of being made of bronze or even gold.[96] Whilst all the masks and resulting portraits discussed here were found in secure funerary contexts, the process of producing portraits for display in other contexts, such as the home, would not have been any different.

Infants do not always appear on their own as statues or portrait busts; there is also a tiny surviving group of statues of a mother and an infant. The earliest of these is the one about which the least is known. This statue is made of

[95] Dasen 2010, 131–2, figs. 5.8(a)–(b); Carroll 2011b, 68, fig. 4.2.
[96] Drerup 1980, 87, pl. 37.2.

Fig. 5.16 Tufa statue of a mother with an infant and a child from Rome.
Photo: Musei Capitolini, Centrale Montemartini, © Roma, Sovrintendenza Capitolina ai Beni Culturali—Archivio Fotografico dei Musei Capitolini.

volcanic tufa stone (pepperino) and depicts a standing woman with a child of a few years standing next to her and an infant in her left arm who suckles at her breast (Fig. 5.16).[97] The statue was found in 1878 near the basilica of San Lorenzo on the Via Tiburtina in Rome with other pieces of tufa statues

[97] Bertoletti et al. 2006, 28–31, fig. 21.

that had been broken up and reused in a wall. These included a statue of Orpheus surrounded by various animals, and the heads of three barbarians, two of whom have long and wild hair, while the third has a pronounced moustache and a skull-cap or tight fitting helmet over his wavy hair.[98] In the catalogue of the Centrale Montemartini museum, where the group is housed, the identity of the woman is suggested as the mythical Hypsipyle, queen of Lemnos, whose twins were fathered by Jason before he abandoned her and left the island with his Argonauts.[99] Although Orpheus, the musician and tamer of animals, was indeed a companion of Jason on the ship Argo, it seems a great leap to identify the female figure as Hypsipyle simply because she may have been associated with the group of statues to which Orpheus belonged. This is especially doubtful because the children associated with the female figure are not the same age and, therefore, not twins. An inscribed tufa statue base was found in the vicinity naming Marcus Minucius, dictator, as the dedicator of a vowed gift (of a now missing statue) to Hercules, leading to the interpretation of the entire group as a victory monument in the sanctuary of Hercules, possibly to celebrate Municius' defeat of Hannibal in 217 BC.[100] This interpretation does not coincide with the information provided on the labels accompanying the statues and statue fragments in the museum. These suggest that two main themes were represented in the sculptural group: mythological themes and a battle scene with barbarians. The statue of the woman with two children is interpreted here as a barbarian prisoner who was paired with the statue of the moustachioed barbarian man. There is nothing about the clothing of the woman or her older child, however, to indicate that they cannot be Roman, in contrast to the appearance of the man with wavy hair, skull cap, and a moustache, who is most definitely not. But what his ethnic origin was or how he could be tied to a Carthaginian victory is unclear, and there is too much uncertainty to decide who the woman actually could be.

A second statue of a breast-feeding mother, dating to the early first century AD, is now in the Museo Chiaramonti in the Vatican. This marble group depicts a seated woman holding a very young child on her lap. She exposes her left breast to feed him, whilst he reaches up with his hand to touch her. The child still has lots of baby fat, but is no longer a tiny baby; he appears to be about a year old. The woman's features are very idealized, so it is unlikely that the statue represents a real person. It has been suggested that she is a goddess or a *dea nutrix*, a nursing goddess, because of the diadem she wears on her head.[101] Liverani hypothesized that it might be Juno and

[98] Bertoletti et al. 2006, 28–31, figs. 19–20.

[99] Bertoletti et al. 2006, 29. Hypsipyle later fled for her life and her sons were taken by pirates and sold to Lycurgus, king of Nemea.

[100] *CIL* I^2.607.

[101] Andreae et al. 1995, 392–5, cat. no. 241, pl.

"una statua di culto".[102] The statue was found near the church of San Clemente possibly as early as the thirteenth century, and became part of the Quirinal Gardens laid out by Pope Sixtus in the late sixteenth century.[103] Despite this general localization of a find spot, we cannot determine the original context of this statue which hampers a proper understanding of the function of this piece.

A bronze statue of Eirene (Peace) cradling her infant Ploutos (Wealth) in her arms was made for the Athenians in the early fourth century BC by the Greek sculptor Kephisodotos, and it proved to be a popular image in Rome and was copied at least thirteen times in marble in the first century AD.[104] A surviving adaptation of the image, now in the Louvre, combined Greek Classical idealized human forms with Roman portrait features in a representation of real people. The empress Valeria Messalina appears in the guise of Eirene and her little son Britannicus, born in AD 41, replaces Ploutos. The imagery was appealing to imperial Roman women for its dynastic and political symbolism, and may have been used already by Agrippina the Elder before Messalina adopted this guise.[105] Messalina represents a traditional Roman *matrona*, her heavy drapery and her covered head suggesting respectability and modesty, and the infant reflecting her fertility and maternal qualities, all of which may have stood in contrast to her moral character and ambitions as they have been conveyed in hostile historical sources compiled after her death. Having been condemned and executed in AD 48 by her husband, Claudius, for adultery and political intrigue, Messalina suffered a *damnatio memoriae*.[106] While other inscriptions and images of this disgraced imperial wife were mutilated, damaged, and destroyed when her memory was erased, the excellent state of preservation of this particular statue of Messalina and Britannicus indicates that it must have been taken out of official circulation and kept somewhere for safekeeping by persons unknown, possibly her family.[107] Although the *damnatio memoriae* pertained only to Messalina, and not her young son Britannicus, within a year, Messalina had been replaced as empress by another ambitious imperial woman, Agrippina the Younger, and within seven years, Britannicus had been murdered by his step-brother, Nero, removing him from the imperial line of succession and damning also his fading memory to obscurity.

[102] Liverani 1989, 90. [103] Lanciani 1924, 189.

[104] Vierneisel-Schlörb 1979, 255–67, figs. 119–27; De Grummond 1990, 667, fig. 6; Picón et al. 2007, 140, 435, no. 158; A. C. Smith 2012, 447–9, fig. 22.4.

[105] S. E. Wood 1992, 219–26; S. E. Wood 2001a, 227, 280, figs. 123–5.

[106] Flower 2006, 182–9. [107] Varner 2004, 96.

6

Mors Immatura I

Contextualizing the Death and Burial of Infants

INFANT MORTALITY AND AGE AT DEATH

Infant mortality in the Roman world was very high. Modern estimates suggest that 50 per cent of children would not have lived to see their tenth birthday, and in the first year of life alone, an infant mortality rate between 20 and 30 per cent has been suggested.[1] But there also is archaeological evidence that infant mortality, in some places, could have been higher than this. Excavations of a necropolis of the imperial period at Piano di Castiglione-Quarto Cappelle del Prete in the eastern *suburbium* of Rome showed that almost 60 per cent of children died before the age of six, and 38 per cent of the population buried in this cemetery had not reached their first birthday.[2] At Velia in Campania, children under the age of one comprised 31 per cent of the total assemblage of the first and second centuries AD in the Porta Marina Sud cemetery.[3] In the cemetery on the hill of Saint-Jean at Soissons, 34.4 per cent of the inhumation burials from the early first to the mid-second century AD consisted of foetuses, premature births, and neonates.[4] Estimated Roman infant mortality rates seem to be quite high at these sites, but, as Frier notes, the patterns throughout the empire are insufficiently consistent for us to have absolute confidence about them.[5]

It can be difficult to determine how many infants died at some sites, for various reasons. In Italy, for example, some publications of cemetery excavations leave out the skeletal analysis altogether; in other reports, the excavators and specialists do not provide precise age at death data, preferring, instead, to refer to infants/children as *infans* I, i.e. 0–6 years of age.[6] In those cases, any

[1] Parkin 1992 suggested 30%. Parkin (2010, 113 and 2013, 49–50) later corrected his earlier estimate to 20%. Golden 1987 quotes 30%–40% infant mortality; Hopkins (1983, 225) proposed that 28% of all babies born alive did not survive their first year.

[2] Catalano et al. 2006; Musco and Catalano 2010, 389.

[3] Craig et al. 2009.

[4] Gissinger 2012, 15.

[5] Frier 1982, 230–1.

[6] Passi Pitcher 1987; Minozzi et al. 2012.

study of infants under the age of one is impossible. Furthermore, not all cemeteries have been excavated in their entirety, nor were all dead infants necessarily buried in them. At Argenton (Table 3), 26 per cent of the second-century burials in the Champ de l'Image cemetery were of infants, but there are no infants at all in the cemeteries excavated at Vallerano and San Vittorino in Rome's eastern suburbs in the second and third centuries AD.[7] Equally, the high proportion of infant burials in some cemeteries can hardly reflect demographic realities. At Sétif in Algeria, for example, 39 per cent of the burials in the east necropolis belonged to children under one year of age.[8] Such circumstances suggest that something very special was going on, even if we are at a loss to explain it.

Poor infant health can be attributed to nutritional deficiencies and infections which led to anaemia, rickets, and other illnesses (see Chapter 3). Newborns, especially, were very vulnerable, as their immune system was not yet fully developed. But ill health did not necessarily end in death, and the bioarchaeological evidence of adult skeletons indicates that many sick babies survived, even if with lasting health problems. Determining the cause of death of those infants who did not survive is no easy task, particularly because the excavated remains often offer no clue. For example, specialists could find nothing to indicate what caused the death of a three-month-old baby buried in an amphora at Podere Minghetti (Ravenna) in the first century AD.[9] At Poundbury near Dorchester, infective disease may have been the cause of death for five neonates or infants, as their bones showed gross periostitis or inflammation of the layer of connective tissue surrounding the bone, but this is just a hypothesis.[10] We are on surer footing with the cause of death of a child twelve to eighteen months of age at Douch in the Kharga Oasis in Egypt; the child, possibly a boy, most likely died of a blow to the head, indicated by the fractured parietal bone, but how or under what circumstances that blow was delivered is completely unknown.[11]

Many variables would have a considerable impact on infant mortality as well as fertility. Because women are less likely to conceive when they are breastfeeding, for example, by delegating that task to a wet-nurse, a mother would also have been able to conceive more quickly and this might have played a role in family planning.[12] Parkin has suggested that women in the ancient world gave birth five or six times on average to counteract high infant mortality, and a number of those children would not survive, resulting in a greater spacing of offspring in the mother's lifetime.[13] In some cases, it is

[7] Allain et al. 1992; Catalano et al. 2001; Cucina et al. 2006.

[8] Février and Guéry 1980.

[9] Fasold et al. 2004, 22.

[10] Farwell and Molleson 1993, 160.

[11] Dunand et al. 1992, 124, 196, pl. 29. For a probable case of physical child abuse involving a child of two or three years of age at Kellis 2, see Wheeler et al. 2013.

[12] Parkin 2013, 50–7; Sparreboom 2014, 148.

[13] Parkin 2010, 106–7.

possible to reconstruct an age profile and mortality rate in particular households. Pudsey was able to show from the census material of the first three centuries AD in Roman Egypt that parents had a greater number of children to compensate for expected child mortality.[14] The papyrus documents reveal relatively large numbers of children in most households with noticeable age gaps between some siblings. Furthermore, from an examination of thirteen skeletons found huddled together where they perished in AD 79 in the House of Julius Polybius in Pompeii, Henneberg and Henneberg concluded that this small sample represented quite effectively the age structure of the Roman population.[15] The family group consisted of a woman 45–55 years old (skeleton 1A), two men 60–70 years old (skeletons 1B, 4A), a woman of 30–40 (skeleton 5–6A), a man aged 25–30 (skeleton 3A), a young pregnant woman 16–18 years of age with her baby still inside her (skeletons 3B and 3C), and six children of 3 (2C), 8–9 (2A), 10–12 (3D), 12–14 (2B and 5–6B), and 15–18 (3E) years. Couples can be identified as 1A and 1B, 4A and 5–6A, and 3A and 3B. The children follow a pattern of birth spacing, with one child born to a couple about every three years and with a missing (i.e. dead) five-year-old between 2A and 2C.

This birth spacing could be a result of death at a very early age, but it also might reflect a prematurely born baby who did not survive. In modern medicine, babies born before thirty-seven or thirty-eight weeks are deemed premature and they are particularly prone to respiratory failure because their lungs cannot inflate properly to deliver oxygen to the body.[16] Such premature infants in antiquity, unable to breath independently, and without a ventilator or breathing machine to help them, certainly would have died. Recent research on the present population suggests that babies born early-term at thirty-seven or thirty-eight weeks are still physiologically immature and at significantly higher risk for long-term adverse outcomes, such as hypoglycaemia, respiratory distress, and gastrointestinal disorders.[17]

In view of the negative value judgements of infants commonly expressed in Roman literary sources and even in modern childhood studies, of particular interest to me in studying Roman funerary evidence are the foetuses, premature babies, and stillborns found in various contexts. For if the youngest members of society truly were deemed of little value or lacking in social significance until they were a few years old, how do we explain the fact that even those children who did not live long enough to be born or who survived birth for only a very short time were, in some places and in some periods, given a proper burial and not simply discarded? And how could we possibly explain the embryotomy in the Poundbury cemetery?[18] This unborn baby,

[14] Pudsey 2013, 487–8. [15] Henneberg and Henneberg 2001.
[16] Allen et al. 1993; Moss 2005. [17] Boyle et al. 2012; Sengupta et al. 2013.
[18] Redfern 2010, 462–3, figs. 15–16.

removed surgically from its mother's womb to save her life, was not disposed of as if it were rubbish, despite the fact that it had not yet entered the world; it was, instead, buried carefully in a wooden coffin. There are, of course, problems inherent in studying such evidence. For example, it is not always clear whether an infant was born dead at full term or died in the womb shortly before birth, especially if the osteological analysis lacks depth or detail, or if the condition of the bones does not allow such precision. And the terminology used in various publications is often confusing and inexact. At Sétif, Guéry claimed that just over 14 per cent of children found here were premature or died at birth, and he classified them either as foetus or stillborn/foetus in the site publication (Table 7).[19] Perhaps greater precision was not possible, but this does leave the age at death somewhat open.

Birth normally takes place in the tenth lunar month, by ancient reckoning, so a baby only six lunar months old, as at Sontheim in Germany, clearly represents a foetus far from nearing full term.[20] A few very small and immature babies at Poundbury, thought to represent miscarriages around the fifth or sixth month of pregnancy, can also be termed 'foetuses' (Table 8).[21] But at Marseille, a number of children in the cemetery report are aged between nine and ten lunar months (thirty-six to forty weeks), so it is not clear whether these infants should be referred to as premature babies or foetuses (Table 2).[22] And when Zanier refers to skeletons belonging to infants between nine and a half and ten lunar months of age as foetuses, I wonder if they should instead be designated as full term or slightly premature births.[23] As far as so-called stillborn babies are concerned, the only thing we can really say with some certainty is that *very* premature babies as young as only six months gestation were stillborn, as they are highly likely to have exited the womb dead. But it is impossible to recognize whether an infant eight or nine gestational months was dead when it was expelled, or whether it died very shortly after birth because it could not survive.

Despite these difficulties, the evidence for the proper burial of foetuses, stillborns, and babies of perinatal age (born alive or not) is varied and insightful. Precise data on the ages of infants buried in a Roman cemetery have been retrieved at Kellis in Egypt. In the East Cemetery (Kellis 2), in use between AD 100 and the middle of the fifth century, 450 skeletons were excavated by 2002, of which (at least) eighty-two were aged between twenty-four gestational weeks (five lunar months) and six weeks after birth. Although Tocheri et al. use the term "foetal skeleton" for all these individuals, the very precise details allow a fine-grained analysis of the burial data.[24] In the first six

[19] Guéry 1985, for example 84, fig. 74 (grave 51); 73, fig. 58 (grave 26); 60, fig. 44 (grave 13).
[20] Hölschen 2002a; Hölschen 2002b. [21] Farwell and Molleson 1993, 171.
[22] For example, Moliner et al. 2003, 313 (tomb 182), 338 (tomb 327), 378 (tomb 518).
[23] Zanier 1992. [24] Tocheri et al. 2005. See also Dupras et al. 2015.

weeks of life, 23 per cent of babies at Kellis died. Seventy-three per cent of the babies here died between the third trimester of pregnancy and full term, and this peak mortality between thirty-six and forty weeks corresponds to a natural mortality profile. The excellent osteological data at Kellis also allow us sometimes to recognize the cause of death in foetal skeletons, such as the genetic disorder brittle bone disease (*osteogenesis imperfecta*).[25]

BURIAL SITES OF INFANTS: INTEGRATION OR EXCLUSION?

There is ample physical evidence for infant burials in cemeteries outside Roman towns and farms, but an intramural location in Roman forts, settlements, and workshops is also attested. Studying this evidence allows us not only to determine the presence of infants in any of these contexts, but also to gain information about the treatment of the body and any protection offered the tiny corpse, as well as evidence of care invested in providing these children with grave-goods. The importance of such remains for understanding familial, social, and cultural attitudes towards infancy is obvious.

Before I move on to the archaeological evidence for infant burials, a short discussion on the funeral rites for the very young is warranted, not least because it has become an apparent fact in both scholarly and popular literature that babies were buried "chiefly at night and by torchlight".[26] There is no evidence for this, either historically or archaeologically. As Baills-Talbi and Dasen put it, this is "un *topos* moderne".[27] This idea appears to come from a notion, as expressed in 1909 by the anthropologist Arnold van Gennep, that in many societies those who die prematurely, without being named or initiated (or baptized!), are not accorded normal funerary rites and are dangerous and harmful to the living.[28] This idea of the universal dangerous dead, including those who died in infancy, was taken up and applied to Roman antiquity by Emile Jobbé-Duval in 1924.[29] A passage in Vergil's *Aeneid* was seen to support this. Aeneas hears voices, sobs and "a loud crying of voices . . . , the spirits of weeping infants" who had been torn from life to abide in the underworld.[30] Not only infants belonged in the category of premature deaths, however, as Vergil also put people wrongly accused and suicides in this group. In the second century AD, the Christian writer Tertullian also referred to souls taken by premature death who, in pagan thought, wandered restlessly.[31] Anyone

25 Cope and Dupras 2011: skeleton B532 at 38 gestational weeks.
26 Turcan 2001, 27.
27 Baills-Talbi and Dasen 2008, 597.
28 Van Gennep 1909, 229–30.
29 Jobbé-Duval 1924, 68–72.
30 Vergil, *Aeneid* 6.426–6.429.
31 Tertullian, *On the Soul* 56.

who died before their time, without fulfilling their destiny, shared this restless fate, but neither Vergil, nor Tertullian suggest that they were evil, and least of all that infants were a malign presence. Then there is the reference in a late fourth- or early fifth-century commentary by Servius on the *Aeneid* which explains the custom of carrying *funalia* (torches) at nocturnal funerals, among other things, at funerals of those who died before they had reached puberty.[32] All this tells us is that funerals could take place at night, and torches would have lit the way, but it does not say that infants were buried routinely at night by torchlight or that they were polluting or harmful. Furthermore, torches were used at Roman funerals in daylight too, and they feature in the lying-in-state and funeral procession also of adults, as we can see in the images on the monument of the Haterii of *c.* AD 100 in Rome.[33] As John Scheid has shown, torches used in funerary ritual symbolically created a space that separated the mourning family from the living.[34] The whole idea of hurried, marginal, and torch-lit burials for babies does not hold up to critical scrutiny and should be rejected.

Infant Burials in Communal Cemeteries

For any discussion of the role and importance of the youngest children in Roman society, and for insight into the existence and creation of an infant's social persona, it is important to be able to ascertain whether children who were only beginning their lives were perceived as persons and members of the community, and whether their presence in the community of the dead—the necropolis—is as tangible as the presence of older children and adults in that context.

Children older than one year are routinely found in excavations of Roman cemeteries. The remains of infants younger than twelve months also survive in many regions, although they are not everywhere present in the same numbers or percentages (Fig. 6.1). Infant burials are normally found scattered throughout a cemetery, rather than concentrated in one area, and they often are buried together with older children and adults. To introduce this section, it is worth having a brief look at just such groups of families and households buried as a close community of the dead in family plots at Pompeii. Excavations conducted from 2003–7 by William Van Andringa and Sébastien Lepetz in four neighbouring enclosures (enclosures 21, 23, 25a, 25b) outside the Porta Nocera revealed seventy-two graves in which sixty-four individuals were buried in the first century AD, including thirteen children between the ages of three months and thirteen years.[35] Infants, children, and adults were buried

[32] A. J. Rose 1923. [33] Sinn and Freyberger 1996, 45–51, cat. no. 5, pls. 8–10.
[34] Scheid 1984. [35] van Andringa et al. 2013.

Fig. 6.1 McMaster University excavation of the skeletal remains of an infant, in the Roman cemetery at the imperial estate at Vagnari.
Photo: Maureen Carroll.

next to and close to each other, and almost everyone was given an above-ground marker and a terracotta pipe for libations to be poured as part of funerary ritual. A cremated infant possibly aged only three to six months, in grave 10, for example, had its own basalt *columella*, a roughly anthropomorphic *stele* typical of this region, as a marker.[36] The back of the stylized head of this *columella* was carved to represent hair styled in a chignon or bun, probably indicating that the dead baby was a little girl. She was the recipient of libations poured in commemorative rituals, as the terracotta libation pipe at the foot of the *columella* indicates.

The burial of infants with other age groups is attested in Gaul, Egypt, North Africa, and Britain, too. At the rural site of Chantambre, many perinatal burials are concentrated in a peripheral zone to the west of the cemetery, but infants this age also can be found buried in other areas of the cemetery in the midst of adults, and adults are also buried in the western peripheral zone.[37] In the Champ de l'Image cemetery at Argenton, thirty-eight premature babies and neonates were buried in a sector of the western part of the cemetery that

[36] van Andringa et al. 2013, 356–67, esp. 361–2; De Larminat 2010, 69.
[37] Girard 1997, 216.

Fig. 6.2 Excavated adult female and adjacent infant burial in reused roof tiles at Vagnari, both *alla cappuccina* burials.
Photo: Tracy Prowse.

appears to have been reserved for them, although infants under the age of one are found also with other children and adults in other parts of the necropolis (Table 3).[38] Also at the Sainte-Barbe cemetery of Marseille, infants can be found throughout the cemetery, although there is a concentration of them in the east.[39] At Kellis 2, the remains of foetuses, premature babies, and newborns are found throughout the cemetery, with no apparent zoning.[40] In the Yasmina cemetery at Carthage, children's burials of the fifth century are restricted to the centre of the area excavated, where they are nestled around cremation monuments of other individuals dating to the second century AD.[41] In the Poundbury Camp cemetery outside Dorchester, children of all ages, including perinatal infants, were included in presumed family groups and were distributed throughout the cemetery.[42]

A further indication of the social and familial cohesion of very young children is the burial of infants with adults, both male and female, and other children; these may represent the parents and siblings of the deceased (Fig. 6.2). The burials of a man, woman, and child side by side at Chantambre is a good example of such a familial group.[43] In the necropolis of Valladas

[38] Allain et al. 1992. [39] Moliner et al. 2003, 108–9, fig. 95.
[40] Tocheri et al. 2005, 329; Wheeler et al. 2011, 113.
[41] Norman 2002, 306–7. [42] Molleson 1989, 28.
[43] Girard 1997, 220–1, fig. 8 (graves 419/420/421).

outside the Roman town of Augusta Tricastinorum (modern St-Paul-Trois-Châteaux), four of seven perinatal babies in the late first or early second century AD were inhumed together with an adult who had been cremated.[44] The burial of mother and child, particularly when they died together, is occasionally recognizable in the funerary record. A couple of examples here may suffice to illustrate this (for further examples see Chapter 3). The double burial of a roughly twenty-five-year-old woman and a newborn in a fourth-century sarcophagus in Arles is likely to represent a case of death in child-birth.[45] On Great Dover Street in London, the inhumation of a woman eighteen to twenty-five years of age together with a foetus about twenty-eight weeks old placed at her right foot is also fairly clearly a case of double birth-related death in the mid-second century AD.[46] A woman with a perinatal child at Chantambre may have been the infant's mother, and two newborns interred with adult females in the northern cemetery at Kempten have been interpreted also as double burials of mother and infant (Table 6).[47] In the Saint-Martin-des-Champs cemetery in Bourges, an infant two to four months of age at the feet of an adult woman in a sarcophagus may be a child who did not die at birth, but survived a little while, possibly after her death.[48]

Infants also are found in close association with men. At Chantambre, a perinatal infant and a man are buried together.[49] In the late Roman cemetery at Poundbury, two infants aged twelve months and eighteen months (243B) were buried with an adult male about fifty years old (243A) who may have been the father or a grandfather or some other male relative (Table 8).[50] Sibling children were also buried together. At Marseille, an eight-year-old child was interred with a full-term baby, both of them in wood coffins (Table 2).[51] A single stone sarcophagus was used at Bourges for the burial of three infants under the age of one.[52] Also at Carnuntum, three infants occupied the same stone sarcophagus, two of them between seven and nine months of age and a third just four to six months old.[53] Although no analysis of the bones has been conducted to determine a familial relationship, it is likely that these three were siblings, although they may have died at different times. At Kempten, it is not unusual to see infants buried together with other infants or older children (Table 6). These include a child aged four to five years old with a perinatal infant lying on its lower arm (graves 238 and 239), a cremated child younger than six and an inhumed perinate in grave 208, and

44 Bel 1992. 45 Sintès 1996, cat. no. 156.
46 Mackinder 2000, 19–20, 42–3, figs. 20, 32 (graves 22 and 23); Gowland 2014, 73, fig. 2.
47 Mackensen 1978a, 147, 242–3 (graves 153 and 154); 150, 260 (graves 213 and 214).
48 Durand 2003, 113–14, fig. 4. 49 Girard 1997, 220, fig. 7 (graves 18/452).
50 Farwell and Molleson 1993, 151, 260, fig. 52.
51 Moliner et al. 2003, 40, 286, pl. 21, tomb 42.
52 Durand 2003, 112, fig. 1. 53 Schweder and Winkler 2004, 40.

two perinatal infants (possibly twins) in grave 95.[54] Twins also may be represented by the two cremated infants aged six to nine months buried together at Mainz-Weisenau in the first half of the first century AD.[55]

Despite this evidence for infant inclusion in communal cemeteries, claims have been made for the existence of burial grounds exclusively for the burial of infants, so-called baby cemeteries. Possibly the first scholar who claimed to have recognized a baby cemetery of the Roman period was Abbot Joseph Joly. He referred to the remains of a dozen infants found in a rock shelter near Alesia as a "*cimetière de bébés*".[56] However, as we have seen in Chapter 3, the skeletal remains are those not only of perinatal infants, but also of an adolescent, suggesting that Joly had discovered only part of a larger assemblage of burials of individuals of varying ages.[57] Scholarship now tends to discredit the idea of baby cemeteries, particularly because excavations have shown that infant burials are not segregated, but mixed with individuals of other age groups. Furthermore, modern and precise ageing methods give us a much more nuanced picture of the ages of babies present at sites that were explored decades ago, demonstrating that foetuses, perinatal, neonatal, and post-neonatal infants were among the dead in so-called baby cemeteries.

If we accept the general accuracy of a 30 per cent mortality rate in the first year of life, however, communal cemeteries often do not contain enough babies of the right age. Many variables, including shallow grave pits, fragility of infant bones, and the disturbance of graves from agricultural activities could be possible reasons for the dearth of recovered baby burials in some cemeteries. But, careless excavation techniques and a lack of awareness of (and interest in) very fragile and very young human remains certainly have contributed to some extent to the underrepresentation of baby burials. Nevertheless, some statistics are available to us. Infants less than one year old make up a mere 1.6–2.2 per cent of the burials at Gubbio (Umbria) and Portorecanati (Marche), for example, and in the Viale Serenissima cemetery in the *suburbium* of Rome, only about 12.5 per cent of the burials here are of children younger than one year.[58] At Carnuntum, neonates and foetuses represent 7.9 per cent of the population in the cemetery south of the civilian town, whilst at Kempten, 15 per cent of the burials are those of infants.[59] So, with these cemeteries and others that exhibit too few burial examples of this age category, questions arise: What are we actually seeing here? Why are there so few children? Were they buried elsewhere? These questions are addressed in the following sections.

[54] Mackensen 1978a, 147, 268, pl. 170.24 (graves 238 and 239); 147, 258, pls. 169.15–16 (grave 208); 226, pl. 166.15 (grave 95).

[55] Witteyer and Fasold 1995, 25 (grave 5).

[56] Joly 1951 and 1954.

[57] Jaeggi 2012a; Jaeggi 2012b; Gadacz 2013.

[58] Mercando et al. 1974; Cipollone 2002; Musco 2006b. On percentages of infants in various cemeteries, see Carroll 2011a, 103–5.

[59] Mackensen 1978a; Schweder and Winkler 2004.

Infant Burials in Settlements and Buildings

Burials of infants within a settlement and in or next to buildings are what a Roman literary source of the late fifth or sixth century AD refers to as *suggrundaria*. The author, Fabius Planciades Fulgentius, has been quoted repeatedly and uncritically in modern scholarship. As the title of his treatise indicates—*The Explanation of Obsolete Words*—Fulgentius was writing about words that no longer found usage in contemporary Latin, and, apparently, words about which there was some confusion in his day. This should warn us about adopting his definition in an archaeological sense, especially because there were obvious problems with it. He wrote: "What *suggrundaria* are: In former times the ancients called *suggrundaria* the burial places of infants who had not yet lived forty days, because they could not be called graves since there were no bones to be cremated nor a big enough corpse for a cenotaph to be raised". But babies *do* have bones which can be burnt, and a cenotaph was a memorial to commemorate a body *in absentia*, so if a corpse was present, no matter how small, the monument above it was never a cenotaph.

According to Roman law, corpses were neither to be buried nor cremated within a settlement, and we find this law adhered to in the charters of Roman towns not just in Italy, but in the provinces too.[60] There is no mention in the original twelve tablets of Roman law of any exemptions to this rule based on age, but Fulgentius seems to suggest that children under the age of forty days were outside burial law, because they were not recognized entities in Roman society. Wiedemann, perhaps influenced by Fulgentius' writings, claimed that children this age were normally buried in the city and within domestic buildings, "at the 'edge' of the house, as they had been at the 'edge' of the household", but the evidence discussed earlier in this chapter demonstrates that babies and infants often are well represented in the extramural cemeteries where, by law, they should be.[61]

The fact remains, however, that infant burials have been retrieved in various places within settlements, usually not in large urban conglomerations—although there are exceptions—but in settlements, villages, or manufacturing complexes and workshops. This latter location is a recurring one, especially in Roman Gaul, and we can trace the practice back to the Iron Age (Chapter 2).[62] They are known at Nyon in Switzerland, where about fifty metres east of the amphitheatre a workshop area contained fourteen graves of neonates.[63] More

[60] See, for example, the city charter of Urso in Spain (Lex Ursonensis), dating to 44 BC, *CIL* II.5349, sections 73–4.

[61] Wiedemann 1989, 179.

[62] In north-east Spain, the tradition of burying babies in dwellings continued in the Roman period, well into the second century AD. See Minguez Morales and José 1989–90; Conde 2010–11, 202–4; Ruiz 2013, 1003.

[63] Musée Romain de Nyon 2003.

information exists at Lezoux in Gaul, where the burials of almost a dozen perinatal and young infants were associated with *terra sigillata* pottery workshops of the first and second centuries AD.[64] In one atelier of the first century, an infant burial was inserted into the debris covering a disused kiln; the child lay in a make-shift container made of three *terra sigillata* moulds. The other babies of the second century were buried simply in pits or in containers, such as bowls, a cist of two inverted querns, tiles, and a wooden coffin. Some of the infants had been given grave goods, including rings, a lamp, miniature vessels, and a feeding bottle. Since the pottery kilns at Lezoux also manufactured feeding bottles, this one may have been made in the workshop itself.[65] It is unclear why infant burials were located in and around the workshops, when, parallel to this, a cemetery with individuals of mixed ages was in use for the whole community, but the treatment of the infant bodies and the gifts accompanying them do not speak for hasty or careless disposal.

At Sallèles d'Aude, a settlement with dwellings separated from pottery workshops and kilns, numerous infant burials in one of those workshops, Building III, have been retrieved (Fig. 6.3).[66] The large size and number of the kilns suggest that several families must have lived and worked here. A total of thirteen babies, usually covered with a tile or a tile fragment, were buried in the

Fig. 6.3 Plan of a ceramic workshop at Sallèles d'Aude with infant burials indicated. The parts of the bodies in light grey are reconstructed.

Drawing: Irene de Luis.

[64] Vertet 1974. [65] Rouquet and Loridant 2000.

[66] Duday et al. 1995; Laubenheimer 2004, 311–13, figs. 9–12.

second half of the first century AD under the beaten earth floor along the walls of the building. Over half the infants died around birth or just days thereafter, four within the first three months of life, and one at six to nine months. The youngest usually were buried in a contracted position, although, based on the position of their legs and arms, two of them appear to have been swaddled or wrapped when they were interred. Only two infants were buried with some grave goods: the oldest infant was found with a jug and a cup at its feet and a perfume flask and an oil lamp near its head, and a three-month-old child had a bronze *fibula* or brooch with macroscopic fragments of textile—either linen or hemp—adhering to the *fibula*. Although the excavators estimated a population of about sixty-six individuals living and working at Sallèles d'Aude at its peak, their burial places have not been found, nor can it be ruled out that more infants might have been buried together with adults in a community cemetery that has yet to be located. At any rate, in the second century, Building III was demolished, but, perhaps because there was a memory of infant burial associated with the building, two more newborns were interred in the ground covering the remains of the structure.

In Iron Age Britain, there was a tradition of burying infants in settlements, and this continued in urban and rural locations in the Roman period. Infant burials, for example, are scattered throughout the Iron Age and Roman settlements at Wattle Syke in West Yorkshire, usually in ditch fills, gullies, and small pits, sometimes in contexts associated with roundhouses.[67] Five infant burials are clustered around Roundhouse 6 in the late Iron Age and early Roman periods, and others of the fourth century AD were found in ditch fills of Enclosure 18.[68] At Barton Court in Oxfordshire, only in the late Roman period, in the mid-fourth century AD, do children of this age category appear to have been buried outside the buildings in one specific location in the south-east part of the paddock. Here, near a corn drier, the excavators found at least twenty-six newborn babies or very young infants. A cemetery for adults and other children has not been located, although it must have existed. At the *civitas* capital of Chichester, excavations in the town also have revealed infant burials of differing dates associated with buildings.[69] The majority of these infants were buried in pits, including pre-existing ones, or under floors, although one was buried in a cist made of reused roof tiles below the eaves of a building in Chapel Street.[70]

Infant burials in small towns are not uncommon in Roman Switzerland, although in earlier excavations they were often missed or only detected in the post-excavation phase, as in the *vicus* at Vitudurum (Oberwinterthur) where several neonates and infants were found in or near houses from the early first to

[67] Martin et al. 2013, 287. [68] Martin et al. 2013, 40–1, 64–5, 57.
[69] Down 1988, 59. [70] Down 1988, 59, pl. 45.

the early second centuries AD.[71] But infant burials are much more commonly found in Roman Switzerland on rural sites, particularly on farmsteads. At Dietikon, near Zürich, for example, thirteen newborns were recovered on the site of a *villa rustica*; they were buried in buildings located along the two outer enclosure walls of the outer precinct (*pars rustica*) outside the enclosure of the owner's residence (*pars urbana*).[72] In one house alone, eight infants were discovered. Sixteen infants were buried in the first and early second centuries AD at the Swiss *villa rustica* at Neftenbach, most of them being interred in or just outside buildings in the *pars rustica* or just inside the boundary wall marking off the *pars rustica* from the *pars urbana*.[73] These babies, both slightly premature, and infants one to two months of age, were placed in simple pits, new and reused, or on fragments of tile, with one deposited in a tile-lined pit.

An intriguing site in this context is the rural site at Sontheim on the Upper Rhine, a settlement which the excavators characterized as a combination of road station, agricultural complex, and sanctuary, dating to the period around AD 100–250 (Fig. 6.4).[74] The settlement consisted of several buildings

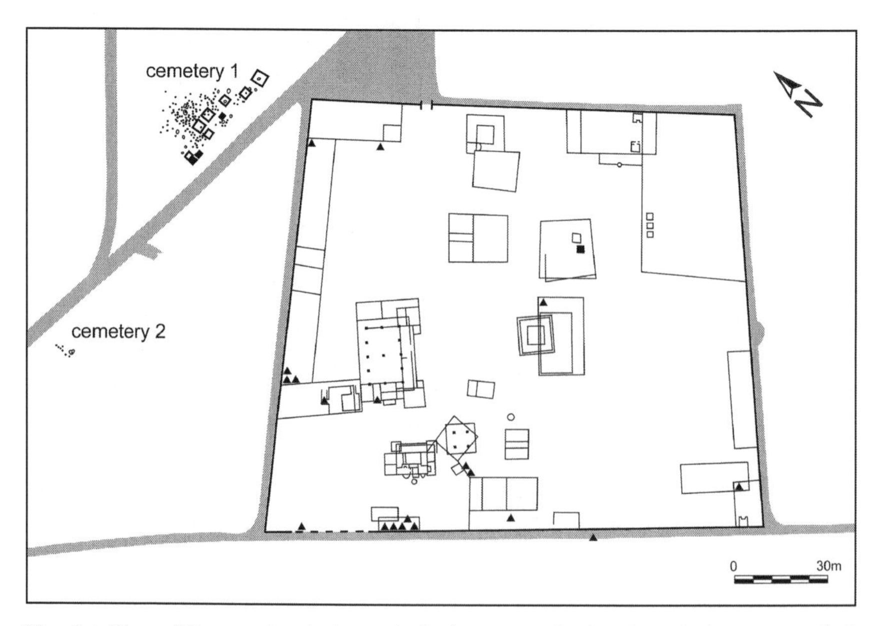

Fig. 6.4 Plan of Roman Sontheim with the location of infant burials (open triangles) in the settlement indicated.

Drawing: Irene de Luis.

[71] Etter 1991, 179–89, figs. 91–2; Berger 1993, 320, fig. 2. See also Pfäffli 2013a, 92, for intramural burials in Augst.

[72] Berger 1993, 320, fig. 4. [73] Langenegger 1996; Langenegger 1999.

[74] Hölschen 2002a; Hölschen and Becker 2006.

(including a Gallo-Roman temple in the middle) arranged within a roughly square area surrounded by an enclosure, with two known cemeteries outside the enclosure. Forty-one infants under the age of one year were found, both in the north-west communal and extramural cemetery, along with other child and adult burials, and in the settlement itself, where only babies were deposited. In both areas, some of these were premature babies of eight to ten lunar months or newborns, although only in the cemetery were there foetuses as young as six lunar months. The infants in the extramural cemetery were buried in wooden coffins and given grave goods. The settlement babies were positioned next to walls or in corners of rooms, with one perinatal infant in a stable. Hölschen, who studied the human remains, suggested that the children who had died before their *dies lustricus* (eighth or ninth day after birth) were buried in the settlement, but those who died after that and had been given a name were buried in the extramural cemetery with the wider community.[75] This is unlikely because there are very premature babies in the extramural cemetery who also had died before they reached their naming day, and Hölschen contradicts himself when he suggests that foetuses might be in the extramural cemetery after all because their mothers may have died with them.[76] In the end, there is no obvious or logical reason why the babies were buried in different locations. There is no anthropological indication that any of these babies were seriously ill or deformed, and neither did the excavators conclude that those buried in the settlement might be the result of infanticide to rid the family of unwanted children.[77]

The burial of infants on Roman farms and villas is well attested in Roman Gaul. At Champ Madame at Beaumont, twenty-seven babies were buried in the first and second centuries AD in an area adjacent to the external wall of a villa enclosure, with almost half of them interred in timber coffins or on amphora pieces and with accompanying grave goods (Table 4; Fig. 6.5).[78] Many of these infants had died at birth or in the early post-neonatal phase. At the Roman farm of the first to third centuries AD at des Béziaux à Langeais, seventeen infants in Gallic amphorae and fragmentary storage vessels (*dolia*) were buried in association with a farm building, either outside its northern and western walls or just inside the building in the north-western sector.[79] And at Sommesous (Marne), twenty-one baby burials in simple pits have been retrieved; these, too, were found outside the enclosure wall of the villa, and over 40 per cent had accompanying grave goods.[80] At least one additional cemetery area at all four sites is to be expected, even if it has not yet been found, as adults and older children have to have been buried somewhere too, just as they were

[75] Hölschen 2002a, 227; Hölschen 2002b, 168.
[76] Hölschen 2002b, 166.
[77] Hölschen 2002b, 167.
[78] Blaizot et al. 2003, 8, fig. 2; Alfonso and Blaizot 2004.
[79] Guiot et al. 2003, 100–4.
[80] Guillier 1992.

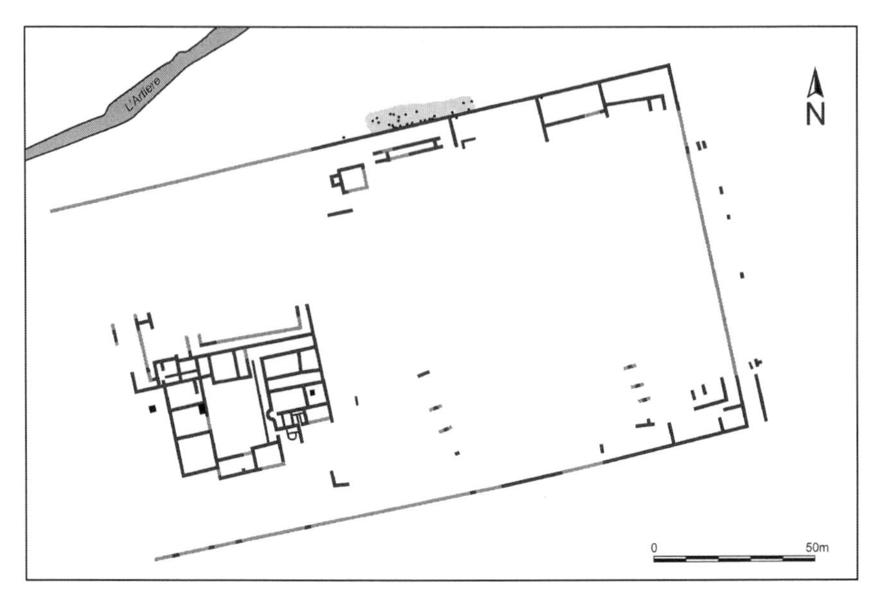

Fig. 6.5 Plan of the Roman rural estate at Beaumont with the location of the infant burials outside the perimeter walls (grey shaded area with black dots).
Drawing: Irene de Luis.

at rural Tavant near Tours (Table 5). Here, at Tavant, a cemetery possibly associated with a Roman villa of the later first century to the third century AD contained the graves of twenty-six adults, younger children, and infants, reflecting a picture of normal life, death, and social cohesion.[81] We have no real grounds to claim that cemeteries at these sites, even those with a high proportion of infants, were what one might call a baby cemetery, without the discovery of truly communal burial grounds for all residents with which to compare them.[82]

There appears to have been a resurgence of intra-settlement burials in the late Roman and post-Roman period. Several sites are attested in Italy. At rural Mezzocorona (Trentino), three neonatal graves were found in habitations that were still in use and not yet abandoned at the end of the third century AD.[83]

[81] Riquier and Salé 2006.

[82] A burial area recently discovered in rescue operations near the modern village of Laquenexy east of Metz appears to have housed only the graves of very young infants (pre-term and perinatal). Only three skeletons in grave pits were sufficiently preserved well enough to age them definitively, but the other five grave pits are of similar size to those with baby skeletons, suggesting that they too were dug for infants. The excavators propose that this cemetery lay between two rural estates of the second and third centuries AD, although the burial grounds appear to me to be quite distant from either of them (500 m and 100 m respectively). At any rate, not enough of the cemetery has been investigated to rule out the existence of other burials of older children and adults nearby. See Brkojewitsch et al. 2014.

[83] Cavada 1994 (tombs 1, 2, and 4).

The so-called slave barracks at late Roman Villa Magna near Rome were also still inhabited when babies were buried under the floors of individual rooms, two infants in one room (room 13) and four in another (room 23).[84] These ranged in age from newborn to between twelve and eighteen months, and there was no sign of careless disposal; instead, they were buried in pits containing rudimentary coffins made of broken tiles.[85] But there is evidence to suggest that abandoned villas and farms were searched out in the late Roman and early post-Roman period for use as burial grounds. Perhaps the most well-known of these is Lugnano where the skeletons of forty-seven premature infants, neonates, and post-neonatal children were excavated in five rooms of a Roman villa no longer in use when it was reused for burials in the mid-fifth century AD.[86] Twenty-two of the infants were probably aborted foetuses. These infants were buried in simple pits, or in arrangements of reused roof tile, or in an amphora, and there was no sign of greater care having been taken for any of the infants on the basis of age.[87] The excavator, David Soren, suggested that these were victims of a malaria epidemic, and the extraction of DNA from the oldest child (two or three years old) confirmed that at least this child had suffered from the disease.[88] Further south, on the site of the rural estate abandoned in the second century AD at Settefinestre near Cosa, spoliation activity was taking place between the end of the fourth and the sixth century AD when several adults and children, including a newborn baby, were deposited in the rubble.[89]

Infant Burials in Roman Forts

A Roman fort is often perceived as a space in which soldiers and male support staff lived and worked, but from which women and children were excluded. In this view, the settlements outside the fort—the *vici* and the *canabae*—were the

[84] Andrews 2016, 132–5.

[85] Andrews 2016, 132–4, figs. 5.73 and 5.74.

[86] Soren and Soren 1999.

[87] Soren 2015, 242.

[88] Soren 2015, 245–6. Soren's (2015, 242–3) suggestion that magic had been involved is not convincing. A raven's claw and the skeleton of a small toad found with two of the burials need not represent remnants of magic rituals, as such things could find their way into the soil easily under normal conditions, especially when it has been churned up and redeposited, as here. The bone doll found in one of the infant burials is missing its articulated legs and arms, but the doll need not be an apotropaic offering with its appendages intentionally removed. If the doll was old and had been used by any child previously, its arms and legs could easily have been lost in play. The twelve puppies and one dog, may, however, have had a ritual significance, especially since we know of dogs being buried with or near infants at Hellenistic Greek sites (for example, Athens, Messene) and at several Roman sites.

[89] Di Gennaro and Griesbach 2003, 163, cat. no. 71. See also the twelve child burials in amphorae of the fourth and fifth centuries AD at the abandoned Cazzanello villa near Tarquinia, many of which are newborns or late-term foetuses: Di Gennaro and Griesbach 2003, 158, cat. no. 54; Becker 2004.

only place where non-military personnel and the possible common-law partners and illegitimate children of soldiers could have lived, because ordinary soldiers were not permitted to marry officially as actively serving military personnel, at least until the ban on marriage was lifted by Septimius Severus in AD 197.[90] Officers, however, could marry legally during service. Wooden writing tablets from the fort at Vindolanda on Hadrian's Wall indicate that commanding officers there had their wives with them before AD 103, and the residences of such officers, and of centurions, were always laid out in more generous fashion than any of the quarters for ordinary soldiers to accommodate a household.[91]

Jürgen Trumm and Regine Fellmann Brogli connected the writing tablet evidence for women in the legionary fort at Vindonissa in Switzerland with the recent discovery of the graves of three newborn infants in the vicinity of the *praetorium* and the centurions' quarters in the southern half of this fort.[92] At least two of the burials belong to the second stone-built phase of the fort, *c.* AD 70–101. Given the proximity of the infant burials to the dwellings of officers, the evidence here strongly suggests the presence of wives and children of men who were entitled to marry in a military context. But writing tablets from Vindonissa reveal also that women with no apparent marital links to officers were running businesses and operating within the fort.[93] In general, there is also broader physical evidence for women and infants associated with the quarters of regular soldiers. At military sites, such as Vindolanda, for example, childrens' shoes found within the barracks of ordinary soldiers have been linked to the presence of families.[94]

Not everyone, however, is willing to accept that women and children lived in the forts. Nick Hodgson, for example, has denied the existence of any artefactual or structural evidence for the routine accommodation of women and children in the barracks of ordinary soldiers in Roman forts on Hadrian's Wall.[95] Norbert Zanier has suggested that the infant bones at Ellingen, an auxiliary fort of the second and early third centuries AD in Germany, must have been brought into the fort from disturbed burial grounds outside the civilian *vicus*, along with other deposits, to level the ground in the fort, dismissing such remains as an indication that women were in the fort.[96]

[90] For discussions, see Garnsey 1970; Southern and Dixon 1996, 85; Phang 2001, 16–17; Tomas 2009–10; Allison 2011.

[91] Bowman and Thomas 1994, no. 291; Hoffmann 1995; Hassall 1999, 35–6; Phang 2001, 130–2.

[92] Trumm and Fellmann Brogli 2008.

[93] Speidel 1996, 180–90, letters 41–5. Letters 41 and 44 are written to women whose abode or place of work is given as inside the fort; letter 45 is an invitation from a female hostelry owner with an address in the fort, and letters 42 and 43 are written by and to a woman whose location was near the fort.

[94] Van Driel Murray 1994; Van Driel Murray 1995; Van Driel Murray 1997.

[95] Hodgson 2014. [96] Zanier 1992, 70–2.

Several newborns and perinatal infants are attested here, although their bones on discovery were often disarticulated and mixed with other material, only to be recognized for what they were during post-excavation analysis in the lab. But partial skeletons also were retrieved at Ellingen, from pits in buildings B and C, identified as soldiers' barracks, and in the south-east corner of the fort, as well as in a well. The latter contained the remains of a baby between nine and a half and ten lunar months, so this baby died shortly before term. Although Hölschen and Becker were willing to believe that women and children lived in the fort here, they suggested that most of the children will have been in the *vici* outside forts.[97] Because of the disturbed contexts of the infant bones, it is difficult to prove that babies lived and died within the accommodations of the fort at Ellingen, but, as Penelope Allison rightly notes, at least some of the infant burials were deliberate and placed in pits dug for them, in some cases probably under the floors of buildings.[98] The soldiers' barracks, buildings B and C, at Ellingen also had considerable quantities of female- or child-related artefacts, and they were the site of most of the infant burials. For me, this brings with it the implication that women and families were living in this fort, probably with ordinary soldiers, before Septimius Severus' marriage reforms, regardless of the legitimacy of such families.

Evidence for infants having died in or around forts is present at other sites with a broad geographical range. On the Upper German *limes* at Osterburken, the remains of three infants were found in the Affeldürn cemetery, one of them being buried very simply, perhaps in a cloth bag or piece of fabric, and another laid on a large amphora sherd.[99] In Britain, at the Roman fort at Reculver, the remains of eleven infants several months old were found, although only six of them can be attributed with certainty to occupation of Roman date in the fort.[100] Their interpretation as so-called foundation burials with ritual significance seems to be another attempt to dismiss the presence of women and children in a military context. Even the retrieval of a baby feeding bottle close to one of the infant skeletons failed to convince the excavator otherwise.

INFANT SACRIFICE, INFANTICIDE, AND EXPOSURE

The classic site for the possible practice of infant sacrifice in antiquity, and still the focus of a long-running debate, is the sanctuary of the Phoenician goddess Tanit, or Tinnit, at Carthage, the so-called tophet. Other sanctuaries of Tanit

[97] Hölschen and Becker 2006, 40–1.
[98] Allison 2006; Allison 2008; Allison 2011, 177–8.
[99] Hölschen and Becker 2006, 37, fig. 31; Schallmayer 2006, 59, fig. 7.
[100] Philp 1966, 7.

and Baal Hamon, also referred to in the modern literature as tophets, are known at Phoenician colonies in Sardinia and Sicily, but the site at Carthage is the most famous.[101] The site, excavated in 1921 and again in the 1970s, had a long history from the fifth to the second century BC, the most intriguing finds from the excavations being the thousands of ceramic urns containing the burnt bones of very young children or young animals and the stone *stelae* that marked the burial site of many of them.[102] Lawrence Stager and others have taken this as proof of the veracity of reports by Roman authors, such as Diodorus Siculus and Plutarch, among others, who state that the Carthaginians sacrificed their children to the Phoenician god Baal Hammon and the goddess Tanit.[103] Of course, these Roman accounts of the enemy Carthaginians and their character and habits are not without enormous bias, written long after events or customs had occurred, and, without a Carthaginian literary or historical narrative, the Roman written record is to be used with caution.[104] On the other hand, infant sacrifice is well attested in textual sources in the Iron Age Levant, and the reality of ritual infant killing in this context is generally accepted.[105] But there has been much debate whether the Carthaginians actually regularly ritually killed their children for religious reasons or whether the children deposited in the tophet were placed here because it was sacred burial ground primarily for foetuses and very young infants who had died of natural causes.[106]

Recent scientific examinations of the cremated skeletal remains in the urns found in the Carthage tophet have reopened the debate. What is important here is the age at death of the individuals. For Schwartz et al., one of the main criteria for determining the age of the infants and whether they had been brought to full term is the absence or presence of a neonatal line in the teeth, an accentuated enamel incremental ring in the tooth crowns separating the enamel formed during intrauterine life from that formed after leaving the womb.[107] This team of researchers concluded in 2010 that most of the sample (of 540 individuals) were either prenatal (23 per cent) or perinatal (31 per cent) infants, with 32 per cent being children who died in the first five or sixth

[101] On tophets in the West, see Aubet 2001, 250–6; Quinn 2011; D'Andrea and Giardino 2013; Quinn 2013; B. D. Shaw 2013, 239–43; Xella et al. 2013.

[102] Stager 1980; Stager 1982; Brown 1991; Lancel 1992.

[103] Stager and Wolff 1984; Diodorus Siculus 20.14; Plutarch, *On Superstition* 13.

[104] One of these, Justin's *Epitome of the Philippic History of Pompeius Trogus*, may be of second- or even fourth-century AD date. For a good discussion of the dangers of relying on the Graeco-Roman view of the Carthaginian Empire, see Pilkington 2013, 1–8, 37–76 and on child sacrifice based on Graeco-Roman sources, see his comments, esp. 62–71.

[105] Stavrakopoulou 2004; Xella 2013b, 263–5.

[106] Moscati 1987; Ribichini 1990.

[107] Schwartz et al. 2010. B. D. Shaw 2013, 242–3, expresses the hope that, in future, the osteological data might shed light on whether the infants were deceased at the time of their sacrifice, but he seems not to be aware of the work of Schwartz et al. 2010.

months after birth. Older children up to the age of six years were also present, but they made up only about 5 per cent of the total. Schwartz et al. suggest, therefore, that the tophet was a cemetery for those who died shortly before or around birth, reflecting 'normal' perinatal and newborn mortality, whatever the cause, rather than indicating sacrifice as the agent of death.[108] Their results were called into question by another research team led by Smith et al. in 2011.[109] They used a method of identifying tooth age, based on estimates of tooth shrinkage during cremation, concluding that Schwartz and his team had under-estimated the age of the tophet sample. The shrinkage they noted represented about four to six weeks of growth and they argued that a minimum of four weeks should be added to the age estimates of the children at the Carthage tophet. For that reason, they aged the Carthagian infants at one and one-and-a-half postnatal months and suggested that most of the babies in the tophet had already been born and, therefore, had been available for sacrifice.

There are, however, methodological problems with the approach by Smith et al. The material they used to establish an estimate of tooth shrinkage consisted of samples in which cremation was conducted in modern ovens which reach a high and consistent temperature. Schwartz et al. had noted, however, that the burning on the bones from the urns at Carthage was actually quite variable and the bones had not always been greatly affected by heat, suggesting that the cremation of the bodies likely took place on small open-air pyres which had not been constructed to achieve a maximum heat or were not able to burn evenly.[110] This same un-evenness of burning was determined earlier by Hélène Bénichou-Safar who studied the cremated remains in the tophets at Carthage and Sousse.[111] In addition, some of the tophet urns contained the remains of several infants, often comingled with animal remains, suggesting that the pyres used to burn them were communal, rather than individual. This could also contribute to irregular burning and varying heat. Smith et al.'s age correction, therefore, is not very convincing.

On balance, I accept Schwartz et al.'s conclusions concerning the estimated ages of the individuals in the Carthage tophet. The mortality curve of the infants in this tophet declines very steeply after the age of one year. The first year of an infant's life in antiquity was perilous, as I have stressed already, particularly at birth and in the first month thereafter. But they were also vulnerable already in the womb, so it is not surprising that prenatal infants

[108] Schwartz et al. 2010, 1.
[109] P. Smith et al. 2011; R. Smith et al. 2013.
[110] Schwartz et al. 2012, 739.
[111] Bénichou-Safar 1988, 60–2. She also determined that the bones of the examined skeletons were always burned in the same place, concluding that the babies had been placed deliberately in one position, namely, lying on their back. In her 2004 publication of the tophet at Carthage, she reiterated that children had been laid whole on the fire, wrapped or dressed in textiles, and that nothing about the skeletal remains can tell us whether these infants were dead or alive when cremated: Bénichou-Safar 2004, 155.

figure among the dead in the tophet. In my opinion, the age distribution at the tophet *could* reflect natural deaths due to all manner of health threats and present a picture of normal infant mortality.[112]

But is the Carthage site really, therefore, a necropolis for youngsters?[113] If that were the case, there should be more infants buried in this and in other tophets in line with infant mortality rates in antiquity. At Mozia in Sicily, for example, little more than 200 infant cremations were made in the excavated part of this tophet, about a quarter or third of the whole site; projecting these numbers onto the original extent of the site and dividing them by four centuries of use would mean that only about two individuals would have been deposited here annually.[114] This does not suggest a regular use of the area for infant burial. The *stelae* set up over the burial sites of infants in tophets, moreover, are not of a funerary nature; instead they are votive in character, stating that something had been given, dedicated, done, vowed, or offered, as Paolo Xella et al. make clear.[115] The dead children in the pots at Carthage are never named in the inscriptions, and this contrasts with funerary epitaphs; only the devotee's name is given, in line with votive inscriptions.[116] What has been vowed or offered is sometimes stated in the inscriptions and that can include a lamb or "a person who has not yet reached maturity".[117] Certainly, the animals found in the tophets, almost always newborn lambs or kids, were killed as sacrificial offerings, and that suggests a seasonal focus once or twice a year on the payment of a vow. It follows, logically, that the vow of offering a young human being meant that that individual would also be killed as a sacrifice. Very young sheep or goats might, under certain circumstances, be offered as substitutes.

But what about the prenatal infants found in the Carthage tophet? How could they be, to quote Smith et al., "available for sacrifice"? Xella argued that parents could vow to sacrifice their child in return for divine assistance for something, possibly offering their as yet unborn child as payment.[118] If the vowed child died in the womb or the mother miscarried, the dead infant or foetus nevertheless would be sacrificed (metaphorically) and taken to the tophet to fulfil the contractual arrangement.

[112] This is also the conclusion of Bénichou-Safar 2004, 160.

[113] Xella 2013b, 268, argues against their use as a necropolis, but he is wrong in stating that animal sacrifice is incompatible with a necropolis or that rich rites, offerings, and *stelae* are unknown for infants or foetuses in cemeteries elsewhere in the ancient world.

[114] Xella 2010, 268; Xella 2013b, 274. Stager 1980, 3, estimated that about one hundred child sacrifices took place annually at the Carthage tophet, but this is entirely based on the density of excavated urns of the period 400–200 BC that is projected onto a surmised total surface area of 5000–6000 sq. m.

[115] Xella et al. 2013. See also in more detail Xella 2013b, 269–71.

[116] Bonnet 2011, 383–4. [117] Xella et al. 2013, 1204. [118] Xella 2013b, 271.

Taken together, the cultural and religious context of the tophets, as well as the epigraphic evidence, point to the Phoenician custom of offering of infants or very young children in fulfilment of a vow sworn to the gods for aid, but it cannot be concluded that the sacrifice of infants took place regularly or even often or that such vows were sworn in response to anything but a serious personal problem or family crisis. Corinne Bonnet suggests that the Carthaginian religious customs explored here do not represent "cruel and primitive rites where children were thrown in the fire" to the amusement of their cold parents.[119] For her, the tophet was a place where the Carthaginians, as former exiles from the Phoenician city of Tyre, performed religious rites, including feasting and libations, to secure protection as a community from the ancestral gods. It was only during a crisis or struggle that Carthaginians may have decided to offer very young children to compel the gods to grant salvation to them.[120]

Even though the Carthage tophet, and other tophets in the central Mediterranean, were in use before the Roman period and, strictly speaking, they might not seem to be immediately relevant to a discussion of Roman infanticide, I have spent some time discussing them because there are later, Roman sites—tophets or so-called *stele*-sanctuaries—in North Africa in which infants and young children predominate. This is the case, for example, at the sanctuary of Baal Hammon (the Roman Saturn) at Henchir el-Hami in central Tunisia where, from the second and first centuries BC to the late second century AD, babies younger than six months were cremated and buried in ceramic urns.[121] Three quarters of the 268 urns buried in the sanctuary contained the cremated remains of children, and these were being offered by people with Libyan, Phoenician, and Latin names. The practice of cremating infants and burying them as votive gifts to the gods is attested also at Hadrumetum (modern Sousse) on the east coast of Tunisia, where the custom finally ended in the late first century AD.[122] A mixture of infants and young lambs as offerings predominated throughout the history of the sanctuary, with animal sacrifices becoming increasingly common until they had replaced the human offerings completely by the late first century AD. Thereafter the ritual of making a vow and an offering involved the deposition of perfume flasks and *stelae*, a feature also of the late phase of the sanctuary of Saturn at Henchir el-Hami.[123]

The Roman necropolis at Thysdrus in Tunisia, in which about a hundred children were buried in the first three centuries AD, has been interpreted by Latifa Slim as a possible tophet.[124] Here, one child of five months, one of ten months, four infants between eight and twelve months, and a newborn were found mixed in with older children. It might appear, at first glance, that there is some kind of sanctuary context because several epitaphs mention a

[119] Bonnet 2011, 383. [120] Bonnet 2011, 384.
[121] Ferjaoui 2007; Quinn 2011, 402–3; McCarty 2013.
[122] McCarty 2011. [123] McCarty 2013, 5. [124] Slim 1983.

templum, and others name a child as an initiate (*initiata*), and also a female divinity (*dea*), but the reference to a *templum* is part of a propitiatory formula about the non-violation of the bones and it clearly referred to the funerary monument or the cemetery itself. Furthermore, the inscriptions on the *stelae* are funerary, not votive, because they name the deceased, unlike the votive *stelae* from the Carthaginian tophet. Naomi Norman rightly pointed out that this necropolis fits comfortably within Roman funerary practices and there is nothing in layout or in the material record of the site to allow the identification of it as a sanctuary or a tophet.[125]

This discussion has focused on the killing of infants as part of a religious ritual. However, there was another practice which involved the intentional killing of newborns, and that was infanticide. Infanticide could be a reaction to situations such as a deformity or the non-viability of the baby, and it was an immediate and effective way of ending an infant's life. In the ancient world, it was not limited to Graeco-Roman society, nor did it end in antiquity.[126] In fact, a recent case in medical ethics was made to legalize the killing of severely disabled infants and re-label the practice as "after-birth abortion".[127] Another way of disposing of infants was the exposure or placing out of a child, *expositio* in Latin, whereby it was taken somewhere and left or given up. Death of the infant was not necessarily the only outcome of *expositio*, especially when a baby was put in a place in which it was likely to be found and raised by someone other than the parents, but it may well have been a frequent result.[128] For the purposes of this book, infanticide and exposure reflect differing parental intentions and they are not considered to be the same thing.[129] Discussions of infanticide and exposure have relied almost exclusively on textual and historical evidence for the simple reason that there is almost no archaeological evidence for either practice. What evidence does exist will be discussed in the remainder of this chapter.

Some Roman texts reveal why and under what circumstances a baby might be killed. Dionysius of Halicarnassus, for example, referred to a probably fictitious law of Romulus, the first king of Rome, which prohibited the killing of any child under the age of three, except one that might be "deformed and monstrous".[130] But this was not a decision the parents could make on their own; rather, the deformity of the child and the likelihood that it could not survive had to be determined by a committee of five neighbours who examined the infant. This association with Romulus suggests that the idea was very old, and perhaps it was somehow related to early Roman laws recorded in the

[125] Norman 2003, 42. [126] Boswell 1984. [127] Giubilini and Minerva 2013.

[128] Patterson 1985 grouped infanticide and exposure in ancient Greece together, saying that both practices were acts of violence against the newborn.

[129] For an excellent discussion of the differences between exposure and infanticide, see Evans Grubbs 2013. See also W. V. Harris 1994.

[130] Dionysius, *Roman Antiquities* 2.15.

Twelve Tables in the sixth century BC. Cicero in the mid-first century BC mentioned a recommendation in the Twelve Tables that a conspicuously deformed child should be killed quickly or removed.[131] In the first century AD, Seneca the Younger wrote that "children who at birth are weak and abnormal" were drowned, further noting that it was a reasonable social measure to separate the damaged from the healthy.[132] By AD 228, however, the emperor Alexander Severus revoked the right of the head of the family (*pater familias*) to impose a death sentence on a child, presumably even with witnesses confirming its deformity or disability. A problem with dealing with terms and concepts such as deformity, however, is that there was no clear definition of disability in antiquity; instead it was a fluid and culturally determined concept, and is so even today.[133] Moreover, many health problems, sensory problems, and disabilities would not have been recognized at birth by the family or the midwife. Years could pass until a disability or impairment manifested itself, and the family would have had to raise and care for the individual as long as he or she lived, as is demonstrably the case at a number of sites in Roman Britain where adolescents and young adults with long-term problems, such as clubfoot, scoliosis, and various cranial deformities, have been identified in the burial record.[134]

Broadly speaking, then, we can say that infants, for a variety of reasons, could be killed at birth, under very specific circumstances and with measures in place that were deemed legal and just, although all of our written sources really only refer to the situation in Rome and Italy. By no means does the *possibility* of infanticide justify popular headlines today such as "Infanticide Common in Roman Empire" or "The tragically common practice of Roman infanticide".[135] The Roman texts do *not* tell us that it was common or even widespread, and the archaeological sources provide little concrete physical evidence, if any, of the practice.[136]

One of the main Roman archaeological sites flagged up as a place where infanticide was practised is Ashkelon in Israel. At Ashkelon, around 100 infants who died within days after or around birth were deposited in a subterranean masonry canal or drain (sometimes, for effect, referred to as a "sewer") that ran under the floor of a bath-house.[137] Although this site lies

[131] Cicero, *On the Laws* 3.19. [132] Seneca, *Of Anger* 1.15.

[133] Laes 2013, 125–6, 129–30.

[134] Southwell Wright 2014. Laes 2013 discusses literary references and historical cases of child disability throughout the ancient world.

[135] http://www.nbcnews.com/id/42911813/ns/technology_and_science-science/t/infanticide-common-roman-empire/#.WAdMEsmdLIU; http://knowledgenuts.com/2014/02/13/the-tragically-common-practice-of-roman-infanticide.

[136] Haentjens 2000, 264: Infanticide "should never be regarded as common practice linked to a specific way of life".

[137] P. Smith and Kahila 1992.

somewhat outside the chronological parameters of this book, I include it here because it has been very influential in the study and interpretation of other archaeological sites with infant remains. The bath-house and drain were built possibly in the fourth century AD over the remains of an earlier house, and the infant skeletons were found at the bottom of the drain. Although the excavators originally speculated that baby girls would have been in the majority, in the belief that girls must have been worth less than boys, a team of scientists examining the DNA in the leg bones of the skeletons found that in the nineteen cases that were successfully sexed fourteen of them were boys and five were girls.[138] In a desire to explain this surprising result, the bath-house was subsequently interpreted as a brothel in which pregnant prostitutes disposed of their unwanted boys, keeping and raising the girls to be future sex workers.[139] This interpretation has been criticized soundly, not only because there is no real evidence to suggest the bath was used as a brothel in the first place, but also because a case of preferential male infanticide does not exist. The whole scenario was "conceptualized within the context of female sexual commodification", suggesting that the only value of female infants was their later sexual exploitation as girls and women.[140] Even if prostitutes really did inhabit the bath, furthermore, one could rightly assume that in their particular trade they would have used contraceptives and methods of birth control, rather than falling pregnant repeatedly and being forced to kill their unwanted babies. Riddle, for example, has identified a whole range of plants used in contraception in the Graeco-Roman world, although it is uncertain how reliable, widespread, or common they generally were.[141]

The original publications suggested that the bath-house was still functioning, and also its drain, when the babies were killed and dumped in it; it was even postulated that the bath-house was in the so-called red-light district of Ashkelon.[142] Later, however, this was revised, and the drain was said to have been disused and served as a rubbish dump by the time the infants were disposed of.[143] In that case, was there anyone even using the bath-house at that time? Was the drain simply an available underground space in a non-functioning building used by local inhabitants as a convenient burial site for infants who died around birth, much like the reused Hellenistic wells in

[138] Faerman et al. 1997; Faerman et al. 1998.

[139] Faerman et al. 1997, 213; Faerman et al. 1998, 864–5.

[140] Scott 2001, 11–12. See also more brief criticism of the brothel theory in M. Rose 1997b. Donald Engels (1980, 118–20) rejected significant female infanticide, claiming that even low rates of it would increase the death rate and lower the birth rate, and in a stable or nearly stable population, this would cause the population to decline at a geometric rate. William Harris (1982) rejected Engels' hypotheses on female infanticide for what he considers fallacious arguments. For a more recent discussion of femicide, see Scheidel 2010.

[141] Riddle 1994. For a critique of Riddle, see Frier 1994, who looks primarily at fertility within legitimate marriage. Hopkins 1965 discusses contraception in medical practice among the upper class.

[142] Faerman et al. 1998, 864–5.

[143] P. Smith and Kahila 2005, 84.

Athens and Messene in which babies who died naturally were placed (see Chapter 2)? That a well could be reused as a burial site also in the Roman period is illustrated by the discovery of one in Augst in Switzerland containing human skeletons, including eight newborns, in the mid-third century AD (where no suggestion of infanticide is made by the excavators).[144] In the end, all we know is that perinatal and newborn infants were put in that drain at Ashkelon, and everything else—the who, the why, the circumstances—is speculation and sensationalism.

Another recent case for infanticide has been made in regard to Yewden Roman farm at Hambleden in Buckinghamshire. Here, in 1912, ninety-seven infants were found on the north side of the site, outside the perimeter wall of the farm, with a further few infants just inside the perimeter wall or under the floor of a building. At the time they were largely ignored until about a third of them were studied by Simon Mays in 2011.[145] Rather than seeing these burials as a reflection of high infant mortality, however, Mays and Eyers claimed that the Yewden babies were victims of infanticide because, according to Mays' age reckoning, they all appear to have died between thirty-eight and forty gestational weeks of age (slightly premature to full term).[146] Gowland and Chamberlain, by using a Bayesian approach to reassess ages at death, demonstrated that these babies did not all die at birth; rather, there are premature babies, newborns, and infants some months old among them, representing a normal picture of infant death.[147] Of the thirty-three infants studied at Yewden, twelve could be sexed, and of these seven were female and five were male.[148] There was clearly no manipulation of the sex ratio as a motivation for putative infanticide here; the numbers tell us simply that almost equal numbers of boys and girls were born and died at Yewden.

Much has been made in the press about the Yewden site, with revelations that both shock the modern psyche and perpetuate notions of Roman coldheartedness. Cocks, the excavator, claimed that the infant bodies must have been disposed of surreptitiously, but for this there is not the slightest evidence.[149] A recent online newspaper piece claimed that "the burials had been done at night, and in secret, a conclusion developed from the irregular and

[144] Pfäffli 2013a, 10–11; Kramis and Trancik 2014, 9–10. [145] Cocks 1921.

[146] Mays and Eyers 2011. See also Hassan et al. 2014. For an earlier discussion of infanticide in Roman Britain, see Mays 1993. W. V. Harris 1994 rejected the evidence at Yewden as an indication of widespread Roman infanticide, stating that it was the Roman practice to bury infants, but to cremate older children and adults. For him, the concentration of infant burials can be explained by these customs.

[147] Gowland and Chamberlain 2002. Mays responded with comments in 2003. See also Gowland et al. 2014 and Gowland 2016 for a sound evaluation of the evidence for infanticide in Roman Britain which is at odds with the views presented by Mays.

[148] Mays and Faerman 2001. [149] Cocks 1921.

sometimes overlapping graves".[150] In reality, all the overlapping of graves tells us is that there had been no surface marker to indicate to later grave diggers where the earlier graves were. Add to that Shepherd Frere's suggestion that the building complex at Yewden might have been a "slave-run establishment" and Eyers's Ashkalon-influenced idea that the villa possibly functioned as a brothel, and we end up with a gruesome picture of infant bloodshed, with pregnant slaves and/or prostitutes killing and disposing of their unwanted offspring.[151] Just as at Ashkelon, there is no independent evidence whatsoever that Yewden farm had been used as a brothel, or, indeed, that it even was slave-run; instead, it was a normal productive farmstead in the countryside, frequented by farmers, labourers, and perhaps merchants, but hardly by a stream of eager men looking for prostitutes out in the sticks. None of the fantastic claims for infanticide or prostitution can be substantiated here, nor, I think, have the burial practices at Yewden been contextualized properly or related to more general customs applicable to infant burial in Roman continental Europe.

In my view, there is little difference between the burial situation at Yewden and at Roman farms discussed earlier at Beaumont, des Béziaux à Langeais, and Sommesous in Gaul, where infant burials are in their own area, together and outside the limitations of or on the periphery of the area for the living. In those places where more extensive areas of the grounds of a farm have been excavated, such as at Tavant, another burial ground for older children and adults was found too, in addition to a distinct concentration of infant burials. This mixed-age communal cemetery has not been found at Yewden or Beaumont or Sommesous, but it certainly will have existed. If infants were buried in their own area at Yewden and at rural sites in Gaul, this does not suggest that they were just killed and dumped, rather that they were given a particular area that was appropriate for this young age category and in which they were deposited with proper care in grave pits and containers. Moreover, since the farm at Yewden was inhabited from the mid-first to the late fourth centuries AD, the occurrence of ninety-seven infant deaths in about three and a half centuries really cannot be seen as anything unusual or as an "infant mass burial".[152]

Let us turn to infant exposure. *Expositio* is mentioned in Classical and Hellenistic Greek texts. In his late fifth century BC *Republic*, a utopian projection, Plato recommended, for example, that the children of "inferior guardians" should be exposed, whereas his contemporary Isocrates regarded the

[150] D. Kelly, "The Tragically Common Practice Of Roman Infanticide", http://knowledgenuts.com/2014/02/13/the-tragically-common-practice-of-roman-infanticide.

[151] Frere 1967, 266–7; Eyers is quoted as saying to BBC news on 25 June 2010 and in the *Mail Online* on 26 June 2010: "The only explanation you keep coming back to is that it's got to be a brothel": http://www.bbc.com/news/10384460 and http://www.dailymail.co.uk/sciencetech/article-1289603/Romans-killed-100-unwanted-babies-English-brothel.html.

[152] http://www.thehistoryblog.com/archives/6582.

exposure of infants as a horrendous crime.[153] How much exaggeration is in Polybius' statement that infant exposure contributed to the depopulation of Greece in the second century BC we cannot tell, but it seems rather unlikely that this was the case.[154]

A handful of Roman writers convey some of the reasons why parents might expose their infants,[155] one being that poor parents might have feared they were not in a position to bring up their children appropriately.[156] The Stoic philosopher Gaius Musonius Rufus wrote a whole treatise on the topic in the first century AD entitled *Whether all children who are born should be reared*, suggesting that there was a debate about the acceptability of exposure.[157] Musonius Rufus appears to have taken the moral high ground in this debate in condemning not only the poor, but especially the wealthier parents "who do not even have poverty as an excuse" and who do not rear "later-born offspring in order that those born earlier may inherit greater wealth". In reality, however, his arguments were meant to encourage senatorial and equestrian families, the elites, to reproduce and provide society with legitimate and socially promising children, and he may have been less concerned about the poor and lower echelons of society.[158] A theme of Plautus' play *Cistellaria* is the rape of a woman who instructed her servant to abandon the child once it was born, presumably because it was a reminder of her violation.[159] Illegitimacy of an infant also might be a reason, and perhaps children born to slaves might be given up by the slave owner. A funerary epitaph in Carthage, for instance, names a slave-girl, Daphnis, who gave birth to a baby by her slave husband, but against the wishes of her master.[160] She asks "who will now feed the son" and take care of him and raise him? If such a child were unwanted by the slave owner, and he had no obligation to keep it, it might well be abandoned to be raised by someone else. Grief or conflicts in the family might furthermore prompt people to give up their children, like a man from Spoletium whose parents abandoned him because of their "*discordia*".[161] The supposed widespread exposure of infants by distraught parents in Italy in response to the sudden death of their beloved Germanicus, adopted son of the emperor Tiberius, in AD 19, on the other hand, sounds implausible.[162] Two centuries later, the jurist Paulus equated the exposure of an infant with killing, but it was not until AD 374 that *expositio* became a punishable crime.[163]

[153] Plato, *Republic* 5.460; Isocrates, *Panathenaicus* 121–2.
[154] Polybius, *Histories* 36.17.5–9.
[155] W. V. Harris 1994, 11–13; Evans Grubbs 2013, 84–92.
[156] Plutarch, *On Affection for Offspring* 497E, 5; Pliny, *Panegyrics* 26.5.
[157] Lutz 1947. [158] Harrill 1995, 40. [159] Plautus, *The Casket.*
[160] *CIL* VIII.24734. [161] Suetonius, *On Grammarians* 21.
[162] Suetonius, *Caligula* 5. W. V. Harris 1994, 14, seems to accept this anecdote as reflecting reality.
[163] Paulus (*Views* 2), *Digest* 25.3.4; W. V. Harris 1994, 21–2, on the edict. W. V. Harris 1994 contains a wealth of information on infant exposure in the textual sources.

There is no way of knowing how many exposed infants died, from cold or heat, or from malnutrition, or even from animal attacks, but it is clear that in many cases these babies were left in a place where they had a very good chance of being found and reared by someone other than the natal family.[164] But they might just as easily be rescued, however, to lead the rest of their lives as slaves. Suetonius' man from Spoletium ended this way, and it happened often enough in Bithynia that Pliny the Younger, governor of the province, wrote a letter to the emperor Trajan in which he asked for advice on what to do about "those who, having been born free, were exposed, then picked up by someone and brought up in slavery".[165] Harris conjectured that during the second and first centuries BC, with so many slaves entering the empire through conquest, there was no shortage of manual labour, but later in the imperial period the exposure of infants was increasingly motivated by the demand for slaves, making the rescuing of foundlings more common.[166]

Wet-nursing contracts from Roman Egypt show that slave babies were often exposed infants, called *anairetoi* in Greek (picked-up ones), who were sometimes explicitly said to have been picked up off the dung-heap (*κοπρία*), in other words taken from the rubbish tip.[167] Presumably, then, it was general knowledge that babies could be found in this less than salubrious location in Egyptian settlements. Such babies would need to be fed as soon as they were found, if they were to survive, and wet-nurses were crucial here. The *lactaria columna*, the nursing column, in Rome was a place where wet-nurses could be hired by families for the infants they kept, as well as for *expositi* who had been picked up and needed feeding.[168]

Not all *expositi* were lost to the natal family forever. Judith Evans Grubbs concluded that some parents who exposed a baby knew all along where it had been taken and who raised it, sometimes reclaiming the child when it was older.[169] Even if the child had worked as a slave in the meantime, the law recognized its free status when it was reclaimed and reunited with the birth family. Those who had raised the child in the meantime, however, would have had the expense of feeding and clothing and perhaps educating or training it, and this led to a problem that prompted Pliny as governor to write that letter to Trajan, asking specifically if the child were reclaimed as free, would those who raised it be owed compensation? Later, in the third century, this issue was still being debated in rhetorical schools.[170]

[164] Boswell 1984, 13–14, is perhaps a bit too optimistic about the chances of an abandoned baby surviving.

[165] Pliny the Younger, *Letters* 10.65–10.66.

[166] W. V. Harris 1994, 6.

[167] Masciadri and Montevecchi 1984; Evans Grubbs 2013, 93–4. On the Kopr- names in Roman Egypt, once thought to indicate that people with this in their personal name had been foundlings from the dung heap, see Pomeroy 1986; W. V. Harris 1994, 8.

[168] Corbier 2001, 62–3.

[169] Evans Grubbs 2010.

[170] Evans Grubbs 2013, 97.

The examination of the evidence in this chapter has shown that infants were buried regularly in community cemeteries with their families and siblings, although that is not uniformly the case across the empire. In some regions, especially Egypt, even foetuses were carefully interred as part of the community. The pre-Roman regional tradition of burying babies within settlements, close to the living, continued in some parts of the Roman world, such as Gaul and Britain, indicating some degree of continuity in attitudes to and relationships with very young children. Although Roman written sources suggest that infants could be killed at birth under very specific circumstances, a critical examination of the archaeological evidence does not substantiate any of the fantastic claims for the practice of infanticide, nor is there any concrete indication that dead infants were disposed of with the rubbish. Indeed, in Chapter 7 on burial ritual and the funerary treatment of infants, it becomes even clearer that Roman families invested in and were attached to their children.

7

Mors Immatura II

The Treatment of the Infant Body in Death

MARSEILLE: GREEK AND ROMAN BURIALS IN CULTURAL COMPARISON

The cemetery under discussion here lies in the modern Sainte-Barbe quarter of Marseille. The site excavation and publication of the data allow us to compare the treatment of the body and the provision of goods for the afterlife of infants in two different periods and under different cultural influences (see Tables 1 and 2). The city was established *c.*600 BC by Greek colonists from Phocaea and it continued as a Roman city after it lost its independence under Julius Caesar in 49 BC. The Sainte-Barbe cemetery functioned as a burial site for the Greek colonists and their descendants from the fourth century BC to about the middle of the second century BC, and, after a hiatus, burial resumed in the latter part of the first century BC and continued until the second century AD for the Roman population. Although it is possible that many of the people living in Marseille in the Roman period were descendants of the earlier inhabitants, and, therefore, of Greek cultural origin, there will have been Roman newcomers as well, and I have divided the cemetery into the "Greek" period and the "Roman" period, based solely on the political chronology of the city. The data presented in this section have been extracted from the detailed publication of the cemetery by Manuel Moliner et al.[1]

As we have seen in Chapter 2, throughout the last centuries BC in Gaul, the indigenous Gallic practice of disposing of infants was to bury them within settlements, but the Greek colonists brought their own burial habits with them, depositing infants in a communal cemetery, rather than in intramural buildings. From the fourth century BC, inhumation was the preferred practice for all age categories, although cremation began to crop up in the third and

[1] Moliner et al. 2003.

second centuries; from the late first century BC to the middle of the first century AD, the Roman inhabitants cremated their dead until about AD 100 when inhumation once again became dominant.

In the Greek period, all infants under the age of one year were inhumed, and they account for about 38 per cent of the sixty-five inhumation burials that could be aged, making this age group only slightly smaller than the adults with 40 per cent. This includes two foetuses of only six-and-a-half lunar months, presumably twins, buried together in the same grave, each in its own ceramic vessel. Of these infants, only 16 per cent are one month or over, the others being mainly perinatal or less than a month old. Overall, with eighty-three individuals in total who could be aged, including cremations, infants make up 30 per cent in the Greek period. Also in the Roman period of the cemetery, all infants were inhumed, as they had been before. Of the inhumation burials with skeletons that could be aged accurately (241), 16 per cent of the Roman burials belong to infants under the age of one year, a clear under-representation compared to the preceding period, and well behind the adults who make up 66 per cent. Of these infants, 21 per cent of them are older than one month of age. Roman burials whose age could be determined, including cremations, total 351, of which 11 per cent are under-one-year-olds.

We can flesh out these bare statistics by studying the various containers used for burial in the two periods. In the Greek phase of the cemetery, 60 per cent of the infants were buried in local Massaliote wine amphorae whose necks had been removed for the insertion of the body, or in fragments of these amphorae; cists of stones or amphora fragments sometimes protected these containers. Other ceramic vessels were used for 12 per cent of the infants, but only for the very youngest (two foetuses, one newborn); thus well over half of all babies were interred in some kind of a ceramic container. This relates to the Greek custom of burying children in pots, *enchytrismos* (see Chapter 2). Wood coffins, all of the fourth century BC and of local Aleppo pine (where identifiable), were used for 12 per cent of infant burials. Some prematures, newborns, and very young infants (16 per cent) also were buried simply in a pit with no recognizable container.

In the Roman phase of the cemetery, 21 per cent of infants were buried in an amphora or part of an amphora (usually a Gallic wine amphora or a Dressel 20 Spanish oil amphora), or had a fragmentary amphora as a cover over the body. Amphorae were used primarily for the burial of perinatal babies, rather than for older infants, indicating that, in the Roman period, there was no longer a prevalence of ceramic-related burial containers. Wooden coffins total 23 per cent, almost twice as many as in the Greek phase, but wood coffins are more prevalent in general for the Roman burials of all age groups, including adults. In the Roman period, cists of tile alone, or of stone, or a rubble mixture of broken tile, amphora pieces, and stones, account for 44 per cent of the containers; several of the wooden coffins are protected by just such a cist.

Infants buried without a recognizable container make up 21 per cent, noticeably more than in the Greek period.

There are differences also in the choice of grave goods in the two phases of the cemetery. In the Greek period, 60 per cent of the infants were given no grave goods at all. Shells were the most common offering (24 per cent), with 12 per cent having a ceramic vessel, including one feeding bottle. In the Roman phase, 67 per cent of the buried infants have no grave goods at all, making this group larger than in the Greek phase, but the variety of grave goods in Roman burials is significantly larger. Ceramic vessels were most common (18 per cent), and, for the first time, coins, lamps, *balsamaria*, and jewellery, such as a bracelet and amulet necklaces(?) appear. Items of clothing, such as shoes, appear in only one Roman burial of a one-year-old, none having been encountered in the Greek period. No Roman infants were buried with shells, unlike their Greek predecessors (see Chapter 2 for shells in Greek burials).

In summary, the Greek colonists of Marseille preferentially buried their infants in ceramic containers, whilst the Roman inhabitants chose mainly coffins and cists for theirs. A greater investment in the outfitting of an infant grave is apparent in the Roman period, and the noticeable scarcity of grave goods in the Greek burials stands in contrast to the variety and abundance of objects buried with infants in the Roman period. These differences in age, container, and grave goods are subtle, but nonetheless significant, and they indicate attitudes toward the very young and what was considered appropriate for them.

CREMATION VS. INHUMATION...AND MUMMIFICATION

Roman textual sources suggest that there were cultural reservations about cremating very young children, and they infer that infants under the age of six months were not disposed of in this way. The reasons given for this apparent prohibition are rather confused and tenuous, especially because cremation and the formation of teeth at around six months are linked together as being significant in some way.[2] Juvenal, too, refers to babies being "too young for the funeral pyre".[3] The examination of burial evidence offers an excellent opportunity to determine whether this differential treatment according to age, as described in contemporary literature, was adhered to in reality anywhere in the empire.

[2] Pliny, *Natural History* 7.16.68, 70, 72.

[3] Juvenal, *Satires* 15.139.

The recent excavations by the École Française de Rome in the tomb precinct of P. Vesonius Phileros outside the Porta Nocera at Pompeii have revealed evidence for a variety of disposal methods in the first century AD.[4] Both inhumation and cremation were practised for infants and children, but it was not always just the older children who were cremated, as we would expect. In fact, a baby less than six months of age (no. 10) was cremated, contrary to the prohibition recorded in primary sources, but another infant aged six months (no. 24) was inhumed in an amphora (Fig. 7.1).[5] Not only this, but also a child between eleven and fifteen months was inhumed (no. 29), although, if we gave credence to the Roman texts, we would expect children in that age category to be cremated.[6] Based on this evidence, the age of six months as the cut-off point for the change in disposal rite from inhumation to cremation was not strictly observed in Italy, or, at least, in Pompeii.

It was not universally adhered to outside Italy, either. Newborns were burned on a funeral pyre at several excavated sites in Roman Gaul, for example at Martigny in Switzerland.[7] At Argenton, 92 per cent of children aged two to

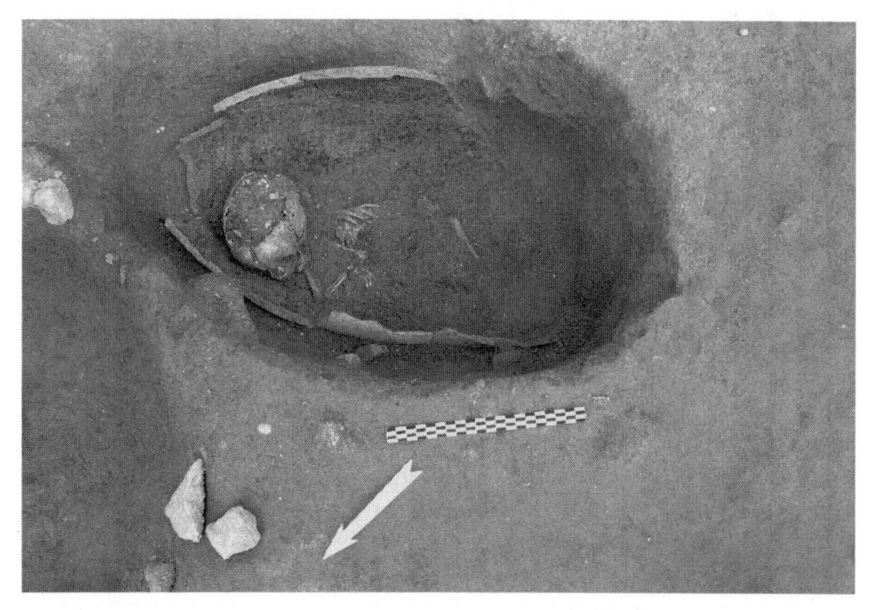

Fig. 7.1 Skeleton of an infant buried in an amphora in a tomb precinct outside the Porta Nocera at Pompeii.

Photo: A. Gailliot, Mission archéologique Porta Nocera 1, and the Soprintendenza Archeologica di Pompei.

[4] Van Andringa et al. 2013.

[5] Van Andringa et al. 2013, 357–67 (no. 10), 322–30 (no. 24).

[6] Van Andringa et al. 2013, 512–15, 527–8 (no. 29).

[7] Durand 2004–5, 17, with fig.

twelve years were cremated, but 15 per cent of newborns also were burnt on a pyre.[8] And in the cemetery of the *vicus* at Stettfeld, where 87 per cent of all child burials from the early second to the mid-third century AD were those of infants of perinatal and neonatal age, 18 per cent in this youngest age group were cremated.[9] In the north cemetery of Worms, four children less than a year old were cremated and buried in urns with a set of grave goods in the late first century AD.[10] Grave 82 was a triple cremation burial, containing an infant, an adult, and a four-year-old child, although the excavators recognized a difference in the cremation procedures, as the newborn appears to have been burnt at a low temperature of around only 300°C, possibly on a separate pyre.[11]

Just as infants, who had not yet begun to teethe, were not universally buried, rather than cremated, children beyond teething age were not cremated everywhere. At Marseille, not only infants, but also children as old as one or two and even four years were inhumed too in the Roman period, although we might expect them to have been cremated at those ages.[12] Likewise, at Avenches inhumation was practised both for infants and for children up to the age of four.[13] Mackensen viewed the inhumation of infants up to the age of seven months as a Mediterranean practice, and suggested that the lack of cremation for children in this age category outside Italy can be interpreted as a new custom introduced by the Romanized population or by Mediterranean newcomers.[14] But the evidence from Pompeii and many other sites in Gaul suggests that there is no fixed Mediterranean practice of this kind, rather there is more variation possible for the burial of infants and children than the Roman written sources indicate.

Mummification was practised regularly in pre-Roman and Roman Egypt not only for adults and children, but also for foetuses and newborns. The procedure involved the preservation of the body and the wrapping of it in resin-coated bandages. A double mummy burial is unusual, but one example comprises a newborn (perhaps stillborn or died at birth), and a foetus only five months old; they were interred together, the foetus lying on the chest of the newborn.[15] Infants could also be eviscerated, embalmed, and mummified, and buried in decorated coffins, just like adults.[16] Varying degrees of mummification appear to have been the practice for infants of differing ages at Douch in the Kargha Oasis. Considerable numbers of foetuses, newborns, and infants

[8] For example, tomb 74: Allain et al. 1992, 170, 172, figs. 62–4.

[9] Wahl and Kokabi 1988, 93–4.

[10] Grünewald 1990, 20, 102–4, 174–5, 253–5, 269–71 (graves 5, 39, 91B, 82A).

[11] Grünewald 1990, 20–1, 67.

[12] Moliner et al. 2003, 99, 285, fig. 84, grave 37 with an adult and a child 10–14 years of age; 99, 286, pl. 21, grave 42 with a child 8 years old.

[13] Castella 1999, 87.

[14] Mackensen 1978b.

[15] Spieser 2008, 542.

[16] Spieser 2008, 542–3.

under the age of one year were recovered in the 1980s in chamber tombs here.[17] Tomb 19 contained the hardly mummified remains of a dozen infants and children, from newborns to around two years old—they were deposited with grave goods in small burial pits. Tomb 73 preserved the remains of thirty foetuses, newborns, and children up to five or six years of age. The very youngest appears not to have been mummified. This led Dunand to posit that, at Douch, children between twelve and eighteen months were mummified, whilst infants younger than that were not.[18]

CONTAINERS, COFFINS, AND WRAPPINGS FOR THE INFANT BODY

By exploring the ways in which infants were placed in the ground and in what kind of protective covering, we gain important insight into the care invested in their burial. Of course, not all babies were buried in containers or coffins. Many were simply interred in a pit in the ground, but even here the effort made to dig a hole for the body indicates the wish to give the infant a proper burial, rather than dispose of it on a rubbish heap.

Once the body had been prepared for burial, choices needed to be made concerning the type of container in which to bury it. In general across the Roman world, the three most popular forms of containers for the bodies of infants were amphorae, or parts of amphorae; ceramic tiles, either on top of or underneath the body or put together to form a cist or box; and wooden coffins. Amphora burials are encountered throughout North Africa, Spain, and Italy, as well as in some regions of Gaul. Infant burials protected by tiles or containers made of tiles are common in Italy, some parts of Gaul, and North Africa. Wooden coffins have been detected in various places, including Gaul, Germany, and Britain, but less frequently in Italy.

The recently discovered infant in an amphora (grave 24) in Enclosure 23 in the Porta Nocera cemetery at Pompeii was about six months of age (see Fig. 7.1).[19] The vessel is a Vesuvian Dragendorff 2-4 wine amphora which had been truncated top and bottom and its neck removed, so that it had a length of fifty centimetres and a maximum width of thirty-two centimetres. It was put into a pit dug especially for this size of vessel, the pit measuring sixty-eight by fifty-three centimetres. The corpse would have been inserted through the top cut, as it was the widest. The opening at the foot of the amphora was sealed with a pebble, possibly wrapped in textile, and the top closed perhaps

[17] Dunand 2004; Dunand et al. 2005.
[18] Dunand 2004; Dunand et al. 2005.
[19] Van Andringa et al. 2013, 322–30, figs. 222b, 225e.

with a piece of wood held in place by chunks of basalt still *in situ*. Henri Duday, who conducted the osteological analysis of the baby's remains, concluded from the position of the bones that the baby's head originally rested on a cushion (since disappeared), with a cluster of sherds placed under the vertebrae and head to hold the infant in that position.[20]

Amphorae were the only type of container used between the end of the first century BC and the middle of the first century AD in the burial of perinatal infants in a chamber tomb at Iasos in western Asia Minor.[21] A total of eleven perinates were buried in amphorae of Coan type that had been cut at the shoulder to insert the tiny body and then closed with a stone slab or with the lower part of a second amphora. This container was used only for infants of this age, whereas older children were buried in simple pits covered with ceramic tiles or stones. Baldoni relates the use of this vessel to the much older Greek tradition of *enchytrismos*.[22]

It is also not uncommon to find parts of amphorae as a base on which infants were deposited or as covers above the body. At Beaumont, several babies under the age of six months were laid to rest on half an amphora or on a large piece of an amphora; two of them were placed in a complete amphora, but of relatively small format (see Table 4).[23] These amphorae usually were of local manufacture, but amphorae imported from more distant locations—because of their primary contents—were also used secondarily for burial. In the Sainte-Barbe cemetery at Marseille, for example, an imported Dressel 20 Spanish oil amphora served as an infant's container in tomb 296.[24] But, in some areas, amphorae were not used at all as burial containers, for example at Kempten, where infants were either buried simply in an earthen pit or in a wood coffin or in a pottery vessel.[25] Neither are they present at Tavant, where, instead, there is evidence for the use of wood coffins and limestone sarcophagi, or at Argenton in central Gaul where wood coffins, jars, and stone and tile cists are prevalent (see Tables 3, 5, and 6).[26] Perhaps the absence of amphora burials in some places is related to the lack of access to or the limited availability of amphorae as imported one-way food packaging, as not all settlements are located on the coast or near trading hubs where we might expect such containers to come into the local economy. This would appear to be the case at Vagnari in Puglia, for example, the central village of a large

[20] Van Andringa et al. 2013, 325–7. [21] Baldoni 2013. [22] Baldoni 2013, 298.

[23] Alfonso and Blaizot 2004, 160–1, fig. 108 (SP 30); 215, fig. 127 (SP 1); 249–50, fig. 161 (SP29); 253, fig. 164 (SP 31); 238–9, fig. 149 (SP 16); 251–2, fig. 162 (SP 30).

[24] Moliner et al. 2003, 331. See also a North African olive oil amphora reused as a coffin for a newborn in Augst, Switzerland, in the fourth century: Pfäffli 2013a, 18–19, cat. no. 8.

[25] Mackensen 1978a, 203, pl. 164.1 (grave 2, earth pit); 217–18, pl. 165.10 (grave 65, wood coffin); 277–8, pl. 171.10 (grave 278, pot).

[26] Tavant: Riquier and Salé 2006, 27–9, figs. 23–6 (grave 6); Argenton: Allain et al. 1992, 119, fig. 27 (tomb 85).

Roman imperial estate that lay very near the Via Appia, where few amphora fragments are present in the ceramic assemblage, either in the village or in the cemetery.[27] Long-distance food stuffs probably were not entering the site in substantial quantities, so their containers were not available for reuse in burials. Instead, tile was produced in quantity at Vagnari, and it is not surprising that tile and brick were used almost exclusively for infant and child burials (and adult burials too, see Figs. 6.2, 7.4).[28]

Infant burials in amphorae, on the other hand, are very common in North Africa, particularly in coastal locations. And African amphorae, having been shipped to other parts of the Roman Empire, were used for infant burials outside North Africa, as at Metaponto in southern Italy where African oil amphorae were reused as containers for the bodies of infants between the ages of about three months and two years.[29] In her study of late Roman infant burials in amphorae in North Africa, Susan Stevens determined that infants who died under the age of one year were given differential treatment according to age.[30] Perinatal infants were buried in small ovoid vessels with grooved or ridged exteriors or in larger amphorae that were cut down to fit the length of the baby, whilst older infants could be buried in smooth, elongated amphora types. She suggests that the smaller vessels were chosen because they resembled *uteri* and acted as a kind of substitute for the mother's womb. She is not the first to recognize the womb-like shape of amphorae and vessels used for infant burials and to connect their symbolic meaning as a provider of maternal protection to rebirth; Roman texts also refer to the shape of the womb as a vessel.[31] In her survey of the Spanish evidence for amphora burials, or amphora-coffins, as she calls them, it appears that here, too, smaller or larger sizes were selected for infants or children, with age being an important choice criterion.[32]

Amphorae were also popular at Pupput and some other North African sites studied by Solenn de Larminat (Fig. 7.2). According to her data, African amphorae were used for children from the age of newborn to three years; however, very few were used for the burial of foetuses or perinatal infants.[33] The smaller the amphora, the younger the infant placed in it. At Pupput, infants under a month were deposited in Dressel 30 and Gallic amphorae less than 90 centimetres tall, whilst children two and three years of age were buried in the large African amphorae 90–110 centimetres in size and Hammamet amphorae reaching a height of 1.20 metres. Other ceramic vessels, such as

[27] Disantarosa 2012, 387–406: amphorae from Italy, Gaul, Spain and North Africa from the landscape survey and the site total only 35.1 kg, from the sixth century BC to the end of the seventh century AD. See also Disantarosa 2014.

[28] Small and Small 2007; Brent and Prowse 2014. For the most recent short overview of the cemetery, see Carroll and Prowse 2016, 334–5. On the tile kilns, see Small 2012b.

[29] Becker 1997. [30] Stevens 2013. [31] Norman 2002, 310.

[32] Stevens 2013. [33] De Larminat 2012a, 517–18.

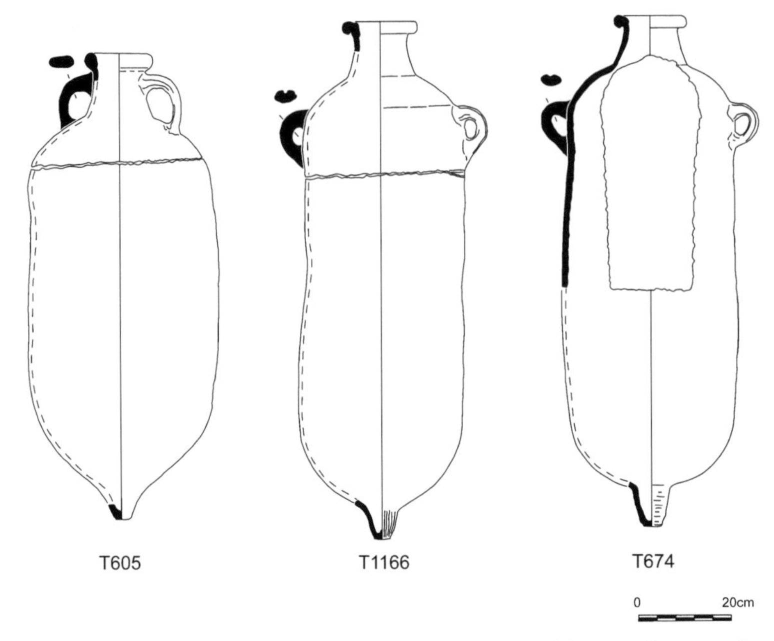

Fig. 7.2 North African amphorae at Pupput, with parts of the vessels cut and cut out to insert the body of an infant.
Drawing: Irene de Luis.

pitchers only thirty-eight or thirty-nine centimetres tall, were used exclusively for foetuses or perinatal infants.

Amphorae were used in various places not only for the burial of older children, but also for adults. Of the twenty-one amphora burials in the late Roman El Castellet necropolis at Ampurias, one (no. 4) was of a woman and a newborn between her legs, both of them having been laid to rest in two long, slim Dressel 27 amphorae placed end to end.[34] Here, at least, the mother was present symbolically to accompany and protect the baby, so an appropriate choice for the pair was a larger amphora type.

Other pottery containers, including small amphorae or jars, were used for infant burials in Roman Gaul. In the Rue de Reverdy cemetery at Chartres, one hundred infants, including forty-five premature babies and newborns, were buried in the second and third centuries AD in regionally produced amphorae and jars. These have been studied (using 3D models) with reference to the position of the skeletons and the ways in which the vessels were broken or cut open to allow the insertion of the corpse.[35] The majority of the baby burials were in vessels with a narrow neck, many of them having been broken

[34] Almagro 1955. [35] Portat et al. 2013.

at the base of the neck to accommodate the baby shortly after death and before rigor mortis had set in. The length and width of the vessel determined to what extent the infant's legs and arms were bent up against its torso or chest, but since the containers are never very big, the position of the body was always tightly contracted. The body was inserted head first or feet first, and may have been wrapped in textile. Like Stevens, Portat et al. suggested that the amphorae and jars at Chartres may have been symbolic of the womb.[36]

Roman ceramic tile and brick, primarily roof tiles or large pieces of roof tile, appear as the cover on infant burials in burial pits, as at Argenton and Langeais in Gaul.[37] Recently discovered burials of pre-term and perinatal infants near Laquenexy near Metz also utilized tile; each burial pit was covered and sealed by a *tegula* (Fig. 7.3).[38] At Kellis 2, some foetuses and newborns had a single mud brick placed over them.[39] Flat *tegula* roof tiles were common either as a base and a cover for infant burials, as at Sétif in North Africa.[40] At Marseille, *tegulae* or tile pieces sometimes were used to construct chests in which wooden baby coffins were inserted.[41] Excavations in the Rue de la Porcelaine between the Roman amphitheatre and lake at

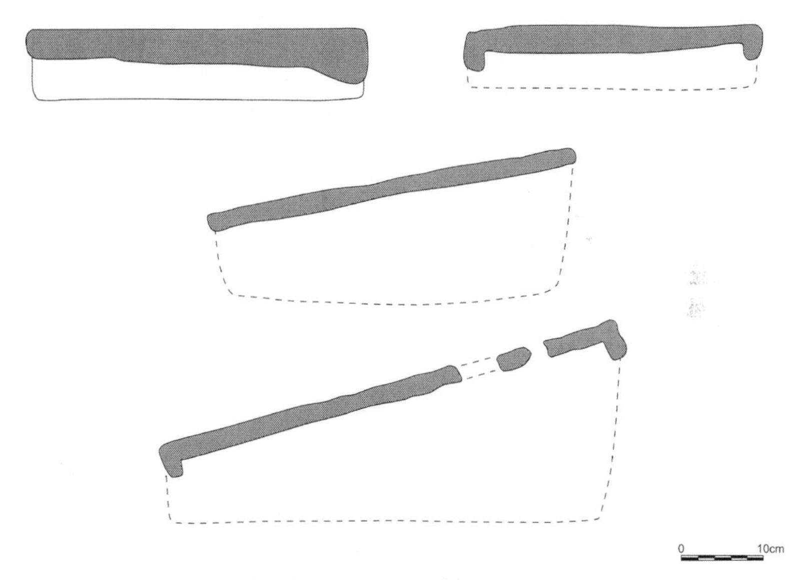

Fig. 7.3 Inhumation burials of infants covered by a roof tile (*tegula*) at Laquenexy.
Drawing: Irene de Luis.

[36] Portat et al. 2013, 53.
[37] Allain et al. 1992, 89, tomb 23 (Argenton); Guiot et al. 2003, 106 (Langeais).
[38] Brkojewitsch et al. 2014, 221–7, figs. 6–9.
[39] Wheeler et al. 2011, 113.
[40] For example, Guéry 1985, 77 (grave 35); 281–2, fig. 228 (grave 314).
[41] Moliner et al. 2003, 55–6, 281, pl. 19 (tomb 12); 363–4, pl. 56 (tomb 444).

Nyon in Switzerland revealed an inhumed newborn of the first century AD in a particularly carefully constructed rectangular cist of *tegulae*.[42] This kind of container is also found in Italian cemeteries, as at Pompeii (Porta Nocera, tomb 29) for a child between eleven and fifteen months.[43]

Particularly prevalent in Italy in the second and third centuries AD were tile burials *alla cappuccina*, that is, the inhumed body lay on a bed of flat roof tiles and was covered with flat roof tiles that stood upright and were angled in to meet over the middle of the body, like a roof. These are very common for inhumation burials for individuals of all ages throughout Italy in the second and third centuries AD, as in the *necropolis* at Lucrezia Romana I and Osteria del Curato outside Rome.[44] As mentioned above, tile was one of the products manufactured in the *vicus* of the imperial estate at Vagnari, and many of these tiles, either whole or partial, were used routinely not only for adult and adolescent burials, but also for infants, including for a newborn baby and infants of six months and more (Fig. 7.4).[45]

Fig. 7.4 Infant burial *alla cappuccina* at Vagnari, as in Fig. 6.2, opened to show the skeleton. Vagnari.
Photo: Tracy Prowse.

[42] Hauser and Rossi 1998, 22, 25; Durand 2004–5, 16, with fig.
[43] Van Andringa et al. 2013, 513–14, figs. 288, 293.
[44] Egidi et al. 2003, 86, cat. no. 19 (Via Lucrezia Romana I, tomb 42), with various amulets.
[45] Small and Small 2007, 172–3, burial F36 (*c.*9 months old).

Curved u-shaped roof tiles, *imbrices*, originally made to cover the roof ridge of buildings, are found in some quantity as containers for infant bodies, particularly in Roman Gaul. We have seen such tiles used for infant burials already in the pre-Roman period, but only in Italy (see Chapter 2). A large assemblage of these was found at the des Bolards necropolis at Nuits-Saint-Georges, where 113 out of 120 infants were buried in this way in the second and third centuries.[46] The *imbrex* tiles, thirty-eight to forty-five centimetres long, were placed in a grave pit with the convex side facing down in the ground, making a shallow trough-like container. When a second *imbrex* was placed on top with the edges of the *imbrices* turned against and meeting each other, a cylinder was created that was just the right size for the bodies of newborns and perinatal infants. Sometimes, other smaller pieces of tile or stone were placed at either end or around the cylinder to protect it. These *imbrex* coffins occur elsewhere in Gaul, in a rural necropolis at Tavaux near Besançon and in Augst in Switzerland (Fig. 7.5).[47] But they also were used in

Fig. 7.5 Infant burial within two *imbrex* tiles, Augst.
Photo: Ausgrabungen Augst/Kaiseraugst; Augusta Raurica.

[46] Planson et al. 1982, 170–6, figs. 34–6.

[47] Tavaux: Barbet et al. 2014, 199–201, fig. 205; Augst: Pfäffli 2013a, 92, fig. 22; Pfäffli 2013b, 73; Lyon: Blaizot 2009, 174, fig. on p. 177. One was found also in Worms in the Rhine: Grünewald 1990, 253–5 (grave 82).

Italy, as in the Porta Palio cemetery outside Verona.[48] It appears that this arrangement was used only for perinatal or newborn infants. The perinatal infant in grave 22 at Tavaux, buried between two *imbrices*, is particularly remarkable, as it appears not to have been the only protective container used for this baby.[49] In the tile container were thirteen little rings, lined up in a row on each of the long sides of the lower *imbrex*, which must point to their original use on the sides of a cradle. It is possible that these are all that remain of a cradle made of perishable materials, the rings having served the purpose of holding ropes or bands pulled across the baby's body to keep it in place, much like the situation depicted on a stone figurine from Nuits-Saint-Georges (see Fig. 4.8).[50]

Small-format wood coffins for babies can only survive when the conditions are favourable. They survive in dry conditions, as at Sétif in North Africa, where we find coffins made of cedar wood from the Atlas Mountains.[51] But even under normal soil conditions in temperate Europe, and when carefully excavated, minute traces of wood can be detected. Some traces of Aleppo pine remain in the coffin burials of infants at Marseille, and at Vindonissa evidence has been found for a wooden box containing the remains of a cremated one-year-old.[52] But the best conditions for the preservation of wood coffins are those when the soil is waterlogged and no bacteria have developed to erode the wood. This was the case at the Drapers' Gardens site in the northern part of Roman London where four small caskets made of oak were excavated in the clayey, wet soil along the Walbrook River; three of them contained skeletons and the fourth was empty (Fig. 7.6).[53] The infants buried in them in the first century AD included a baby slightly less than full term, a newborn, and an infant less than six months of age. Three of the coffins were rectangular, measuring sixty by twenty-five, sixty by twenty-seven, and sixty-five by seventeen centimetres, and were made of radially cleft oak boards less than eighteen millimetres thick and tacked into place (tack holes survived). The wood for the coffins may have been cut from fence posts. The fourth coffin, measuring eighty-two by twenty-four centimetres, was an oval bentwood container, constructed of oak boards bent around an oval baseboard. It has been suggested that these boxes may have been used originally for something else, and were recycled as coffins, but it is more likely that at least the rectangular boxes would have been made especially for the infants when they died.[54]

[48] Cavalieri Manasse and Bola 1998.

[49] Barbet et al. 2014, 89–90, 204–5, fig. 212.

[50] Coulon 2004a, 49; Barbet et al. 2014, 205, fig. 213.

[51] Guéry 1985, 60, fig. 44 (grave 13).

[52] Marseille: Moliner et al. 2003, 334 (tomb 308); 353–64, pl. 56 (tomb 444); Vindonissa: Hintermann 2000, 49, fig. 50, tomb 93-84.

[53] Ridgeway 2009, 10. I thank Jonathan Butler, Pre-Construct Archaeology, for sending me the internal report on the burials and the coffins.

[54] Ridgeway 2009, 10.

Fig. 7.6 Tiny wood coffin excavated at the Drapers' Gardens site, London.
Photo: Pre-Construct Archaeology.

Generally, however, wooden caskets do not survive in anything approaching this intact condition, and they are more likely to be detected archaeologically through other details associated with them. This includes the stains of rotted wood in a rectangle around the body, or, as in the case of the eastern cemetery in Roman London, the rectangular shape of a bed of white chalk (a slurry or powder of marine calcite) which once lay on the bottom of the coffin under, and possibly on, the infant's body.[55] Additionally, the iron nails used to hold together the planks of wood sometimes are all that survives of the coffin, the nails surviving in a rectangle and revealing the shape and size of the original container (Fig. 7.7). Iron nails arranged in a rectangle have been noted in the excavations of many cemeteries.[56] The body of the newborn infant in grave 150 at Gubbio, for example, was surrounded by a rectangle of ten iron nails indicating the shape and size of the coffin.[57] The same was the case for a baby two-and-a-half to three months old at Avenches (en Chaplix);

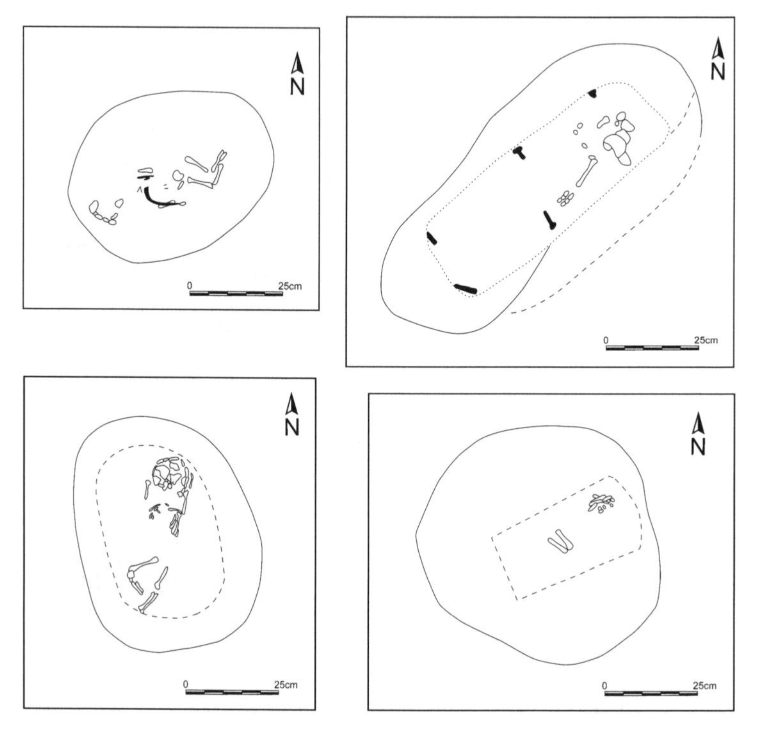

Fig. 7.7 Burial pits and remains of wood coffins for infants at Évreux. The two graves on the right offer the clearest evidence for a coffin, due to the outline of the container and/or the preservation of its nails.

Drawing: Irene de Luis.

[55] Barber and Bowsher 2000, 320–1, figs. 108, 112. This may continue an Iron Age custom of lining infant graves with chalk: Tibbetts 2008, 193.

[56] In Gaul: Argenton (Allain et al. 1992, 92-3, tomb 42); Beaumont (Alfonso and Blaizot 2004, 223–4, fig. 134, grave SP5; 226–8, fig. 137, grave SP7); Lyons-la-Forêt (Dollfus and Guyot 1968); Alesia (Jaeggi 2012a, 230–1, graves 6, 7, 11); in Tunisia: Pupput (De Larminat 2012b, 519–20, fig. 8); in Italy: Vagnari (Small and Small 2007, 180–6, fig. 27, burial F41).

[57] Cipollone 2002, 202, fig. 198.

the rectangle left by the nails where they fell out of the rotting wood is clear.[58] In order to further protect the perishable wooden coffin, it could be placed within another container of more durable material, such as a cist of tiles or tiles, stones and fragmented amphorae.[59] Farwell examined the number of nails associated with wooden coffins for adults and children at Poundbury from the second to fourth century AD (see Table 8), concluding that children of one year or less were buried in coffins with an average of nine nails, whilst the coffins of adults were held together with an average of sixteen nails (for females) and nineteen (for males).[60] Despite the small size of infant coffins, there was a proportionally high outlay of material.

There can be considerable differences in the size of wood coffins. The wood coffins fashioned for infants and very young children at Rottweil in Germany at fifty-five to eighty-five centimetres in length and twenty-five to forty centimetres in width are of a comparable size to those found at the Drapers' Gardens site in London.[61] One of the wood coffins at Colchester Butt Road (grave 503) also fits into this group at seventy by thirty centimetres.[62] At the lower end of the range, however, are coffins at Alesia measuring forty by thirty and forty-five by thirty-three centimetres, at Colchester Abbey Road measuring thirty-five by thirty centimetres, and at Évreux where the coffin in grave 85 was thirty-five by thirteen centimetres.[63] Presumably the difference in proportion has to do with the age of the infant and its size, although the smallest coffin for a perinatal infant at Évreux measures twenty-seven by eighteen centimetres, whilst two slightly premature and smaller babies were contained in larger boxes measuring thirty-two by ten and forty-one by twelve centimetres.[64]

A range of other materials and containers were utilized in infant burials, in addition to the three main categories of ceramic vessels, tiles, and timber. Even metal vessels, such as a bronze bucket, were used.[65] More common, however, are ceramic vessels, such as the lidded ceramic urns (*olla*) used at Pompeii for the cremated remains of infants, children, and adults.[66] Other ceramic containers include a mortarium, a *terra sigillata* bowl, jars, storage vessels such

[58] Castella 1999, 318 (grave ST 444).

[59] Argenton: Allain et al. 1992, 95, fig. 27, tomb 85; Marseille: Moliner et al. 2003, 281, pl. 19, tomb 12, and pp. 64–6.

[60] Farwell and Molleson 1993, 15.

[61] Fecher and Burger-Heinrich 2010, 79–98.

[62] Crummy 2010, 47–8.

[63] Alesia: Jaeggi 2012a, 230–1 (graves 7 and 11); Colchester: Crummy 2010, 38–9 (feature 25); Évreux: Pluton et al. 2008, 255.

[64] Pluton et al. 2008, 256 (grave 126: 27 × 18 cm); 253 (grave 51: 32 × 10 cm); 253–4 (grave 52: 41 × 12 cm).

[65] Vertet 1974, 86.

[66] For a cremated infant in an *olla* at Pompeii (burial no. 10), see Van Andringa et al. 2013, 362, figs. 238, 240. This definitive publication of all the burials in a precinct outside the Porta Nocera contains numerous examples of ceramic cinerary urns.

as *dolia*, a handmade ceramic basin, and two ceramic bee-hives placed end to end.[67] At Chantambre, ceramic urns or jars were used almost exclusively for perinatal or neonatal individuals.[68] Ceramic basins or deep dishes are common as containers at Sousse and nearby sites in north-east Tunisia, and they are also, but far less frequently, represented at Pupput.[69] Occasionally, the same type of vessel was turned upside down on the lower basin to form a kind of sarcophagus. Because of the size of the containers (thirty-six to forty-five centimetres in length) and the poorly preserved human remains or even lack of bones in them, it is assumed that they were primarily intended for premature births or foetuses and for babies dying at birth. Icard was the first to refer to such a vessel as "un grand plat en forme de baignoire", a large dish in the shape of a bath basin.[70] The similarity with a bath basin may be fortuitous, but it is worth considering whether these basins were reused vessels, perhaps originally having been used to give the newborn its first bath or to collect the baby at birth. These basins crop up regularly as containers for infants in the Auvergne in central France as well, where they are interpreted either as reused cooking or storage vessels or as basins made for the care of the baby's personal hygiene.[71]

Stone is another material that could be used to protect the infant body. Stones of various shapes and sizes occasionally were arranged around the body or to line the grave pit, or were combined with amphora fragments, tiles, and stone slabs to make a cist. At Tavant, seven out of twenty-two infants were interred in a sarcophagus made of shelly limestone (see Table 4).[72] At Camí de la Platja del Cossis near Tarragona, a stone sarcophagus formed the outer protective shell of an infant burial; inside the sarcophagus was a second container made of lead.[73] One single limestone sarcophagus was used for a triple burial of two babies seven to nine months old and one infant only four to six months of age at Carnuntum; fragments of wool textiles in this container suggest that one or more of them had been wrapped up in textiles.[74]

Very ephemeral materials used to make containers are sometimes detected in excavations, such as wicker baskets and reed mats in Cambridge.[75] Wicker

[67] Mortarium: Schallmayer 2006, 59, fig. 6 (Schwabmünchen); *terra sigillata* bowl: Allain et al. 1992, 52–3, 170, figs. 36, 64, tomb 74 (Argenton); jars: Hugoniot et al. 1975, 85 (Bruère-Allichamps); *dolium*: Guiot et al. 2003, 103–4, fig. 18 (Langeais); handmade ceramic basin: Alfonso and Blaizot 2004, 254–6, figs. 166–7 (Beaumont, grave SP 32); two ceramic beehives placed end to end: Garland 2001, 78, fig. 17 (Vrana).

[68] Murail and Girard 2000, 107–8.

[69] De Larminat 2012b, 515.

[70] Icard 1904, 165.

[71] Wittmann 2009, 179–80. See a hand-made oval ceramic basin for the burial of a baby at Beaumont (Champ Madame): Alfonso and Blaizot 2004, 254–6, figs. 166–7, grave SP 32.

[72] Riquier and Salé 2006.

[73] Macías and Menchón 2002, 244–5, figs. 9–10.

[74] Schweder and Winkler 2004, 40, 60, 133–5, pls. 28.1–4 (sarcophagus 2).

[75] Struck 1993b, 314; Goodburn et al. 1976, 340–1; Anon. 1978, 58–9.

trays and baskets, equally and perhaps originally at home in domestic contexts, served as burial containers for infants in late Roman Egypt.[76] Of Roman date, although not within the frontiers of the Roman Empire, is the unique second-century burial of an infant aged four to six months in an ovoid trough made of birch wood from Tofting in the marsh area of coastal Schleswig-Holstein in northern Germany.[77] Based on the position of the fragile bones, the excavators concluded that one of the babies at Neftenbach in Switzerland possibly had been buried in a bag of textile or organic material (burial 10).[78]

The rarest type of container used for infants are lead sarcophagi. These sarcophagi, generally dating to the period between the second and the fourth centuries AD, are not distributed widely for either adults or children, probably because they were expensive items that few could afford. Infants in lead sarcophagi are known in Britain, Gaul, and North Africa. The infant in a lead sarcophagus at Arrington Bridge in Cambridgeshire was between ten and eleven months of age, and was inhumed in a wool blanket or wrappings dyed with madder and indigo.[79] Traces of an aromatic resin from the genus *Pistacia*, originating in the Mediterranean or the Levant, were found on the head of the infant, indicating some kind of treatment of the body, possibly one denoting high status.[80] Lead was also used to contain the body of a one-year-old child in Mausoleum R10 in the late Roman cemetery at Poundbury, the lead lining evident in both an outer and inner wooden coffin (see Table 8).[81] The lead sarcophagus used for a child at Avenches (St. 167), aged between one and two years of age, was sixty-eight centimetres long and made of one sheet of lead folded over.[82] The child lay on its back with two glass bowls at foot level. De Larminat, in her survey of child burials in Roman North Africa, flagged up the existence of only four lead sarcophagi used for children in that region, postulating that these must have been the offspring of families who could afford to bury their dead in mausolea or in family enclosures.[83] The age of the youngest of these children is uncertain, but the smallest sarcophagus of only sixty centimetres in length at Thina in Tunisia suggests that this child was an infant.[84]

A type of container that is known exclusively in Roman Egypt is the decorated anthropoid coffin made of wood, and either painted and/or gilded. A Roman mummy coffin of this type from Akhmim contained a mummified

[76] Spieser 2008, 516–17, figs. 2a–b.
[77] Beilke-Voigt 2007; Rubel 2013, 238–9, fig. 2b.
[78] Langenegger 1996, 158, fig. 2; Langenegger 1999, 489–94.
[79] Taylor 1993. The infant was at first claimed to be hydrocephalic, but that was later revised: Brettell et al. 2014, 2.
[80] Brettell et al. 2014. Myrrh and frankincense were found as droplets in the linen wrappings of an infant at Kellis: B542, Wheeler et al. 2011, 114.
[81] Farwell and Molleson 1993, 61, fig. 43 (grave 525).
[82] Castella 1999, 241–2, fig. 231 (grave ST 167).
[83] De Larminat 2012b, 514.
[84] Fortier and Malahar 1910, 96–7.

newborn infant; the body, face, and dress painted on the coffin, however, represent the baby as a little pharaoh or Osiris, god of the dead, with royal attributes and even a beard.[85] This infant is symbolically divinized. From the New Kingdom, terracotta anthropoid coffins were produced for mummified newborns and foetuses, and they continued to be produced into the Roman and late Roman period for infants and babies.[86] The most remarkable wooden containers for foetuses and newborns are the statues, about fifty centimetres tall, in the form of the god Bes; the mummified individual was inserted in a cavity in the back of the statue.[87] Bes had a particular connection with childbirth and young children, and perhaps in this context he was thought to continue to protect even the dead infant.

Part of the preparation for burial could include some kind of dressing or wrapping of the dead, as we have seen. It is, nevertheless, unusual to find physical evidence for textiles in Roman graves, whether they are graves of adults or children. Much of our evidence for textiles in a funerary context is indirect, as it is in the burial of a newborn in a wooden coffin at Avenches (À la Montagne cemetery). A pierced coin with the infant indicates that it had been worn as an amulet, and this coin preserved evidence for a wool blanket in which the child had been wrapped, as a few organic remains stuck very fortuitously to the corrosion on the coin.[88] At Leptiminus in Tunisia, a few small snippets of black(?) textile around a newborn indicate some sort of wrapping or clothing.[89] It is only in Roman Egypt, where the dry heat and sand create ideal conditions for the preservation of organic materials, that we have a better idea of the dressing of the dead through samples of textiles and in some cases whole shrouds and garments. In the East Cemetery at Kellis, all the foetal and perinatal infants were wrapped in pieces of linen cloth, and a single cotton blanket was recovered from the burial of an infant under the age of one year.[90] Although quite late for our consideration here, newborns were wrapped in shrouds of white, blue, red, or green pieces of cloth in the eighth and ninth centuries AD at Tebtunis, this situation almost certainly continuing a much older practice of providing textile protection for the little bodies.[91]

Impressions of swaddling bands and bonnets or head coverings are sometimes preserved in plaster and gypsum in graves and sarcophagi. At a number of Roman sites in Tunisia, such as Carthage, Kef, and Haïdra, liquid or soft plaster and chalk were either poured over the bodies of adults and children once they were in the grave, or the grave was filled with liquid plaster and the bodies plunged into it; in either case, outlines of the bodies and the textiles in

85 Spieser 2008, 537–8, fig. 18.
86 Spieser 2008, 538–40, figs. 19–20.
87 Spieser 2008, 541–2, fig. 21.
88 Blanc 2002, 155, fig. 11.
89 Ben Lazreg and Mattingly 1992, 214.
90 Wheeler et al. 2011, 113; Wheeler 2012, 228.
91 Gallazzi and Hadji-Minaglou 2012, 395, figs. 8–9.

which they were wrapped are left as negative imprints.[92] These plaster baths were employed for children also at Pupput, albeit rarely, preserving the body outline and shape of the now decomposed wood coffin of a child two or three years old and the remains of infants in amphorae, one of them a prematurely born baby and the other an infant of six months.[93] These plaster impressions, however, are not as clear as some examples of similar treatment of infants in Britain and Germany. A late Roman sandstone sarcophagus from York no longer contains the skeletal remains of its inhabitants, but the practice of pouring liquid gypsum or plaster over bodies has preserved the impressions in the hardened gypsum of two adults and an infant in the container (Fig. 7.8).[94] The baby had been wrapped in bandages that encircled its body, head, legs, and feet. In late Roman Trier, as a result of a similar process of pouring gypsum or plaster on bodies in sarcophagi, the negative form of a very small child has survived.[95] The modern plaster cast of this form shows that the

Fig. 7.8 Negative impressions of two adults (whose legs are visible here) and an infant wrapped in textiles, as preserved in gypsum in a sarcophagus from Roman York.
Photo: Maureen Carroll/Collection: York Museums Trust (YORYM: 2007.6126).

[92] De Larminat 2012b, 505–6. [93] De Larminat 2012b, 510–11, 522–3, figs. 4, 9.
[94] Henshall 1962; Carroll 2012b: 138–40, pl. 21.
[95] Cüppers 1984, 212; Schallmayer 2006, 63, fig. 11.

infant was tightly and completely wrapped in diagonally wound textile bands from head to toe. Its face was also enveloped in fabric, which, of course, it would not have been in life.

But also the position of the body may shed light on the use of shrouds or swaddling clothes for dead babies, as a textile wrapping would have held the individual body parts together during decomposition. Perinatal infants at Évreux in Normandy, for example, were buried in the foetal position in the first century AD, and some of them appear to have been relatively tightly wrapped in a shroud of some kind.[96] The deposition of bone and bronze pins near the legs of infants and young children in Roman Gaul and Italy may also indicate that they had been wrapped in a shroud and fastened with a pin.[97] It is difficult to ascertain whether an infant was simply wrapped in textile or enveloped in swaddling bands at the time of burial, but Duday opted for the latter in the case of a newborn buried in the floor of the pottery workshop at Sallèles d'Aude, because the limbs of the baby were positioned parallel to its body, which would be consistent with swaddling.[98] The contracted posture and the lack of bone movement in the components of the bodies of a pre-term infant and a baby less than three months at Laquenexy suggest that both individuals had decomposed within a textile bag or shroud.[99]

INVESTMENT AND EXPENSE

The types of containers and materials used to bury the most vulnerable in Roman society must be considered in the context of expense and attention paid to funerary treatment. Some containers were specifically made for infants, such as the small lead and timber coffins and the Egyptian mummy coffins. The made-to-order nature of these coffins reveals anything but a disinterest in giving infants an adequate burial. Lead and timber coffins, and mummy cases, of course, were also made in larger formats for adult corpses, and it is clear that there was an industry for the production of burial containers that was capable of adjusting sizes to suit even the smallest occupant. However, none of the other containers discussed in this chapter were custom made for infants, although many of them show evidence of having been altered in ways that involve an input of labour and time to render them appropriate in size or shape for the burial of tiny corpses.

[96] Pluton et al. 2008, 252–3 (grave 47); 253 (grave 50); 253 (grave 51); 253–4 (grave 52); 257 (grave 126).

[97] Riquier and Salé 2006, 23–7, figs. 19–22 (Tavant, grave 5); Cipollone 2002, 202, 203–5, figs. 198, 199a (Gubbio, tombs 150, 151); Small and Small 2007, 144, 191–5, fig. 36 (Vagnari, burial F43).

[98] Duday 2009, 63–9.

[99] Brkojewitsch et al. 2014, 222–3, fig. 6.

This is the case for amphora burials, all of the amphorae clearly having been used for their primary purpose as containers for edible commodities before being opened, sometimes reduced in size, and reused as a burial vessel.[100] It is difficult, if not impossible, to estimate what the cost of procuring a used amphora might have been, and in coastal and riverine places such as Rome, Ostia, or Marseille, where amphorae entered the harbours and docks in large shipments to be emptied of their contents, there was an extensive supply of this commodity. But whether used amphorae actually were to be had free of charge, as de Larminat suggests, or whether they had to be purchased from the docks, merchants, or distributors, is unclear.[101] The small amphorae used for baby burials at Chartres were seconds and of lesser quality than those found in domestic contexts, and Portat et al. suggest that they were chosen to serve a secondary purpose as burial containers for that reason.[102] But the reuse of amphorae was not just a cheap solution for disposing of individuals, such as babies, who might be thought of as relatively unimportant in social terms, because amphorae were also used for older children and adults. Also the tile and brick deposited in *alla cappuccina* and cist burials of infants in Italy and elsewhere is a material that was produced primarily for use in roofing domestic and public buildings. Second-hand and even fragmentary brick and tile from ruinous or dismantled buildings cannot have been very costly to procure, but we neither understand the mechanisms of this procurement, nor do we have any information about prices for this material. But it, too, is not just a shoddy solution for the disposal of infants and the very young, as older children and adults are also buried under and on top of tiles in many places throughout the second and third centuries AD. Brick and tile are widespread and clearly appropriate for regular burials of all ages. And, finally, the scraps and pieces of textile used to wrap the foetuses and infants at Kellis 2 seem to be offcuts and remnants of the clothing of adults, rather than pieces of specially woven burial shrouds.[103] The latter appear to be reserved for adults, although adults, too, were sometimes wrapped in remnants of whatever textiles were available.

GRAVE GOODS AND OFFERINGS

In Chapter 4, objects of material culture were discussed in the context of feeding, clothing, protecting, entertaining, and socialising the youngest members of society. A considerable amount of knowledge about these things, in

[100] The amphora in burial 24 at Porta Nocera in Pompeii possibly had been broken before it was used: Van Andringa et al. 2013, 327.

[101] De Larminat 2012b, 516.

[102] Portat et al. 2013.

[103] Wheeler et al. 2011, 113–14.

effect, comes from the funerary context. Without wishing to duplicate the information in that chapter here, and keeping in mind that there is considerable diversity in the types of grave goods and offerings in infant graves, it is important to examine the full range of things deposited with the infant at death, as this allows us to recognize parental and familial expressions of affection and loss and to explore artefacts that may have been chosen to compensate for a life cut short. Studying the grave goods in burials also enables us to recognize potential cultural differences in the type of things given to infants in death and whether their absence or presence is related to local and regional customs. The rarity of grave goods in infant burials at Poundbury, for example, is striking, but, given that these children were frequently interred in wood coffins made for them, the lack of objects in the graves cannot be interpreted as a reflection of the low value placed on children this young (see Table 8). It was simply not customary at this site in Britain to include objects in the burials of babies.

Amuletic jewellery is often found in the grave in a position relevant to the original part of the body on which the objects were worn. Amulets and *crepundia* are found on the clavicle, near the neck and head, suggesting that these were part of necklaces.[104] But the infant was not always wearing amuletic jewellery when it was buried; instead, the discovery of amulets of various kinds in a little heap near the feet, or near the hand, or outside the burial container may indicate that objects were once put in a cloth bag and placed in the grave.[105]

Some grave goods appear to have been intended to ease the passage from life to death, and even the negotiation of the afterlife. Coins placed in the hand or mouth of the deceased to pay the ferryman, Charon, for passage across the Styx are known from adult graves throughout Italy and the Roman provinces. In rare cases, they are found in precisely the same physical position in graves of infants, suggesting that their passage into the afterlife was perceived in a similar manner. At Fidene, for example, an inhumed child of one year had a coin (an *as* of Domitian) in its mouth, as did an infant the same age at Roman Marseille.[106] At Alesia (Mont Auxois), the infant in grave 7 still held a coin of Claudius in its left hand.[107] An unusual case is the infant in grave 289 at Lankhills in Britain who was buried with three coins in its mouth.[108] Also,

[104] Marseille: Moliner et al. 2003, 172, 309, pl. 31, grave 169. This infant had a group of amulets around the head, and another group on the level of its lower limbs, suggesting perhaps a necklace, still strung, and another bag of amulets. Kempten: Mackensen 1978a, 57, grave 212.

[105] Near the feet: Hintermann 2000, 275–6, pl. 46 (Vindonissa, grave 93-100); Moliner et al. 2003, 172, 380–1, pl. 61 (Marseille, grave 534, possibly a two-year-old); or near the hand: Crummy 2010, 47–8, fig. 10 (Colchester Butt Road, grave 503); or outside the burial container, possibly once in a little bag: Riquier and Salé 2006, 47–9, figs. 52–5 (Tavant, grave 15).

[106] Fidene: Ceci 2001, 81–96; Marseille: Moliner et al. 2003, 357, pl. 54 (tomb 409).

[107] Jaeggi 2012a, 230, 236 (grave 7).

[108] Crummy 2010, 66.

extremely young babies could be buried with coins. At Soissons, a possible stillborn infant was found with a coin in its mouth, and, perhaps even more remarkably, two coins found next to the head of a prematurely born infant suggest that it had been buried with a coin on each eye.[109]

In other cases, it is not certain whether the coins in burials represent ferry money if they are simply scattered or not placed in the grave in close contact with the infant. Coins do not seem to have been put in the graves because of their monetary value, and many of them were, actually, quite old when they went into the ground. Most of the coins with infants under the age of one year in the cemetery at Mainz-Weisenau were already between ten and twenty years old when they were deposited in the graves.[110] Coins in the fourth-century child burials at Colchester were quite a bit older, dating to the second and third centuries AD.[111] Crummy suggested that the coins in these graves at Colchester were chosen for the reverse images of male and female deities and personifications, all of which symbolically acted as guardians and substitute parents for the dead children, but no such pattern could be recognized at Marseille.[112] According to Perassi, a female allegorical figure, such as *Felicitas*, on a coin reverse would have been chosen intentionally for deposition in child burials, as she represented a maternal protector, and this interpretation is applied by Jaeggi to an infant burial at Alesia in which a coin of Vespasian with *Felicitas* on the reverse was found.[113]

Lamps also might be interpreted as something for use in the afterlife or to light up the dark in the world of the dead. Children older than six months in Italy occasionally have ceramic oil lamps in their assemblages, and they are not uncommon in infant graves in Gaul and Germany, but they never are regularly deposited with them.[114] They might, in some places, have been deemed appropriate even for premature or newborn babies, as at Sétif; the clay lamp in grave 49 had traces of soot on it, indicating that it had been used before deposition with the baby (see Table 7).[115] At Soissons, the newborn in grave 742 was buried with a ceramic oil lamp at its feet.[116] One infant under six months at Beaumont was given something much rarer, an iron hanging lamp.[117]

[109] Gissinger 2012, 19, fig. 13.

[110] Witteyer and Fasold 1995, 30, cat. no. 7: a coin of Tiberius in a grave of *c.* AD 50; 55, cat. no. 28, grave 68: a Claudian coin in a grave of *c.* AD 70–90; 55, cat. no. 29, grave 71: a coin of Vespasian in a burial dating to *c.* AD 75–90.

[111] Crummy 2010, 62–6. [112] Moliner et al. 2003, 173; Crummy 2010, 60, 69–74.

[113] Perassi 1999, 66; Jaeggi 2012a, 237.

[114] Rome, Osteria del Curato IV: Egidi et al. 2003 (tomb 103); Gubbio: Cipollone 2002, 208, fig. 203 (tomb 156); Mainz-Weisenau: Witteyer and Fasold 1995, 25, cat. no. 5 (grave 40); 55, cat. no. 28 (grave 68).

[115] Guéry 1985, 83, fig. 71. [116] Gissinger 2012, 20, figs. 15–16.

[117] Alfonso and Blaizot 2004, 228–32, figs. 140, 142 (SP 8); Blaizot 2009, 178, fig. on p. 178.

One other offering may be associated with funerary rituals and rites of passage, namely the *balsamarium* or small flask of ceramic or glass. In Roman Marseille, almost 61 per cent of the glass found in the graves of individuals of all ages in the Sainte-Barbe necropolis is made up of *balsamaria*.[118] They are known widely throughout the Roman world in adult graves, and they crop up in infant graves too. In the Valladas cemetery of Augusta Tricastinorum, one of the infants buried with an adult had been given a feeding bottle, a cup, and a *balsamarium*; these were nicely separated from the offerings for the adult which consisted of thirteen vessels, a lamp, and six *balsamaria*.[119] The glass *balsamaria* buried with infants at Mainz-Weisenau have been interpreted as remnants of a ritual performed by the survivors that would have involved pouring a liquid sacrifice over the body when taking leave of it, just before the grave was closed.[120] This is entirely possible when the glass flasks are placed outside the coffin, as at Tavant, and when objects lie outside and on top of the container, as at Alesia (grave 11) where a glass *balsamarium*, three *fibulae*, and burnt animal offerings were revealed on its lid.[121] But when a glass *balsamarium* and ceramic jug are carefully placed at the feet of an infant in a wood coffin, as in the En Chaplix cemetery at Avenches, it may also be that the vessels were given to the child for its future needs in the afterlife.[122]

It was not very common to bury infants in Roman Italy with items of food and drink. There are no food offerings in any of the infant burials in the suburban cemeteries of Rome at Osteria del Curato or Lucrezia Romana, for example, and such offerings in Pompeii are meagre and simple.[123] Sometimes we can infer by the type of ceramic vessels in the graves whether liquids or solids were involved, but, when the actual remains of food survive no guesswork is needed. A one-year-old infant in the Via Triumphalis cemetery on Vatican hill was interred with a chicken egg, although the excavators have focused more on the rebirth symbolism of the egg, than on its role as a food offering.[124] When edible grave goods are published as part of the grave assemblage, as at Nave in Lombardy, the skeletal remains might not be aged any more precisely than *infans* I (under six years), so it is difficult to know whether food offerings were more customary for older children than for babies. Nevertheless, the range of edible commodities is broad, as, for example, in tomb 19, where the excavators recovered sheep/goat bones, as well as evidence for a wide range of cereals (barley, wheat), fruits (figs), vegetables (broad beans), and nuts (walnuts, hazelnuts).[125] The deposition of vessels associated

[118] Moliner et al. 2003, 137. [119] Bel 1992, 110.

[120] Witteyer and Fasold 1995, 25.

[121] Tavant: Riquier and Salé 2006, 56–7, figs. 66–8 (grave 20); Alesia: Jaeggi 2012a, 231, 235, fig. 14.

[122] Castella 1999, 314–15, figs. 289–90 (grave ST 370). [123] Lepetz 2012, 322.

[124] Liverani and Spinola 2010, 64–6, fig. 65.

[125] Passi Pitcher 1987, 40, fig. on p. 41. There were also bones of a sheep or goat in the tomb.

with food and drink is also not very common in infant graves in Italy. These include individual feeding bottles in graves at Portorecanati.[126] An early second-century burial of a neonate at Urbino (Marche) contained two *terra sigillata* plates (form Dragendorff 31) and two ceramic cups.[127] A cup formed part of the burial assemblages of newborns at Gubbio.[128]

In contrast to the situation in Roman Italy, the inclusion of food and drink, and the vessels used for them, can be studied particularly well in Roman Gaul. Of the sixty infants at Kempten, twenty-four were given one or two ceramic jugs, fourteen had one or more bowls, and three were accompanied by plates (see Table 6). Especially notable is the little set of one *terra sigillata* bowl, one *terra sigillata* plate, and a beaker buried in the early first century AD with each of the two perinatal babies in grave 95.[129] One of the perinatal infants at Chantambre was buried with a feeding bottle.[130] Feeding bottles also accompanied children who had not yet been weaned, for example a child of between the ages of one and a half and two years at Roman Rottweil.[131] At the rural cemetery at Tavant, many babies were buried with offerings of food, ranging from joints of pork and mutton and cuts of chicken, to a whole chicken egg and/or vessels for food and drink, such as beakers, bowls, plates, jugs, and pots (see Table 5).[132] One of the cuts of pork in grave 5 was from a young pig, the bones showing traces of butchery, but no evidence of having been cooked in a fire. Some of the vessels clearly had been used before deposition in the grave; these include a pot with soot on it in grave 7, a used feeding bottle, and a mixture of used and new beakers, bowls, and jugs in graves 15 and 20. These grave goods most often were put together as a package in a ceramic storage vessel, a *dolium*, separate from the burial container.

Food and food containers are also present in the rural cemetery at Beaumont (see Table 4).[133] Five of the twenty-seven infants here were interred with food, as witnessed by the bones of pigs and sheep or goats. Ten of the Beaumont babies had one or more jugs with them; four had drinking vessels,

[126] Cipollone 2002, 252–4, figs. 112, 140–1, 144 (tomb 70, a neonate), and also 284, figs. 154, 183, 191 (tomb 119, a child).

[127] Mercando et al. 1982, 163–4, figs. 43–4 (tomb 37).

[128] Cipollone 2002, 62–3, figs. 62–3 (tomb 43); 202, fig. 198 (tomb 150).

[129] Mackensen 1978a, 166, 226, pl. 178.1 (grave 95).

[130] Girard 1997, 218 (grave 241).

[131] Fecher and Burger-Heinrich 2010, 99–100, pl. 105 (grave 223). See also 142, pl. 152, grave 383, a grave of a small child (the skeleton had disappeared) with a feeding bottle; and 174, pl. 193, grave 501 of a baby three to nine months old with a feeding bottle. Elsewhere, in the necropolis near the port at Avenches, an infant four to six months of age in a wooden coffin appears to have been given a feeding bottle, although the vessel was not immediately next to the burial: Castella 1987, 84–6, figs. 84–8 (grave 32).

[132] Riquier and Salé 2006: for example, 23–7, figs. 19–22 (grave 5); 29–31, figs. 27–30 (grave 7); 34–6, figs. 34–6 (grave 9); 37–8, figs. 37–9 (grave 10); 91, fig. 97 (grave 11); 91 (grave 16); 53–5, 91, figs. 62–4 (grave 18).

[133] Alfonso and Blaizot 2004.

and the two tripod pots suggest that also typical Gallic cooking vessels were part of the provision. Two babies had a feeding bottle and another was buried with two feeding bottles.[134] A child between twelve and eighteen months of age at Soissons was particularly well provisioned with food (Fig. 7.9).[135] Here, in grave 964, a complete chicken had been placed along the left side of a child, on top of a cut of pork from a young pig (part of the vertebra). There were also three pots that perhaps once contained liquids or stews and a large plate, now also empty. Cuts of meat—chicken and pork—were found in several of the infant graves at Kempten.[136] A crusty mass in grave 230 of a child under six (*infans* I) at Kempten has been interpreted as pablum or porridge-like material.[137] Food was not only placed in inhumation burials, but also burned on the pyre. The neonate in grave 82A at Worms, for example, had several jugs, cups, and a beaker buried with it, as well as cuts of pork and poultry which had been exposed to fire.[138]

A food offering is presumably what the snails in infant graves at Lyons-la-Forêt in Normandy represent. In the graves of these babies, buried possibly in the fourth century in the remains of a second-century theatre at this site, a variety of land snails was found, including *helix nemoralis*, *helix limbata*, *hyalinia cellaria*, and *cyclostoma elegans*.[139] Graves 2, 3, 5, and 6 contained these snails, usually just one or two, although there were five in grave 6 and many more in grave 2. In this burial, an infant less than two months old had eight snails arranged around the body and there was a concentration of ninety-eight snail shells just outside the grave pit, as if they had been gathered there in a heap or been kept in a now decomposed bag or container of organic material. Whilst live snails can find their way into graves to consume what is buried within, the way these snails were found is highly suggestive of the remains of a meal or meals for the infants, especially because two of the graves also contained a single oyster shell which can only be the remains of a food offering. In addition, two tusks and a bone of a wild boar, as well as a cow molar, were found in graves 5 and 6 which might point to meat offerings.

It is interesting to note that not all of the animal bones in the funerary context of infant burials come from animals that would have provided meat for human consumption. At Argenton, for example, in addition to bones of

[134] Alfonso and Blaizot 2004, 226–8, fig. 137 (SP 7); 246–8, figs. 156–7 (SP 22); 258, fig. 170 (SP 40).

[135] Gissinger 2012, 22–3, 43, fig. 21; Lepetz 2012, 322–4, figs. 9–10.

[136] Mackensen 1978a, 172–7.

[137] Mackensen 1978a, 172, 266, grave 230.

[138] Grünewald 1990, 20. The burnt pig bones in the grave of an infant younger than a year in grave 91B at Worms (Grünewald 1990, 20) indicate that the food had been cremated with the infant.

[139] Dollfus and Guyot 1968. Other finds included a glass aryballos, a glass bracelet, and a coin of Constantine II.

Fig. 7.9 Excavated burial of an inhumed infant with food, including a complete chicken (to the right of the infant) and a cut of pork, as well as vessels for food and drink, Soissons.

Photo: Bastien Gissinger, Conseil Générale de l'Aisne.

pigs, cows, horses, and chickens, two complete dog skeletons were recovered, as well as a dog skull (see Table 3).[140] Also at Kempten, a baby was buried in

[140] Allain et al. 1992, 92–3, tomb 39, dog skeleton; 92, tomb 41, dog skull; 95, tomb 82-83, dog skeleton.

grave 413/414 with a dog in a wooden coffin.[141] It is tempting to associate the dog skeletons with family pets, as Faber does, referring to the dog at Kempten as the baby's playmate and protector.[142] Certainly the baby in a cradle with its pet dog is a motif seen in Hellenistic and Roman figurines (see Fig. 4.8).[143]

At some sites, individual animal teeth can be found in infant graves; these include pig and cow teeth.[144] It is unknown whether these single teeth were part of a meat offering or had a more symbolic meaning. However, individual teeth that have a hole drilled in them can be interpreted as amulets, especially when they are found *in situ* with other types of amulets (see Figs. 4.12, 4.13, 4.16, bottom row). Drilled animal teeth are most frequently dog teeth, or those of wild animals, but the teeth of domesticates, such as bovids (cattle, sheep/goat), also occur as amulets.[145] A wider range of amuletic jewellery is discussed in Chapter 4.

Objects of personal adornment and jewellery of precious metals are extremely rare in infant graves. Items made of gold include simple finger rings and earrings, as found with newborns and children between one and two years of age at Sétif, in the suburbs of Rome, and at Urbino.[146] In some cases, jewellery of gold accompanied that made of bronze and various other materials, as at Rec de Ligno à Valros, where an infant only a few months old was buried not only with an amulet necklace, but also with two gold finger rings, a gold bracelet, a bronze bracelet, a bronze ring, a bronze *fibula*, and two discs made of antler.[147] Silver jewellery also appears very rarely in the form of a lunula pendant and other necklace pendants.[148] And it was not always female infants who wore jewellery. The child twelve to eighteen months of age at Douch in Egypt, who may have been a boy and died from a blow to the head, wore a bronze earring in each ear.[149]

Much rarer jewellery and dress accessories include anklets made of iron, found only in Algeria and Tunisia, where even infants only a few months old

[141] Faber 1998, 155–8, graves 413 and 414.

[142] Faber 1998, 157–8. For a dog buried with an adult and two children at Clermont-Ferrand (Pâtural) in the first century AD, see Foucras 2014.

[143] Graepler 1997, 107 (fn. 202), 111 (fn. 230), 229, fig. 263 (grave 64); Deyts 2004, 234, figs. 6–7. A baby in Rottweil was buried with a terracotta dog figurine: Fecher and Burger-Heinrich 2010, 99–100, pl. 105, grave 223.

[144] Cipollone 2002, 208, fig. 203, tomb 156, pig tooth; 240, fig. 233d, tomb 190, pig tooth (Gubbio); Allain et al. 1992, 90–1, tomb 29, pig tooth (Argenton); Mackensen 1978a, 206, grave 18, cow tooth (Kempten); De Larminat 2012b, 509, pig tooth, boar tooth (Tipasa).

[145] Bel 2012, 204, fig. 14.

[146] Egidi et al. 2003, two gold earrings (Rome, Lucrezia Romana I, tomb 117); Mercando et al. 1982, 135–42, figs. 17, 20a, 21–5, gold finger ring (Urbino, tomb 13); Guéry 1985, 287, fig. 330c, pl. 71 (Sétif).

[147] Bel 2012, 199, 202, fig. 11.

[148] For example, at Rottweil: Fecher and Burger-Heinrich 2010, 174, pl. 193, grave 501, silver lunula pendant; and Rome, Via Lucrezia Romana I: Egidi et al. 2003, 86, cat. no. 19, tomb 42.

[149] Dunand et al. 1992, 124, 196, 214, pls. 29, 48.1–3.

were buried with this jewellery still in place.[150] *Fibulae* as dress accessories are associated normally with clothing worn by adults or older children, and they are very rarely associated with children under the age of one. A *fibula* was retrieved from the burial of an infant three to six months old at Sallèles d'Aude, for example, and a group of three *fibulae*, one of which was silver-washed, were objects in the burial of a perinatal infant at Alesia.[151] The single example from Sallèles d'Aude may have held a shroud in place and, therefore, were functional in death, but the *fibulae* at Alesia were placed outside and on top of the coffin of the infant, suggesting that their inclusion had symbolic value, rather than a practical purpose.

The evidence marshalled here has shed light on the ways in which infants could be afforded special treatment based on their tender age. It has also shown that there were regional and possibly cultural differences in the deposition of a range of various grave goods accompanying infants, some of which point to an expression of deep loss and a material compensation for unfinished lives. Information on the age and status of, and aspirations for, those same unfinished lives is provided in Roman funerary commemoration, the meaning and context of which is the focus of Chapter 8.

[150] Guéry 1985, 259–60, 267, 287; De Larminat 2012b, 508.

[151] Sallèles: Duday et al. 1995, 43, fig. 18 (grave 4); Alesia: Jaeggi 2012a, 231, 235, fig. 14 (grave 11). The baby younger than six months in grave 212 at Kempten was also buried with an iron *fibula*: Mackensen 1978a, 154, 259, pl. 86.5.

8

Funerary Commemoration of Infants

AGE AT DEATH IN EPITAPHS

Children sometimes, but by no means regularly, were commemorated with a funerary monument, and these have been used in various ways to explore aspects of Roman childhood. Brent Shaw calculated that 27.7 per cent of funerary inscriptions with an age indication from Rome were for children below the age of ten years, demonstrating clearly that children are not under-represented there in the epigraphic record.[1] However, statistics show that only about 1.3 per cent of the tens of thousands of inscribed funerary monuments from Rome and Italy record the deaths of babies younger than a year.[2] Of the approximately 30,000 surviving funerary inscriptions in the city of Rome, only 109 (0.35 per cent) commemorate children under the age of one, with no evident difference in quantity in regard to the sex of the infant.[3] Infants younger than one year have a stronger presence in the assemblages of funerary inscriptions at Ostia (2.1 per cent), Lyon (2.2 per cent), and Caesarea Mauretaniae (2.8 per cent), for example, although there are less of them than those for children over a year in age.[4] So one could say that the very youngest children are indeed under-represented in the epigraphic record, but to conclude that this is a reflection of their lack of value in society would be erroneous and misleading. In fact, to argue this way would be to ignore that an under-representation in funerary commemoration is apparent in general for any population of any Roman town at any time. Not everyone had a tombstone or a monument with an inscription, for a whole range of reasons, regardless of the age of the individual. This makes age at death information in inscriptions of limited value for demographic studies. And even when older

[1] Shaw 1991, 74–6. [2] Hopkins 1983, 225.

[3] Carroll 2011a, 111, fig. 7; King 2000, 125, came to a similar conclusion (0.4 per cent, that is 128 inscriptions out of 29,250). I calculated only about 1 per cent of the commemorative inscriptions from the Isola Sacra cemetery at Portus to have been for children less than a year old, but that rises to 9.4 per cent when these infants are included in all the inscriptions to children: Carroll 2006, 173.

[4] Laes 2014, 133, table 1.

children or adults are routinely under-represented or are simply absent, an argument is never put forward that anyone who was twenty, or thirty, or sixty and was not commemorated had not been loved or part of a community or social group. It seems that, in modern scholarship, the so-called lack of attachment to individuals is used solely in conjunction with the thin epigraphic evidence for children of a very young age. If infants are under-represented in funerary commemoration, there were clearly other factors at play and we need to try to ascertain what they were and what the commemoration of very young children reveals to us about their familial and social context, their value and role, and the emotions elicited in those left behind.

Stone markers represent a financial outlay, although prices would have varied, depending on the material, skill of the stone-cutter, length of the inscription, and the elaborateness of the memorial.[5] But they always would have been beyond the possibilities of the poor who may just have been able to find the money to bury the child properly and nothing more. Equally, it may not have been the cultural custom in some families or some regions to commemorate the dead with permanent stone monuments, so the absence of memorials for infants in the archaeological record may reflect something other than available funds. The low numbers of inscribed monuments for children under one year in various Roman cities cited above indicate that it was not necessarily to be expected that an inscribed stone would be commissioned and erected, and, for that reason, families who did so demonstrated their will to preserve the memory of a loved child. Christian Laes, in his study on the youngest children in Latin epigraphy, demonstrates clearly that the decision to erect an inscribed stone for an infant less than a year old was considered very special.[6] If the commemorator is named, most frequently it was the parents who jointly commissioned and set up a memorial, followed by the father as the only named dedicator and then the mother, but occasionally grandparents or the child's *nutrix* are named as commemorators.[7] Among the infant inscriptions in the city of Rome, however, many are individual commemorations in which only the child is named, the parents and other commemorators foregoing the advertisement of their own status in favour of the prominence of the infant.[8]

The engraved monuments of infants and very young children are generally very specific about the age of the deceased, a device that may have been intended to highlight the pathos involved. The fact that Titus Flavius Eunianus died a day before the milestone of his first birthday was probably very poignant, especially since the child was free-born and a citizen, unlike his parents who had once been slaves.[9] Little Diadumenus also had almost

[5] Susini 1973; Duncan-Jones 1974; Carroll 2006, 77–8.

[6] Laes 2014, 134.

[7] Grandparents (*CIL* VI.17557, *CIL* VI.35377), a child's *nutrix* (*CIL* VI.16587, *CIL* VI.17157, *CIL* VI.28120).

[8] King 2000, 140.

[9] *CIL* VI.18053.

reached his first birthday, but died at eleven months, twenty-four days, and eight hours.[10] Some inscriptions are even more detailed and represent the special commissioning of a unique memorial specifically for the child commemorated. The son of Troilus and Pia in Rome died at one year, nine months, six days, and six hours; Cartillia Actilia in Rome lived only one year, eight months, one day, and two hours; and the boy Pagus died in the same city at nine months, four days, and six hours.[11] Somewhat surprisingly, another little boy in Rome is recorded as having lived only one year, three months, twenty days, and two-and-a-*half* hours, the latter detail being particularly specific.[12] Lucius Valerius in Rome was taken at the age of seventy-one days, and the inscription provides the additional information that he had been born during the night in the sixth hour and he died during the night in the sixth hour.[13]

Now this kind of precision is also interesting in the context of the general statement of ages on Roman funerary inscriptions. Richard Duncan-Jones has concluded that on many occasions, the inscribed age at death is divisible by five and that this reflects age-rounding that can be attributed to widespread illiteracy and/or the educational standards of different social classes.[14] According to his data, age-rounding was most prevalent amongst people of servile birth and soldiers of low status, but the highest social group represented in the epigraphic material, the town councillors, were the least likely to round up or round down their ages because they, as members of the educated elite, showed an age-awareness.[15] The vast majority of the infants commemorated with an inscribed stone in this study, however, did not come from upper class, elite families, suggesting perhaps that the specific ages given in their epitaphs reflect something special in the general scheme of funerary epigraphy. Perhaps not only the poignancy of such an early death is to be read into the inscriptions, but also the idea that the family was taking greater care to remember the very young or to express a great loss and attachment to those so vulnerable. And, of course, the more recent the birth of the child, the greater the chance that the stated age at death is accurate, because it was very much still in people's memory. In the end, even if we cannot be certain that the very detailed age at death on funerary monuments to infants is accurate, it should not be dismissed simply as spurious precision or attributed to epigraphic convention.[16]

[10] *CIL* VI.16836. Sometimes, the second birthday seems to have been another milestone, indicated by the very exact ages given: *CIL* VI.20786, a boy of one year, eleven months, sixteen days, and two hours; *CIL* VI.21232, a girl of one year, eleven months, ten days, and eleven hours.

[11] The son of Troilus and Pia: *CIL* VI.14793; Cartillia Actilia: *CIL* VI.14448; Pagus: *CIL* VI.23726.

[12] *CIL* VI.17540.

[13] *CIL* VI.28044 and *Inscriptiones Latinae Selectae* (*ILS*) 8191.

[14] Duncan-Jones 1977, 334–5. [15] Duncan-Jones 1977, 338.

[16] Bodel 1995, 455, 459. Bodel is not commenting on the infant epitaphs here, but he does doubt the accuracy of age statements in funerary epigraphy in rhetorical and cultural contexts.

A very young baby, Vernaclus, lived only nine days and was commemorated in Cologne in the second or third century AD.[17] Vernaclus is referred to as *filius*, so it is clear that Lucius Cassius Tacitus, who set up the marker, is the boy's father, but the child's name might mean "little house-born slave", the diminutive of *verna*; in this case, however, it should, if correctly spelled, be *vernaculus*.[18] But it begs the question why the man would have named his son "little slave" unless he himself was a slave and his status was inherited by the child. Lucius Cassius Tacitus, however, is not a slave name, but a name of a Roman citizen (either free-born or freed), formulated as a *trianomina*. In addition, Vernaclus certainly existed as a personal name, and was used, for example, by Quintus Aemilius Vernaclus in Munigua.[19] Thus, I am inclined to think that the infant's full name would have been Lucius(?) Cassius Vernaclus and that he had just been given his name on his naming day or *dies lustricus*—the ninth day after birth—when he died.

Very occasionally, even babies who died *before* their official naming day were commemorated by name. Perhaps these children were very ill from the day of birth, and a name was chosen for them quickly, before the requisite naming ceremony. Sextus Bebius Stolo's *trianomina* is inscribed as an indication of his citizenship and free birth; he only lived four days and ten hours.[20] His father, a sailor in the Roman fleet in Misenum, and his mother commemorated him. In the same city, but in the Christian period, Aemilius Eulalius was named and commemorated at the age of only eight days, although the *dies lustricus* would have taken place a day later.[21] Even younger is the boy Simplicius who appears to have died in Rome in AD 364 on the same day he was born, having possibly lived for only an hour.[22] Since this epitaph was found in the excavations of the mithraeum under the church of Santa Prisca and is of the Christian period, the baby might have been given urgent Christian baptism as a blameless and innocent soul.[23] In Rome, the freedwoman Julia Donata included the specific information in the epitaph of her son that he had been given a name before he died, presumably on his *dies lustricus*, but does not say what it was.[24]

As we have seen in Chapter 3, once the baby exited the womb and was given its first bath, was swaddled and fed, it had an identity and was part of the family. The *dies lustricus* represented an official, legal, and social convention of recognizing

[17] *CIL* XIII.8375; Galsterer and Galsterer 1975, cat. no. 373, pl. 83; Faust 1998, cat. no. 110, pl. 8.3; Carroll 2006, 172, fig. 58.

[18] On *vernae*, see Sigismund-Nielsen 2013, 293–6.

[19] *AE* 1966.163. [20] *CIL* X.3547; Laes 2014, 141, Italy 2.

[21] *Inscriptiones Christianae Urbis Romae* (*ICUR*) 5.13984; Laes 2014, 135, Christian Rome 9.

[22] *ICUR* 6.15587; Laes 2014, 135, Christian Rome 1. A consular date allows us to fix the year exactly.

[23] Vermaseren and van Essen 1965, 121.

[24] *CIL* VI.20427 and *ILS* 8480; Laes 2014, 134, Rome 3.

the infant's name in the context of the larger community, but there is no reason to assume that pagan or Christian parents had not already chosen their child's name before it was born or that they did not use it before it was ritually fixed.

EXPRESSIONS OF GRIEF AND LOSS

Margaret King's study of the funerary inscriptions set up for children in the city of Rome suggests that the gender, status, and class of a child did not necessarily influence the chances of it being commemorated, and that the decision to commemorate was not a simple material consideration.[25] Even the slave status of some infants did not always preclude them from being remembered with an inscription. Epitaphs in Rome, for example, record slave boys a little older than one year, a one-year-old daughter (Socratia) of an imperial slave, and a house-born slave (*verna*) six months and twenty-nine days old.[26] Nor does the often formulaic language used by the commemorator give us any real insight into the emotions felt by the loss of a child.[27] King rightly flags up the standardization of contemporary British epitaphs, most of them chosen from stock, at the same time pointing out that this cannot be taken as a lack of genuine grief.[28] Typical of the straightforward and brief information in epitaphs are texts that include the name of the infant, the age at death, and the name and relationship to the deceased of the commemorator:

DIS MANIBUS
AELIAE P F
SECUNDILLAE
V D XXXXI
P AELIUS SECUNDUS
FLAVIA SECUNDILLA
PARENTES FECERUNT

"To the Spirits of the Dead (and of) Aelia Secundilla, daughter of Publius Aelius Secundus, lived for 41 days. Publius Aelius Secundus and Flavia Secundilla, the parents, did this."[29]

D M
TI CLAUDI GRATIANI
VIX MENS
V DIE III

[25] King 2000, 121–9.
[26] *CIL* VI.11626; *CIL* VI.11637; *CIL* VI.26618; *CIL* VI.14920; also *CIL* VI.14469.
[27] King 2000, 131. [28] King 2000, 136. [29] *CIL* VI.10978.

"To the Spirits of the Dead (and of) Tiberius Claudius Gratianus, lived five months, and three days."[30]

DM
SATYRI FECIT
JASON PATER
Q V M VIII D VIII
H III

"To the Spirits of the Dead (and of) Satyrus who lived for five months, eight days, and three hours. Jason, the father, did this."[31]

Despite the brevity of these inscriptions, we would be wrong in thinking that parents had no emotional attachment to their infants or that they simply were acting dutifully because it was expected of them. In fact, such inscriptions are of considerable value in allowing us to embed infants and children within their family and to recognize other relationships.[32] They often also reveal the existence of many families who lost several children through premature death. Lucius Numitorius Privatus in Rome commemorated six of his children, the youngest dying at just forty days, the oldest at seven years and twenty days, the rest ranging from two to five years of age.[33] Salvius Felix and Valeria Agathemeris in Lyon, for example, set up a stone for their daughter, Salvia Valeriana, who lived two years, one month, and two days, and their son Salvius Victor who lived one month and twenty-five days.[34] Both children are referred to as "dearest". In epitaphs from the city of Rome, *dulcissimus* (sweetest) and *carissimus* (dearest) were general terms used to commemorate adults as well as children, although Sigismund Nielsen has pointed out that *dulcissimus* was used more often for children.[35] Both terms of endearment might be used slightly differently, however, in other places, such as Lyon, where *carissimus* was used also for children in infancy, such as M. Fraternius Saturninus from Lyon who lived for little more than three months.[36]

More rare is the use of the epithet "most wise", *suavissimus*, and when it is attached to infants as young as three and six months, one wonders whether this had manifested itself in any noticeable way while the children were alive.[37] Also rare is the reference to a baby having been well-deserving, *benemerenti*, as this epithet was used primarily to express the gratitude of the commemorators

[30] *CIL* VI.14983. [31] Thylander 1952, A218; Helttula 2007, 93–4, no. 81.
[32] On expressions of grief for children, see Carroll 2006, 198–202.
[33] *CIL* VI.23142. [34] *CIL* XIII.2255. [35] Sigismund-Nielsen 1997, 192.
[36] *CIL* XIII.2146; see also *CIL* VI.17711; *CIL* VI.18053; *CIL* VI.22330; *CIL* VI.24510; *CIL* VI.34257. On terms of endearment in Latin epitaphs in Lyon and their chronological differences, see Rosenwein 2006, 64–8.
[37] *CIL* VI.17313 (Eucapius, six months and three days); *CIL* VI.18904 (M. Gavius Eurytus, three months and ten days).

to the deceased, and, therefore, the term is used with older individuals.[38] Also unusual for infants is the epithet "most dutiful", *pientissimus*, as this term referred to the kind of support that would be expected from children for their parents. Whilst children who had lived into their teenage years at least were more likely to be referred to as *pientissimus*, infants would not have been expected yet to have demonstrated duty or support at such a tender age.[39]

In Lyon, Mattonius Restitutus died at the age of forty and was survived by his wife Ruttonia Martiola and two children.[40] The inscription is emotionally charged in a subtle way. Cause for lament for Ruttonia Martiola was the short duration of her happy marriage (nine years and nine months) and the very young age of her now fatherless children, a son only three years, one month, and twelve days old, as well as a second son only nine months of age. In the same Gallic capital, Quintus Acceptus Firminus and his wife Satria Venusta lost three children of varying ages.[41] In the inscription on their sarcophagi, much is made of the pain of the parents at the loss of a son whose premature death at eleven years, six months, and twenty-six days left them bereft, but the information on the death of another son, dead at a year, three months, and two days, and a daughter at a year, two months, and twenty-six days, is much briefer. It may be that the parents' investment in the older child, who had survived infancy, the most dangerous phase of life, made his death even more bitter and a loss worth vocalizing more explicitly. Parents and family who had lost an infant sometimes referred to themselves as unhappy or most unhappy, as did a *mater infelicissima* commemorating her eleven-month-old son in Rome.[42] Lucius Precilius Pothinus in Rome declared himself *infelicissimus* at the triple loss of a son at four months, a daughter at ten months, and another son at seven years and ten months.[43] For the anonymous commemorator of a child in Carthage, it was too painful and unsettling to state the name of the deceased or his/her age at death. Thus, we do not know the precise age of the dead child, but the epitaph reveals that as a baby he or she was sweet and "within a short time death overcame life".[44]

The parents of Speratus who died in Rome at five months grieved infinitely, according to the infant's epitaph, and the text of the inscription addresses the passerby, expecting him or her also to shed tears over the child's remains.[45] The parents of a "sweetest little daughter" (*filia dulcissima*) in Mainz had a touching and poignant poem inscribed on a tall grave altar to commemorate

[38] Sigismund Nielsen 1997, 185. See *CIL* VI.20029, a boy eleven months and fifteen days old, and *CIL* VI.34442, a boy of only two months and twelve days.

[39] *CIL* VI.23726; *CIL* VI.28229; *CIL* VI.34442; *CIL* VI.35558; Sigismund Nielsen 1997, 197–8.

[40] *CIL* XIII.2018; Wierschowski 2001, 249–50, cat. no. 484.

[41] *CIL* XIII.1910.

[42] *CIL* VI.25377 (*mater infelicissima*, in reference to a boy of eleven months). See also parents and grandparents as *infelices*, *CIL* VI.21465 (*parentes et avia et avos infelices*, in reference to a boy of one year, five months, and eighteen days).

[43] *CIL* VI.24911.

[44] *CIL* VIII.25006.

[45] *CIL* VI.26680. For stones addressing the visitor, see Carroll 2007/8.

their child: "One is compelled to lament (the passing of) the sweet girl. Oh, had you never been born, when you were to become so loved, and yet it was determined at your birth that you would shortly be taken from us, much to your parents' pain. She lived half a year and eight days. The rose bloomed and soon wilted" (see Fig. 4.5).[46] The same parents record the loss of a second infant daughter on another grave altar, but without a poetic lamentation.[47] Although Seneca might chastise a contemporary of his, the consul designate Marullus, for grieving openly for his dead son who represented nothing more than a lost "fragment of time", parents of the non-elite classes clearly felt less bound to restrain themselves in expressing grief, as this verse epitaph clearly reveals.[48]

Parental sorrow is the focus of another moment to an infant in Mérida in southern Spain.[49] The stone was carved in the second half of the second century or in the early third century AD with two inscriptions, one in Greek and one in Latin. The Greek text reads: "You who are passing by this tomb, my mother Gaiena together with my father Sosthenes set this *stele* up for me, much lamenting the loss of a small child. For my seventh month was not yet complete (when I died). My name is Iulianus." The Latin text is briefer: "My name is Iulianus. I was not permitted to live beyond seven months. Both my parents lamented greatly." The Greek inscription and the Greek single names of the parents suggest that they may have come originally from the eastern Mediterranean to Mérida as peregrine *incolae* (inhabitants from outside the area) of the colony. Their son, however, was given a common Latin name in the new community.

FUNERARY IMAGES OF INFANTS

This little boy from Mérida is also portrayed in his funerary portrait as a chubby child with a round face and folds of fat on his legs, but he looks older than seven months and he is no mere mortal boy. In fact, he has wings and is, therefore, represented in divine guise as a cupid. This is a clear case of *consecratio in formam deorum*, a phrase used by Henning Wrede to characterize individuals who are shown as or identified with gods and goddesses.[50] As we shall see in the following section, this device was not uncommon in the Roman funerary portraiture of children, and especially children of freedmen.[51] Behind Iulianus is a vine laden with grapes, and he holds an enormous bunch

[46] *CIL* XIII.7113; Selzer 1988, 127; Boppert 1992, 120–2, cat. no. 88, pl. 54; Carroll 2006, 169, 198, fig. 56; Mander 2013, 29–30, cat. no. 453, fig. 13.

[47] *CIL* XIII.7114; Selzer 1988, 126; Boppert 1992, 123–4, cat. no. 89, pl. 55; Carroll 2006, 169–70, fig. 57; Mander 2013, 29–30, cat. no. 452, fig. 14.

[48] Seneca, *Letters* 99.2. On infants and verse epitaphs, see King 2000, 146–50.

[49] *CIL* II.562 and *IG* XIV.2541.

[50] Wrede 1981. See Mander 2013, 55–9, cat. no. 266.

[51] Kleiner 1987a.

that he has just plucked in his left arm. This motif has obvious Dionysiac connotations, again lifting the boy into an elevated divine realm. As Janet Huskinson concludes in her study of imagery in the reliefs on children's sarcophagi, cupids were attractive figures in this medium because they were "perpetual children" and they offered "opportunities to display the prettiness and sentimentality which adults often like to associate with children".[52] Iulianus, thus, is mortal, but he appears here immortal and forever young. He is approached on his right by a snake which also alludes to immortality and rebirth, as a snake can shed its skin and emerge revitalized.

The elevation of a child to quasi-divine status is made explicit in the text of a second-century funerary altar to a little boy named Hipponicus, slave of Dignilla, wife of the legate of the twenty-second legion (*legio XXII Primigenia Pia Fidelis*) in Mainz.[53] His slave parents, Hedyepes and Genesia, are recorded as dedicators, but the sheer size (over two metres tall) and elaborateness of the altar suggests that this child was loved and cherished not only by his parents, but also by his privileged and high status owners. The text reads: "As he grew up, strong in frame and of handsome appearance, with Cupid's face and manner, I was not afraid to say he was like Apollo." But the process of growing up did not last very long as he died shortly before his first birthday at the age of three-hundred-and-thirty days. His full frontal portrait, complete with wings, however, depicts a child older than the stated age, with a pose and demeanour reminiscent of statues of Apollo.[54]

Sextus Rufius Achilleus, who died in Rome in the first half of the second century AD at the age of seven months and nine days and was commemorated by his father, is represented as a little boy who looks older than an infant that age (Fig. 8.1).[55] The boy holds a winged staff with two snakes entwined around it (*caduceus*) in his left arm and a money bag (*marsupium*) in his right hand, both attributes of the Graeco-Roman god Hermes/Mercury, the god of commerce and profit, of travellers, and the conductor of souls to the underworld. This form of *consecratio* was popular amongst freedmen and descendents of freedmen, the probable status of father and son here.[56] Sextus Rufius Decebalus, the boy's father, therefore, could have chosen this motif to commemorate his wealth and social position by associating his son with the god of wealth, but the allusion to Hermes/Mercury accompanying the soul of his child may also have been a factor in selecting this imagery.[57]

[52] Huskinson 1996, 105, 107. See L. Papirius Speratus, a three-year-old, as cupid with grapes approaching his dead mother: *CIL* VI.23979; Mander 2013, cat. no. 122.

[53] *CIL* XIII.6808; Boppert 1992, 118–20, cat. no. 87, pls. 52–3; Mander 2013, cat. no. 454, fig. 4.

[54] Mander 2013, 14.

[55] *CIL* VI.25572; Carroll 2011a, 112, fig. 8; Mander 2013, 57, cat. no. 94.

[56] Kleiner 1987a, 88, cat. no. 46; German and Last 2000, 250; Mander 2013, 56.

[57] German and Last 2000.

Fig. 8.1 Funerary monument Sextus Rufius Achilleus, seven months and nine days old, Rome.

Photo: Maureen Carroll, with permission of the Ministero dei beni e delle attività culturali e del turismo—Soprintendenza Speciale per il Colosseo, il Museo Nazionale Romano e l'Area archeologica di Roma.

Another child who received the special treatment with divine attributes is Hateria Superba, dead at one year, six months, and twenty-five days.[58] Her

[58] *CIL* VI.19159; Kleiner 1987a, 183–4, cat. no. 58, pl. 36.2; Backe-Dahmen 2006, 155–6, cat. no. A19, pl. 14; Mander 2013, 153–4, cat. no. 70, fig. 131.

"most unhappy parents" set up a large marble altar around AD 100 for her and themselves on the Via Flaminia north of Rome. Hateria Superba stands enveloped in a child's *toga*, crowned with a wreath by two winged cupids who appear to deify her with this gesture. The elaborate ornament on the parting of her hair suggests that she, or rather her parents, might have been followers of Isis, a goddess who offered the hope of rebirth in the next world. The *toga* reflects her status as a citizen girl, a particularly privileged achievement, considering her parents probably were of ex-slave status, and the pet dog and birds allude to the wealth and leisure time this little girl was afforded.

Common to all the infants depicted in divine guise discussed above is the fact that the age of the child in the text does not correspond to the physical representation of the child's body. The early second-century grave *stele* of Quintus Fabius Proculus dedicated by his grandmother in Rome is another particularly good instance of this, as the nine-month-old appears to be a boy of some years, wearing a *chlamys* or cloak, often worn as adult military dress, over his shoulder.[59] This might be understood as the inability of the sculptor to represent the true ages of children. However, Roman sculptors certainly were able to represent infants and very young children of varying ages. We need only examine the portraits of the three children as portrait busts on the reliefs from the tomb of the Haterii in Rome to see accurate depictions of different ages.[60] One little boy is clearly a toddler, perhaps between one and two years of age, as his chubby cheeks and round head suggest; the other boy is about four or five, and the girl is about two or three years old. Interestingly, it is the little girl who appears in a pose and dress that links her to the divine. Her tunic slips off her right shoulder, alluding to Venus, a model of feminine beauty, and the portrait is also in a seashell, another clear steer towards Venus.[61]

A second-century marble sarcophagus from Rome with vignettes of a boy's short life also demonstrates the ability of the sculptor to depict ages convincingly.[62] At the far right, mother and father take an excursion in a wagon with their son as a swaddled infant of two or three months of age, and at the left they venture forth again with the child as a little boy when he died (see Fig. 5.12). In between, he is shown at two intermediary stages: short and pudgy, having learned to walk and playing with a wheeled scooter, and subsequently a bit taller and less plump, playing with the family's pet goose. A winged cupid accompanies the little boy on his final journey, or perhaps the viewer is meant to read the image as the little boy transformed into cupid

[59] *CIL* VI.17557; Kleiner 1987a, 188–9, cat. no. 62, pl. 37.2; Mander 2013, 28, cat. no. 68; Fittschen and Zanker 2014, 139, cat. no. 151, pl. 143.

[60] Sinn and Freyberger 1996, 51–9, pls. 11–16.

[61] Kleiner 1987b, 551–2.

[62] Amedick 1991, 153, cat. no. 190, pl. 45; Huskinson 1996, 10, 22, cat. no. 1.29, pl. 1.3; Huskinson 2011, 534–45, fig. 31.8; Carroll 2011a, 101, fig. 2.

and heading towards immortality. Like the biographical sarcophagus for M. Cornelius Statius discussed in Chapter 3 (see Fig. 4.6), a selection of images from the life cycle of a child fits the format of the long rectangular side of the coffin, enabling the sculptor to depict infancy and earliest childhood in stages.

Nor did Roman sculptors shy away from depicting infants in the very earliest stage of life. On a relief-decorated gravestone in Metz, the named infant Aeliola is tightly swaddled from head to toe, putting her in the group of infants forty to sixty days old, as described by Soranus, even though her age is not recorded in the epitaph (Fig. 8.2).[63] Another swaddled infant appears on a probable gravestone from Chauvigny, but there is no accompanying inscription to name him or state his age.[64] These monuments are not only extremely rare in realistically portraying an individual in earliest infancy, but also in commemorating someone this young without any accompanying family members. The infant is the complete focus of the depiction, on its own, and in its own right. The image of an infant only weeks old and tightly swaddled could be used, however, to depict something other than itself or highlight the pathos of early death, as the second-century funerary altar of a woman in Mérida illustrates.[65] Iulia Saturnina was a *medica*, a midwife or doctor, and a very good one at that (*optima*), as the epitaph tells us. However, it is not her that is portrayed in relief on the monument, but rather an infant apparently standing upright and enveloped tightly in swaddling bands. The baby may, of course, be hers, but because it is the only image on the altar, and is not seen with the *medica*, but entirely on its own, it is more likely that the infant alludes to Iulia Saturnina's profession and her career in successfully delivering babies like this one who is just at the beginning of its first year of life.

MOTHER AND INFANT COMMEMORATED

Swaddled infants appear far more commonly in the context of the family, and especially with their mothers. Images of mother and baby on monuments, usually *stelae* and altars, are distributed in Italy and especially in the Roman provinces of Gaul and Pannonia, and very occasionally in Greece.[66] A *stele* of the first century AD from Poitiers, for example, depicts Lepida and her swaddled infant daughter, also named Lepida, commemorated by Reginus, who is

[63] *CIL* XIII.11363; Baills 2003, 126, fig. 3; Mander 2013, 28, cat. no. 350, fig. 12; Carroll 2014, 162, fig. 2.
[64] Coulon 2004a, 46–7, fig. on p. 46; Mander 2013, 28, cat. no. 314.
[65] *CIL* II.497.
[66] Carroll 2014. See Holtzmann 2012, 411, fig. 5, for a mother and swaddled infant on a Roman funerary medallion portrait.

Fig. 8.2 Gravestone and "portrait" of Aeliola as a swaddled infant, Metz.
Drawing: Irene de Luis.

both husband and father to them (Fig. 8.3).[67] The baby lies on its back in front of its mother, and the image is probably meant to be seen as a mother holding her infant; the sculptor may not have been particularly talented, and the swaddling looks more like a fur wrap than textile bands. Another *stele* from Metz

[67] Deyts 2004, 236, fig. 10; Coulon 2004a, 157; Carroll 2014, 168, fig. 5.

Fig. 8.3 Gravestone of Lepida and her daughter Lepida, from Poitiers.
Drawing: Irene de Luis.

portrays a woman named Carantodia and her infant son Sextus (Fig. 8.4).[68] Carantodia and her baby are seen from the chest up, little Sextus standing next to her all wrapped up in swaddling bands. Each of these babies must have lived long enough to be named. But their portrayal with their mothers suggests that they

[68] Baills 2003, 126, fig. 2.

Fig. 8.4 Gravestone with portraits of Carantodia and her swaddled son Sextus, Metz.
Drawing: Irene de Luis.

both died, perhaps as a result of complications in childbirth. These double portraits commemorate the close personal relationship mother and infant had shared very briefly or symbolically continued to share for posterity.

There also are other monuments of mothers cradling a swaddled infant in which the dead woman and the commemorator are named. These can be the husband, as in the case of Antistia Firma from Budapest, or the cousin and brother, as in the case of Flavia Aiulo from Aquincum, or the parents, as attested by the *stele* of Claudia Iulia from Scarbantia.[69] In none of these three cited monuments is there any mention of the depicted infant. Other portraits might have no inscription at all surviving, so we cannot know names of the mother, the infant, or the commemorators. This includes a marble relief panel walled up into the bell tower of the cathedral at Benevento which is graced with a portrait of a woman who holds her swaddled infant conspicuously in

[69] Flavia Aiulo: *CIL* III.14352; Krüger 1974, 16–17, cat. no. 15, pls. 8–9; Carroll 2012b, 141, pl. 22; Mander 2013, 97, cat. no. 662, fig. 81; Carroll 2014, 169, fig. 6. Claudia Iulia: Mander 2013, 96–7, cat. no. 605, fig. 80; Carroll 2014, 169–70, fig. 8.

Fig. 8.5 Funerary portrait of an unnamed mother and her swaddled infant, from Benevento.

Drawing: Irene de Luis.

her arm and faces the viewer (Fig. 8.5).[70] Such portraits may be understood as images of mothers and infants who died together or soon after one another. If the baby is not named, it is possible that it had died before its *dies lustricus*, but it is equally possible that only the mother was privileged enough to be named

[70] Frenz 1985, 117–18, cat. no. 71, pl. 30.4; Carroll 2014, 170, fig. 9.

in the inscription because her death in her reproductive years might have represented a greater loss to the family.

But, in some cases, we may be looking not at women who had given birth to a child or children, but at a pictorial device used to compensate for an early death that robbed these women of the chance of having offspring in the first place. They might be depicted in death as mothers as a way of symbolically fulfilling their natural social role in Roman society. It is possible in only one case to check the depiction of a mother and infant on the grave *stele* against the contents of the grave above which the marker stood, and that is in Cologne where, in 1962, both grave and stone were excavated (Fig. 8.6).[71] This *stele*, dating to about AD 20, commemorates a woman named Bella who, in her portrait, holds an unnamed baby in swaddling clothes tightly to her breast. The excavators found no evidence of an infant in the grave, only the skeleton of the roughly twenty-year-old Bella herself. So the motif of the baby in her arms could be simply a wish for what could have been and Bella is shown as a virtual mother, or Bella could have died, but the baby survived and was not buried with her. It is impossible to say for certain which scenario is the correct one.

A most remarkable Roman depiction of the mid-third century of a woman with a tiny infant is that on the funerary monument of Aelius Munatius and his wife Aurelia Cansauna from the civilian settlement outside the Roman fort at Intercisa in Pannonia (Fig. 8.7).[72] She is shown with her husband and small children, the youngest being a baby held in the crook of her left arm. The infant is clearly dressed in swaddling clothes, and is therefore only two or three months of age. Aurelia Cansauna not only holds the infant, she has lifted up her dress with her right hand to bare her breast as if to begin feeding her baby. The folds of dress fabric that swirl around the breast, its prominent nipple, and her exaggeratedly long index finger pointing at her breast are devices to ensure that attention is paid to this part of her anatomy and, by inference, her ability to nurture children.

The depiction of Aurelia Cansauna is unique in Pannonia, and I know of no comparable portrait in the other western provinces, but there is a striking similarity between her pose with an infant and that of a woman on a second-century funerary relief from Palmyra, now in the Fitzwilliam Museum in Cambridge (Fig. 8.8), and with a funerary portrait of the second or third century of a woman and her infant from Daraya near Damascus (Fig. 8.9).[73] Both are from Syria and depict a Syrian family, and they are extremely rare portrayals of the explicit maternal nurturing of a child in this region. Funerary

[71] Carroll 2001, 91, fig. 43; Höpken 2007, 299, fig. 245; Carroll 2014, 173.

[72] *RIU* 5.1153; Boatwright 2005, 287–9, fig. 10.1; Mander 2013, 98, cat. no. 733, fig. 82; Carroll 2014, 174, fig. 11.

[73] Budde and Nicholls 1967, 86, cat. no. 139, pl. 46; Heyn 2012, 439–40, fig. CS VI.2; Weber 2006, 30, cat. no. 9, pl. 6A.

Fig. 8.6 Funerary *stela* of Bella cradling her swaddled infant, Cologne.
Photo: © Rheinisches Bildarchiv Köln (www.rheinischesbildarchiv.de).

Fig. 8.7 Funerary monument of Aurelia Cansauna and her family, Budapest. Hungarian National Museum, Inv. Nr. MNM 22.2905.3.

Photo: Ortolf Harl, *ubi erat lupa*, © Hungarian National Museum.

portraits of elaborately dressed women not shown in the act of breastfeeding their child, but simply holding it their arms, were much more common in the second and third centuries in Syria.[74] The child in the arm of the woman on

[74] Sadurska and Bounni 1994, 143–4, cat. no. 188, fig. 159; 164, cat. no. 217, fig. 181; 130–1, cat. no. 173, fig. 194.

Fig. 8.8 Funerary relief from Palmyra of a breastfeeding mother.
Photo: © The Fitzwilliam Museum, Cambridge.

the Fitzwilliam relief rests his hand on her bare breast. Like Aurelia Cansauna, the fabric of her dress is bunched up in a circular pattern, and also the elongated index finger of her right hand points to her breast. The woman on the relief from Daraya also pulls her garment away from her breast to let her baby suckle, and she also has rather large hands and long fingers. These women, therefore, convey the message that they were fertile and nurturers of children.

Such similar poses and messages from funerary monuments of different regional origins require an explanation. Aurelius Munatius, the husband of Aurelia Cansauna and a soldier in the *cohors I milliaria Hemesenorum*, was a Syrian from Samosota, one of many who came to Intercisa in the late second and third centuries AD with the army. At Intercisa, in particular, there appears to have been what Mocsy calls a Syrian enclave that was supplemented repeatedly with new recruits from Syria.[75] A study of the epigraphic evidence for Syrians on the Danube suggests that their wives also came from Syria.[76] So

[75] Mocsy 1974, 227. [76] Tentea 2012; Agócs 2013.

Fig. 8.9 Funerary portrait of a woman breastfeeding from Daraya (Damascus).
Drawing: Irene de Luis.

Aurelia Cansauna may also have been from the east, and perhaps the inspiration for her pose is to be sought in an eastern, Syrian funerary context. The funerary monuments of the Syrian soldiers and their families are large and elaborate, and their production over the years would have kept sculptors at Intercisa in business. Might these sculptors have been Syrian? We know that Palmyrene artists were operating far from home in northern Britain, producing some of the best funerary portraits at South Shields.[77] And at South Shields, details such as hand gestures and drapery styles invite parallels with contemporary funerary sculpture at Palmyra. Many of the Palmyrene women hold a spindle and distaff in front of them, their hand gestures also in these cases drawing attention to the instruments they are holding and inferring their domestic skill in wool-working.[78] And their index and middle fingers are often exaggeratedly large and long as if to emphasize the display of wool-working tools. These features can also be seen in the funerary portrait of Regina at South Shields which may have been carved by a Palmyrene sculptor.[79] If Syrian, or, more specifically, Palmyrene, sculptors contributed to or influenced the funerary art of Intercisa, this may account for some similarities between the two portraits of mother and child at Intercisa and Palmyra. But the array of children of various ages in the foreground of the monument of Aurelia Cansauna and Aurelius Munatius is a feature characteristic of Pannonian, not Syrian, funerary art in which large families with many offspring play an important role.[80] Thus, varying traditions may have been blended together here.

With the notable focus on children in funerary commemoration on the Danube, it is perhaps not surprising that infants are included also in family groups in funerary portraits in the region. On another grave *stele* from Intercisa, for example, a woman with a babe in arms is flanked by two soldiers, possibly a husband and son or brother.[81] The ethnic attire of the woman indicates clearly that she is local. Another Pannonian woman, Toutomara, and her Pannonian husband, Nertomarus, are also depicted in the first half of the second century with their children (Fig. 8.10).[82] Toutomara holds an infant in her right arm, whilst putting her left arm around the shoulder of her adolescent son next to her; on the right is Nertomarus.

Part of the extended Roman family might include a wet-nurse (*nutrix*) who acted as a surrogate mother in the nurture and care of the infant. She not only cared for the infant from the beginning, but could maintain personal bonds with her former charge afterwards. The wet-nurse Trophima, for example, was one of the commemorators of a little girl named Domitia Felicitata who lived for one year, five months and sixteen days in Rome; whether she helped pay for the monument, or the girl's father, who is named as the main dedictor, simply included Trophima out of affection for his daughter, is unknown.[83] Perhaps the most famous monument of a *nutrix* in funerary commemoration is Severina who appears on a third-century altar in Cologne.[84] The inscribed text identifies her as "Severina *nutrix*". Severina, who may have been a slave,

[77] Phillips 1976; Carroll 2013. [78] Heyn 2010.
[79] Carroll 2013. [80] Boatwright 2005; Mander 2012.
[81] Mander 2013, 309, cat. no. 713.
[82] Mander 2013, 286, cat. no. 603. On families on the Danube, see Carroll 2015.
[83] *CIL* VI.35123. See also *CIL* VI.10554.
[84] *CIL* XIII.8356; Mander 2013, 139–40, cat. no. 415, figs. 122–4.

Fig. 8.10 Funerary portraits of Toutomara (left) with an infant in her arm, her older son (middle), and her husband Nertomarus (right), Budapest.
Drawing: Irene de Luis.

appears on two sides of the altar, once bending over lovingly to a swaddled infant tucked up in a wicker cradle (see Fig. 4.9), and in the second image giving the baby the breast. Attention is drawn to this activity because her breast on which the baby sucks is exaggeratedly large. Debate has focused on whether this monument was put up to commemorate Severina by the now adult person(s) she had nursed or whether Severina herself commissioned the altar to commemorate her former charge(s). The confusion stems from the portrait bust on the front side of the altar. Most scholars have interpreted the portrait as that of a man, but Ursula Rothe has argued convincingly that the portrait wears female clothing and that this person is Severina herself.[85] Thus, it is likely that Severina was commemorated by a grateful former owner or employer for her services to the family. There was no biological relationship between Severina and the child or children, but the two images of her rocking a baby in its cradle and breastfeeding it created the illusion of maternal love

[85] Rothe 2011.

and tenderness for which a natal link was not needed. If Severina, as a slave, never had legitimate children of her own, this splendid monument dedicated to her by a grateful surrogate child elevates her symbolically to the status of a Roman matron.

CHILDREN AND THE SOCIAL STATUS OF THE FAMILY

Funerary monuments of infants also commemorate biological familial relationships and they shed light on dashed hopes and aspirations for the future of the child and its parents, especially when the children remembered are from families of low status. Even if the infant was a slave and of the lowest social status, the commemorator of that child might attempt to improve reality and have it depicted as a Roman citizen in death. For those who had been slaves, legitimate marriage and legitimate children were of enormous importance. A secure family life with a hope of the family's survival is exactly what a slave could not have as long as he or she was of servile status, so the desire to establish a family is entirely understandable. Manumission was key, as children born of freed parents would be not only legitimate, but also have Roman citizenship and benefit from many open avenues in life that had been beyond their parents' grasp. For that reason, the early death of a free-born child must have been particularly devastating for the parents. For example, the eight-month-old T. Helvius Lupus, briefly introduced in Chapter 1, was born of a mother whose name, Helvia Secundilla, indicates she was in possession of Roman citizenship.[86] The boy is Roman and he is a citizen of Mérida, despite his very young age. His mother, however, might have been a former slave of the Helvii attested elsewhere in Augusta Emerita, gaining her citizenship upon manumission.[87] It is likely that the boy's father, Probus, was still a slave, as his single name suggests, possibly associated with the Rio Tinto copper and iron mines, where the inscription was found (modern Huelva), but the child inherited the status of Roman citizen from his mother. Thus, the combination of free-born status, citizenship, and corporate membership are important features of the boy's identity—he had been entitled to all those social markers and symbolized the family's upward trajectory, thwarted by his death. Many funerary portraits of freedman families visually underscore the importance of family and children in non-verbal ways.[88]

[86] *AE* 1965, 298; Rothenberg and Blanco-Freijeiro 1981, 18, fig. 3; Edmondson et al. 2001, 139–41, cat. no. 10, pl. 10A–C.

[87] Edmondson 2007, 549.

[88] George 2005a.

A funerary altar set up by a possible freedwoman named Publicia Glypte in the early second century AD in Rome is a relevant monument to consider here, especially since it commemorates two children of the relevant age.[89] In the funerary portraits we see Nico, who was eleven months and eight days old, and Eutyches, who lived for one year, five months, and ten days (Fig. 8.11). Nico was her son (he is referred to in the epitaph as *filius*), but his single name suggests he may not have been free-born; Eutyches is specifically referred to as Publicia Glypte's house-born slave (*verna*). Yet both boys wear the *toga praetexta*, a garment reserved for citizen children. It is possible that her *verna* could be her own biological son, born before she was freed, therefore still retaining his slave status, but equally the little boy may be the son of one of Publicia Glypte's household slaves of whom she was particularly fond. Perhaps she intended to free Eutyches, but he died before she could make this a reality. Both boys look the same age, although there is a difference of six months. Both stand like little learned orators, with a script roll in the hand and more rolls in a container between them. Neither boy would have been able to read, let alone stand and recite anything at their age. Both little boys are made older, of higher status, and well educated, thus altering reality and perhaps reflecting what Publicia Glypte would have hoped they could achieve one day. The fact that both boys also stand on a little pedestal even makes them look like statues, and this is, perhaps, an allusion to life-size honorific statues erected for and to the elite in public places.[90] Neither boy was of the elite class, however, so this representation is aspirational and, at the same time, a device to compensate for ambitions for futures that were thwarted by early deaths.

Another funerary altar from Rome commemorating two infants is that of Maena Mellusa, a freedwoman.[91] The monument was set up in the mid-first century by the husband of Maena Mellusa, Gaius Oenucius Delus, as the first two lines of the inscription reveal; the names of the two boys appear below. One was named Dexter and he lived for eleven months; the other was Sacerdos who died at three months and ten days. Both boys are referred to as sons (*filii*). The baby in Maena Mellusa's arm must be the three-month-old Sacerdos, and the little boy standing in front of her must be Dexter, even though he looks much older than eleven months. The single names of the boys suggest that they were slaves, born before Maena Mellusa had been freed, and yet the image chosen by the commemorator was one of tender and intimate maternal interaction with no hint at all of illegitimate status or a threatened

[89] *CIL* VI.22972; Kleiner 1987a, 195–6, cat. no. 68, pl. 40.1; Rawson 2003b, 286–8, fig. 2; Backe-Dahmen 2006, 156–7, cat. no. A21, pl. 15b; Carroll 2012b, 142, fig. 7; Mander 2013, 107, cat. no. 73, fig. 92.

[90] Bol 1989, 121–3, cat. no. 34, pls. 59–61.

[91] *CIL* VI.21805; Carroll 2012a, 49, fig. 4.5; Mander 2013, 111, cat. no. 25, fig. 97.

Fig. 8.11 Funerary reliefs of Publicia Glypte and her two infant sons, Rome.
Drawing: Irene de Luis.

future for the little slave boys. In fact, the scene stresses more than anything else the close emotional attachment to even the youngest children, regardless of free or servile status.

The inclusivity of family iconography is well illustrated by the funerary monument set up by Sextus Titius Primus, a successful freedman and *sevir Augustalis* in Ancona, to commemorate his partner, a child, and another adult

Fig. 8.12 Gravestone of Sextus Titius Primus and family from Ancona. Lucania Benigna, his wife, may be the woman on the left who holds a small child.
Drawing: Irene de Luis.

freedwoman (Fig. 8.12).[92] His partner, Lucania Benigna, according to the inscription was his *concubina*, suggesting that she may not yet have been freed when she died, or that they were not in a legitimate marriage. The child Chloe may not have been his legitimate offspring, although she could be his biological child; equally, she could be the slave child of someone else in the household. She is referred to as his *delicium*, his "favourite", "darling", or "pet", a term used for favoured slave children.[93] But only the inscription makes this clear. The image says something else. Lucania Benigna, the *concubina*, who may be the woman to the left of Sextus Titius Primus, is being embraced tenderly by the child in her arms, presumably Chloe, although the hairstyle of the child looks more like that of a boy. The motif of mother and infant as represented here conveys none of the negativity or insecurity present in a precarious situation of slavery. Instead, the portraits convey a coherent

[92] *CIL* XI.6176; Mander 2013, 73–4, cat. no. 190, fig. 55.
[93] Sigismund-Nielsen 1990; Laes 2003; Sigismund-Nielsen 2013, 297–8.

image of family closeness and attachment that would be expected in a legal marriage, and, as such, they perhaps improve reality and elevate the status of mother and child by inference. The images create the impression of biological family connections, whether they existed or not. As Mander has demonstrated, the iconography of the family often only allows us to recognize family members in general, and only inscriptions, should they survive, clarify if the familial links were natal or surrogate.[94] The relationship between the freedwoman Titia Chreste and Sextus Titius Primus cannot be clarified. She could be a fellow former slave of the same owner of Sextus Titius Primus, or she could be his former slave, based on her family name. At any rate, she was part of this extended family and perhaps one of the surrogate carers of Chloe and other children in the household.

Funerary portraits of children who had survived infancy, in particular, could project ideas about status and reveal aspirations for the social advancement of the family. For the free-born offspring of ex-slaves, for example, the display of citizenship and legal status is extremely important, and this could be signalled in funerary monuments by nomenclature and dress. The inscription on the travertine limestone slab of the mid-first century BC of the freedman Epictes in Rome, for example, depicts a father, mother, and child.[95] This young child of about two years of age at the most, perhaps a girl or possibly a boy with long, curly hair, is positioned between its parents and is the focal point of this nuclear family grouping. The *bulla* suspended from a strap around the child's neck immediately establishes his/her Roman citizenship and free-born status.

On another tomb relief of *c*.40–*c*.30 BC in Rome, the iconography of which also points to a family of ex-slave status, the father wears the *toga* to which he was entitled only after his manumission and the mother is dressed modestly in a tunic and *palla* as a Roman matron.[96] The boy between them, no longer an infant, but born free after his parents were released from slavery, is dressed in the *toga praetexta* and wears a *bulla*, both devices stressing the fact that the child is a Roman citizen and therefore holds a privileged status (Fig. 8.13). The tactile poses of parents and child, the pet birds, and the rich array of fruit offered to the child, also highlight his specialness. The tragedy of the death of a child, who might well be the only offspring and in whom the family placed its hopes of survival and upward social mobility, is patently obvious.

Children were important for the continuation of the family line in any part of the Roman Empire. Here, I would like to look briefly at a particular city in

[94] Mander 2013, 132.

[95] *CIL* I.3010/*CIL* VI.17211; Kockel 1993, 126–7, cat. no. F12, pl. 31c; Backe-Dahmen 2006, 139, cat. no. R6, pl. 3b.

[96] Kockel 1993, 196–7, cat. no. M1, pls. 111a, 112a; Backe-Dahmen 2006, 143–4, cat. no. R18, pls. 7a–b; Larsson Lovén 2013, 307, fig. 15.3.

Fig. 8.13 Relief panel from a tomb in Rome, depicting father, mother, and free-born son.
Drawing: Irene de Luis.

the east—Palmyra—to explore the portrayal of children in funerary portraits and in texts as guarantors of the survival and social eminence of powerful and wealthy families and clans. Smith has demonstrated that a strong sense of kinship pervaded Pergamene society, with lineage groups being of major significance.[97] Palmyrene tombs were shared by related kin, and their erection and sculptural decoration reinforced the relationships between families and clans and their ancestral founders. Names, blood relations, and genealogical details are included in the inscriptions on every stone slab sealing individual burials (*loculi*). Children appear on *loculus* slabs not just of women, but also of men who were fathers and even uncles. Yarhibôlâ is depicted in a himation, for example, and his young son, Yarhai, who stands behind him to the right, is dressed in the same garment; this slab of the mid-second century AD seals his *loculus* in the *hypogaeum* of the families of Sassan and Mattai.[98] Usually an adult will be seen with one or occasionally two children; extremely rare is the depiction of three children on the *loculus* slab of a mother in the *hypogaeum* of Šalamallat.[99] Boys and girls are depicted as equals in position and stature.[100]

The production of heirs and the establishment or maintenance of clan alliances would be important also in the case of remarriage. In the shared *hypogaeum* of the family of Bôlbarak at Palmyra, for example, two *loculus* slabs with a portrait commemorate two different women who had been married to the same man, ʻOgeilû, son of the founder of the tomb. Each

[97] A. M. Smith 2013, 88.
[98] Sadurska and Bounni 1994, 50–1, cat. no. 57, fig. 53.
[99] Sadurska and Bounni 1994, 163–4, cat. no. 216, fig. 195.
[100] A. M. Smith 2013, 96.

woman wears traditional, ornate Palmyrene costume, and each is accompanied by a small child. One woman, whose inscribed name is damaged, is portrayed as a mother who holds a little boy in the crook of her left arm. The child, depicted as a little adult in a tunic, grasps his mother's dress with his right hand.[101] The other woman, Šullâ, holds a little girl dressed in a long chiton and jewellery, holding a bird in her left hand.[102] It is difficult to know how old either child was, and whether they were both, in fact, infants, but were depicted, as was the Palmyrene tradition, as older children or miniature adults. Both *loculus* slabs have been dated to the mid-second century AD, and it is impossible to know which wife died first, but they each produced at least one heir and, therefore, fulfilled their maternal role in the union of two families, even if the child died young. This was worth advertising for posterity.

Thus, Roman funerary monuments contextualize and commemorate both biological and non-biological familial relationships and they reveal frustrated plans for the future of the child and the *familia*. Funerary images of freedman families, especially in Rome, visually highlight the importance of family and children in non-verbal ways, but group portraits with numerous children that are prevalent in some frontier regions, such as Pannonia, also reveal tangible attitudes towards children and their integral role in indigenous families far from the centre of empire. The poignancy of the death of an infant or very young child is relayed by both the often explicit inscriptions and the age-appropriate depiction of babies and their activities. Ambitions for the future of an infant were frequently thwarted by early death, and the monuments explored here demonstrate clearly that parents and carers took care to remember the very young and, in doing so, expressed their attachment to those so vulnerable.

[101] Sadurska and Bounni 1994, 143–4, cat. no. 188, fig. 159.
[102] Sadurska and Bounni 1994, 144–5, cat. no. 190, fig.158.

9

Integrated Perspectives on Roman Infancy

It has been my aim throughout this book to integrate archaeological evidence, material culture, and the iconography of infancy with social and cultural history. Written sources, when immediately relevant to the life and circumstances of an infant, have been cited throughout, but they have not dominated the discussion. The burial evidence and material culture assessed here provide us with a data set that is better and more meaningful than texts on their own for an exploration of a range of issues. Having investigated the archaeological evidence for infancy and earliest childhood and the material culture of this life-stage in the previous chapters, we are in a good position to evaluate the reliability and validity of the texts in a nuanced way. In this final chapter, therefore, it is appropriate to assess a particular group of Roman texts that have been influential in our own judgement of the relationship between Roman parents and their offspring and to contextualize them with the other strands of evidence. These are sources that were written primarily in response to infant death and that appear to record the general Roman attitude towards children below the age of one year.

RE-EVALUATING LAWS ON MOURNING

Plutarch wrote that the Romans ("our people") by custom did not perform any of the rites for children who died in infancy "that the living are expected to perform for the dead".[1] One rite that he mentions specifically as not being performed is the pouring of libations. According to Plutarch, neither are the graves of infants given much attention, nor do the surviving parents invest in the laying out of the bodies of their children or sit by them (before burial?). He wrote this, perhaps quite surprisingly, in a letter of consolation to his wife on the death of their two-year-old daughter, although we might wonder how

[1] Plutarch, *Consolation to his Wife* 11. For a discussion of the text, see Baltussen 2009b.

much consolation such dismal comments or his advice on grieving inconspicuously might have given her. Plutarch has given us a list of things not to do or that were not expected of the surviving family when infants died, and some of this, at least, can be assessed in conjunction with the physical evidence for infant death and burial.

The wealth of archaeological and artefactual evidence marshalled in Chapters 6 and 7 contradicts completely the claim that children dying in infancy were not the object of ritual attention. The inclusion of grave goods pertaining to the afterlife, religious beliefs, and protection—such as coins, *balsamaria*, amulets, lamps, and food offerings, to name just a few—demonstrates clearly that families certainly did perform rites for their young children (Figs. 4.3, 4.12–17, 7.9). And they provided libations for their infants, as the archaeological evidence shows. A ceramic libations tube directly above the body of a six-month-old child in the Porta Nocera cemetery at Pompeii, for example, clearly refutes the notion that this particular rite was inappropriate for children so young.[2] The glass *balsamaria* in infant graves in Roman Gaul may also attest to a ritual pouring of oils or unguents over the body just before the sealing of the grave.[3] Furthermore, the archaeological evidence demonstrates that infant graves were indeed given attention and that efforts were made to find suitable containers for the bodies, some of them not just reused or repurposed, but made especially and specifically for babies. To the former group belong the amphorae and other ceramic containers that were altered, cut open, and resealed for a baby, and to the latter belong the wood coffins tailor-made to fit the size of a tiny body (see Figs. 7.1–2, 7.6–7). Whether in communal cemeteries or in settlements, the bodies of infants generally were protected by some kind of material or combination of materials, even if the results were sometimes makeshift (see Figs. 7.3, 7.5). And there clearly were regional preferences in the rites of cremation or inhumation, in the predominant type of burial container, and in the range of grave goods given infants, underscoring the fact that what we commonly see as universal Roman customs were, in reality, more varied, and these practices need to be contextualized in a wider world beyond Rome and even Italy if we want to understand how infants were raised, socialized, cared for, and buried.

The jurist Ulpian noted that the performance of a burial was a public demonstration of *pietas* or duty.[4] Cicero defined *pietas* as "that feeling under the influence of which kindness and careful attention is paid to those who are united to us by ties of blood", and this extended to attention paid to

[2] De Larminat 2010, 69; Van Andringa et al. 2013, 356–67, especially 361–2.

[3] Witteyer and Fasold 1995, 25; Riquier and Salé 2006, 56–7, figs. 66–8; Jaeggi 2012a, 231, 235, fig. 14.

[4] Ulpian (*Edict* 25), *The Digest of Justinian* (*Digest*) 11.14.7.

proper burial.[5] So, here, too, there appears to be a discrepancy between Plutarch's claim that Roman parents invested little or no effort in burying their children who died in infancy and the social obligation of the family to bury their relatives and afford them funerary rites, regardless of the age of the deceased.

This obvious investment in the proper burial of an infant stands also in contrast to Plutarch's comment that "the laws forbid us to mourn for infants".[6] This appears to stem from a legal recommendation in the writings of the jurist Ulpian that "children younger than three are not formally mourned, but are mourned in marginal form; a child less than a year receives neither formal mourning nor marginal mourning".[7] And it is Plutarch again, citing early Roman law, who says that the periods of mourning were regulated so that "over a child of less than three years there was to be no mourning at all; over one older than that, the mourning was not to last more months than it had lived years, up to ten".[8] The impression is given that it was against Roman law to mourn a baby, and that only children who had reached their third birthday were worthy of mourning, although there are inconsistencies here because another jurist, Paulus, stated that "minors up to the age of three years should be mourned for one month for each year of their age at the time of their death".[9] This means that a one-year-old child would indeed be mourned, even if just for a month, but for children who had not yet lived a year there was no mourning period according to law.

Yet, in other literary sources, specific mention is made of grieving fathers and especially distressed mothers who, with breasts still full of milk, carry their newborns to the grave, faltering in their steps and beating their chests.[10] Does this behaviour represent mourning? If mourning is equated with emotion and a sense of loss, it is clear that this cannot be regulated by law, in any period, so "mourning" as it is used by the jurists and Plutarch must mean something else. Grief is personal and can be expressed in ways that are not obvious to others, and this can be neither prescribed nor banned; however, grief and sorrow can be displayed boldly and ostentatiously in public, and it was this that was decidedly frowned upon by elite Roman society, particularly by those who adhered to the Stoic belief that life was to be lived and death performed in moderation and with a sense of decorum. Seneca's *Moral Letters* contains advice on how to deal with death, stating in *Letter* 99 (*On Consolation to the Bereaved*) "that which we Stoics advise, is honourable: when emotion has prompted a moderate flow of tears, and has, so to speak, ceased to effervesce, the soul should not be surrendered to grief".[11] The "sweet caresses" of babyhood should be remembered by parents, but they should not be dwelled

[5] Cicero, *On Invention* 2.53. [6] Plutarch, *Consolation to his Wife* 11.
[7] Ulpian, *FIRA* 2.536. [8] Plutarch, *Numa* 12.2. [9] Paulus, *Opinions* 1.21.13.
[10] Statius, *Silvae* 5. [11] Seneca, *Letter* 99.

upon if they are taken away from them.[12] Composure was to be maintained, self-control being one of the things in which good Roman children were to be trained by parents, nurses, and teachers.[13] Moderation and acceptance are stock elements of Stoic consolatory correspondence throughout the first and second centuries AD.

But very obvious public outpourings of grief and mourning in conjunction with child death are recorded quite often in Roman texts, so it is obvious that not everyone took the stiff upper lip approach. The childless poet Statius wrote a whole poem in the late first century AD on the loss and sadness he felt on the death of his adopted son, a little slave whom he had freed.[14] His sorrow is such that he admits to being excessive, "weeping past the bounds of decency". He is intolerant of those who criticize his "tears and moans", and dismissive of those who dare "to make laws against sorrow, and decree there should be boundaries to grief". Social norms on grieving openly and in public are disregarded by Statius, and he found them unnatural. Not being a member of the Roman elite and perhaps less constrained by the Stoic philosophical tenets so evident among the upper echelons of society in Rome, Statius had a different attitude towards family and familial behaviour, and one that was more widespread than the few surviving texts would suggest.

It was really only the social elite of Rome, and, even then, perhaps only a subset of this class, who cared about public decorum and composure so much. Members of the upper class in Rome scrutinized each other constantly, and the weight of their social disapproval could come down on individuals who overstepped the mark with public outpourings of grief and shows of mourning. Pliny the Younger was particularly scathing about his contemporary, the senator M. Aquilius Regulus, who was seemingly mad with grief at the loss of his young son: "The boy had a number of ponies, some in harness and others not broken in, dogs both great and small, nightingales, parrots and blackbirds—all these Regulus slaughtered at his pyre. Yet an act like that was not caused by his grief; it was but a public display of his grief."[15] Even a grieving emperor could be ridiculed, as was Nero who "greeted a daughter, presented to him by Poppaea, with more than human joy".[16] The baby died in less than four months, however, and the "emperor showed himself as incontinent in sorrow as in joy". The openness with which Nero mourned, apparently out of control, stood in contrast to the exemplary behaviour of the empress Livia at the death of her son Drusus; Livia "grieved no more than was becoming to a Caesar or due to a son".[17] For Seneca, "sorrow for the loss of one's own children is natural", but it had to be "reasonable", and not exaggerated or

[12] Seneca, *Consolation to Marcia* 6.5.

[13] Tacitus, *Dialogue on Oratory* 29.

[14] Statius, *Silvae* 5.

[15] Pliny, *Letters* 4.2. On Regulus and his social context and activities, see Hoffer 1999, 55–63.

[16] Tacitus, *Annals* 15.23.

[17] Seneca, *Consolation to Marcia* 6.3.

played out in public.[18] Seneca was very hard on the bereaved consul designate, Iunius Marullus, on the death of his little son, accusing him of behaving in a womanly fashion and reproaching him for turning "a mere sting" into pain.[19] After all, the son, no longer an infant, had been but "a fragment of time" that had been lost.[20] One wonders what the loss of an infant in childbirth or within the first weeks and months of life would have been called by Seneca! In his opinion, "the mourning which public opinion prompts is more than nature insists upon".[21] And here we have this word "mourning" again, clearly meaning things done, showed, or performed openly and without constraint, and it is against this kind of behaviour that Seneca, Plutarch, Ulpian, and Paulus took a stand. The oft-quoted passages in their writings pertaining to an apparent ban on mourning for infants, in reality, do not refer to sorrow and grief, as both are normal human reactions to the death of someone very young; instead, they are statements about finding a measured and controlled way of publicly expressing loss. They do not seek to regulate emotions or forbid the family to mourn in private or to invest care and effort in the burial of their youngest children, as the many examples of personalized graves examined in this book clearly attest. Elsewhere in the *Digest*, Ulpian noted that "parents, children of either sex, as well as all other agnates or cognates should be mourned in accordance with the sense of propriety, grief of mind, and wish of each individual", which looks even less like a state regulation on mourning according to age and more like individual and personal reactions to death.[22]

Parents were very aware that the life of a child was precarious and that things could go wrong. Various written documents confirm that even those of the most elevated social standing worried about losing their children and tried to enjoy them while they could. The emperor Marcus Aurelius, himself a Stoic, and paraphrasing the Stoic philosopher Epictetes, was acutely aware that a child kissed good-night "may be dead in the morning".[23] He had much experience with infant death, as he and his wife, Faustina, lost several children as babies or young children between AD 147 and 160. He attempted to free himself of the fear of losing children, advising that one should not ask oneself "how may I not lose my child", but "how may I not dread to lose him".[24] Epictetes suggested another tack in dealing with the death of loved ones: "Never say of anything, 'I lost it', but say, 'I gave it back'. Has your child died? It was given back."[25] These clearly are coping mechanisms devised to stop a bereaved parent being consumed by grief; they are not expressions of a lack of engagement or concern for one's children. Epictetes, Seneca, Plutarch,

[18] Seneca, *Consolation to Marcia* 6.7.
[19] Seneca, *Letter* 99.2. On Seneca's letters, including this one, see Wilson 1997.
[20] Seneca, *Letter* 99.2.
[21] Seneca, *Consolation to Marcia* 6.7.
[22] Ulpian (*Edicts* 8), *Digest* 3.2.23.
[23] Marcus Aurelius, *Meditations* 11.34; Epictetes, *Enchiridion* 3.
[24] Marcus Aurelius, *Mediations* 9.40.
[25] Epictetes, *Enchiridion* 11.

and Marcus Aurelius all would have believed that external events in life were beyond their control and that they needed to be accepted calmly through rigorous self-discipline. But they were not mouthpieces for Romans everywhere of varying status and backgrounds and many would have disagreed with their philosophy and attitudes.

COMPENSATING FOR LIVES UNLIVED?

Chapter 3 explored the religious and social aspects of fertility and conception as attested in the material culture and texts, highlighting the tangible desire for children and ideas about the developing foetus. According to the *Digest*, the foetus had legal rights, and a baby still in the mother's body was to be taken care of just as much as it would be when born.[26] The *Digest* states that children not yet born were, in almost every branch of the civil law, regarded as already existing, and that they were allowed to take statutable inheritances.[27] If a father had made a will not knowing his wife was pregnant and if he died before the baby was born, for example, an existing will lost its validity and the newborn child then became the heir. In fact, the text of the *Edictum Carbonianum* explicitly states that the unborn child of a deceased father ought to receive financial resources and aid because "he or she is born not only for the benefit of the ascendant male to whom he or she is alleged to belong but also for the community".[28] The reference here to the child belonging to and benefiting society suggests clearly that an infant, whether or not already born, was not looked upon as something of little consequence or of negligible importance. Its death would not change this situation. In fact, even if the mother died with her baby still in her womb, her offspring was to be excised from her body, otherwise one would run the risk of having "destroyed the prospects of the offspring being alive" when the pregnant mother was buried.[29]

A baby's prospects, therefore, were important and people were mindful of them. Infants would have meant different things to people of different social standing, of course, and there may well have been varying degrees of importance of a very young child. This perhaps manifested itself in different ways that cannot always be measured and which may not be apparent in the archaeological record. Different factors of a cultural, regional, religious, and social nature would have played a role in forming attitudes towards and relationships with the youngest members of society. The elite classes would

[26] Paulus (*Shares Which Are Allowed to the Children of Condemned Prisoners*), *Digest* 1.5.7.

[27] Julian (*Digest* 69), *Digest* 1.5.26. See Hirt 2004 for a discussion of the rights of foetuses and infants.

[28] McGinn 2013, 351.

[29] Marcellus (*Digest* 28), *Digest* 11.8.2.

have thought of their offspring especially in terms of the continuity of the family name and the opportunities for marriage alliances with other elite families, and there might have been concerns over inheritance and legacies, but there is no reason to think that elite parents did not keenly love their children or grieve for them when they died. The orator Quintilian makes this quite clear when he says that he had "nothing but pain to bear" at the death of his ten-year-old son and the loss of his charm, pleasantness, and wit, but a source of the pain was also the dashed hopes for the boy's future career in the high offices of state.[30] Lower down the social scale, the freedman class placed a great deal of hope in their children born after manumission, as the door to social mobility and advancement for the whole family could be opened by their free-born children, yet there is no evidence to suggest that such children were valued only for that reason or that true sorrow was not felt when they died. Several funerary epitaphs examined in Chapter 8 attest to the devastation felt by non-elite parents at the death of an infant. And Statius in his collected poems, *Silvae*, gives us valuable insight into the lives and relationships of slaves and freedmen at the end of the first century AD.[31] Statius, the son of a teacher, and from a family that might have descended from a freedman, expresses deep love and affection for children, even the youngest infants. In *Silvae* 5, it is made clear that his adopted slave child was loved from the start of his life: "From the first moment of your birth, you seized my heart, and fixed yourself there. I taught you sounds and words, saw to your complaints and hidden hurts, stooped down and raised you to my lips as you crawled along the ground, and in my loving lap saw you close your drooping eyelids, as I summoned sweet sleep." Statius tried to console himself when the child died, but, unlike the Stoic writers of consolatory texts, he failed to do so.

An infant's perceived prospects and the family's hopes and plans for the child manifest themselves to some degree in the remains in infant burials. A special and recurring theme in this context is the sense of a child having been robbed of a future by premature death, *mors immatura*, and this is apparent both in the material culture of the burials and in the funerary commemoration of infants. In many cases, it is as if the attention paid to the dead infant and the things given to it in death in some small way compensated for a life unlived. It is as if these infants were perceived as "a person who would have been", to use a phrase coined by Henley and Kohner.[32]

Chapter 7 explored a range of grave goods that accompanied infants, and these can be interpreted as expressing frustration and the loss of a child who was cheated of future prospects. Some families deposited items of food, attire, and play in the graves of infants, suggesting that they projected their baby's future needs or that they gave their dead offspring things that they would have

[30] Quintilian, *Institutes of Oratory* 6.13.
[31] Gibson 2006, xxxviii–xlii, 62–70.
[32] Henley and Kohner 2001.

needed had they not been claimed by untimely death. It is noticeable that babies and infants could be provisioned with food which they would have been too young to eat. Infants under the age of six months would not even have begun to be weaned, relying instead on mother's milk or some milk substitute. In that sense, the feeding bottles found with some weaning-age infants would be appropriate, especially if they had belonged to the child during its short life (see Fig. 4.1). But, in reality, the cuts of chicken and joints of pork and mutton at Beaumont, or the snails at Lyons-la Forêt, for example, would not have been appropriate nourishment at all for a baby.[33] There is perhaps an element of compensation here whereby the infants whose lives could not be lived to maturity were being given provisions for a projected future life-stage when they would have been able to consume such food. A projected future need for other objects placed in the grave might also be read into the deposition of hob-nailed shoes with infants. Hob-nailed shoes appear in both male and female adult graves at Roman Marseille, but a one-year-old here is absolutely unique in also having been buried with a pair of them.[34] They are not baby booties, but a size suitable for an older child. The shoes deposited with a baby one or two months old at Bézanne are, in fact, of adult size, even though the child would have had no use for such things until much later in life.[35] The infant under six months of age in grave 50 at Worms would have had no use or need for its *Scheitelschmuck*, a decorative metal band with gems worn on the head on the central parting of the hair, as this generally was worn by children who were already some years old, up to the age of puberty.[36] The bone dice and glass gaming pieces buried with a child one to two years old at Urbino might also have been more appropriate for an older child.[37] That is also true for the gaming piece and bone die deposited with a child between six and eighteen months in the Porta Palio cemetery outside Verona.[38] And one wonders why a perinatal infant at Iasos would need a bronze arrow head, unless this object perhaps projected some kind of (masculine) activity of the future.[39] Equally, the bone spindle whorl buried in an amphora outside Rome with an infant only about five months old might point to a future gendered activity as wife and home-maker.[40]

Other objects allow us to pursue this avenue of enquiry further. The female character in Plautus' *Rudens*, Palaestra, abducted from her parents at the age of three, had a box of things she had kept since childhood, which included

[33] Dollfus and Guyot 1968; Alfonso and Blaizot 2004.

[34] Moliner et al. 2003, 363–4, pl. 56 (tomb 444). On shoes in North African child burials, see De Larminat 2012a, 302–3, fig. 7.

[35] Baills-Barré 2013, 48, with fig.

[36] von Gonzenbach 1969, 904–12.

[37] Mercando et al. 1982, 135–42, figs. 23, 25 (tomb 13).

[38] Giovannini 2006, 326.

[39] Baldoni 2013, 301, fig. 13 (tomb 8).

[40] Egidi et al. 2003, 125–6, no. 107, Osteria del Curato V (tomb 20). Admittedly, the sex of the baby cannot be determined, but, if female, this interpretation is very plausible.

miniature examples of a gold sword, a gold axe, and a silver knife; these are referred to as *crepundia*.[41] This reference to a little gold sword and a little silver knife links well to the discovery of diminutive knives and a *gladius* in infant graves of the late first and early second centuries AD at Tavant in Gaul (see Table 5; Fig. 9.1). In grave 7, which contained the remains of an infant between

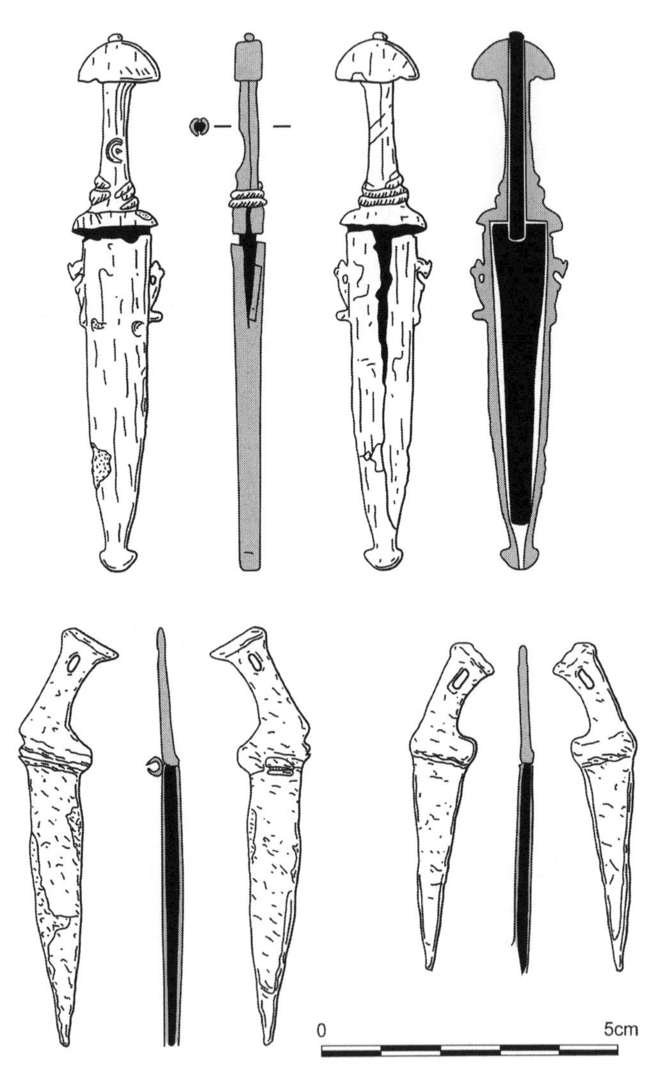

Fig. 9.1 Miniature knives and a *gladius* (top) in infant burials at Tavant.
Drawing: Irene de Luis.

[41] Plautus, *Rudens* 1156–71.

six and twelve months of age, a miniature iron knife (five-and-a-half centimetres) with a small suspension hole on the grip, an iron ring, and a large bone bead were found near the baby's neck, suggesting that these objects had been strung on a cord or thread.[42] And also in grave 6, a child between the age of one and two years was buried with a miniature iron knife (seven centimetres) with a suspension ring on the back; it lay on the child's left clavicle, and its location on the body and some traces of wool found adhering to the suspension ring clearly point to it being worn around the neck on a cord.[43] The small size of the knives given to children at Tavant and described in Roman fiction suggests that these objects were deemed suitable gifts even for infants. Perhaps like the miniature *gladius* (nine centimetres) found in a contemporary grave of an infant three to six months old at Tavant, these objects reveal a projection of future needs and a life, ultimately unlived, in which adult-size equipment would replace the childhood versions.[44] In fact, Tavant furnishes us with an example of an adult-sized iron knife just over forty-three centimetres long that was buried, along with an iron spear and various cuts of pork, with an adult individual, perhaps as a sign of his elevated status.[45] The two knives buried with the infants, although of miniature format, are of the exact same type, suggesting emulation of and aspiration to an adult male's social status.

We can infer also in the texts and images on funerary monuments of infants discussed in Chapter 8 a sense of compensating for a life too short. The often very precise statement of age at death feels like an attempt to make more of the brief time infants had lived. Likewise, the use of certain epithets in epitaphs for infants alludes to the developing or future qualities of children. The epithet "most wise", *suavissimus*, to describe a virtue of the deceased, for example, is fairly rare even for adults, so its use with an infant can only be a projection.[46] It is also a *topos* of Roman literature that children might be wiser, kinder, and more sophisticated than expected of such young individuals. Plutarch's daughter, Timothena, for example, was mild, good tempered, generous, and kind already before she died at the age of two.[47] Equally rare in funerary epigraphy is the reference to a baby having been well-deserving, *benemerenti*, as this epithet was used primarily to express the gratitude of the commemorators to the deceased for what he or she had done.[48] Likewise unusual for infants is the epithet "most dutiful", *pientissimus*, as this term referred to the

[42] Riquier and Salé 2006, 29–31, figs. 27–30 (grave 7).

[43] Riquier and Salé 2006, 27–9, figs. 23–6 (grave 6).

[44] Riquier and Salé 2006, 34–6, figs. 34–6 (grave 9).

[45] Riquier and Salé 2006, 40–3, 88–90, figs. 43, 95 (grave 11).

[46] *CIL* VI.17313 (Eucapius, six months and three days); *CIL* VI.18904 (M. Gavius Eurytus, three months and ten days).

[47] Plutarch, *Consolation to his Wife* 2.

[48] Sigismund Nielsen 1997, 185. See *CIL* VI.20029, a boy, eleven months and fifteen days old, and *CIL* VI.34442, a boy, only two months and twelve days.

kind of support that would be expected from children for their parents, but usually older children and not from tiny babies.[49] This group of epithets, then, suggests that some future qualities were being projected in the face of *mors immatura*, qualities that the children could have developed had they lived longer and which would have seen their parents hopes fulfilled, rather than frustrated. Thus, both the material culture and the epigraphic record indicate that for infants within the first year of their life, and even within the first weeks and months, identities and a social personhood were being constructed and developed.

As we have seen in Chapters 5 and 8, the youngest children, from newborn to toddler, could be depicted accurately and age-appropriately in private portraits and in funerary art which suggests interest in and careful observation of this age group (see Figs. 4.5, 5.14, 8.2). But sometimes infants were portrayed in their funerary reliefs older than they were in reality, and if we do not assume that gravestones were just bought off the shelf from available stock in the workshop, there must be other reasons for this phenomenon (see Figs. 8.1, 8.11). Jason Mander refers to those portraits that depict the child older than its actual age as "prospective".[50] I see them not only as prospective, but also compensatory for the unlived future of the infant. Kleiner interprets them as a way for parents to lament "unfinished lives".[51] Roman commemoration in text and images was often used to correct or even improve the reality experienced by people in various social situations and this concept may have been applied to those people also who were just starting out in their lives. Thus, children dying before their first birthday might be transformed in their funerary portraits into older boys and girls who had already accomplished something in life and whose family had looked forward to a bright future for them.[52]

Far from being only "a fragment of time", the first year of life was packed full of challenges, achievements, and, sometimes, disappointments. From birth (see Fig. 3.1) and the first cleansing of the baby's body (see Figs. 5.9–10), the year was marked by a series of milestones that helped shape the child's physical and social development. By the eighth or ninth day, the baby had been given a name, one that may have been chosen even before the *dies lustricus*, and within thirty days its birth had been officially and publicly registered. By the end of the second or third month, the swaddling bands had been removed, the completion of that period in the life-course being a cause for celebration and a time when religious dedications of thanks were made to the gods (see Figs. 1.1, 3.4a–b, 3.5, 4.4). At half a year, the baby had begun the weaning process, other new foods supplementing the milk of its

[49] *CIL* VI.23726; *CIL* VI.28229; *CIL* VI.34442; *CIL* VI.35558; Sigismund Nielsen 1997, 197–8.
[50] Mander 2013, 28. [51] Kleiner 1987b, 553. [52] Hope 2001, 89–91.

mother or nurse, issuing in the next phase of an increasingly independent life. The completion of the first year ended in the infant's first birthday. In Roman society, birthdays were celebrated by young and old, but the marking of this particular *dies natalis* would have been an important event after a year-long negotiation of many health hazards and dangers, a celebration which perhaps 30 per cent of children did not live to experience.

APPENDIX

Tables 1–8

List of Tables

Table 1 Infant burials in the Greek necropolis in Marseille, Sainte-Barbe, fourth to mid-second century BC.

MARSEILLE GR

Tomb no.	Age	Crem./Inh.	Container	Object
19	8–9.5 LM	inh.		shell
36	perinatal	inh.	amphora fragment	olpe
52	neonate	inh.	amphora	none
54	neonate	inh.	amphora	none
104	neonate	inh.	amphora	none
105	9 months +/− 3	inh.	wood coffin	shell
106	neonate	inh.	amphora	shell
109	neonate	inh.	amphora fragment	none
112	neonate	inh.	amphora	none
115	6.5 LM	inh.	pitcher	pot
115	6.5 LM	inh.	pot	none
118	neonate	inh.		feeding bottle, shell
119	8–8.5 LM	inh.	amphora	none
120	neonate	inh.	amphora	none
122	1 month	inh.	amphora	none
122	perinatal	inh.	amphora	none
133	perinatal?	inh.		none
230	9 LM	inh.	wood coffin	none
233	few weeks	inh.	stone and tile cover	none
254	neonate	inh.	hydria, wood coffin; rubble cover	terracotta head ornament
286	neonate	inh.	amphora	none
288	neonate	inh.	amphora	none
305	6 months +/− 3	inh.		3 shells
319	neonate	inh.	amphora	none
545	neonate	inh.	amphora	shell

Table 2 Infant burials in the Roman cemetery in Marseille, Sainte-Barbe, *c.*30 BC to *c.* AD 200.

MARSEILLE ROM

Tomb no.	Age	Crem./Inh.	Container	Object
12	perinatal	inh.	wood coffin/tile cist	none
42	10 LM	inh., w. 8-yr child	wood coffin/stones cist	TS cup, urn
123	10 LM	inh.		none
169	1 year	inh.		feeding bottle, lamp, cup, glass beads, coin, iron ring; bronze, bone and amber amulets
182	9.5 LM	inh.	tile cist	none
184	9 LM	inh, w. crem. adult	tile cover?	none
296	6 months	inh.	amphora	none
299	6 months	inh.	cist amph., tile, stone	none
308	10 LM	inh.	wood coffin	glass beads, coin, amber amulet, bracelet
316	10 LM	inh.		none
327	9 LM	inh.	wood coffin?	none
332	9.5 LM	inh.		bowl, cup, metal object
344	1 month	inh.	slate cist	none
366	9 LM	inh.	amphora	none
374	10 LM	inh.	amphora	none
375	10 LM	inh.	stone packing	none
385	6–12 months	inh., w. crem. adult		glass beads
394	9.5 LM	inh.	stone cover	none
395	10 LM	inh.	tile cist	none
397	perinatal	inh.	amphora	none
400	10 LM	inh.	wood coffin	coin
401	9 LM	inh.	stones, stone cover	none
403	10 LM	inh.	tile, stones cist	none
409	1 year	inh.		coin (in mouth), cup
419	9 months	inh.	wood coffin	none
433	9.5 LM	inh.	tile cist	none
435	9.5 LM	inh.	wood coffin	none
443	perinatal	inh.	stones cist	none
444	1 year	inh.	wood coffin, in tile cist	shoes, glass *balsamarium*
447	9.5 LM	inh.	amphora frag. and slate cover	none
452	9.5 LM	inh.	wood coffin	none
459	10 LM	inh.	stone cover	TS cup
464	10 LM	inh.	tile cist	jug
483	perinatal	inh.	amphora	none
511	perinatal	inh.	amphora	none
514	10 LM	inh.		African RS plate
518	9 LM	inh.	amphora frag. cover	none
519	perinatal	inh.		none
527	perinatal	inh.	tile cist	pierced coin, glass bead

Table 3 Infant burials in the Roman cemetery in Argenton, Champ de l'Image, mid-first to early third century AD.

ARGENTON

Tomb no.	Age	Crem./Inh.	Container	Objects
1	infant	crem.		urn, sherd
47	infant	crem.		terracotta bust
74	neonate	crem.	TS bowl	6 terracotta figurines
78	neonate	crem.	urn with bowl lid	TS bowl, pot
85	neonate	crem.		2 terracotta Venus figurines
117	infant	crem.	urn with lid	none
121	infant	crem.	urn with lid	TS sherds, terracottas, nail
133	infant	crem.	glass urn, stone surround	TS cup, nails, lead
17	infant	inh.		none
19	neonate	inh.		none
22	stillborn?	inh.	stone on baby	none
23	1 month	inh.	tiles as cover, coffin? (nails)	TS bowl
24	infant	inh.	in large jar fragment	TS bowl
25	1 year	inh.	wood coffin (nails), tiles	TS bowl
26	foetus	inh.	wood coffin (nails), tiles	none
27	3 months	inh.	wood coffin (nails)	bowl base
28	neonate	inh.	jar/amphora, stone border	nail, nail cleaner?
29	1 year	inh.	jar/amphora cover	goat and cow bones, pig tooth
31	infant	inh.		dog or fox bone
32	2 months	inh.		jug neck, pot base
33	10 months	inh.	stone on baby, coffin? (nails)	bovid bone
34	6 months	inh.		dog skeleton, other bones
38	neonate	inh.		none
39	infant	inh.		none
40	4 months	inh.		none
41	1 month	inh.	stone surround	dog skull, sherds
42	infant	inh.	wood coffin (nails)	none
43	4 months	inh.	wood coffin (nails)	none
44	stillborn	inh.	tile cover, amphora frag.	TS plate, other sherds
45	4–5 months	inh.	coffin? (nails)	none
46	6 months	inh.	coffin? (nails)	none
47	6 months	inh.	stone cover	fragmentary jug, terrac. figurine, sherds
52	infant	inh.	against W enclosure wall	horse bone, chicken bone, nails
64	infant	inh.	wood coffin (nails)	horse molar
70	1 year	inh.	stone bedding	TS bowl, jug, 1 large nail
82/83	6 months	inh.	wood coffin (nails)	dog skeleton
85	infant	inh.	tile cist and wood coffin	2 terrac. figurines, feeding bottle, iron ring
86	infant	inh.	coffin? (nails)	jug, rock-crystal bead, pierced coin amulet
88	infant	inh.	stone surround, + coffin?	TS cup, jug
92	infant	inh.	wood coffin (nails)	pig bones
122	perinatal	inh.	coffin? (nails)	dog bone
134	infant	inh.	stone surround?	nails
154	1 year	inh.		none
164	neonate	inh.		3 jug necks
165	infant	inh.		glass and ceramic sherds, bones

Table 4 Infant burials in the Roman cemetery at Tavant, mid-first to third century AD.

TAVANT				
Tomb no.	**Age**	**Crem./Inh.**	**Container**	**Objects**
5	9–15 months	inh.	limestone sarcophagus	2 glass *balsamaria*, iron needle and ring, 30 glass beads (in sarc.); 5 ceramic vessels, pig bones (in *dolium*)
6	1–2 years	inh.	wood coffin? (nails) within limestone sarcophagus	miniature knife, iron ring and bracelet, coin (in sarc.); 2 ceramic vessels (in *dolium*); glass flagon outside
7	6–12 months	inh.	limestone sarcophagus	miniature knife, iron ring, bone bead/spindle whorl (in sarc.); 2 ceramic vessels, chicken egg (in *dolium*)
9	3–9 months	inh.	limestone sarcophagus	miniature gladius, coin (in sarc.); 3 ceramic vessels (in *dolium*); glass flagon, iron implement outside
10	infant	inh.	wood coffin? (nails)	4 ceramic vessels, 2 glass flagons
12	perinatal	inh.		*dolium*
13	9–15 months	inh.	wood coffin? (nails)	ceramic beaker and jug (in *dolium*)
15	infant	inh.	limestone sarcophagus	glass flagon, bronze ring, iron nail (in sarc.); 8 ceramic vessels, incl. feeding bottle, 2 bronze rings bronze bell (in sarc.); iron bracelet, 9 glass beads, 2 bone objects (outside)
18	8–16 months	inh.	limestone sarcophagus	5 ceramic vessels, chicken carcass, goat/sheep bones (in *dolium*)
20	6–12 months	inh.	wood coffin	3 glass *balsamaria* (in coffin); 3 ceramic vessels outside

Table 5 Infant burials in the Roman cemetery at Beaumont, Champ Madame, late first/early second century AD.

BEAUMONT				
Tomb no.	**Age**	**Crem./Inh.**	**Container**	**Objects**
1	perinatal	inh.	large amphora sherd, wood coffin?	pig bones
2	infant	inh.	wood coffin (nails)	jug, antler disk
3	infant	inh.	wood coffin (nails)	jug
4	infant	inh.	poss. wood coffin (nails)	7 ceramic vessels, glass flagon, pig mandible
5	0–6 months	inh.	wood coffin (nails)	jug
6	perinatal-premature	inh.		none
7	infant	inh.	wood coffin (nails)	11 ceramic and glass vessels, incl. feeding bottle, pig and sheep bones
8	infant	inh.	wood coffin (nails)	8 ceramic vessels, metallic lamp, antler disc
9	0–6 months	inh.		jug, nails
10	infant		wood coffin(?) under tiles	pottery fragments
11	0–6 months	inh.	wood coffin (nails)	jug
15	0–6 months	inh.	tile lined pit	none
16	0–6 months	inh.	small amphora	none
18	0–6 months	inh.		2 jugs, nails
19	perinatal	inh.	on large amphora sherd	pig bone
20	perinatal	inh.		jug, TS cup
21	infant	inh.	*tegula* cover	none
22	infant	inh.	wood coffin (nails)	6 vessels, including feeding bottle
26	infant	inh.		none
27	infant	inh.		none
28	3–6 months	inh.		none
29	infant	inh.	on large amphora sherd	none
30	0–2 months	inh.	on half amphora	none
31	3–6 months	inh.	on Gallic amphora sherd	none
32	infant	inh.	oval ceramic basin	none
34	infant	inh.		jug, pot base
40	0–6 months	inh.		jug, pot, 2 feeding bottles

Table 6 Infant burials in the Roman cemetery at Kempten, Auf der Keckwiese, first century AD.

KEMPTEN

Tomb no.	Age	Crem./Inh.	Container	Object
2	7–7¼ LM	inh.		none
17	<1 year	crem.		2 bowls, pot, jug
18	<1 year	crem.		2 pots, bowl, beaker, cow tooth and bone
26	8–9 LM	inh.		partial chicken (burned)
65	6 months	inh.	wood coffin	glass *balsamarium*, 3 pots, jug
77	6 months	inh.		glass *balsamarium*, pot, jug
79	8¼–8½ LM	inh.		none
83	7–9 LM	inh.	coffin? (nails)	jug
86	neonate	inh.		glass *balsamarium*
87	8¾ LM	inh.		none
92	infant (<6 months)	inh.		beaker, pot, jug
95	neonate no. 1	inh.		TS plate, TS bowl, beaker
95	neonate no. 2	inh.		
96	neonate 9¾ LM	inh		chicken bone (burned), beaker, bowl
103	neonate	inh.		chicken bone (burned), TS bowl, iron fragment
104	8–9 LM	inh.		none
105	neonate	inh.	wood coffin	pot, bronze ring
109	infant (<6 months)	inh.	wood coffin	none
111	infant (<6 months)	inh.	wood coffin	jug, iron ring
115	6 months	inh.		jug, pot
116	neonate	inh.	wood coffin	fibula, iron fittings from wood box(?)
117	infant (<6 months)	inh.	wood coffin	jug, bowl, bronze bell, coin
134	infant (<6 months)	inh.		bronze/iron fittings from wood box, coin
143	<1 year	crem.		glass flagon, beaker, pot, coin
145	9 months	crem.	urn	bowl, 3 pots, jug, iron/bronze frags., pig/chicken bones (burned)
148	neonate	inh.		bowl, jug
154	infant (<6 months)	inh.		none
155	infant (<6 months)	inh.		fragmentary pot
164	9 LM	inh.	wood coffin	jug
166	infant (<6 months)	inh.	wood coffin	bowl
172	max. 1 year	crem.	urn	glass *balsamarium*, glass frags., 3 pots, 2 jugs, pig bones (burned)
174	6 months	inh.	wood coffin	2 jugs, pot, fibula
186	8–9 LM	inh.		pot

187	infant (up to 6 months)	inh.		none
197	infant (up to 6 months)	inh.		jug, burned pig bone
199	8½ LM	inh.		bowl, jug
200	9 LM	inh.		none
205	infant (up to 6 months)	inh.	wood coffin	bowl
206	infant (up to 6 months)	inh.	wood coffin	bronze amulet ring, frag. iron hinges, 2 shoe nails
208	neonate	inh. (+ crem. child)		none (grave goods with child cremation)
211	6 months	inh.	wood coffin	pot, jug
212	neonate	inh.		bowl, fibula, 2 bronze amulet rings, bronze amulet, bronze bell
214	9¾ LM	inh.		none
226	up to 6 months	inh.		glass *balsamarium*
239	neonate	inh. (+ 4–5-year-old child)		none (grave goods with other child)
242	up to 6 months	inh.		none
244	infant (<6 months)	inh.		jug
249	9¾ LM	inh.		none
251	infant (<6 months)	inh.		none
252	infant (<6 months)	inh.		bowl
276	up to 6 months	inh.	wood coffin	none
278	>6 months	crem. (+ crem. adult)	urn	lamp, silver pendant, glass *balsamarium* (more with adult)
290	neonate	inh.		none
294	infant up to 6 months	inh.		coin, bowl, plate, jug
328	infant up to 6 months	inh.		jug, bowl
337	infant up to 6 months	inh.		jug
364	infant up to 6 months	inh.		jug, coin
376	infant up to 6 months	inh.		jug
378	infant up to 6 months	inh.		jug, lamp
395	8¾ LM	inh.	wood coffin	jug, coin

Table 7 Infant burials in the Roman cemetery at Sitifis/Sétif, second century AD.

SITIFIS				
Tomb no.	**Age**	**Crem./Inh.**	**Feature/Container**	**Objects**
2	1 year	inh.	*loculus*, stones cover	plate
7	few months	inh.	rect. rock cut	plate
9	1–3 months	inh.	stones cover	none
11	foetus	inh.	pit, stones cover	none
13	foetus/stillborn	inh.	*loculus* cut, tile seal, cedar coffin	none
14	foetus/stillborn	inh.	stones seal	none
15	3–12 months	inh.	rect. rock cut	none
18	few months	inh.	rect. rock cut, shist slab cover	none
26	foetus/stillborn	inh.	rect. rock cut	small plate
29	3–12 months	inh.	clay slab seal	none
30	stillborn/perinatal	inh.	clay slab seal	none
31	few months	inh.	rect. rock cut, *tegula* cover	none
35	stillborn	inh.	rect. rock cut, *tegula* cover	none
39	foetus/stillborn	inh.	stones, schist slab	none
40	3–12 months	inh.	rect. pit in rock	none
47	foetus/stillborn	inh.	rect. pit in natural soil	none
49	foetus/stillborn	inh.	rect. rock cut, stones seal	lamp (used, with soot)
50	few months	inh.	rect. rock cut	none
51	foetus/stillborn	inh.	rect. rock cut, stones seal	none
53	1 year +	inh.	rock pit	lamp, bowl, coin
54	1 year +	inh.		none
56	foetus/perinatal	inh.	rect. rock cut, schist and stone	none
59	1 year +	inh.		none
60	foetus	inh.	rect. pit in rock, schist slab	none
61	1 year	inh.	irregular pit in rock, *tegula*	plate, coin, shells
64	stillborn/perinatal	inh.	pit in virgin soil, stone surround	none
69	few months	inh.	rect. rock pit, *tegula* and stone	plate, coin, iron nail, lamp, glass vess., cup
70	1 year	inh.	rock-cut pit, stones, *tegula*	worked bone, plate, jug, lamp, ostrich shells
73	few weeks	inh.	pit in rock, stones and mortar	none
74	*c.*3 months	inh.	soil, stones cover	none
75	stillborn/neonate <3 months	inh.	pit, stones	none
78	stillborn/perinatal	inh.	rock pit, schist cover	none
79	foetus/stillborn/ perinatal	inh.	pit in rock, wood coffin	lamp, plate
99	few months	inh.	pit in soil	marble plaque
100	foetus/premature	inh.		none
240	few months	inh.	rock pit	13 small nails (bonnet on head)?

241	few months—max. 1 year	inh.	rock pit	plate, 2 cups, lamp
248	stillborn/neonate	inh.		plate and lamp
253	few months—max. 1 year	inh.	pit in soil	plate, lamp, pitcher
259	foetus	inh.	rock pit, *tegula* cover	none
264	few months	inh.	pit, stone cover	iron bracelet, copper bracelet
267	foetus/perinatal	inh.	under stones	none
268	foetus	inh.	stones and tile	none
271	1–2 years	inh.	tile base and tile cover	none
272	at least 1 year	inh.	*tegula* cist, stones	none
273	few months	inh.	stones enclosing grave	none
274	stillborn	inh.	under flat stone	none
275	*c.*3 months	inh.	schist pieces, stones	none
276	stillborn/neonate <3 months	inh.	reused gravestone cover	none
278	foetus	inh.	stones cover	none
279	1 year	inh.	cist	iron bracelet
289	3–12 months	inh.		none
299	premature	inh.		none
301	foetus	inh.		none
302	premature	inh.		none
304	foetus	inh.	rock pit, stones and tile cover	none
305	3–12 months	inh.	rock pit, tile and rock frags. cover	none
306	1 year +	inh.	rect. rock pit, rubble cover	none
311	foetus	inh.	soil, stones surround, schist top	none
314	foetus	inh.	tile base, *tegula* cover	none
315	foetus	inh.	stone surround	none
316	few months	inh.	stone surround, stone top	none
318	1 year +		stones cover	none
330	1–3 months	inh.		copper bracelet, iron ring, earrings
337	few months (max. 1 year)	inh.		none
339	3–12 months	inh.	tile fragments	none
340	1–3 months	inh.		none
341	neonate	inh.		none
344	foetus or neonate	inh.		none

Table 8 Infant burials in the Roman cemetery at Poundbury, Dorset. The light grey entries date to the late Iron Age and early Roman periods (mid-first to early second century AD). The others date to the late second to early fourth century AD.

POUNDBURY

Tomb no.	Age	Crem./Inh.	Container	Object
253	<12 months	inh.		none
1214	1½ years	inh.		none
1249	stillborn	inh.		none
1366	perinatal	inh.		none
1368	foetus/miscarriage	inh.		none
1371	perinatal	inh.		none
1372	perinatal	inh.		none
1375	perinatal	inh.		none
1376	perinatal	inh.		none
1377	perinatal	inh.		none
1379	perinatal	inh.		none
1380	perinatal	inh.		none
1382	perinatal	inh.		none
1383	stillborn	inh.	wood coffin	none
1386	stillborn	inh.		none
1387	<12 months	inh.		none
1388	perinatal	inh.		none
1389	6 months	inh.		none
1390	1 year	inh.		none
1391	1 year	inh.	wood coffin	ceramic vessel
1392	perinatal	inh.		none
1393	perinatal	inh.		none
1394	neonate	inh.		none
1395	perinatal	inh.		none
596	foetus/neonate	inh.		none
28	1 year	inh.	wood coffin, flint packing	none
29A	foetus/miscarriage	inh.		none
52	<12 months	inh.		none
131A	foetus/neonate	inh.		none
161	foetus/neonate	inh.	stone-lined pit	none
186	perinatal	inh.		none
187	<12 months	inh.	wood coffin	none
188	perinatal	inh.		none
189	<12 months	inh.	wood coffin	none
191	perinatal	inh.	wood coffin	none
194	perinatal	inh.	stone-lined pit	none
210	1 year	inh.	wood coffin	none
241	<12 months	inh.		none
243B	1 year	inh.		none
243B	1½ years	inh.		none
254	stillborn	inh.		none
263	<12 months	inh.		none
264	foetus/miscarriage	inh.		none
267	9 months	inh.	wood coffin	none

288	6 months	inh.	wood coffin	none
296	perinatal	inh.		none
308	foetus/neonate	inh.		none
312	6 months	inh.		none
315	1½ years	inh.	wood coffin	none
339	<12 months	inh.	wood coffin	none
347	stillborn	inh.	wood coffin	none
348	under 12 months	inh.	wood coffin	none
353	foetus/neonate	inh.		none
358B	1 year	inh.	wood coffin	none
361	neonate	inh.		none
365B	perinatal	inh.		none
366	1½ years	inh.	wood coffin	none
368	6 months	inh.	wood coffin	none
375	9 months	inh.	wood coffin	none
378	1 year	inh.	wood coffin	none
380	<12 months	inh.	wood coffin	none
382A	1 year	inh.		none
384	perinatal	inh.	wood coffin	none
418	9 months	inh.	wood coffin	none
428	<12 months	inh.	wood coffin	none
430	<12 months	inh.		none
433	neonate	inh.	wood coffin	none
440	stillborn	inh.		none
441	6 months	inh.	wood coffin	none
443	neonate	inh.	wood coffin	none
444	perinatal	inh.	wood coffin	none
445	perinatal	inh.	wood coffin	none
446	perinatal	inh.		none
449	perinatal	inh.		none
456	perinatal	inh.	stone-lined pit	none
457	foetus/neonate	inh.		none
458	foetus/neonate	inh.		none
461	perinatal	inh.		none
462	perinatal	inh.		none
470A	<12 months	inh.		none
476	foetus/neonate	inh.		none
484	<12 months	inh.	wood coffin	none
491	foetus/neonate	inh.		none
493	perinatal	inh.	stones on body	none
523	foetus/neonate	inh.		none
525	1 year	inh.	lead/wood coffins, gypsum	none
539	foetus/neonate	inh.		none
540	under 12 months	inh.	wood coffin	none
541	infant	inh.	wood coffin	none
549	9 months	inh.	wood coffin	bone bracelet
551?	infant	inh.	wood coffin	bronze brooch, bone pin, coin
555	9 months	inh.		none

(*continued*)

Table 8 Continued

POUNDBURY

Tomb no.	Age	Crem./Inh.	Container	Object
557	9 months	inh.	wood coffin	none
565	9 months	inh.		none
569	foetus/neonate	inh.		none
570	perinatal	inh.		none
572	foetus/stillborn	inh.		none
573	<12 months	inh.		none
575	perinatal	inh.		none
577	perinatal	inh.		none
582	stillborn	inh.		none
583	perinatal	inh.		none
584	perinatal	inh.		none
585	perinatal	inh.		none
586	perinatal	inh.		none
587	6 months	inh.		none
588	foetus/neonate	inh.	wood coffin	none
589	perinatal	inh.		none
590	perinatal	inh.		none
591	6 months	inh.	wood coffin	none
592	neonate	inh.		none
594	<12 months	inh.	wood coffin	none
597	perinatal	inh.	wood coffin	none
603	foetus/neonate	inh.	wood coffin	none
605	foetus/neonate	inh.		none
606	foetus/neonate	inh.		none
607	perinatal	inh.	wood coffin	none
624	12 months	inh.	wood coffin	none
675	foetus/neonate	inh.	pit, flint and chalk lined	none
694	6 months	inh.	wood coffin	none
697	1½ years	inh.	wood coffin	none
742	6 months	inh.	wood coffin	none
744	6 months	inh.	wood coffin	none
745	9 months	inh.	wood coffin	none
746	9 months	inh.		none
763	foetus/neonate	inh.	wood coffin	none
764	1 year	inh.	wood coffin	none
768	foetus/neonate	inh.		none
770	6 months	inh.	stone-lined pit	none
786	1 year	inh.	wood coffin	none
802	1 year	inh.	wood coffin	none
805	9 months	inh.	wood coffin	none
806	foetus/neonate	inh.	wood coffin	none
807	6 months	inh.		none
812B	perinatal	inh.		none
818	foetus/neonate	inh.	wood coffin	none
820	stillborn	inh.		none
827	perinatal	inh.		none
828	<12 months	inh.	wood coffin	none

829	foetus/neonate	inh.		none
821	foetus/neonate	inh.		none
824	foetus/neonate	inh.		none
835	<12 months	inh.		none
836	foetus/neonate	inh.	wood coffin	none
848	foetus/neonate	inh.		none
860	perinatal	inh.	wood coffin, stone base	none
874	6 months	inh.		none
882	6 months	inh.	wood coffin	none
887	9 months	inh.	wood coffin	none
915	1 year	inh.	wood coffin	none
939	9 months	inh.	wood coffin	none
944	6 months	inh.	wood coffin	none
948	9 months	inh.	wood coffin	none
966	<12 months	inh.	stone-lined pit	none
967	6 months	inh.	wood coffin	none
969	6 months	inh.	wood coffin	none
971	6 months	inh.	wood coffin	none
972	6 months	inh.	wood coffin	none
1002	foetus/neonate	inh.	wood coffin	none
1003	6 months	inh.		none
1005	perinatal	inh.	wood coffin	none
1008	6 months	inh.		none
1026	foetus/neonate	inh.	wood coffin	none
1051	stillborn	inh.		none
1058	perinatal	inh.		none
1061	foetus/neonate	inh.		none
1062	6 months	inh.		none
1072	stillborn	inh.		none
1076	6 months	inh.		none
1077	6 months	inh.		none
1078	6 months	inh.	wood coffin	none
1083	9 months	inh.	wood coffin	none
1084	1 year	inh.	wood coffin	none
1084A	foetus/miscarriage	inh.		none
1097	6 months	inh.	wood coffin	none
1101	6 months	inh.		none
1103	9 months	inh.		none
1105	perinatal	inh.	stone surround	none
1109	9 months	inh.	wood coffin	none
1124	3 months	inh.		none
1126	1 year	inh.		3 bronze bracelets, bronze frags., glass
1133	9 months	inh.	wood coffin	none
1134	<12 months	inh.	wood coffin	none
1151	9 months	inh.	wood coffin	none
1166	9 months	inh.	wood coffin	none
1174	1¼ years	inh.	wood coffin	none

(*continued*)

Table 8 Continued

POUNDBURY				
Tomb no.	**Age**	**Crem./Inh.**	**Container**	**Object**
1180	6 months	inh.	wood coffin	none
1209	6 months	inh.	wood coffin	none
1211	foetus/neonate	inh.		none
1221	6 months	inh.		none
1318	1 year	inh.	wood coffin	none
1326	perinatal	inh.	stone-lined pit	none
1329	9 months	inh.	wood coffin, stone surround	none
1342	stillborn	inh.	stone-lined pit	none
1345	foetus/neonate	inh.		none
1413	neonate	inh.		none
1414	foetus, dismembered	inh.	wood coffin	none
1416	perinatal	inh.	wood coffin, rubble surround	none

Bibliography

Abraham, E., Hendler, T., Schipra-Lichter, I., Kanat-Maymon, Y., Zagoory-Sharon, O., and Feldman, R. (2014), 'Father's Brain is Sensitive to Childcare Experiences', *Proceedings of the National Academy of Science* 111(27): 9792–7.

Adams, J. N. (2007), *The Regional Diversification of Latin, 200 BC–600 AD*. Cambridge: Cambridge University Press.

Adriani, A. (1939), *Cataloghi illustrati del Museo Campano, I: Sculture in Tufo*. Naples: Museo Campano.

Agócs, N. (2013), 'People in Intercisa from the Eastern Part of the Roman Empire', in Visy, Z. (ed.), *Specimina Nova Dissertationum ex Institutis Historiae Antiquae et Archaeologiae Universitatis Quinqueecclesiensis, Pars Prima, XXI–XXII*, Pécs: University of Pécs, 9–28.

Agustí, B., Martín, A., and Pons, E. (2008), 'Dipòsits infantils als poblats ibers empordanesos (Catalunya)', in Gusi, F., Muriel, S., and Olària, C. R. (eds.), *Nasciturus, infans, puerulus vobis mater terra: La muerte en la infancia*. Castelló: Servei d'Investigacions Arquelògiques i Prehistòriques, 117–42.

Ajootian, A. (2006), 'Male *Kourotrophoi*', in Mattusch, C. C., Donohue, A. A., and Brauer, A. (eds.), *Common Ground: Archaeology, Art, Science and Humanities. Proceedings of the XVIth International Congress of Classical Archaeology*, Oxford: Oxbow, 617–20.

Alesan, A., Malgosa, A., and Simó, C. (1999), 'Looking into the Demography of an Iron Age Population in the Western Mediterranean. I: Mortality', *American Journal of Physical Anthropology* 110(3): 285–301.

Alexandridou, A. (2012), 'The north necropolis of Vari revisited', *Αρχαιολογικη εφημερις* 15: 1–73.

Alfonso, G. and Blaizot, R. (eds.) (2004), *La villa gallo-romaine de Champ Madame à Beaumont (Puy-de- Dôme): habitat et ensemble funéraire des nourrissons* (Documents d'Archéologie en Rhône-Alpes et en Auvergne 27). Lyon: L'Association Lyonnaise pour la Promotion de l'Archéologie en Rhône-Alpes.

Allain, J., Fauduet, I., and Tuffrau-Libre, M. (1992), *La nécropole gallo-romaine du Champ de l'Image à Argentomagus (St-Marcel, Indre)*. Saint-Marcel: Musée d'Argentomagus.

Allen, M. C., Donohue, P. K., and Dusman, A. E. (1993), 'The Limit of Variability: Neonatal Outcome of Infants Born at 22 to 25 Weeks' Gestation', *The New England Journal of Medicine* 329(22): 1597–601.

Allison, P. M. (2006), 'Artefact Distribution within the Auxiliary Fort at Ellingen: Evidence for Building Use and for the Presence of Women and Children', *Bericht der Römisch-Germanischen Kommission* 87: 387–452.

Allison, P. M. (2008), 'The Women and Children Inside 1st- and 2nd-Century Forts: Comparing the Archaeological Evidence', in Brandl, U. (ed.), *Frauen und römisches Militär: Beiträge eines Runden Tisches in Xanten vom 7. bis 9. Juli 2005* (BAR International Series 1759). Oxford: Archaeopress, 120–39.

Allison, P. M. (2011), 'Soldiers' Families in the Early Roman Empire', in Rawson, B. (ed.), *A Companion to Families in the Greek and Roman Worlds*. Oxford: Blackwell, 161–82.

Alonso, E. (2006), 'Les médaillons en bois de cerf de l'est et du centre-est de la Gaule romaine: Étude d'apres l'ensemble d'Alésia', *Revue Archéologique de l'Est* 55: 197–223.

Alonso, E. (2008), 'Travail et décor des médaillons en bois de cerf: Analyse et essai typologique', in Bertrand, I. (ed.), *Le travail de l'os, du bois de cerf et de la corne à l'époque romaine: Un artisanat en marge? Actes de la Table ronde Instrumentum, Chauvigny (Vienne, F), 8–9 décembre 2005*. Chauvigny: Monique Mergoil Montagnac, 275–81.

Almagro, M. (1955), *Las necropolis de Ampurias: Necropolis romanas y necropolis indigenas, Vol. 2* (Monografías Ampuritanas 3). Barcelona: Seix Barral.

Amedick, R. (1991), *Vita Privata. Die Sarkophage mit Darstellungen aus dem Menschenleben*. Berlin: Gebrüder Mann.

Ammerman, R. M. (1993), *The Sanctuary of Santa Venera at Paestum II: The Votive Terracottas*. Ann Arbor: University of Michigan Press.

Andreae, B., Anger, K., De Angelis, M. A., Geominy, W., Granino, M. G., Köhler, J., Kreeb, M., Liverani, P., Mathea-Förtsch, M., Stadler, M., and Uncini, A. (1995), *Bildkatalog der Skulpturen des Vatikanischen Museums, Vol. 1, Museo Chiaramonti*. Berlin: Walter de Gruyter.

Andreae, B., Anger, K., Granino, M. G., Köhler, J., Liverani, P., and Spinola, G. (1998), *Bildkatalog detr Skulpturen des Vatikanischen Museums, Vol. 2, Museo Pio Clementino Cortile Ottagono*. Berlin: Walter de Gruyter.

Andrews, M. (2016), 'The Infant Burials', in Fentress, E., Goodson, C., Maiuro, M., Andrews, M., and Dufton, J. A. (eds.), *Villa Magna: An Imperial Estate and its Legacies, Excavations 2006–10*. Oxford: Oxbow, 132–5.

Angeli, M. and Quarante, P. (2006), 'Necropoli della III Casa Circondariale di Rebibbia (Municipio V)', in Tomei, M. A. (ed.), *Roma. Memorie dal sottosuolo: Ritrovamenti archeologici 1980–2006*. Rome: Electa, 261–2.

Anon., 'The Cambridge Shrine', *Current Archaeology* 61, 1978, 58–9.

Arvanitopoulos, A. S. (1928), *Graptai stelai Demetriados-Pagason*. Athens: Archaeological Society.

Aubet, M. E. (2001), *The Phoenicians and the West: Politics, Colonies and Trade* (2nd edn). Cambridge: Cambridge University Press.

Backe, A. (2015), 'Römische Kinderkleidung zwischen Realität und Repräsentation', in Paetz gen. Schieck, A. and Bergemann, U.-C. (eds.), *Das Bild vom Kind im Spiegel seiner Kleidung von prähistorischer Zeit bis zur Gegenwart*. Regensburg: Schnell und Steiner, 56–75.

Backe-Dahmen, A. (2006), *Inocentissima Aetas: Römische Kindheit im Spiegel literarischer, rechtlicher und archäologischer Quellen des 1. bis 4. Jahrhunderts n. Chr.* Mainz: Philipp von Zabern.

Baggieri, G. and Rinaldi Veloccia, M. L. (eds.) (1996), *Speranza e Sofferenza: Nei votivi anatomici dell'Antichità*. Rome: Ministero per i Beni e le Attività Culturali.

Baills, N. (2003), 'Stèles épigraphiques dedieés aux enfants en base âge', in Gourevitch, D., Moirin, A., and Rouquet, N. (eds.), *Maternité et petite enfance dans l'Antiquité romaine*. Bourges: Éditions de la Ville de Bourges, 122–8.

Baills-Barré, N. (2013), 'Les enfants en bas âge en Gaule romaine: des lieux d'ensevelissement spécifiques', *La petite Enfance dans le Monde Grec et Romain* (*Dossiers d'Archéologie* 356): 46–9.

Baills-Talbi, N. and Dasen, V. (2008), 'Rites funéraires et practiques magiques', in Gusi, F., Muriel, S., and Olària, C. R. (eds.), *Nasciturus, infans, puerulus vobis mater terra: La muerte en la infancia.* Castelló: Servei d'Investigacions Arquelògiques i Prehistòriques, 595–618.

Baker, B. J., Dupras, T. L., and Tocheri, M. W. (2005), *The Osteology of Infants and Children.* College Station: Texas A&M University Press.

Balch, D. L. and Osiek, C. (eds.) (2003), *Early Christian Families in Context.* Grand Rapids: William B. Eerdmans Publishing Company.

Baldoni, D. (2013), 'Considerazioni su alcune sepolture infantile a *enchytrismos* rinvenute a Iasos', in Graziadio, G., Guglielmino, R., Lenuzza, V., and Vitale, S. (eds.), *Φιλική Συναυλία: Studies in Mediterranean Archaeology for Mario Benzi* (BAR Int. Series 2460). Oxford: Archaeopress, 291–307.

Baltussen, H. (2009a), 'A Grief Observed: Cicero on Remembering Tullia', *Mortality* 14(4): 355–69.

Baltussen, H. (2009b), 'Personal Grief and Public Mourning in Plutarch's *Consolation to his Wife*', *American Journal of Philology* 130: 67–98.

Barber, B. and Bowsher, D. (2000), *The Eastern Cemetery of Roman London: Excavations 1983–1990.* London: Museum of London.

Barbet, G., Joan, L., and Ancel, M.-J. (eds.) (2014), *La nécropole gallo-romaine des "Charmes d'Amont" à Tavaux (Jura).* Montagnac: Éditions Mergoil.

Barral, P., Dedet, B., Delrieu, F., Giraud, P., Le Goff, I., Marion, S., and Villard-Le Tec, A. (eds.) (2010), *Gestes funéraires en Gaule au second âge du Fer. Actes du XXXIIIe colloque international de l'AFEAF. Caen 20–24 mai 2009.* Besançon: Presses universitaires de Franche-Comté.

Batziou-Efstathiou, A. (1981), 'Two New Grave Stelae of Larisa Museum', *Athens Annals of Archaeology* 14–15: 47–54.

Baxter, J. E. (2005), *The Archaeology of Childhood: Children, Gender and Material Culture.* Walnut Creek: AltaMira Press.

Beaumont, L. (2003), 'The Changing Face of Childhood', in Neils, J. and Oakley, J. H. (eds.), *Coming of Age in Ancient Greece: Images of Childhood from the Classical Past.* New Haven: Yale University Press, 59–84.

Beaumont, L. (2012), *Childhood in Ancient Athens.* London: Routledge.

Becker, M. J. (1997), 'Roman Period Amphora Burials of Young Children Dating to the Third Century CE at Metaponto (Basilicata) Italy', *Archaeological News* 21–2: 20–6.

Becker, M. J. (2004), 'The Cazzanello Perinatal Cemetery: Continuities of Etruscan Mortuary Practices into the Late Antique Period and Beyond', *Studi Etruschi* 70: 255–67.

Beer, C. (1994), *Temple-Boys, A Study of Cypriote Votive Sculpture Part 1: Catalogue*, Jonsered: Paul Åströms Förlag.

Beilke-Voigt, I. (2007), 'Kinderdefizite und Kinderfriedhöfe–Zur Sonderstellung des Kindes im Bestattungsritual anhand archäologischer und ethnologischer Quellen', *Ethnologisch-Archäologische Zeitschrift* 45: 271–95.

Bel, V. (1992), 'Les sépultures', in Odiot, T., Bel, V., and Bois, M. (eds.), *D'Augusta Tricastinorum à Saint-Paul-Trois-Châteaux (Drôme)*. Lyon: Service régional de l'Archéologie de Rhône'Alpes, 105–14.

Bel, V. (2012), 'Les dépôts de mobilier dans les tombes d'enfants et d'adolescents en Gaule Narbonnaise au Haut-Empire', in Hermary, A. and Dubois, C. (eds.), *L'enfant et la mort dans l'Antiquité III: Le materiel associé aux tombes d'enfants. Actes de la table ronde internationale organisée à la Maison Méditteranéenne de Sciences de l'Homme (MMSH) d'Aix-en-Provence, 20–22 janvier 2011*. Arles: Éditions Errance, 193–216.

Ben Lazreg, N. and Mattingly, D. (1992), *Leptiminus (Lamta): A Roman Port City in Tunisia. Report no. 1* (JRA Supplement 4). Ann Arbor: Journal of Roman Archaeology.

Bénichou-Safar, H. (1988), 'Sur l'incinération des enfants aux tophets de Carthage et de Sousse', *Revue de l'Histoire des Religions* 205(1): 57–67.

Bénichou-Safar, H. (2004), *Le Tophet de Salammbô à Carthage. Essai sur reconstruction*. Rome: École française de Rome.

Berger, L. (1993), 'Säuglings- und Kinderbestattungen in römischen Siedlungen der Schweiz–ein Vorbericht', in Struck, M. (ed.), *Römerzeitliche Gräber als Quellen zu Religion, Bevölkerungsstruktur und Sozialgeschichte*. Mainz: Johannes Gutenberg-Universität.

Bertoletti, M., Cima, M., and Talamo, E. (2006), *Centrale Montemartini: Musei Capitolini*. Milan: Mondadori Electa.

Bianchi Bandinelli, M. T. and Bianchi Bandinelli, R. (1968), 'La kourotrophos Maffei del museo di Volterra', *Revue Archéologique* 2: 225–40.

Bisel, S. C. and Bisel, J. F. (2002), 'Health and Nutrition at Herculaneum: An Examination of Human Skeletal Remains', in Jashemski, W. F. and Meyer, F. G. (eds.), *The Natural History of Pompeii*. Cambridge: Cambridge University Press, 451–75.

Blaizot, F. (2009), 'Rites et pratiques funéraires à Lugdunum du Ier au IVe siècle', in Goudineau, C. (ed.), *Rites Funéraires à Lugdunum*. Paris: Éditions Errance, 155–85.

Blaizot, F., Alix, G., and Ferber, E. (2003), 'Le traitement funéraire des enfants décédés avant un an dans l'Antiquité: études de cas', *Bulletins et Memoires de la Société d'Anthropologie de Paris* 15(1–2): 49–77.

Blanc, P. (2002), 'Avenches: a la Montagne, aux Conches Dessus, Creux de la Vigne', *Bulletin de l'Association Pro Aventico* 44: 152–8.

Blandin, B. (2010), 'Les Enfants et la Mort en Eubeé au Debut de l'Âge du Fer', in Guimier-Sorbets, A.-M. and Morizot, Y. (eds.), *L'Enfant et la mort dans l'Antiquité I: Nouvelles recherches dans les nécropoles grecques: Le signalement des tombes d'enfants. Actes de la table ronde internationale organiseé à Athènes, École française d'Athènes, 29–30 mai 2008*. Paris: de Boccard, 47–65.

Boatwright, M. (2005), 'Children and Parents on the Tombstones of Pannonia', in George, M. (ed.), *The Roman Family in the Empire: Rome, Italy and Beyond*. Oxford: Oxford University Press, 287–318.

Bobou, O. (2015), *Children in the Hellenistic World: Statues and Representation*. Oxford: Oxford University Press.

Bodel, J. (1995), 'Minicia Marcella: Taken Before her Time', *American Journal of Philology* 116(3): 453–60.

Bol, P. C. (ed.) (1989), *Forschungen zur Villa Albani. Katalog der antiken Bildwerke I.* Berlin: Gebrüder Mann Verlag.

Bolla, M. (2013), 'Bronzetti in contesti funerari di età romana', *LANX* 15: 1–50.

Bonfante, L. (1986), 'Votive Terracotta Figures of Mothers and Children', in Swaddling, J. (ed.), *Italian Iron Age Artefacts in the British Museum.* London: British Museum Publications, 195–203.

Bonfante, L. (1997), 'Nursing Mothers in Classical Art', in Koloski-Ostrow, A. O. and Lyons, C. L. (eds.), *Naked Truths: Women, Sexuality and Gender in Classical Art and Archaeology.* London: Routledge, 174–96.

Bonfante, L. (2006), 'Etruscan Inscriptions and Etruscan Religion', in De Grummond, N. T. and Simon, E. (eds.), *The Religion of the Etruscans.* Austin: University of Texas Press, 9–26.

Bonfante, L. (2013), 'Mothers and Children', in MacIntosh Turfa, J. (ed.), *The Etruscan World.* London: Routledge, 426–46.

Bonnet, C. (2011), 'On Gods and Earth: The Tophet and the Construction of a New Identity in Punic Carthage', in Gruen, E. S. (ed.), *Cultural Identity in the Ancient Mediterranean.* Los Angeles: J. Paul Getty Trust, 373–87.

Bookidis, N. (2010), *Corinth, Volume XVIII, Part V, The Sanctuary of Demeter and Kore: The Terracotta Sculpture.* Princeton: The American School of Classical Studies at Athens.

Boppert, W. (1992), *Zivile Grabsteine aus Main und Umgebung* (Corpus Signorum impreii Romani II, 6, Deutschland). Mainz: Verlag des Römisch-Germanischen Zentralmuseums.

Boschung, D. (1987a), *Antike Grabaltäre aus den Nekropolen Roms.* Bern: Verlag Stämpfli et Cie.

Boschung, D. (1987b), 'Römische Glasphalerae mit Portätbüsten', *Bonner Jahrbücher* 187: 194–258.

Bosnakis, D. (2013), 'L'Allaitement maternel: Une image exceptionalle dans l'iconographie funéraire?', *La petite Enfance dans le Monde Grec et Romain* (*Dossiers d'Archéologie* 356): 58–61.

Bossert, M. (1998), *Die figürlichen Reliefs von Aventicum. CSIR 1.1, Schweiz.* Lausanne: Cahiers d'Archéologie Romande.

Bossert-Radtke, C. (1992), *Die figürlichen Reliefs und Rundskulpturen aus Augst und Kaiseraugst* (Forschungen in August 16). Augst: Römermuseum.

Boswell, J. E. (1984), 'Expositio and Oblatio: The Abandonment of Children and the Ancient and Medieval Family', *American Historical Review* 89: 10–33.

Bouisset, P. (1969), 'Un jouet d'enfant en terre cuite', *Bulletin de la Société des Etudes Scientifiques de l'Aude* 69: 119–21.

Bouisset, P. (1977), 'Note sur une deuxième poupée trouvée en Narbonnais', *Bulletin de la Société des Etudes Scientifiques de l'Aude* 77: 91–3.

Bouma, J. W. (1996), *Religio Votiva: The Archaeology of Latial Votive Religion.* Groningen: University of Groningen.

Bourbou, C. (2013), 'The Imprint of Emotions Surrounding the Death of Children in Antiquity', in Chaniotis, A. and Ducrey, P. (eds.), *Unveiling Emotions II: Emotions in Greece and Rome: Texts, Images, Material Culture.* Stuttgart: Steiner Verlag, 331–50.

Bourbou, C. and Themelis, P. (2010), 'Child Burials at Ancient Messene', in Guimier-Sorbets, A. M. and Morizot, Y. (eds.), *L'Enfant et la mort dans l'Antiquité I: Nouvelles recherches dans les nécropoles grecques: Le signalement des tombes d'enfants. Actes de la table ronde internationale organiseé à Athènes, École française d'Athènes, 29–30 mai 2008*. Paris: de Boccard, 111–28.

Bowen, G. E. (2002), 'Some Observations on Christian Burial Practices at Kellis', in Hope, C. A. and Bowen, G. E. (eds.), *Dakhleh Oasis Project: Preliminary Reports on the 1994–1995 to 1998–1999 Field Seasons*. Oxford: Oxbow, 167–82.

Bowersock, G. W. (2011), 'Infant Gods and Heroes in Late Antiquity: Dionysos' First Bath', in Schlesier, R. (ed.), *A Different God? Dionysos and Ancient Polytheism*. Berlin: Walter De Gruyter, 3–14.

Bowman, A. K. and Thomas, J. D. (1994), *The Vindolanda Writing Tablets (Tabulae Vindolandenses II)*. London: British Museum Press.

Boyle, E. M., Poulsen, G., Field, D. J., Kurinczuk, J. J., Wolke, D., and Quigley, M. A. (2012), 'Effects of Gestational Age at Birth on Health Outcomes at 3 and 5 Years of Age: Population Based Cohort Study', *British Medical Journal* 344: 1–14.

Bradley, K. R. (1986), 'Wet-Nursing at Rome: A Study in Social Relations', in Rawson, B. *The Family in Ancient Rome*. Oxford: Oxford University Press, 201–29.

Bradley, K. R. (1998), 'The Sentimental Education of the Roman Child: The Role of Pet-Keeping', *Latomus* 57: 523–57.

Brandl, U. (ed.) (2008), *Frauen und Römisches Militär: Beiträge eines Runden Tisches in Xanten vom.7. bis 9. Juli 2005* (BAR Int. Series 1759). Oxford: Archaeopress.

Brent, L. and Prowse, T. (2014), 'Grave Goods, Burial Practices and Patterns of Distribution in the Vagnari Cemetery', in Small, A. M. (ed.), *Beyond Vagnari: New Themes in the Study of Roman South Italy*. Bari: Edipuglia, 99–110.

Brettell, R. C., Stern, B., Reifarth, N., and Heron, C. (2014), 'The "Semblance of Immortality"? Resinous Materials and Mortuary Rites in Roman Britain', *Archaeometry* 56(3): 444–59.

Brkojewitsch, G., Marquié, S., Naji, S., and Adam, F. (2014), '*Funera Acerba* dans les campagnes de la cité des Mediomatrici? Le cas de Laquenexy "La Noiseraie" (Moselle)', *Revue Archéologique de l'Est* 63: 213–36.

Brown, S. S. (1991), *Late Carthaginian Child Sacrifice and Sacrificial Monuments in their Mediterranean Context*. Sheffield: JSOT Press.

Brunn, C. (1996), 'A Temple of Mater Matuta in the *regio sexta* of Rome', *Zeitchrift für Papyrologie und Epigraphik* 112: 219–23.

Buccellato, A., Catalano, P., Arrighetti, B., Caldarini, C., Colonelli, G., Di Bernardini, M., Minozzi, S., Pantano, W., Santandrea, S., and Torri, C. (2003), 'Il comprensorio della necropolis di via Basiliano (Roma): un'indagine multidisciplinare', *Melanges d'Archeologie et d'Histoire de l'Ecole Francaise de Rome* 115: 311–76.

Buchner, G. and Ridgway, D. (1993), *Pithekoussai and the First Western Greeks* (Pithekoussai I). Rome: Giorgio Bretschneider.

Budde, L. and Nicholls, R. V. (1967), *Catalogue of the Greek and Roman Sculpture in the Fitzwilliam Museum*. Cambridge: Cambridge University Press.

Budin, S. L. (2011), *Images of Woman and Child from the Bronze Age: Reconsidering Fertility, Maternity, and Gender in the Ancient World*. Cambridge: Cambridge University Press.

Buljević, Z. (2013), 'Glass Phalerae in the Roman Province of Dalmatia', in Sanader, M., Rendić-Miočević, A., Tončinić, D., and Radman-Livaja, I. (eds.), *Weapons and Military Equipment in Funerary Context: Proceedings of the XVII Roman Military Equipment Conference, Zagreb, 24th–27th May, 2010*. Zagreb: Arheološki musej u Zagrebu, 289–97.

Burton, D. (2003), 'Public Memorials, Private Virtues: Women on Classical Athenian Grave Monuments', *Mortality* 8(1): 20–35.

Cacciatore, J. and Bushfield, S. (2007), 'Stillbirth: The Mother's Experience and Implications for Improving Care', *Journal of Social Work in End-of-Life and Palliative Care* 3(3): 59–79.

Caminneci, V. (2012a), 'Enchytrismos: Seppellire in vase nell'antica Agrigento', in Caminneci, V. (ed.), *Parce Sepulto: Il rito e la morte tra passato e presente*. Agrigento: Soprintendenza di Agrigento, 111–32.

Caminneci, V. (ed.) (2012b), *Parce Sepulto: Il rito e la morte tra passato e presente*. Agrigento: Soprintendenza di Agrigento.

Caneva, S. G. and Delli Pizzi, A. (2014), 'Classical and Hellenistic Statuettes of the So-Called "Temple Boys": A Religious and Social Reappraisal', in Terranova, C. (ed.), *La presenza dei bambini nelle religioni del Mediterraneo antico*. Rome: Aracne, 495–521.

Capasso, L. (2001), *I Fuggiaschi di Ercolano: Paleobiologia delle Vittime dell'Eruzione Vesuviana del 79 d.C.* Rome: L'Erma di Bretschneider.

Carè, B. (2012), 'L'astragalo in tomba nel mondo Greco: un indicatore infantile? Vecchi problem e nuove osservazioni a proposito di un aspetto del costume funerario', in Hermary, A. and Dubois, C. (eds.), *L'Enfant et la mort dans l'Antiquité III: Le materiel associé aux tombes d'enfants. Actes de la table ronde internationale organisée à la Maison Méditteranéenne de Sciences de l'Homme (MMSH) d'Aix-en-Provence, 20–22 janvier 2011*, Arles: Éditions Errance, 403–16.

Carlon, J. M. (2009), *Pliny's Women: Constructing Virtue and Creating Identity in the Roman World*. New York: Cambridge University Press, 157–74.

Carroll, M. (1989), 'Chous', in Rudolph, W. and Calinescu, A. (eds.), *Ancient Art from the V.G. Simkhovitch Collection*. Bloomington: Indiana University Art Museum, 155–6.

Carroll, M. (2001), *Romans, Celts and Germans: The German Provinces of Rome*. Stroud: Tempus.

Carroll, M. (2006), *Spirits of the Dead: Roman Funerary Commemoration in Western Europe*. Oxford: Oxford University Press.

Carroll, M. (2007/8), 'Vox Tua Nempe Mea Est: Dialogues with the Dead in Roman Funerary Commemoration', *Accordia Research Papers* 11: 37–80.

Carroll, M. (2011a), 'Infant Death and Burial in Roman Italy', *Journal of Roman Archaeology* 24: 99–120.

Carroll, M. (2011b), 'Memoria and Damnatio Memoriae: Preserving and Erasing Identities in Roman Funerary Commemoration', in Carroll, M. and Rempel, J. (eds.), *Living through the Dead: Burial and Commemoration in the Classical World*. Oxford: Oxbow, 65–90.

Carroll, M. (2012a), '"No part in earthly things": The Death, Burial, and Commemoration of Newborn Children and Infants in Roman Italy', in Harlow, M. and

Larsson Lovén, L. (eds.), *Families in the Roman and Late Antique World*. London: Continuum, 41–63.

Carroll, M. (2012b), 'The Roman Child Clothed in Death', in Carroll, M. and Wild, J. P. (eds.), *Dressing the Dead in Classical Antiquity*. Stroud: Amberley, 134–47.

Carroll, M. (2013), '"The Insignia of Women": Dress, Gender and Identity on the Roman Funerary Monument of Regina from Arbeia', *The Archaeological Journal* 169: 281–311.

Carroll, M. (2014), 'Mother and Infant in Roman Funerary Commemoration', in Carroll, M. and Graham, E.-J. (eds.), *Infant Health and Death in Roman Italy and Beyond* (JRA Supplementary Series 96). Portsmouth: Journal of Roman Archaeology, 159–78.

Carroll, M. (2015), 'Commemorating Military and Civilian Families on the Danube Limes', in Vagalinski, L. and Sharankov, N. (eds.), *Limes XXII: Proceedings of the XXIInd International Congress of Roman Frontier Studies held in Ruse, Bulgaria (September 2012)*. Sofia: National Archaeological Institute, 501–9.

Carroll, M. and Graham, E.-J. (eds.) (2014), *Infant Health and Death in Roman Italy and Beyond* (JRA Supplementary Series 96). Portsmouth: Journal of Roman Archaeology.

Carroll, M. and Prowse, T. (2016), 'Research at the Roman Imperial Estate at Vagnari, Puglia (Comune di Gravina in Puglia, Provincia di Bari, Regione Puglia)', *Papers of the British School at Rome* 84: 333–6.

Carroll, M. and Rempel, J. (eds.) (2011), *Living through the Dead: Burial and Commemoration in the Classical World*. Oxford: Oxbow.

Carroll, M. and Wild, J. P. (eds.) (2012), *Dressing the Dead in Classical Antiquity*. Stroud: Amberley.

Carter, J. C. (1998), *The Chora of Metaponto, Vol. 2: The Necropoleis*. Austin: University of Texas Press.

Castagnoli, F. (1979), 'Il culto della Mater Matuta e della Fortuna nel Foro Boario', *Studi Romani* 27: 145–52.

Castella, D. (1987), *La nécropole du port d'Avenches. Cahiers d'Archéologie Romande 41: Aventicum IV*. Avenches: L'Université de Lausanne.

Castella, D. (1999), *La nécropole gallo-romaine d'Avenches 'En Chaplix': Fouilles 1987–1992, Vol. 1, Etude des sépultures* (Cahiers d'archéologie romande 77, Aventicum IX). Lausanne: Cahiers d'Archéologie Romande.

Castella, D. and Blanc, P. (2007), 'Les pratiques funéraires à Avenches (*Aventicum*) et dans sa Région durant le Haut-Empire', in Faber, A., Fasold, P., Struck, M., and Witteyer, M. (eds.), *Körpergräber des 1.–3. Jahrhunderts in der römischen Welt: Internationales Kolloquium Frankfurt am Main, 19.–20. November 2004*. Frankfurt: Archäologisches Museum Frankfurt, 323–40.

Catalano, P., Amicucci, G., Benassi, V., Caldarini, C., Caprara, M., Carboni, L., Colonnelli, G., De Angelis, F., Di Giannantonio, S., Minozzi, S., Pantano, W., and Porreca, F. (2006), 'Gli insiemi funerari d'epoca imperiale: L'indagine antropologica di campo', in Tomei, M. A. (ed.), *Roma. Memorie dal sottosuolo: Ritrovamenti archeologici 1980–2006*. Rome: Electa, 560–3.

Catalano, P., Minozzi, S., and Pantano, W. (2001), 'Le necropoli romane di età imperiale: un contributo all'interpretazione del popolamento e della qualità della

vita nell'antica Roma', in Quilici, L. and Quilici Gigli, S. (eds.), *Urbanizzazione delle Campagne nell'Italia Antica (Alante tematico di topografia antica* 10). Rome: L'Erma di Bretschneider, 127–37.

Catalano, P., Pantano, W., Calderini, C., De Angelis, D., Battastini, A., and Iorio, A. (2012), 'The Contribution of the Anthropological Study to the Analysis of Ancient Cemeteries: The Demographic Profile of Six Roman Imperial Age Necropolis', *Journal of Biological Research* 85(1): 224–6.

Cavada, E. (1994), '"Sit tibi terra levis": la casa come luogo funerario', in Cavada, E. (ed.), *Archeologia a Mezzocorona: Documenti per la storia del popolamento rustico di eta romana nell'area atesina.* Trento: Provincia autonoma di Trento, 267–74.

Cavalieri Manasse, G. and Bola, M. (1998), 'Osservazioni sulle necropolis veronesi', in Fasold, P., Fischer, T., von Hesberg, H., and Witteyer, M. (eds.), *Bestattungssitte und kulturelle Identität: Grablagen und Grabbeigaben der frühen römischen Kaiserzeit in Italien und den Nordwest-Provinzen* (Xantener Berichte 7). Cologne: Rheinland Verlag, 103–41.

Ceci, F. (2001), 'L'interpretazione di monete e chiodi in contesti funerari: esempi dal suburbio romano', in Heinzelmann, M., Ortalli, J., Fasold, P., and Witteyer, M. (eds.), *Römischer Bestattungsbrauch und Beigabensitten in Rom, Norditalien und den Nordwestprovinzen von der späten Republik bis in die Kaiserzeit (Culto dei morti e costumi funerari romani: Roma, Italia settentrionale e province nord-occidentali dalla tarda Repubblica all'età imperiale).* Wiesbaden: Dr Ludwig Reichert Verlag, 87–97.

Ceci, F. (2006), 'Lotalità Settecamini, Via Tiburtina KM 14,700 (Municipio V)', in Tomei, M. A. (ed.), *Roma. Memorie dal sottosuolo: Ritrovamenti archeologici 1980–2006.* Rome: Electa, 265.

Cesarano, M. (2010–11), 'Aspects and Implications of Funerary Ritual for Infants during the Samnite Period in the "Ronga" Necropolis of Nola', *Etruscan Studies* 14: 155–83.

Chaniotis, A. (ed.) (2011), *Ritual Dynamics in the Ancient Mediterranean* (Heidelberger Beiträge und epigraphische Studien 49). Heidelberg: Franz Steiner Verlag.

Chapa-Brunet, T. (2008), 'Presencia infantil y ritual funerario en el mundo ibérico', in Gusi, F., Muriel, S., and Olària, C. R. (eds.), *Nasciturus, infans, puerulus vobis mater terra: La muerte en la infancia.* Castelló: Servei d'Investigacions Arquelògiques i Prehistòriques, 619–42.

Choi, X. J., Kim, M. K., and Jeong, S. J. (2013), 'Vitamin D Deficiency in Infants Aged 1–6 Months', *Korean Journal of Pediatrics* 56(5): 205–10.

Cianfriglia, L. and De Cristofaro, A. (2013), 'I crepundia dalla tomba 37 della necropoli di Castel Malnome: Usi funerari e rituali magici', in Simón, F. M. and Piranomonte, M. (eds.), *Contesti magici, Contextos magicos* (Atti del Convegno internazionale). Rome: De Luca, 233–45.

Cianfriglia, L., De Cristofaro, A., and Di Mento, A. (2013), 'La necropoli imperiale di Castel Malnome (Ponte Galeria): risultati preliminari. Il sepolcreto dei *saccarii salarii*? (Municipio XI ex XV)', *BCom* 114: 414–23.

Ciarallo, A. and De Carolis, E. (eds.) (2001), *La Casa di Giulio Polibio: Studi Interdisciplinari.* Tokyo: Centro Studi Arti Figurativi.

Cichorius, N. (1896), *Die Reliefs der Trajanssäule.* Berlin: Verlag von Georg Reimer.

Cipollone, M. (2002), 'Gubbio (Perugia), Necropoli in località Vittorina: Campagne di scavo 1980–1982', *Notizie degli Scavi di Antiquità* (Series 9) 11: 5–372
Clairmont, C. W. (1993), *Classical Attic Tombstones*. Kilchberg: Akanthus.
Clarke, N. M. P. (2014), 'Swaddling and Hip Dysplasia: An Orthopaedic Perspective', *Archives of Disease in Childhood* 99, 5–6.
Cleland, L. (2005), *The Brauron Clothing Catalogues: Text, Analysis, Glossary, and Translation* (BAR International Series 1428). Oxford: John and Erica Hedges Ltd.
Coarelli, F. (1988), *Il Foro Boario dalle Origini alla Fine della Repubblica*. Rome: Edizioni Quasar.
Coarelli, F. (1995), 'Venus Iovia, Venus Libitina? Il santuario del Fondo Patturelli a Capua', in Marino, A. S. (ed.), *L'Incidenza dell'Antico. Studi in memoria di Ettore Lepore. Atti del Convegno Internazionale Anacapri 24–28 marzo 1991*. Naples: Luciano Editore, 371–88.
Coarelli, F. (1999), *La Colonna Traiana*. Rome: Editore Colombo.
Cocks, A. H. (1921), 'A Romano-British Homestead in the Hambleden Valley, Bucks', *Archaeologia* 71: 141–98.
Cohen, A. (2011), 'Picturing Greek Families', in Rawson, B. (ed.), *A Companion to Families in the Greek and Roman Worlds*. Oxford: Blackwell, 465–87.
Cohen, A. and Rutter, J. (eds.) (2007), *Constructions of Childhood in Ancient Greece and Italy* (Hesperia Supplement 41). Princeton: Princeton University Press.
Comella, A. (1978), *Il materiale votivo tardo di Gravisca*. Rome: Giorgio Bretschneider.
Comella, A. (1981), 'Tipologia e diffusione dei complessi votivi in Italia in epoca medio- e tardo-repubblicana', *Melanges d'Archeologie et d'Histoire de l'Ecole Francaise de Rome* 93: 717–803.
Conde, A. S. (2010–11), '*Mors Immatura* en el Mundo Romano: Provincia Tarraconensis', *Annales de Arqueología Cordobesa* 21–2: 197–220.
Cope, D. J. and Dupras, T. L. (2011), 'Osteogenesis Imperfecta in the Archaeological Record: An Example from the Dakhleh Oasis, Egypt', *International Journal of Paleopathology* 1: 188–99.
Corbier, M. (2001), 'Child Exposure and Abandonment', in Dixon, S. (ed.), *Childhood, Class and Kin in the Roman World*. London: Routledge, 52–73.
Cordell, A. S. and Thomas, N. (1990), 'Fathers and Grieving: Coping with Infant Death', *Journal of Perinatology* 10(1): 75–80.
Cordie-Hackenberg, R. and Haffner, A. (1991), *Das keltisch-römische Gräberfeld von Wederath-Belginum. 4. Teil: Gräber 1261–1817 ausgegraben 1978–1980*, Mainz: Verlag Philipp von Zabern.
Cordie-Hackenberg, R. and Haffner, A. (1997), *Das keltisch-römische Gräberfeld von Wederath-Belginum. 5. Teil: Gräber 1818–2472 ausgegraben 197, 1981–1985*, Mainz: Verlag Philipp von Zabern.
Coşkunsu, G. (ed.) (2015), *The Archaeology of Childhood: Interdisciplinary Perspectives on an Archaeological Enigma*. New York: State University of New York Press.
Costanzo, D. and Dubois, C. (2014), 'Fra Greci, indigeni e Greci d'Occidente: Parures e amuleti dalle sepolture infantili del Mediterraneo antico', in Terranova, C. (ed.), *La presenza dei bambini nelle religioni del Mediterraneo antico*. Rome: Aracne, 141–83.
Couilloud, M. T. (1974), *Les monuments funéraires de Rhénée: Exploration archéologique de Délos* 30. Paris: École française d'Athènes.

Coulon, G. (2003), 'L'emmaillotage', in Gourevitch, D., Moirin, A., and Rouquet, N. (eds.), *Maternité et petite enfance dans l'Antiquité romaine*. Bourges: Éditions de la Ville de Bourges, 152–4.

Coulon, G. (2004a), *L'enfant en Gaule romaine*. Paris: Éditions Errance.

Coulon, G. (2004b), 'Images et imaginaire de la naissance dans l'Occident romain', in Dasen, V. (ed.), *Naissance et petite enfance dans l'Antiquité: Actes du colloque de Fribourg, 28 novembre–1 décembre 2001*. Fribourg: Academic Press, 209–25.

Counts, D. B. (2012), 'A History of Archaeological Activity in the Athienou Region', in Toumazou, M. K., Kardulias, P. N., and Counts, D. B. (eds.), *Crossroads and Boundaries: The Archaeology of Past and Present in the Malloura Valley, Cyprus* (Annual of ASOR 65). Boston: American Schools of Oriental Research, 45–54.

Cox, S. (2016), 'The Infants: Osteology', in Fentress, E., Goodson, C., Maiuro, M., Andrews, M., and Dufton, J. A. (eds), *Villa Magna: An Imperial Estate and its Legacies, Excavations 2006–10*. Oxford: Oxbow, 183–97.

Craig, O. E., Biazzo, M., O'Connell, T. C., Garnsey, P., Martinez-Labarga, C., Lelli, R., Salvadei, L., Tartaglia, G., Nava, A., Reno, L., Fiammenghi, A., Rickards, O., and Bondioli, L. (2009), 'Stable Isotopic Evidence for Diet at the Imperial Roman Coastal Site of Velia (1st and 2nd Centuries AD) in Southern Italy', *American Journal of Physical Anthropology* 139: 572–83.

Crawford, S. and Lewis, C. (2008), 'Childhood Studies and the Society for the Study of Childhood in the Past', *Childhood in the Past* 1: 5–16.

Crielaard, J. P. (1998), 'Cult and Death in early 7th-Century Euboea: The Aristocracy and the Polis', in Marchegay, S., Dinahet, M. T., and Salles, J. F. (eds.), *Nécropoles et pouvoir: Idéologies, pratiques et interpretations. Actes du colloque Théories de la nécropole antique Lyon,21–25 janvier 1995*. Lyon: Maison de l'Orient et de la Méditerranée Jean Pouilloux, 43–58.

Cristofani, M. (1975), *Satue-Cinerario Chiusine di età classica*. Rome: Giorgio Bretschneider.

Crummy, N. (2010), 'Bears and Coins: The Iconography of Protection in Late Roman Infant Burials', *Britannia* 41: 37–93.

Cucina, A., Vargiu, R., Mancinelli, D., Ricci, R., Santandrea, E., Catalano, P., and Coppa, A. (2006), 'The Necropolis of Vallerano (Rome, 2nd–3rd Century AD): An Anthropological Perspective on the Ancient Romans in the *Suburbium*', *International Journal of Osteoarchaeology* 16: 104–17.

Cüppers, H. (1984), *Trier, Kaiserresidenz und Bischofssitz: Die Stadt in spätantiker und frühchristlicher Zeit*. Mainz: von Zabern.

Curdy, P., Mottet, M., Nicoud, C., Baudais, D., Lundström-Baudais, K., and Moulin, B. (1993), 'Brig-Glis/Waldmatte, un habitat alpin de l'âge du Fer. Fouilles archéologiques N9 en Valais', *Archéologie suisse* 16: 138–51.

Currie, S. (1996), 'The Empire of Adults: The Representation of Children on Trajan's Arch at Beneventum', in Elsner, J. (ed.), *Art and Text in Roman Culture*. Cambridge: Cambridge University Press, 153–81.

D'Andrea, B. and Giardino, S. (2013), 'Il Tofet dove e perché: L'identità fenicia, il circolo di Cartagine e la fase Tardo Punica', *Bolletino di Archeologia online Direzione Generale per l'Antichità* 4(1): 1–29.

D'Ercole, V. (1999), 'Nella terra dei Marsi e dei Frentani', *Archeo* 168: 30–41.

Dasen, V. (1993), *Dwarfs in Ancient Egypt and Greece.* Oxford: Oxford University Press.

Dasen, V. (1997), 'A propos de deux fragments de *Deae nutrices* à Avenches: déesses mères et jumeaux dans le monde italique et gallo-romain', *Bulletin de l'Association Pro Aventico* 39: 125–40.

Dasen, V. (2003a), 'Les amulettes d'enfants dans le monde gréco-romain', *Latomus* 62(2): 275–89.

Dasen, V. (2003b), 'Protéger l'enfant: amulettes et crepundia', in Gourevitch, D., Moirin, A., and Rouquet, N. (eds.), *Maternité et petite enfance dans l'Antiquité romaine.* Bourges: Éditions de la Ville de Bourges, 172–7.

Dasen, V. (ed.) (2004), *Naissance et petite enfance dans l'Antiquité: Actes du colloque de Fribourg, 28 novembre–1 décembre 2001.* Fribourg: Academic Press.

Dasen, V. (2009), 'Roman Birth Rites of Passage Revisited', *Journal of Roman Archaeology* 22: 199–214.

Dasen, V. (2010), 'Wax and Plaster Memories: Children in Elite and non-Elite Strategies', in Dasen, V. and Späth, T. (eds.), *Children, Memory and Family Identity in Roman Culture.* Oxford: Oxford University Press, 109–46.

Dasen, V. (2011), 'Childbirth and Infancy in Greek and Roman Antiquity', in Rawson, B. (ed.), *A Companion to Families in the Greek and Roman Worlds.* Oxford: Blackwell, 291–314.

Dasen, V. (2012), 'Cherchez l'enfant! La question de l'identité à partir du materiel funéraire', in Hermary, A. and Dubois, C. (eds.), *L'Enfant et la mort dans l'Antiquité III: Le materiel associé aux tombes d'enfants. Actes de la table ronde internationale organisée à la Maison Méditteranéenne de Sciences de l'Homme (MMSH) d'Aix-en-Provence, 20–22 janvier 2011.* Arles: Éditions Errance, 9–22.

Dasen, V. (2013a), 'Becoming Human: From the Embryo to the Newborn Child', in Evans Grubbs, J., Parkin, T., and Bell, R. (eds.), *The Oxford Handbook of Childhood and Education in the Classical World.* Oxford: Oxford University Press, 17–39.

Dasen, V. (2013b), 'Naissance et petite enfance dans l'antiquité. Nouvelles approches', *La petite enfance dans e monde grec et romain* (*Dossiers d'Archéologie* 356): 2–7.

Dasen, V. and Späth, T. (eds.) (2010), *Children, Memory and Family Identity in Roman Culture.* Oxford: Oxford University Press.

Davies, G. (1985), 'The Significance of the Handshake Motif in Classical Funerary Art', *American Journal of Archaeology* 89: 627–40.

Dawodu, A. and Wagner, C. L. (2007), 'Mother-Child Vitamin D Deficiency: An International Perspective', *Archives of Disease in Childhood* 92 (9): 737–40.

De Cazanove, O. (2008), 'Enfants en langes: pour quells voeux?', in Greco, G. and Ferrara, B. (eds.), *Doni agli dei: Il sistema dei doni votivi nei santuari.* Naples: Naus, 271–84.

De Cazanove, O. (2013), 'Enfants au maillot en contextre cultuel en Italie et en Gaule', *La petite Enfance dans le Monde Grec et Romain* (*Dossiers d'Archéologie* 356): 8–13.

De Grummond, N. T. (1990), 'Pax Augusta and the Horae on the Ara Pacis Augustae', *J. Roman Archaeology* 94: 663–77.

De la Genière, J. (ed.) (1994), *Nécropoles et Sociétés Antiques (Grèce, Italie, Languedoc): Actes de la Colloque International du Centre de Recherches Archéologiques de l'Université de Lille III, Lille, 2–3 Décembre 1991.* Naples: Centre Jean Bérard.

De Larminat, S. (2010), 'Signalisation des tombes d'enfants dans un quartier funéraire de la nécropole romaine de Porta Nocera à Pompéi', in Guimier-Sorbets, A.-M. and Morizot, Y. (eds.), *L'Enfant et la mort dans l'Antiquité I: Nouvelles recherches dans les nécropoles grecques: Le signalement des tombes d'enfants. Actes de la table ronde internationale organiseé à Athènes, École française d'Athènes, 29–30 mai 2008*. Paris: de Boccard, 375–85.

De Larminat, S. (2012a), 'Le mobilier deposé dans les sépultures d'enfants en Afrique du Nord à l'époque romaine', in Hermary, A. and Dubois, C. (eds.), *L'Enfant et la mort dans l'Antiquité III: Le materiel associé aux tombes d'enfants. Actes de la table ronde internationale organisée à la Maison Méditteranéenne de Sciences de l'Homme (MMSH) d'Aix-en-Provence, 20–22 janvier 2011*. Arles: Éditions Errance, 293–312.

De Larminat, S. (2012b), 'Gestes et pratiques funéraires autour des inhumations en fosse d'enfants en Afrique romaine à l'époque païenne', in Nenna, M.-D. (ed.), *L'Enfant et la mort dans l'Antiquité II: Types de tombs et traitement du corps des enfants dans l'antiquité gréco-romaine. Actes de la table ronde internationale organisée à Alexandrie, Centre d'Études Alexandrines, 12–14 novembre 2009*. Alexandria: Centre d'Études Alexandrines, 501–38.

Dedet, B. (2008), 'La mort du nouveau-né et du nourrisson dans le sud de la France protohistorique (IXe–Ier siècles avant J.C.)', in Gusi, F., Muriel, S., and Olària, C. R. (eds.), *Nasciturus, infans, puerulus vobis mater terra: La muerte en la infancia*. Castelló: Servei d'Investigacions Arquelògiques i Prehistòriques, 143–82.

Dedet, B. (2012), 'Mobilier funéraire et statut des enfants dans le monde indigène protohistorique du Sud de la France', in Hermary, A. and Dubois, C. (eds.), *L'Enfant et la mort dans l'Antiquité III: Le materiel associé aux tombes d'enfants. Actes de la table ronde internationale organisée à la Maison Méditteranéenne de Sciences de l'Homme (MMSH) d'Aix-en-Provence, 20–22 janvier 2011*. Arles: Éditions Errance, 149–69.

Dedet, B. (2013), 'Petits enfants et usages funéraires dans la société indigene de Gaule du Sud', *La petite Enfance dans le Monde Grec et Romain* (*Dossiers d'Archéologie* 356): 42–5.

Dedet, B., Duday, H., and Tillier, A. M. (1991), 'Inhumations de foetus, nouveau-nés et nourrissons dans les habitats protohistoriques du Languedoc: l'exemple de Gailhan (Gard)', *Gallia* 48: 59–108.

Dedet, B., Gruat, P., and Marty, G. (2001), 'Sépultures d'enfants en bas âge dans l'agglomération du Puech de Mus à Sainte-Eulalie-de-Cernon (Aveyron) au Ve s. av. J.C.', *Documents d'archéologie méridionale* 24: 127–63.

Dedet, B. and Schwaller, M. (2010), 'Les pratiques funéraires en Languedoc et en Provence du Ve au milieu du IIe siècle av. J.-C.', in Barral, P., Dedet, B., Delrieu, F., Giraud, P., Le Goff, I., Marion, S., and Villard-Le Tec, A. (eds.), L'Âge du fer en Basse-Normandie: *Gestes funéraires en Gaule au second âge du Fer. Actes du XXXIIIe colloque international de l'AFEAF, Caen 20–24 mai 2009*. Besançon: Presses universitaires de Franche-Comté, 269–90.

Deiss, J. J. (1993), *Herculaneum: Italy's Buried Treasure*. Malibu: J. Paul Getty Museum.

Deloache, J. S., Pickard, M. B., and LoBue, V. (2011), 'How Very Young Children Think about Animals', in McCardle, P., McCune, S., Griffin, J. A., and Maholmes, V. (eds.), *How Animals Affect Us: Examining the Influence of Human–Animal Interaction on Child Development and Human Health*. Washington: American Physchological Association, 85–99.

Demand, N. (1994), *Birth, Death, and Motherhood in Classical Greece*. Baltimore: Johns Hopkins University Press.

Demangel, R. (1922), 'Un sanctuaire d'Artémis-Eileithyia à l'Est du Cynthe', *Bulletin de Correspondence Hellénique* 46: 58–93.

Derks, T. (1998), *Gods, Temples and Religious Practices: The Transformation of Religious Ideas and Values in Roman Gaul* (Amsterdam Archaeological Studies 2). Amsterdam: Amsterdam University Press.

Derks, T. (2014), 'Seeking Divine Protection against Untimely Death: Infant Votives from Roman Gaul and Germany', in Carroll, M. and Graham, E.-J. (eds.), *Infant Health and Death in Roman Italy and Beyond*. Portsmouth: Journal of Roman Archaeology (JRA Supplement 96): 47–68.

Deyts, S. (2001), 'La Sculpture et les Inscriptions', in Pommeret, C. (ed.), *Le Sanctuaire antique des Bolards à Nuits-Saint-Georges (Côte-d'Or)* (Revue Archéologique de l'Est. Supplement 16). Dijon: Editions S.A.E., 129–39.

Deyts, S. (2004), 'La femme et l'enfant au maillot en Gaul: Iconographie et épigraphie', in Dasen, V. (ed.), *Naissance et petite enfance dans l'Antiquité: Actes du colloque de Fribourg, 28 novembre–1 décembre 2001*. Fribourg: Academic Press, 227–37.

Di Gennaro, F. and Griesbach, J. (2003), 'Le sepolture all'interno delle ville con particolare riferimento al territorio di Roma', in Pergola, P., Santangeli Valenzani, R., and Volpe, R. (eds.), *Suburbium: Il Suburbio di Roma dalla Crisi del Sistema delle Ville a Gregorio Magno*. Rome: École Française, 123–66.

Di Nucci, E. (2013), 'Killing Fetuses and Killing Newborns', *Journal of Medical Ethics* 39(5): 19–20.

Dillon, M. (2002), *Girls and Women in Classical Greek Religion*. London: Routledge.

Dillon, S. (2006), 'Women on the Columns of Trajan and Marcus Aurelius and the Visual Language of Roman Victory', in Dillon, S. and Welch, K. E. (eds.), *Representations of War in Ancient Rome*. New York: Cambridge University Press, 244–71.

Dillon, S. and Welch, K. E. (eds.) (2006), *Representations of War in Ancient Rome*. New York: Cambridge University Press.

Disantarosa, G. (2012), 'Amphorae', in Small, A. M. (ed.), *Vagnari: Il villaggio, l'artigianato, la proprietà imperiale*. Bari: Edipuglia, 387–406.

Disantarosa, G. (2014), 'Contextualizing the Context: Amphorae from the Site of Vagnari and from the Basentello Valley', in Small, A. M. (ed.), *Beyond Vagnari: New Themes in the Study of Roman South Italy*. Bari: Edipuglia, 149–67.

Dixon, S. (1988), *The Roman Mother*. London: Norman and Sydney.

Dixon, S. (ed.) (2001), *Childhood, Class and Kin in the Roman World*. London: Routledge.

Do Sameiro Barroso, M. (2013), 'Post-Mortem Cesarean Section and Embryotomy: Myth, Medicine and Gender in Greco-Roman Culture', *Acta medico-historia Adriatica* 11(1): 75–88.

Dolansky, F. (2012), 'Playing with Gender: Girls, Dolls, and Adult Ideals in the Roman World', *Classical Antiquity* 31(2): 256–92.

Dollfus, M. A. and Guyot, A. (1968), 'Sépultures de nouveau-nés dans les fouilles gallo-romaines de Fleurheim à Lyons-la-Forêt (Eure)', *Annales de Normandie* 18(4): 283–300.

Down, A. (1988), *Roman Chichester*. Chichester: Phillimore & Co.

Drerup, H. (1980), 'Totenmaske und Ahnenbild bei den Römern', *Römische Mitteilungen* 87: 81–129.

Dubois, C. (2012), 'Des objets pour les bébés? Le dépôt de mobilier dans le sépultures d'enfants en bas âge du monde grec archaïque et classique', in Hermary, A. and Dubois, C. (eds.), *L'Enfant et la mort dans l'Antiquité III: Le materiel associé aux tombes d'enfants. Actes de la table ronde internationale organisée à la Maison Méditteranéenne de Sciences de l'Homme (MMSH) d'Aix-en-Provence, 20–22 janvier 2011*, Arles: Éditions Errance, 329–42.

Dubois, C. (2013), 'L'alimentation des enfants en bas âge: Les biberons grecs', *La petite Enfance dans le Monde Grec et Romain (Dossiers d'Archéologie* 356): 64–7.

Duday, H. (2009), *The Archaeology of the Dead: Lectures in Archaeothanatology*. Oxford: Oxbow.

Duday, H., Laubenheimer, F., and Tillier, A.-M. (1995), *Sallèlles d'Aude: nouveau-nés et nourrissons gallo-romains*. Paris: Presses universitaires de Franche-Comté.

Dunand, F. (2004), 'Les enfants et la mort en Egypte', in Dasen, V. (ed.), *Naissance et petite enfance dans l'Antiquité: Actes du colloque de Fribourg, 28 novembre–1er décembre 2001*. Fribourg: Academic Press, 13–32.

Dunand, F., Heim, J.-L., Henein, N., and Lichtenberg, R. (1992), *La nécropole de Douch (Oasis de Kharga): Exploration Archéologique, Vol. 1: Monographie des tombes 1 à 72*. Cairo: Institut Français d'Archeologie Orientale du Caire.

Dunand, F., Heim, J.-L., Henein, N. and Lichtenberg, R. (2005), *La necropole de Douch (Oasis de Kharga): Exploration Archeologique, Vol. 2: Monographie des tombs 73 à 92*. Cairo: Institut Francais d'Archeologie Orientale du Caire.

Duncan-Jones, R. (1974), *The Economy of the Roman Empire: Quantitative Studies*. Cambridge: Cambridge University Press.

Duncan-Jones, R. (1977), 'Age-Rounding, Illiteracy and Social Differentiation in the Roman Empire', *Chiron* 7: 333–53.

Dupras, T. L. (2010), 'The Use of Stable Isotope Analysis to Determine Infant and Young Child Feeding Patterns', in Moffat, T. and Prowse, T. (eds.), *Human Diet and Nutrition in Biocultural Perspective*. New York: Berghahn Books.

Dupras, T. L., Schwarcz, H. P., and Fairgreave, S. I. (2001), 'Infant Feeding and Weaning Practices in Roman Egypt', *American Journal of Physical Anthropology* 115(3): 204–12.

Dupras, T. L., Wheeler, S. M., Williams, L., and Sheldrick, P. (2015), 'Birth in Ancient Egypt: Timing, Trauma, and Triumph? Evidence from the Dakhleh Oasis', in Ikram, S., Kaiser, J., and Walker, R. (eds.), *Egyptian Bioarchaeology. Humans, Animals, and the Environment*. Leiden: Sidestone Press, 53–65.

Durand, R. (2003), 'Les sépultures d'enfants', in Gourevitch, D., Moirin, A., and Rouquet, N. (eds.), *Maternité et petite enfance dans l'Antiquité romaine*. Bourges: Éditions de la Ville de Bourges, 112–14.

Durand, R. (2004–5), 'La place des enfants dans le monde des mortes', *L'Enfant en Gaule et dans d'Empire romain* (l'Archéologue 75): 16–17.

Ede, J., Sobnach, S., Castillo, F., and Bhyat, A. (2011), 'The Lithopedion: An Unusual Cause of an Abdominal Mass', *South African Journal of Surgery* 49(3): 140–1.

Edmondson, J., Nogales Basarrate, T., and Trillmich, W. (2001), *Imagen y Memoria: Monumentos funerarios con retratos en la Colonia Augusta Emerita*. Madrid: Real Academia de la Historia.

Edmondson, J. (2007), 'The Cult of *Mars Augustus* and Roman Imperial Power at *Emerita Augusta* (Lusitania) in the Third Century A.D.: A New Votive Dedication', in T. Nogales and J. González (eds.), *Culto Imperial: política e poder*. Rome: "L'Erma" di Bretschneider, 542–75.

Egidi, R., Catalano, P., and Spadoni, D. (eds.) (2003), *Aspetti di vita quotidiana dalle necropoli della via Latina*. Rome: Museo Nazionale Romano.

Ehmig, U. (2013), 'Risikobewältigung bei Schwangerschaft und Geburt in der römischen Antike: Lateinische dokumentarische und archäologische Zeugnisse', *Arctos* 47: 111–29.

Elia, D. and Meirano, V. (2015), 'Children and Funerary Space: Ritual Behaviour in the Greek Colonies of Magna Graecia and Sicily', in Sánchez Romero, M., Alarcón García, A., and Aranda Jiménez, G. (eds.), *Children, Spaces and Identity*. Oxford: Oxbow, 310–26.

Endenberg, N. and van Lith, H. (2011), 'The Influence of Animals on the Development of Children', *Veterinary Journal* 190: 208–14.

Engels, D. (1980), 'The Problem of Female Infanticide in the Greco-Roman World', *Classical Philology* 75(2): 112–20.

Etter, H. F. (1991), 'Zu den Säuglingsbestattungen im Vicus Vitudurum-Oberwinterthur', in Etter, H. F., Fellmann Brogli, R., Fellmann, R., Martin-Kilcher, S., Morel, P., and Rast, A. (eds.), *Beiträge zum römischen Oberwinterthur—Vitudurum 5* (Monographien der Kantonsarchäologie Zürich 10). Zürich: Orell Füssli Verlag, 179–89.

Evans Grubbs, J. (2010), 'Hidden in Plain Sight: *Expositi* in the Community', in Dasen, V. and Späth, T. (eds.), *Children, Memory, and Family Identity in Roman Culture*. Oxford: Oxford University Press, 293–310.

Evans Grubbs, J. (2013), 'Infant Exposure and Infanticide', in Evans Grubbs, J., Parkin, T., and Bell, R. (eds.), *The Oxford Handbook of Childhood and Education in the Classical World*. Oxford: Oxford University Press, 83–107.

Evans Grubbs, J., Parkin, T., and Bell, R. (eds.) (2013), *The Oxford Handbook of Childhood and Education in the Classical World*. Oxford: Oxford University Press.

Faber, A. (1998), *Das römische Gräberfeld auf der Keckwiese in Kempten*. Kallmünz: Verlag Michael Laßleben.

Fabre, V. (1995), 'Inhumations d'enfants morts en bas-âge dans l'habitat protohistorique de Brig-Glis VS-Waldmatte', *Jahrbuch der Schweizerischen Gesellschaft für Ur-und Frühgeschichte* 78: 186–8.

Facchini, F., Rastelli, E., and Brasili, P. (2004), 'Cribra Orbitalia and Cribra Crania in Roman Skeletal Remains from the Ravenna Area and Rimini (I–IV Century AD)', *International Journal of Osteoarchaeology* 14: 126–36.

Faerman, M., Filon, D., Kahila Bar Gal, G., Greenblatt, C. L., Stager, L., Oppenheim, A., and Smith, P. (1998), 'Determination of the Sex of Infanticide Victims from the Late Roman Era through DNA Analysis', *Journal of Archaeological Science* 25: 861–5.

Faerman, M., Kahila, G., Smith, P., Greenblatt, C., Stager, L., Filon, D., and Oppenheim, A. (1997), 'DNA Analysis Reveals the Sex of Infanticide Victims', *Nature* 385: 212–13.

Fairgrieve, S. I. and Molto, J. E. (2000), 'Cribra Orbitalia in Two Temporally Disjunct Population Samples from the Dakhleh Oasis', *American Journal of Physical Anthropology* 111(3): 319–31.

Farwell, D. E. and Molleson, T. L. (1993), *Excavations at Poundbury 1966–80, Volume II: The Cemeteries*. Dorchester: Dorset Natural History and Archaeological Society.

Fasold, P., Maioli, M. G., Ortalli, J., and Scheid, J. (eds.) (2004), *La necropoli sulla duna: Scavi a Classe romana*. Frankfurt/Ravenna: Soprintendenza per i Beni Archeologici dell'Emilia Romagna.

Faust, W. (1998), *Die Grabstelen des 2. und 3. Jahrhunderts im Rheingebiet* (Bonner Jahbuch Supplement 52). Cologne: Rheinland Verlag.

Fecher, R. and Burger-Heinrich, E. (2010), *Arae Flaviae VII: Die Römischen Gräberfelder*. Stuttgart: Konrad Theiss Verlag.

Fentress, E., Goodson, C., Maiuro, M., Andrews, M., and Dufton, J. A. (eds.) (2016), *Villa Magna: An Imperial Estate and its Legacies, Excavations 2006–10*. Oxford: Oxbow.

Ferjaoui, A. (2007), *Le sanctuaire de Henchir el-Hami: da Ba'al Hammon au Saturne africain, Ier s. av. J.-C.-IVe s. ap. J.-C.* Tunis: Institut National du Patrimoine.

Ferris, I. M. (2000), *Enemies of Rome: Barbarians through Roman Eyes*. Stroud: Sutton.

Ferris, I. M. (2003), 'The Hanged Men Dance: Barbarians in Trajanic Art', in Scott, S. and Webster, J. (eds.), *Roman Imperialism and Provincial Art*. Cambridge: Cambridge University Press, 53–68.

Février, P.-A. and Guéry, R. (1980), 'Les rites funéraires de la nécropole orientale de Sétif', *Antiquités africaines* 15: 91–124.

Field, D., Hockey, J., and Small, N. (eds.) (1997), *Death, Gender and Ethnicity*. London: Routledge.

Finley, M. I. (1981), 'The Elderly in Classical Antiquity', *Greece and Rome* 28: 156–71.

Fiorini, L. (2014), 'Gli dei di Gravisca', in Mercuri, L. and Fiorini, L. (eds.), *Il mare che univa: Gravisca santuario mediterraneo*. Rome: Gangemi Editore, 57–63.

Fischer, K.-D. (1987), 'Nochmals ubuppa und tit(t)ina', *Philologus* 181: 156–7.

Fittà, M. (1998), *Spiele und Spielzeug in der Antike: Unterhaltung und Vergnügen im Altertum*. Stuttgart: Theiss.

Fittschen, K. and Zanker, P. (2014), *Katalog der römischen Porträts in den Capitolinischen Museen und den anderen kommunalen Sammlungen der Stadt Rom, Vol. 4: Kinderbildnisse, Nachträge zu den Bänden I–III, Neuzeitliche odr neuzeitlich verfälschte Bilnisse, Bildnisse an Reliefdenkmälern*. Berlin: Walter De Gruyter.

FitzGerald, C., Saunders, S., Bondioli, L., and Macchiarelli, R. (2006), 'Health of Infants in an Imperial Roman Skeletal Sample: Perspective from Dental Microstructure', *American Journal of Physical Anthropology* 130: 179–89.

Fiumi, E. (1976), *Volterra Etrusca e Romana*. Pisa: Pacini Editore.

Florescu, F. B. (1965), *Das Siegesdenkmal von Adamklissi, Tropaeum Traiani*. Bucharest: Verlag der Akademie der Rumänischen Volksrepublik.

Flower, H. (2006), *The Art of Forgetting: Disgrace and Oblivion in Roman Political Culture*. Chapel Hill: University of North Carolina Press.

Fluck, C. and Finneiser, K. (2009), *Kindheit am Nil: Spielzeug—Kleidung—Kinderbilder aus Ägypten in den Staatlichen Museen zu Berlin*. Berlin: Staatliche Museen zu Berlin.

Foley, H. (2003), 'Mothers and Daughters', in Neils, J. and Oakley, J. H. (eds.), *Coming of Age in Ancient Greece: Images of Childhood from the Classical Past*. New Haven: Yale University Press, 113–37.

Fortier, E. and Malahar, E. (1910), 'Les fuilles à Thina (Tunisie) exécutées en 1908–1909', *Bulletin archéologique du Comité des travaux historiques et scientifiques* 1: 82–99.

Foucras, S. (2014), 'Inhumer des chiens avec des humains? L'exemple du Pâtural, au Ier siècle de notre ère', in Bet, P. and Dousteyssier, B. (eds.) *Éclats Arvernes: Fragments archéologiques (Ier–Ve siècle apr. J.-C.).* Clairmont Ferrand: Presses Universitaires Blaise Pascal, 262–3.

Fox, S. C. (2012), 'The Bioarchaeology of Children in Graeco-Roman Greece', in Nenna, M.-D. (ed.), *L'Enfant et la mort dans l'Antiquité II: Types de tombs et traitement du corps des enfants dans l'antiquité gréco-romaine. Actes de la table ronde internationale organisée à Alexandrie, Centre d'Études Alexandrines, 12–14 novembre 2009*, Alexandria: Centre d'Études Alexandrines, 409–27.

Franco, P., Seret, N., Scaillet, J.-N., Groswasser, S., and Kahn, A. (2005), 'Influence of Swaddling on Sleep and Arousal Characteristics of Healthy Infants', *Pediatrics* 115: 1307–11.

Fraser, A. M., Brockert, J. E., and Ward, R. H. (1995), 'Association of Young Maternal Age with Adverse Reproductive Outcomes', *The New England Journal of Medicine* 332(17): 1113–17.

Frel, J. (1981), *Roman Portraits in the Getty Museum: Exhibition Catalogue for 'Caesars and Citizens'.* Tulsa: Philbrook Art Center.

Frenz, H. G. (1985), *Römische Grabreliefs in Mittel- und Süditalien.* Rome: G. Bretschneider.

Frere, S. (1967), *Britannia: A History of Roman Britain.* London: Routledge & Kegan Paul.

Frier, B. (1982), 'Roman Life Expectancy: Ulpian's Evidence', *Harvard Studies in Classical Philology* 86: 213–51.

Frier, B. (1994), 'Natural Fertility and Family Limitation in Roman Marriage', *Classical Philology* 89: 318–33.

Gabelmann, H. (1985), 'Römische Kinder in Toga Praetexta', *Jahrbuch des Deutschen Archäologischen Instituts* 100: 497–531.

Gadacz, M. (2013), 'L'Âge des individus du "cimetière de bébés"', *La petite Enfance dans le Monde Grec et Romain* (*Dossiers d'Archéologie* 356): 57.

Galinsky, K. (1966), 'Venus in a Relief on the Ara Pacis Augustae', *American Journal of Archaeology* 70: 223–43.

Gallazzi, C. and Hadji-Minaglou, G. (2012), 'Sépultures de nouveaux-nés et d'enfants dans une nécropole de la fin du VIIIe et du IXe s. apr. J.-C. à Umm-el-Breigât', Tebtynis, in Nenna, M.-D. (ed.), *L'Enfant et la mort dans l'Antiquité II: Types de tombs et traitement du corps des enfants dans l'antiquité gréco-romaine. Actes de la table ronde internationale organisée à Alexandrie, Centre d'Études Alexandrines, 12–14 novembre 2009*, Alexandria: Centre d'Études Alexandrines, 389–405.

Galsterer, H. and Galsterer, B. (1975), *Die römischen Steininschriften aus Köln.* Cologne: Greven & Bechtold.

Garland, R. (2001), *The Greek Way of Death* (2nd edn). Bristol: Bristol Classical Press.

Garland, R. (2013), 'Children in Athenian Religion', in Evans Grubbs, J., Parkin, T., and Bell, R. (eds.), *The Oxford Handbook of Childhood and Education in the Classical World.* Oxford: Oxford University Press, 207–26.

Garnsey, P. (1970), 'Septimius Severus and the Marriage of Soldiers', *Californian Studies of Classical Antiquity* 3: 45–53.

Garnsey, P. (1999), *Food and Society in Classical Antiquity*. Cambridge: Cambridge University Press.

George, M. (2000), 'Family and *Familia* on Roman Biographical Sarcophagi', *RömMitt* 107: 191–207.

George, M. (2005a), 'Family Imagery and Family Values in Roman Italy', in George, M. (ed.), *The Roman Family in the Empire: Rome, Italy and Beyond*. Oxford: Oxford University Press, 37–66.

George, M. (ed.) (2005b), *The Roman Family in the Empire: Rome, Italy and Beyond*. Oxford: Oxford University Press.

Gerard, C. M., Harris, K. A., and Thach, B. T. (2002), 'Physiologic Studies on Swaddling: An Ancient Child Care Practice which may Promote the Supine Position for Infant Sleep', *Journal of Pediatrics* 141: 398–404.

German, E. and Last, R. (2000), 'Roman Funeral Stele of a Boy Chrysanthus', *Zeitchrift für Papyrologie und Epigraphik* 130: 249–52.

Gibson, B. (2006), *Statius. Silvae 5. Edited with Introduction, Translation and Commentary*. Oxford: Oxford University Press.

Giovannini, A. (2006), 'Spigolature Aquileisi: Instrumenta domestica dai depositi del Museo Archeologico Nazionale: Vasellame ceramico miniaturistico, giocattoli, giochi', *Histria Antiqua* 14: 323–57.

Girard, L. (1997), 'Les sujets immatures du cimetière Gallo-Romain de Chantambre (Essonne), Pratiques Funéraires', in Buchet, L. (ed.), *L'Enfant, son corps, son histoire. Actes des 7èmes Journées anthropologiques de Valbonne 1994*. Sophia Antipolis: Éditions APDCA, 211–25.

Gissinger, B. (2012), 'Fouille d'un quartier funéraire des Ier et IIe s. dans le *suburbium* de Soissons/*Augusta Suessionum*', *Gallia* 69(1): 3–67.

Giubilini, A. and Minerva, F. (2013), 'After-Birth Abortion: Why Should the Baby Live?', *Journal of Medical Ethics* 39(5): 261–3.

Giuliano, A. (1981), *Museo Nazionale Romano. Le Sculture I.2*. Rome: De Luca Editore.

Giuliano, A. (1985), *Museo Nazionale Romano. Le Sculture I.8*. Rome: De Luca Editore.

Glinister, F. (2006), 'Reconsidering "Religious Romanization"', in Schultz, C. E. and Harvey Jr, P. B. (eds.), *Religion in Republican Italy*. Cambridge: Cambridge University Press, 10–33.

Golani, A. (2014), 'Cowrie Shells and their Imitations as Ornamental Amulets in Egypt and the Near East', in Golani, A. and Wygnańska, Z. (eds.), *Beyond Ornamentation: Jewelry as an Aspect of Material Culture in the Ancient Near East* (Polish Archaeology in the Mediterranean 23/2, Special Studies). Warsaw: Polish Centre of Mediterranean Archaeology, 71–94.

Golden, M. (1987), 'Did the Ancients Care when their Children Died?', *Greece & Rome* 35(2): 152–63.

Golden, M. (2015), *Children and Childhood in Classical Athens*. Baltimore: Johns Hopkins University Press.

Goodburn, R., Wright, R. P., Hassall, M. W. C., and Tomlin, R. S. O. (1976), 'Roman Britain in 1975', *Britannia* 7: 290–392.

Goudineau, C. (ed.) (2009), *Rites Funéraires à Lugdunum*. Paris: Éditions Errance.

Gourevitch, D. (1987), 'La mort de la femme en couches et dans les suites de couches', in Hinard, F. (ed.), *La mort, les morts et l'au-delà*. Caen: Presses d l'Université, 187–93.

Gourevitch, D. (2004), 'Chirurgie obstétricale dans le monde romain: césarienne et embryotomie', in Dasen, V. (ed.), *Naissance et petite enfance dans l'Antiquité: Actes du colloque de Fribourg, 28 novembre–1 décembre 2001*. Fribourg: Academic Press, 239–64.

Gourevitch, D. and Chamay, J. (1992), 'Femme nourrissant son enfant au biberon', *Antike Kunst* 35(1): 78–81.

Gourevitch, D., Moirin, A., and Rouquet, N. (eds.) (2003), *Maternité et petite enfance dans l'Antiquité romaine*. Bourges: Éditions de la Ville de Bourges.

Gowland, R. (2016), 'Ideas of Childhood in Roman Britain: The Bioarchaeological and Material Evidence', in Millett, M., Revell, L., and Moore, A. (eds.), *The Oxford Handbook of Roman Britain*. Oxford: Oxford University Press, 301–20.

Gowland, R. and Redfern, R. (2010), 'Childhood Health in the Roman World: Perspectives from the Centre and Margin of the Empire', *Childhood in the Past* 3: 15–42.

Gowland, R. L. and Chamberlain, A. T. (2002), 'A Bayesian Approach to Ageing Perinatal Skeletal Material from Archaeological Sites: Implications for the Evidence for Infanticide in Roman-Britain', *Journal of Archaeological Science* 29(6): 677–85.

Gowland, R. L., Chamberlain, A.T., and Redfern, R. (2014), 'On the Brink of Being: Re-Evaluating Infanticide and Infant Burial in Roman Britain', in Carroll, M. and Graham, E.-J. (eds.), *Infant Health and Death in Roman Italy and Beyond* (JRA Supplement 96). Portsmouth: Journal of Roman Archaeology, 69–88.

Graepler, D. (1997), *Tonfiguren im Grab: Fundkontexte hellenistischer Terrakotten aus der Nekropole von Tarent*. Munich: Biering and Brinkmann.

Graham, E.-J. (2013), 'The Making of Infants in Hellenistic and Early Roman Italy: A Votive Perspective', *World Archaeology* 45(2): 215–31.

Graham, E.-J. (2014), 'Infant Votives and Swaddling in Hellenistic Italy', in Carroll, M. and Graham, E.-J. (eds.), *Infant Health and Death in Roman Italy and Beyond* (JRA Supplement 96). Portsmouth: Journal of Roman Archaeology, 34–46.

Green, M. A. (1992), *Animals in Celtic Life and Myth*. London: Routledge.

Grossman, J. B. (2001), *Greek Funerary Sculpture: Catalogue of the Collections at the Getty Villa*. Los Angeles: J. Paul Getty Trust.

Grossman, J. B. (2007), 'Forever Young: An Investigation of the Depictions of Children on Classical Attic Funerary Monuments', in Cohen, A. and Rutter, J. (eds.), *Constructions of Childhood in Ancient Greece and Italy* (Hesperia Supplement 41). Princeton: Princeton University Press, 309–22.

Gruen, E. S. (ed.) (2011), *Cultural Identity in the Ancient Mediterranean*. Los Angeles: J. Paul Getty Trust.

Grünewald, M. (1990), *Der römische Nordfriedhof in Worms: Funde von der Mainzer Straße*. Worms: Bücher Bessler.

Guérin, P., Calvo Gálvez, M., Grau Almero, E., Guillén Calatayud, P. M. (1989), 'Tumbas infantiles en el Castellet de Bernabé (Liria, Valencia)', *Inhumaciones infantiles en el ambito mediterraneo espanol (siglos VII a. e. al II d. E.)* (*Cuadernos de Prehistoria y Arqueología Castellonenses* 14). Castellón dela Plana: Servicio de Arqueolo, 63–94.

Guéry, R. (1985), *La nécropole orientale de Sitifis: Fouilles de 1966–1967*. Paris: Éditions du Centre National de la Recherche Scientifique.

Guillier, G. (1992), 'Une nécropole d'enfants d'époque gallo-romaine à Sommesous (Marne)', *Revue Archéologique Sites* 52: 16–29.

Guimier-Sorbets, A.-M. and Morizot, Y. (eds.) (2010), *L'Enfant et la mort dans l'Antiquité I: Nouvelles recherches dans les nécropoles grecques: Le signalement des tombes d'enfants. Actes de la table ronde internationale organiseé à Athènes, École française d'Athènes, 29–30 mai 2008*. Paris: de Boccard.

Guiot, T., Couvin, F., and Blanchard, P. (2003), 'Le site antique (Ier–IIIe s) des Béziaux à Langeais (Indre-et-Loire)', *Revue Archéologique du Centre de la France* 42: 75–119.

Gusi, F., Muriel, S., and Olària, C. R. (eds.) (2008), *Nasciturus, infans, puerulus vobis mater terra: La muerte en la infancia*. Castelló: Servei d'Investigacions Arquelògiques i Prehistòriques.

Hackworth Petersen, L. and Salzman-Mitchell, P. (eds.) (2012), *Mothering and Motherhood in Ancient Greece and Rome*. Austin: University of Texas Press.

Hadzisteliou-Price, T. (1969), 'The Type of the Crouching Child and the "Temple Boys"', *Annual of the British School at Athens* 64: 95–112.

Hänninen, M. (2005), 'From Womb to Family: Rituals and Social Conventions Connected to Roman Birth', in Mustakallio, K., Hanska, J., Sainio, H.-L., and Vuolanto, V. (eds.), *Hoping for Continuity: Childhood, Education and Death in Antiquity and the Middle Ages*. Rome: Institutum Romanum Finlandiae, 49–59.

Haensch, R. (2013), 'Von Poppaea zu Pulcheria–Das Bemühen um göttlichen Beistand bei der Geburt eines kaiserlichen Nachfolgers', *Arctos* 47: 131–52.

Haentjens, A. M. E. (2000), 'Reflections on Female Infanticide in the Greco-Roman World', *L'antiquité classique* 69: 261–4.

Haffner, A. (1971), *Das keltisch-römische Gräberfeld von Wederath-Belginum, 1. Teil: Gräber 1–428 ausgegraben 1954/1955*. Mainz: Verlag Philipp von Zabern.

Haffner, A. (1974), *Das keltisch-römische Gräberfeld von Wederath-Belginum, 2. Teil: Gräber 429–883 ausgegraben 1956/1957*. Mainz: Verlag Philipp von Zabern.

Halcrow, S. E. and Tayles, N. (2008), 'The Bioarchaeological Investigation of Childhood and Social Age: Problems and Prospects', *Journal of Archaeological Method and Theory* 15: 190–215.

Hamilton, R. (1992), *Choes and Anthesteria: Athenian Iconography and Ritual*. Ann Arbor: University of Michigan Press.

Hanson, A. E. (2004), 'A Long-Lived "Quick-Birther" (*okytokion*)', in Dasen, V. (ed.), *Naissance et petite enfance dans l'Antiquité: Actes du colloque de Fribourg, 28 novembre–1 décembre 2001*. Fribourg: Academic Press, 265–80.

Hanson, A. E. (2008), 'The Gradualist View of Fetal Development', in Brisson, L., Congoudeau, M.-H., and Solère, J.-L. (eds.), *L'embryon: Formation et animation. Antiquité grecque et latine traditions hébraïque, chrétienne et islamique*. Paris: Librairie Philosophique J. Vrin, 95–108.

Harlow, M. (2012), 'Death and the Maiden: Reprising the Burials of Roman Girls and Young Women', in Carroll, M. and Wild, J. P. (eds.), *Dressing the Dead in Classical Antiquity*. Stroud: Amberley.

Harlow, M. (2013), 'Toys, Dolls and the Material Culture of Childhood', in Evans Grubbs, J., Parkin, T., and Bell, R. (eds.), *The Oxford Handbook of Childhood and Education in the Classical World*. Oxford: Oxford University Press, 322–40.

Harlow, M. and Larsson Lovén, L. (eds.) (2012), *Families in the Roman and Late Antique World*. London: Continuum.
Harlow, M. and Laurence, R. (eds.) (2010), *A Cultural History of Childhood and the Family, Vol. 1: Antiquity*. Oxford: Berg.
Harrill, J. A. (1995), *The Manumission of Slaves in Early Christianity* (Hermeneutische Untersuchungen zur Theologie 32). Tübingen: Mohr.
Harris, H. A. (1933), *Bone Growth in Health and Disease*. London: Oxford University Press.
Harris, W. V. (1982), 'The Theoretical Possibility of Extensive Infanticide in the Graeco-Roman World', *The Classical Quarterly* 32(1): 114–16.
Harris, W. V. (1994), 'Child Exposure in the Roman Empire', *Journal of Roman Studies* 84: 1–22.
Harvey Jr, P. B. (2006), 'Religion and Memory at Pisaurum', in Schultz, C. E. and Harvey Jr, P. B. (eds.), *Religion in Republican Italy*. Cambridge: Cambridge University Press, 117–36.
Hassall, M. (1999), 'Homes for Heroes: Married Quarters for Soldiers and Veterans', in Goldsworthy, A. and Haynes, I. (eds.), *The Roman Army as a Community* (JRA Supplement 34). Portsmouth: Journal of Roman Archaeology, 35–40.
Hassan, A., Brown, K., Eyers, J., Brown, T., and Mays, S. (2014), 'Ancient DNA Study of the Remains of Putative Infanticide Victims from the Yewden Roman Villa Site at Hambleden, England', *Journal of Archaeological Science* 43: 192–7.
Hatt, J. J., Lebel, P., and Joffroy, R. (1954), '*Et omnes stellas ex cornibus alcinis*: Talismans gallo-romains en bois de cerf ou d'élan trouvés dans les tombes', *Revue Archéologique de l'Est et Centre-Est* 5: 55–66.
Hauser, P. and Rossi, F. (1998), 'Urbanisme et habitat', in *Nyon: Une colonie romaine sur les bords du Lac Léman* (*Dossiers d'Archeologie* 232): 18–25.
Haynes, S. (2000), *Etruscan Civilization: A Cultural History*. Los Angeles: Getty Publications.
Helttula, A. (ed.) (2007), *Le iscrizioni sepolcrali latine nell'Isola Sacra* (Acta Instituti Romani FInlandiae 30). Helsinki: Finnish Institute.
Hemelrijk, E. (2015), *Hidden Lives, Public Personae: Women and Civic Life in the Roman West*. Oxford: Oxford University Press.
Henley, A. and Kohner, N. (2001), *When A Baby Dies: The Experience of Late Miscarriage, Stillbirth and Neonatal Death*. London: Routledge.
Henneberg, H. and Henneberg, R. J. (2001), 'Skeletal Material from the House of C. Iulius Polybius in Pompei, 79 AD', in Ciarallo, A. and De Carolis, E. (eds.), *La Casa di Giulio Polibio: Studi Interdisciplinari*. Tokyo: Centro Studi Arti Figurativi, 79–92.
Hensen, A. and Ludwig, R. (2005), 'Reise ins Jenseits: Totenehrung und Bestattung im Südwesten', in Schmidt, S. (ed.), *Imperium Romanum: Roms Provinzen an Neckar, Rhein und Donau, Begleitband zur Ausstellung des Landes Baden-Württemberg im Kunstgebäude Stuttgart, 1 Oktober 2005 bis 8 Januar 2006*. Esslingen: Archäologisches Landesmuseum Baden-Württemberg, 369–78.
Henshall, A. S. (1962), 'Cloths in Burials with Gypsum', in *An Inventory of the Historical Monuments in the City of York I: Eburacum, Roman York*. London: Royal Commission on Historical Monuments, 108–9.

Hermary, A. and Dubois, C. (eds.) (2012), *L'Enfant et la mort dans l'Antiquité III: Le materiel associé aux tombes d'enfants. Actes de la table ronde internationale organisée à la Maison Méditteranéenne de Sciences de l'Homme (MMSH) d'Aix-en-Provence, 20–22 janvier 2011*. Arles: Éditions Errance.

Heyn, M. K. (2010), 'Gesture and Identity in the Funerary Art of Palmyra', *American Journal of Archaeology* 114(1): 631–61.

Heyn, M. K. (2012), 'Female Portraiture in Palmyra', in James, S. L. and Dillon, S. (eds.), *A Companion to Women in the Ancient World*. Oxford: Malden, 439–41.

Hillson, S. (2009), 'The World's Largest Infant Cemetery and its Potential for Studying Growth and Development: The Notia Kylindra Site on the Island of Astypalaia in the Dodecanese', in Schepartz, L. A., Fox, S. C., and Bourbou, C. (eds.), *New Directions in the Skeletal Biology of Greece* (Hesperia Supplement 43). Athens: American School of Classical Studies, 137–54.

Hintermann, D. (2000), *Der Südfriedhof von Vindonissa: Archäologische und naturwissenschaftiche Untersuchungen im römerzeitlichn Gräberfeld Windisch-Dägerli* (Veröffentlichungen der Gesellschaft pro Vindonissa XVII). Brugg: Aargauische Kantonsarchäologie.

Hirt, M. (2004), 'Le legislation romaine et les droits de l'enfant', in Dasen, V. (ed.), *Naissance et petite enfance dans l'Antiquité: Actes du colloque de Fribourg, 28 novembre–1 décembre 2001*. Fribourg: Academic Press, 281–91.

Hodgson, N. (2014), 'The Accomodation of Roman Soldiers' Wives in Roman Fort Barracks – on Hadrian's Wall and Beyond', in Collins, R. and McIntosh, F. (eds.), *Life in the Limes: Studies of the People and Objects of the Roman Frontiers*. Oxford: Oxbow, 18–28.

Hoffer, S. E. (1999), *The Anxieties of Pliny the Younger*. Atlanta: Scholars Press.

Hoffmann, B. (1995), 'The Quarters of the Legionary Centurions of the Principate', *Britannia* 26: 107–51.

Holdt Sommer, S. (2016), 'Lithopedion: An Unexpected Finding', *American Journal of Obstetrics and Gynecology* 215(4): 524.e1–524.e2.

Hölschen, B. (2002a), 'Säuglinge überall – Bestattungen im Siedlungs- und Gräberfeldareal der römischen Siedlung Sontheim/Brenz "Braike", Kreis Heidenheim', in Wamser, L. and Steidl, B. (eds.), *Neue Forschungen zur römischen Besiedlung zwischen Oberrhein und Enns: Kolloquium Rosenheim 14–16 Juni 2000*. Remshalden: Bernhard Albert Greiner, 223–9.

Hölschen, B. (2002b), 'Wohin mit den toten Kindern? Kinderbestattungen im Siedlungs- und Gräberfeldareal der römischen Siedlung Sontheim/Brenz "Braike", Kreis Heidenheim', in Alt, K. W. and Kemkes-Grottenthaler, A. (eds.), *Kinderwelten: Anthropologie—Geschichte—Kulturvergleich*. Mainz: Böhlau, 164–70.

Hölschen, B. and Becker, T. (2006), '"Grenzkinder": Zu den Nachweismoglichkeiten von Kindern am Obergermanisch-Raetischen Limes', in Seitz, G. (ed.), *Im Dienste Roms: Festschrift für Hans Ulrich Nuber*. Remshalden: Verlag Bernhard Albert Greiner, 35–44.

Holtzmann, B. (2012), 'Les médaillons funéraires de Thasos', in T. Stephanidou-Tiveriou, P. Karanastase, and D. Damaskos (eds.), *Κλασική παράδοση και νεωτερικά στοιχεία στην πλαστική της ρωμαϊκής Ελλάδας. Proceedings of the International Conference in Thessaloniki, 7–9 May 2009*. Thessaloniki: University Studio Press, 409–16.

Hong, Y. (2012), 'Collaboration and Conflict: Discourses of Maternity in Hippocratic Gynecology and Embryology', in Hackworth Petersen, L. and Salzman-Mitchell, P. (eds.), *Mothering and Motherhood in Ancient Greece and Rome*. Austin: University of Texas Press, 71–96.

Hope, V. M. (2001), *Constructing Identity: The Roman Funerary Monuments of Aquileia, Mainz and Nîmes* (BAR International Series 960). Oxford: Archaeopress.

Höpken, C. C. C. (2007), 'Frührömische Gräber in Köln', in Uelsberg, G. (ed.), *Krieg und Frieden: Kelten, Römer, Germanen*. Bonn: Landschaftsverband Rheinland, 295–301.

Hopkins, K. (1965), 'Contraception in the Roman Empire', *Comparative Studies in Society and History* 8(1): 124–51.

Hopkins, K. (1983), *Death and Renewal: Sociological Studies in Ancient History*. Cambridge: Cambridge University Press.

Houby-Nielsen, S. (2000), 'Child Burials in Ancient Athens', in Sofaer Derevenski, J. (ed.), *Children and Material Culture*. London: Routledge, 151–66.

Hugoniot, E., Thevenon, R., and Vannier, G. (1975), 'Les sépultures gallo-romaines tardives de Bruère-Allichamps (Cher)', *Revue archéologique du Centre* numéro spécial: 85–92.

Huntsman, T. (2014), 'Hellenistic Etruscan Cremation Urns from Chiusi', *Metropolitan Museum Journal* 49: 141–50.

Huskinson, J. (1996), *Roman Children's Sarcophagi: Their Decoration and its Social Significance*. Oxford: Clarendon Press.

Huskinson, J. (2011), 'Picturing the Roman Family', in Rawson, B. (ed.), *A Companion to Families in the Greek and Roman Worlds*. Oxford: Wiley-Blackwell, 521–41.

Huttmann, A., Tillmanns, U., Greiling, H., and Riedel, M. (1989), 'Inhaltsanalysen römischer Säuglingstrinkgefässe', *Kölner Jahrbuch Vor- und Frühgeschichte* 22: 365–72.

Icard, S. (1904), 'Note sur une nécropole romaine de Sousse', *Bulletin de la Société Archéologique de Sousse* 3: 165–9.

Jaeggi, S. (2012a), 'Le "cimetière de bébés" d'Alésia: un mobilier funéraire inédit', in Hermary, A. and Dubois, C. (eds.), *L'Enfant et la mort dans l'Antiquité III: Le materiel associé aux tombes d'enfants. Actes de la table ronde internationale organisée à la Maison Méditteranéenne de Sciences de l'Homme (MMSH) d'Aix-en-Provence, 20–22 janvier 2011*. Arles: Éditions Errance, 225–41.

Jaeggi, S. (2012b), 'Le cimetière de bébés d'Alésia, un mythe revisité', *Bulletin der Schweizer Arbeitsgemeinschaft für Klassische Archäologie* 2012: 46–50.

Jaeggi, S. (2013), 'Alésia, un "cimetière de bébés" redécouvert?', *La petite Enfance dans le Monde Grec et Romain* (*Dossiers d'Archéologie* 356): 54–7.

James, S. L. and Dillon, S. (eds.) (2012), *A Companion to Women in the Ancient World*. Oxford: Malden.

Janssen, R. (1996), 'Soft Toys from Egypt', in Bailey, D. M. (ed.), *Archaeological Research in Roman Egypt* (JRA Supplement 19). Ann Arbor: JRA.

Jarva, E. (1981), 'Area di tombe infantili a Ficana', *Archeologia Laziale* 4: 269–73.

Jashemski, W. F. and Meyer, F. G. (eds.) (2002), *The Natural History of Pompeii*. Cambridge: Cambridge University Press.

Jenkins, I., Farge, C., and Turner, V. (2015), *Defining Beauty: The Body in Ancient Greek Art*. London: The British Museum.

Jobbé-Duval, E. M. (1924), *Les morts malfaisants (Larvae, Lémures) d'après le droit et les croyances populaires des Romains.* Paris: Sirey.

Johnson, K. (2003), 'Textile and Papyrus Figurines from Karanis', *Bulletin of the University of Michigan Museums of Art and Archaeology* 15: 49–64.

Joly, J. (1951), 'Un cimetière gallo-romain de bébés à Alise-Sainte-Reine (Côte-d'Or)', *Revue Archéologique de l'Est* 11: 119–20.

Joly, J. (1954), 'Quelques sépultures du cimetière de bébés de la Croix Saint-Charles sur le mont Auxois', *Revue Archéologique de l'Est et Centre-Est* 5: 92–8.

Kaibel, G. (ed.) (1878), *Epigrammata Graeca ex Lapidibus Conlecta.* Berlin: Berolini.

Kalaitzi, M. (2010), 'The Representaion of Children on Classical and Hellenistic Tombstones from Ancient Macedonia', in Guimier-Sorbets, A.-M. and Morizot, Y. (eds.), *L'Enfant et la mort dans l'Antiquité I: Nouvelles recherches dans le nécropoles grecques: Le signalement des tombs d'enfants. Actes de la table ronde internationale organiseé à Athènes, École française d'Athènes, 29–30 mai 2008.* Paris: De Boccard, 327–46.

Kallintzi, K. and Papaikonomou, I.-D. (2010), 'La presence des enfants dans le nécropoles d'Abdère', in Guimier-Sorbets, A.-M. and Morizot, Y. (eds.), *L'Enfant et la mort dans l'Antiquité I: Nouvelles recherches dans le nécropoles grecques: Le signalement des tombs d'enfants. Actes de la table ronde internationale organiseé à Athènes, École française d'Athènes, 29–30 mai 2008.* Paris: De Boccard, 129–59.

Kampen, N. (1981), *Image and Status: Roman Working Women in Ostia.* Berlin: Gebrüder Mann.

Kampen, N. B. (2009), *Family Fictions in Roman Art: Essays on the Representation of Powerful People.* Cambridge: Cambridge University Press.

Kapparis, K. (2002), *Abortion in the Ancient World.* London: Duckworth.

Kaschnitz-Weinberg, G. (1936–7), *Sculture del Magazzino del Museo Vaticano.* Rome: Città del Vaticano.

Katzenberg, M. A., Herring, D. A., and Saunders, S. R. (1996), 'Weaning and Infant Mortality: Evaluating the Skeletal Evidence', *American Journal of Physical Anthropology* 101: 177–99.

Keenleyside, A., Schwarcz, H., Stirling, L., and Ben Lazreg, N. (2009), 'Stable Isotopic Evidence for Diet in a Roman and Late Roman Population from Leptiminus, Tunisia', *Journal of Archaeological Science* 36: 51–63.

Kepartová, J. (1984), 'Kinder in Pompeji: Eine epigraphische Untersuchung', *Klio* 66: 192–209.

Killgrove, K. (2010), *Migration and Mobility in Imperial Rome.* PhD thesis, University of North Carolina at Chapel Hill.

King, M. (1996), *The Behavioural and Emotional Reaction of the Romans to Infant Mortality.* PhD thesis, University of Edinburgh.

King, M. (2000), 'Commemoration of Infants on Roman Funerary Inscriptions', in Oliver, G. J. (ed.), *The Epigraphy of Death: Studies in the History and Society of Greece and Rome.* Liverpool: Liverpool University Press, 117–54.

Kleiner, D. E. E. (1977), *Roman Group Portraiture: The Funerary Reliefs of the Late Republic and Early Empire.* New York: Garland Publications.

Kleiner, D. E. E. (1987a), *Roman Imperial Funerary Altars with Portraits.* Rome: Giorgio Bretschneider Editore.

Kleiner, D. E. E. (1987b), 'Women and Family Life on Roman Imperial Funerary Altars', *Latomus* 46: 545–54.

Kleiner, D. E. E. (1992), *Roman Sculpture*. New Haven: Yale University Press.

Koch, G. (1988), *Roman Funerary Sculpture: Catalogue of the Collections*. Malibu: Getty Museum Press.

Kockel, V. (1993), *Porträtreliefs Stadtrömischer Grabbauten: Ein Beitrag zur Geschichte und zum Verständnis des spätrepublikanisch-frühkaiserzeitlichen Privatporträts*. Mainz: Philipp von Zabern.

Koloski-Ostrow, A. O. and Lyons, C. L. (eds.) (1997), *Naked Truths: Women, Sexuality and Gender in Classical Art and Archaeology*. London: Routledge.

Koukouli-Chrysanthaki, C. (1994), 'The Cemeteries of Abdera', in de la Genière, J. (ed.), *Nécropoles et Sociétés Antiques: Grèce, Italie, Languedoc: Actes de la Colloque International du Centre de Recherches Archéologiques de l'Université de Lille III, Lille, 2–3 Décembre 1991*. Naples: Centre Jean Bérard, 33–77.

Kovács, P. (2005), *Tituli Romani in Hungaria Reperti: Supplementum I*. Budapest: Enciklopédia Kiadó.

Kramis, S. and Trancik, V. (2014), '"Extra locos sepulturae": Literaturreview zu römerzeitlichen Perinatenfunden auf dem Gebiet der heutigen Schweiz', *Bulletin der Schweizerischen Gesellschaft für Anthropologie* 20(2): 5–26.

Krauße, D. (1998), 'Infantizid', in Müller-Karpe, A., Brandt, H., Jöns, H., Krauße, D., and Wigg, A. (eds.), *Studien zur Archäologie der Kelten, Römer und Germanen in Mittel- und Westeuropa*. Rahden: Verlag Marie Leidorf, 313–52.

Krause, J.-U. (2011), 'Children in the Roman Family and Beyond', in Peachin, M. (ed.), *The Oxford Handbook of Social Relations in the Roman World*. Oxford: Oxford University Press, 623–42.

Krüger, M.-L. (1974), *Die Reliefs der Stadtgebiete von Scarbantia und Savaria, CSIR I.5 Österreich*. Vienna: Verlag der österreichischen Akademie der Wissenschaften.

Kutlu, A., Memik, R., Mutlu, M., Kutlu, R., and Arslan, A. (1992), 'Congenital Dislocation of the Hip and its Relation to Swaddling Used in Turkey', *Journal of Pediatric Orthopaedics* 12: 598–602.

Kuttner, A. (1995), *Dynasty and Empire in the Age of Augustus: The Case of the Boscoreale Cups*. Berkeley: University of California Press.

Laes, C. (2003), 'Desperately Different? Delicia Children in the Roman Household', in Balch, D. L. and Osiek, C. (eds.), *Early Christian Families in Context*. Grand Rapids: William B. Eerdmans Publishing Company, 298–324.

Laes, C. (2011a), *Children in the Roman Empire: Outsiders Within*. Cambridge: Cambridge University Press. (Published 2006 as *Kinderen bij de Romeinen: Zes eeuwen dagelijks leven*.).

Laes, C. (2011b), 'Grieving for Lost Children, Pagan and Christian', in Rawson, B. (ed.), *A Companion to Families in the Greek and Roman Worlds*. Oxford: Wiley-Blackwell, 315–30.

Laes, C. (2013), 'Raising a Disabled Child', in Evans Grubbs, J., Parkin, T., and Bell, R. (eds.), *The Oxford Handbook of Childhood and Education in the Classical World*. Oxford: Oxford University Press, 124–44.

Laes, C. (2014), 'The Youngest Children in Latin Epigraphy', in Carroll, M. and Graham, E.-J. (eds.), *Infant Health and Death in Roman Italy and Beyond* (JRA Supplement 96). Portsmouth: Journal of Roman Archaeology, 131–44.

Lally, M. and Moore, A. (eds.) (2011), *Re-Thinking the Little Ancestor: New Perspectives on the Archaeology of Infancy and Childhood.* Oxford: Archaeopress.

Lambert, S. D. (1993), *The Phratries of Attica.* Ann Arbor: University of Michigan Press.

Lancel, S. (1992), *Carthage.* Paris: Fayard.

Lanciani, R. (1924), *Wanderings through Ancient Roman Churches.* Boston: Houghton Mifflin Company.

Langdon, S. (2007), 'The Awkward Age: Art and Maturation in Early Greece', in Cohen, A. and Rutter, J. (eds.), *Constructions of Childhood in Ancient Greece and Italy* (Hesperia Supplement 41). Princeton: Princeton University Press, 173–91.

Langenegger, E. (1996), 'Die Neonatengräber', in Rychener, J. (ed.), *Der römischer Gutshof in Neftenbach* (Monografien der Kantonsarchäologie Zürich 31.1). Zürich: Fotorotar AG, 489–94.

Langenegger, E. (1999), 'Zu den Neonatengräbern im römischen Gutshof von Neftenbach ZH', *Archéologie Suisse* 19(4): 156–8.

Larsson Lovén, L. (2013), 'Children and Childhood in Roman Commemorative Art', in Evans Grubbs, J., Parkin, T., and Bell, R. (eds.), *The Oxford Handbook of Childhood and Education in the Classical World.* Oxford: Oxford University Press, 302–21.

Laubenheimer, F. (2004), 'La mort des tout petits dans l'Occident romain', in Dasen, V. (ed.), *Naissance et petite enfance dans l'Antiquité: Actes du colloque de Fribourg, 28 novembre–1 décembre 2001.* Fribourg: Academic Press, 293–315.

Lawton, C. L. (2007), 'Children in Classcial Attic Votive Reliefs', in Cohen, A. and Rutter, J. B. (eds.), *Constructions of Childhood in Ancient Greece and Rome* (Hesperia Supplement 61). Princeton: Princeton University Press, 41–60.

Lazer, E. (2009), *Resurrecting Pompeii.* London: Routledge.

Lee, M. (2012), 'Maternity and Miasma: Dress and the Transition from Parthenos to Guné', in Hackworth Petersen, L. and Salzman-Mitchell, P. (eds.), *Mothering and Motherhood in Ancient Greece and Rome.* Austin: University of Texas Press, 23–42.

Lee, M. (2015), *Body, Dress and Identity in Ancient Greece.* New York: Cambridge University Press.

Lepetz, S. (2012), 'Les restes animaux dans les tombes d'enfants à la période romaine: l'exemple de trois grandes nécropoles d'Italie, de Tunisie et du Nord de la France', in Hermary, A. and Dubois, C. (eds.), *L'Enfant et la mort dans l'Antiquité III: Le materiel associé aux tombes d'enfants. Actes de la table ronde internationale organisée à la Maison Méditteranéenne de Sciences de l'Homme (MMSH) d'Aix-en-Provence, 20–22 janvier 2011.* Arles: Éditions Errance, 313–28.

Lepper, F. and Frere, S. (1988), *Trajan's Column: A New Edition of the Cichorius Plates.* Stroud: Alan Sutton.

Lewis, M. E. (2007), *The Bioarchaeology of Children: Perspectives from Biological and Forensic Anthropology.* Cambridge: Cambridge University Press.

Lewis, M. E. (2010), 'Life and Death in a Civitas Capital: Metabolic Disease and Trauma in the Children from Late Roman Dorchester, Dorset', *American Journal of Physical Anthropology* 142(3): 405–16.

Lewis, M. E. (2012), 'Thalassaemia. Its Diagnosis and Interpretation in Past Skeletal Populations', *International Journal of Osteoarchaeology* 22: 685–93.

Lewis, M. E. and Gowland, R. L. (2009), 'Infantile Cortical Hyperostosis: Cases, Causes and Contradictions', in Lewis, M. E. and Clegg, M. (eds.), *Proceedings of the Ninth Annual Conference of the British Association for Biological Anthropology and Osteoarchaeology, University of Reading 2007* (BAR International Series 1918). Oxford: Archaeopress, 43–51.

Lewis, S. (2002), *The Athenian Woman: An Iconographic Handbook*. London: Routledge.

Lilimpaki-Akamati, M. (1998), 'Relief Grave Stele from the East Cemetery at Pella', *ArchDelt* 53A: 257–66.

Lillehammer, G. (2000), 'The World of Children', in Sofaer Derevenski, J. (ed.), *Children and Material Culture*. London: Routledge, 17–26.

Lillehammer, G. (2010), 'Archaeology of Childhood', *Complutum* 21(2): 15–44.

Liston, M. A. and Papadopoulos, J. K. (2004), 'The "Rich Athenian Lady" was Pregnant: The Anthropology of a Geometric Tomb Reconsidered', *Hesperia* 73(1): 7–38.

Liston, M. A. and Rotroff, S. (2013a), 'Babies in the Well: Archaeological Evidence for Newborn Disposal in Hellenistic Greece', in Evans Grubbs, J., Parkin, T., and Bell, R. (eds.), *The Oxford Handbook of Childhood and Education in the Classical World*. Oxford: Oxford University Press, 62–82.

Liston, M. A. and Rotroff, S. (2013b), 'Des bébés dans un puits: Un témoignage de l'abandon des nouveau-nés en Grèce hellénistique', *La petite Enfance dans le Monde Grec et Romain* (*Dossiers d'Archéologie* 356): 74–9.

Liverani, P. (1989), *Museo Chiaramonti*. Rome: L'Erma di Bretschneider.

Liverani, P. and Spinola, G. (2010), *The Vatican Necropoles*. Milan: Brepols.

López-Bertran, M. and Vives-Ferrándiz, J. (2015), 'Miniatures from Domestic Contexts in Iron Age Iberia', *Miniaturization* (*World Archaeology* 47(1)): 80–93.

Lovell, A. (1997), 'Death at the Beginning of Life', in Field, D., Hockey, J., and Small, N. (eds.), *Death, Gender and Ethnicity*. London: Routledge, 29–51.

Lundeen, L. E. (2006), 'In Search of the Etruscan Priestess', in Schultz, C. E. and Harvey Jr, P. B. (eds.), *Religion in Republican Italy*. Cambridge: Cambridge University Press, 34–61.

Lutz, C. (1947), 'Musonius Rufus, the Roman Socrates', *Yale Classical Studies* 10: 3–147.

McCardle, P., McCune, S., Griffin, J. A., and Maholmes, V. (eds.) (2011), *How Animals Affect Us: Examining the Influence of Human–Animal Interaction on Child Development and Human Health*. Washington: American Physchological Association.

McCarty, M. M. (2011), 'Representations and the "Meaning" of Ritual Change: The Case of Hadrumetum', in Chaniotis, A. (ed.), *Ritual Dynamics in the Ancient Mediterranean: Agency, Emotion, Gender, Representation* (Heidelberger Beiträge und epigraphische Studien 49). Heidelberg: Franz Steiner Verlag, 197–228.

McCarty, M. M. (2013), 'Continuities and Contexts: The Tophets of Roman Imperial-Period Africa', in Xella, P. (ed.), *The Tophet in the Ancient Mediterranean. Studi Epigrafici e Linguistici* 29–30: 93–118.

McGinn, T. A. J. (2013), 'Roman Children and the Law', in Evans Grubbs, J., Parkin, T., and Bell, R. (eds.), *The Oxford Handbook of Childhood and Education in the Classical World*. Oxford: Oxford University Press, 341–62.

Macías, J. M. and Menchón, J. (2002), 'Excavacions at Camí de la Platja dels Cossis (Tarragona): Noves aportacions a la problemática funeraria del sector nord-oriental

de Tàrraco', in *Tribuna d'Arquelogia 1998–1999*. Generalitat de Catalunya, Department de Cultura: Barcelona, 237–57.

MacIntosh Turfa, J. (2004), 'Anatomical Votives', in *Thesaurus Cultus et Rituum Antiquorum (ThesCRA) I: Processions, Sacrifices, Libations, Fumigations, Dedications*. Los Angeles: J. Paul Getty Museum, 359–68.

MacIntosh Turfa, J. (2006), 'Votive Offerings in Etruscan Religion', in De Grummond, N. T. and Simon, E. (eds.), *The Religion of the Etruscans*. Austin: University of Texas Press, 90–115.

Mackensen, M. (1978a), *Cambodunumforschungen IV: Das römische Gräberfeld auf der Keckwiese in Kempten*. Kallmünz: M. Lassleben.

Mackensen, M. (1978b), 'Körperbestattete Neonaten in der römischen Nekropole von Šempeter', *Arheološki Vestnik* 29: 336–41.

Mackinder, A. (2000), *A Romano-British Cemetery on Watling Street: Excavations at 165 Great Dover Street, Southwark, London*. London: MoLAS.

McWilliam, J. (2001), 'Children among the Dead', in Dixon, S. (ed.), *Childhood, Class and Kin in the Roman World*. London: Routledge, 74–98.

McWilliam, J. (2013), 'The Socialization of Roman Children', in Evans Grubbs, J., Parkin, T., and Bell, R. (eds.), *The Oxford Handbook of Childhood and Education in the Classical World*. Oxford: Oxford University Press, 264–85.

Mafart, B., Kéfi, R., and Béraud-Colomb, E. (2007), 'Palaeopathological and Palaeogenetic Study of 13 Cases of Developmental Displasia of the Hip with Dislocation in a Historical Population from Southern France', *International Journal of Osteoarchaeology* 17: 26–38.

Malamidou, D. and Papaikonomou, I.-D. (2013), 'Femmes enceintes et astragales: Une sépulture à deux urnes cinéraires d'Amphipolis', *La petite Enfance dans le Monde Grec et Romain* (*Dossiers d'Archéologie* 356): 32–5.

Mander, J. (2012), 'The Representation of Physical Contact on Roman Tombstones', in Harlow, M. and Larsson Lovén, L. (eds.), *Families in the Roman and Late Antique World*. London: Continuum, 64–84.

Mander, J. (2013), *Portraits of Children on Roman Funerary Monuments*. Cambridge: Cambridge University Press.

Marlow, C. A. (2001), 'Miscarriages and Infant Burials in the Dakhleh Oasis Cemeteries: An Archaeological Examination of Status', in Marlow, C. A. and Mills, A. J. (eds.), *The Oasis Papers 1: Proceedings of the First International Symposium of the Dakhleh Oasis Project*. Oxford: Oxbow, 105–10.

Martin, L., Richardson, J., and Roberts, I. (2013), *Iron Age and Roman Settlements at Wattle Syke: Archaeological Investigations during the A1 Bramham to Wetherby Upgrading Scheme*. Leeds: West Yorkshire Archaeological Services.

Masciadri, M. M. and Montevecchi, O. (1984), *I Contratti di Balliatico*. Milan: Istituto di Papirologia.

Massa, S. (1997), *Aeterna Domus: Il complesso funerario di età romana del Lugone (Salò)*. Salò: Comune di Salò.

Massar, N. (2012), *L'enfant et la mort dans l'Antiquité I: nouvelles recherches dans les nécropoles grecques: Le signalement des tombes d'enfants* by A.-M. Guimier-Sorbets and Y. Morizot (eds.). Reviewed in: *Bryn Mawr Classical Review*: 2012.03.45.

Mattusch, C. C., Donohue, A. A. and Brauer, A. (eds.) (2006), *Common Ground: Archaeology, Art, Science and Humanities. Proceedings of the XVIth International Congress of Classical Archaeology*, Oxford: Oxbow.

Matz, F. (1969), *Die Dionysischen Sarkophage.* Berlin: Gebrüder Mann Verlag.

Mays, S. (1993), 'Infanticide in Roman Britain', *Antiquity* 67: 883–8.

Mays, S. (2002), *The Archaeology of Human Bones.* London: Routledge.

Mays, S. (2003), 'Comment on "A Bayesian Approach to Ageing Perinatal Skeletal Material from Archaeological Sites: Implications for the Evidence for Infanticide in Roman Britain" by Gowland, R. L. and Chamberlain, A. T.', *Journal of Archaeological Science* 30: 1695–700.

Mays, S. and Eyers, J. (2011), 'Perinatal Infant Death at the Roman Villa Site at Hambleden, Buckinghamshire, England', *Journal of Archaeological Science* 38: 1931–8.

Mays, S. and Faerman, M. (2001), 'Sex Identification in some Putative Infanticide Victims from Roman Britain Using Ancient DNA', *Journal of Archaeological Science* 28: 555–9.

Mays, S., Robson Brown, K., Vincent, S., Eyers, J., King, H., and Roberts, A. (2014), 'An Infant Femur Bearing Cut Marks from Roman Hambleden, England', *International Journal of Osteoarchaeology* 24(1): 111–15.

Maza, G. and Montandon, B. (2011), 'Nuits-Saint-Georges, le sanctuaire romain de Pré de Nuits (Côte-d'Or)', in Reddé, M., Barral, P., Favory, F., Guillaumet, J.-P., Joly, M., Marc, J.-Y., Nouvel, P., Nuninger, L., and Petit, C. (eds.), *Les lieux de culte du Nord-Est de la Gaule à l'époque de la Romanisation* (Collection Bibracte 21). Bibracte: Glux-en-Glenne, 603–17.

Mazarakis Ainian, A. (2010), 'Tombes d'enfants à l'intérieur d'habitats au début de l'Âge du Fer dans le monde grec', in Guimier-Sorbets, A.-M. and Morizot, Y. (eds.), *L'Enfant et la mort dans l'Antiquité I: Nouvelles recherches dans les nécropoles grecques: Le signalement des tombes d'enfants. Actes de la table ronde internationale organiseé à Athènes, École française d'Athènes, 29–30 mai 2008.* Paris: de Boccard, 67–95.

Megow, W.-R. (1987), *Kameen von Augustus bis Alexander Severus.* Berlin: Walter de Gruyter.

Mercando, L., Sorda, S., and Capitanio, M. (1974), 'Portorecanati (Macerata): La necropoli romana di Portorecanati', *Notizie degli Scavi di Antichità* 28: 142–445.

Mercando, L., Luni, M., Taborelli, L., Sorda, S., Corrain, C., Erspamer, G., and Malgeri, G. (1982), 'Urbino (Pesaro). Necropoli romana: tombe al Bivio alle Croce dei Missionari e a San Donato', *Notizie degli scavi di Antichità* 36: 109–420.

Merker, G. S. (2000), *Corinth, Volume XVIII, part IV, The Sanctuary of Demeter and Kore: Terracotta Figurines of the Classical, Hellenistic and Roman Periods.* Princeton: The American School of Classical Studies at Athens.

Messineo, G. (1991–2), 'Puerilia Crepitacula?', *Rivista di Studi Pompeiani* 5: 119–32.

Michalaki-Kollia, M. (2010), 'Un Ensemble exceptionnel d'Enchytrismes de Nouveau-Nés, de Foetus et de Nourrissons découvert dans l'Îsle d'Astypalée en Grèce: Cimetière de Bébés ou Sanctuaire? (Première Approche)', in Guimier-Sorbets, A.-M. and Morizot, Y. (eds.), *L'Enfant et la mort dans l'Antiquité I: Nouvelles recherches dans les nécropoles grecques: Le signalement des tombes d'enfants. Actes de la table ronde internationale organiseé à Athènes, École française d'Athènes, 29–30 mai 2008.* Paris: de Boccard, 161–205.

Michalaki-Kollia, M. (2013), 'Les 3000 bébés d'Astypalée', *La petite Enfance dans le Monde Grec et Romain (Dossiers d'Archéologie* 356): 22–9.

Miclea, I. (1971), *The Column.* Cluj: Publishing House Dacia.

Minguez Morales, J.-A. and José, A. (1989–90), 'Enterramientos infantiles *domésticos en la colonia* Lepida: Celsa (Velilla de Ebro, Zaragoza)', *Caesaraugusta* 66–7: 105–22.

Minozzi, S., Catalano, P., Caldarini, C., and Fornaciari, G. (2012), 'Palaeopathology of Human Remains from the Roman Imperial Age', *Pathobiology* 79: 268–83.

Mocsy, A. (1974), *Pannonia and Upper Moesia: A History of the Middle Danube Provinces of the Roman Empire.* London: Routledge and Kegan Paul.

Modica, S. (2007), *Rituali e Lazio Antico: Deposizioni infantile e abitati.* Milan: CUEM.

Moliner, M., Mellinand, P., Naggiar, L., Richier, A., and Villemeur, I. (eds.) (2003), *La nécropole de Sainte-Barbe à Marseille (IVe s. av. J.-C.-IIe s. ap. J.-C.)* (Etudes massaliètes 8). Aix-en-Provence: Édisud.

Molleson, T. and Cox, M. (1988), 'A Neonate with Cut Bones from Poundbury Camp', *Bulletin de la Société Royale Belge d'Anthropologie et de Préhistoire* 99: 53–9.

Molleson, T. I. (1989), 'Social Implications of Mortality Patterns of Juveniles from Poundbury Camp, Romano-British Cemetery', *Anthropologischer Anzeiger* 47(1): 27–38.

Mols, S. T. A. M. (2002), 'Identification of the Woods Used in the Furniture at Herculaneum', in Jashemski, W. F. and Meyer, F. G. (eds.), *The Natural History of Pompeii.* New York: Cambridge University Press, 225–34.

Mols, S. T. A. M. (2007–8), 'Ancient Roman Household Furniture and its use: From Herculaneum to the Rhine', *Anales de prehistoria y arqueología* 23–4: 145–60.

Morris, I. (1987), *Burial and Ancient Society: The Rise of the Greek City State.* Cambridge: Cambridge University Press.

Moscati, S. S. (1987), *Il sacrificio punico dei fanciulli: Realtà o invenzione?* (Problemi attuali di scienza e di cultura 261). Rome: Accademia Nazionale dei Lincei.

Moss, T. J. M. (2005), 'The Respiratory Consequences of Preterm Birth', *Proceedings of the Australian Physiological Society* 36: 23–8.

Murail, P. and Girard, L. (2000), 'Biology and Burial Practices from the End of the First Century A.D. to the Beginning of the Fifth Century A.D.: The Rural Necropolis of Chantambre (Essonne, France)', in Pearce, J., Millett, M., and Struck, M. (eds.), *Burial, Society and Context in the Roman World.* Oxford: Oxbow, 105–11.

Muriel, S. and Playà, R. M. (2008), 'Els elements marins a les sepultures infantils', in Gusi, F., Muriel, S., and Olària, C. R. (eds.), *Nasciturus, infans, puerulus vobis mater terra: La muerte en la infancia.* Castelló: Servei d'Investigacions Arquelògiques i Prehistòriques, 643–66.

Murphy, S. and Shevlin, M. (2014), 'Psychological Consequences of Pregnancy Loss and Infant Death in a Sample of Bereaved Parents', *Journal of Loss and Trauma* 19(1): 56–69.

Murphy, S. and Thomas, H. (2013), 'Stillbirth and Loss: Family Practices and Display', *Sociological Research Online* 18(1): http://www.socresonline.org.uk/18/1/16.html.

Musco, S. (2006a), 'La mansio di Quarto di Corzano', in Tomei, M. A. (ed.), *Roma: Memorie dal sottosuolo, Ritrovamenti archeologici 1980–2006.* Rome: Electa, 319–23.

Musco, S. (2006b), 'La necropoli Collatina: Viale della Serenissima-Via Andriuli', in Tomei, M. A. (ed.), *Roma: Memorie dal sottosuolo, Ritrovamenti archeologici 1980–2006*. Rome: Electa, 274–5.

Musco, S. (2006c), 'Via di Tor Cervara (Municipio V)', in Tomei, M. A. (ed.), *Roma: Memorie dal sottosuolo, Ritrovamenti archeologici 1980–2006*. Rome: Electa, 291–3.

Musco, S. and Catalano, P. (2010), 'Tombes d'Enfants de l'Époque imperial dans la Banlieue de Rome: Les cas de Quarto Cappello del Prete, de Casal Bertone et de la Nécropole Collatina', in Guimier-Sorbets, A.-M. and Morizot, Y. (eds.), *L'Enfant et la mort dans l'Antiquité I: Nouvelles recherches dans les nécropoles grecques: Le signalement des tombes d'enfants. Actes de la table ronde internationale organiseé à Athènes, École française d'Athènes, 29–30 mai 2008*. Paris: De Boccard, 387–402.

Musée Romain de Nyon (2003), *Nyon: Colonia Iulia Equestris*. Nyon: Éditions Infolio.

Myers, G. (1998), *Children and Animals: Social Development and Our Connections to Other Species*. Boulder: Westview Press.

Nava, M. L. (2012), *Museo Provinciale Campano di Capua. Guida alle Collezioni*. Caserta: Claudio Grenzi Editore.

Neils, J. (2003), Children and Greek Religion, in Neils, J. and Oakley, J. H. (eds.), *Coming of Age in Ancient Greece: Images of Childhood from the Classical Past*. New Haven: Yale University Press, 139–62.

Neils, J. and Oakley, J. H. (eds.) (2003), *Coming of Age in Ancient Greece: Images of Childhood from the Classical Past*. New Haven: Yale University Press.

Nenna, M.-D. (ed.) (2012), *L'Enfant et la mort dans l'Antiquité II: Types de tombs et traitement du corps des enfants dans l'antiquité gréco-romaine. Actes de la table ronde internationale organisée à Alexandrie, Centre d'Études Alexandrines, 12–14 novembre 2009*. Alexandria: Centre d'Études Alexandrines.

Nollé, J. (2003), 'Vielerorts war Bethlehem: Göttergeburten im kaiserzeitlichen Kleinasien', *Antike Welt* 34(6): 635–43.

Noriuchi, M., Kikuchi, Y., and Senoo, A. (2008), 'The Functional Neuroanatomy of Maternal Love: Mother's Response to Infant's Attachment Behaviours', *Biological Psychiatry* 63(4): 415–23.

Norman, N. (2002), 'Death and Burial of Roman Children: The Case of the Yasmina Cemetery at Carthage: Part 1, Setting the Stage', *Mortality* 7(3), 302–23.

Norman, N. (2003), 'Death and Burial of Roman Children: The Case of the Yasmina Cemetery at Carthage: Part 2, The Archaeological Evidence', *Mortality* 8(1): 36–47.

Oakley, J. H. (2003), 'Death and the Child', in Neils, J. and Oakley, J. H. (eds.), *Coming of Age in Ancient Greece: Images of Childhood from the Classical Past*. New Haven: Yale University Press, 163–94.

Oakley, J. H. (2004), *Picturing Death in Classical Athens: The Evidence of the White Lekythoi*. Cambridge: Cambridge University Press.

Oakley, J. H. (2013), 'Children in Archaic and Classical Greek Art: A Survey', in Evans Grubbs, J., Parkin, T., and Bell, R. (eds.), *The Oxford Handbook of Childhood and Education in the Classical World*. Oxford: Oxford University Press, 147–71.

Obladen, M. (2014), 'Technical Inventions that Enabled Artificial Infant Feeding', *Neonatology* 106(1): 62–8.

Opper, T. (2008), *Hadrian: Empire and Conflict*. London: British Museum Press.

Ornan, T. (2007), 'Labor Pangs: The Revadim Plaque', in Bickel, S., Schroer, S., Schurte, R., and Uehlinger, C. (eds.), *Bilder als Quellen, Images as Sources: Studies on Ancient Near Eastern Artefacts and the Bible Inspired by the Work of Othmar Keel*. Fribourg: Academic Press, 215–35.

Ortner, D. J. and Mays, S. (1998), 'Dry-Bone Manifesations of Rickets in Infancy and Early Childhood', *International Journal of Osteoarchaeology* 8(1): 45–55.

Otto, W. F. (1965), *Dionysos: Myth and Cult*. Bloomington: Indiana University Press.

Paine, R. R., Vargiu, R., Signoretti, C., and Coppa, A. (2009), 'A Health Assessment for Imperial Roman Burials Recovered from the Necropolis of San Donato and Bivio CH, Urbino, Italy', *Journal of Anthropological Science* 87: 193–210.

Palagia, O. (2006), 'Baby Out of a Basket in the Athenian Asklepieion', in Mattusch, C. C., Donohue, A. A., and Brauer, A. (eds.), *Common Ground: Archaeology, Art, Science and Humanities. Proceedings of the XVIth International Congress of Classical Archaeology*. Oxford: Oxbow, 606–9.

Palfi, G., Dutour, O., and Berato, J. (1993), 'Étude paléopathologique de la serie Gallo-Romaine de Costebelle (Hyères, Var)', *Paleobios* 9: 1–27.

Palfi, G., Dutour, O., Borreani, M., Brun, J.-P., and Berato, J. (1992), 'Congenital Syphilis from the Late Antiquity in France', *International Journal of Osteoarchaeology* 2: 245–61.

Papageorgopoulou, C., Suter, S. K., Rühli, F. J., and Siegmund, F. (2011), 'Harris Lines Revisited: Prevalence, Comorbidities, and Possible Etiologies', *American Journal of Human Biology* 23(3): 381–91.

Papaikonomou, I. D. (2008), 'Enfance et identité sexuée das les cites grecques', in Gusi, F., Muriel, S., and Olària, C. R. (eds.), *Nasciturus, infans, puerulus vobis mater terra: La muerte en la infancia*. Castelló: Servei d'Investigacions Arquelògiques i Prehistòriques, 683–710.

Parkin, T. (1992), *Demography and Roman Society*. Baltimore: Johns Hopkins University Press.

Parkin, T. (2010), 'Life Cycle', in Harlow, M. and Laurence, R. (eds.), *A Cultural History of Childhood and the Family, Vol. 1: Antiquity*. Oxford: Berg, 97–114.

Parkin, T. (2013), 'Demography of Infancy and Early Childhood', in Evans Grubbs, J., Parkin, T., and Bell, R. (eds.), *The Oxford Handbook of Childhood and Education in the Classical World*. Oxford: Oxford University Press, 46–50.

Passi Pitcher, L. (ed.) (1987), *Sub Ascia: Una necropoli romana a Nave*. Modena: Edizioni Panini.

Patterson, C. (1985), '"Not Worth the Rearing": The Causes of Infant Exposure in Ancient Greece', *Transactions of the American Philological Association* 115: 103–23.

Pautasso, A. (1994), *Il deposito votive presso la Porta Nord a Vulci*. Rome: Bretschneider.

Pease, A. S., Fleming, P. J., Hauck, F. R., Moon, R. Y., Horne, R. S. C., L'Hoir, M. P., Ponsonby, A.-L., and Blair, P. S. (2016), 'Swaddling and the Risk of Sudden Infant Death Syndrome: A Meta-Analysis', *Pediatrics* 137(6): 1–9.

Perassi, C. (1999), 'Monete nelle tombe di etàromana imperial: casi di scelta intenzionale sulla base dei soggetti e delle scritte?', in Dubois, F., Frey-Kupper, S., and Perret, G. (eds.), *Trouvailles monétaires de tombes: Actes du deuxième colloque international du Groupe suisse pour l'étude des trouvailles monétaires, Neuchâtel 3–4 mars 1995*. Lausanne: Éditions du Zèbre, 43–70.

Perkins, P. (2012), 'The Bucchero Childbirth Stamp on a Late Orientalizing Period Shard from Poggio Colla', *Etruscan Studies* 15(2): 146–201.

Pettitt, P. B. (2011), *The Paleolithic Origins of Human Burial.* London: Routledge.

Pfäffli, B. (2013a), *Kinder? Kinder!: Auf Spurensuche in Augusta Raurica. Begleitheft zur Ausstellung im Museum Augusta Raurica.* Augst: Römermuseum.

Pfäffli, B. (2013b), 'Où sont les enfants? Enquête à Augusta Raurica', *La petite Enfance dans le Monde Grec et Romain* (*Dossiers d'Archéologie* 356): 71–3.

Phang, S. E. (2001), *The Marriage of Roman Soldiers (13 BC–AD 235): Law and Family in the Imperial Army.* Leiden: Brill.

Phillips, E. J. (1976), 'A Workshop of Roman Sculptors at Carlisle', *Britannia* 7: 101–8.

Philp, B. (1966), 'Ritual Burials at Reculver', *Kent Archaeological Review* 6: 7.

Picón, C. A., Mertens, J. R., Milleker, E. J., Lightfoot, C. S., and Hemingway, S. (2007), *Art of the Classical World in the Metropolitan Museum of Art: Greece, Cyprus, Etruria, Rome.* New York: The Metropolitan Museum of Art.

Pilkington, N. (2013), 'Growing Up Roman: Infant Mortality and Reproductive Development', *Journal of Interdisciplinary History* 44(1): 1–35.

Pingiatoglou, S. (1981), *Eileithyia.* Würzburg: Königshausen and Neumann.

Planson, E., Brenot, C., Deyts, S., Joubeaux, H., Lejeune, M., and Poulain, T. (1982), *La nécropole des Bolards à Nuits-Saint-Georges.* Lyon: Éditions du Centre National.

Pluton, S., Adrian, Y.-M., Kliesch, F., and Cottard, A. (2008), 'La nécropole gallo-romaine du "Clos au Duc" à Évreux (Eure): des sépultures du Ier siècle apr. J.-C.', *Revue archéologique de l'Ouest* 25: 209–21.

Pomeroy, S. B. (1986), 'Copronyms and the Exposure of Infants in Egypt', in Bagnall, R. A. and Harris, W. V. (eds.), *Studies in Roman Law in Memory of A. Arthur Schiller.* Leiden: Brill, 147–62.

Pommeret, C. (ed.) (2001), *Le Sanctuaire antique des Bolards à Nuits-Saint-Georges, Côte-d'Or* (Revue Archéologique de l'Est Supplement 16). Dijon: Editions S.A.E.

Portat, E., Fouriaux, F., and Simon, J. (2013), 'L'inhumation en vase des bébés gallo-romains: Restitution 3D à partir de l'exemple de Chartres', *La petite Enfance dans le Monde Grec et Romain* (*Dossiers d'Archéologie* 356): 50–3.

Powell, L. A., Redfern, R. C., Millard, A. R., and Gröcke, D. R. (2014), 'Infant Feeding Practices in Roman London: Evidence from Isotopic Analyses', in Carroll, M. and Graham, E.-J. (eds.), *Infant Health and Death in Roman Italy and Beyond* (JRA Supplement 96). Portsmouth: Journal of Roman Archaeology, 89–110.

Prowse, T. L., Saunders, S. R., Schwarcz, H. P., Garnsey, P., Macchiarelli, R., and Bondioli, L. (2008), 'Isotopic and Dental Evidence for Infant and Young Child Feeding Practices in an Imperial Roman Skeletal Sample', *American Journal of Physical Anthropology* 137: 294–308.

Pudsey, A. (2013), 'Children in Roman Egypt', in Evans Grubbs, J., Parkin, T., and Bell, R. (eds.), *The Oxford Handbook of Childhood and Education in the Classical World.* Oxford: Oxford University Press, 484–509.

Quinn, J. C. (2011), 'The Cultures of the Tophet: Identification and Identity in the Phoenician Diaspora', in Gruen, E. S. (ed.), *Cultural Identity in the Ancient Mediterranean.* Los Angeles: J. Paul Getty Trust, 388–413.

Quinn, J. C. (2013), 'Tophets in the Punic World', in Xella, P. (ed.), *The Tophet in the Phoenician Mediterranean. Studi Epigrafici e Linguistici* 29–30: 23–48.

Rajakumar, K. (2003), 'Vitamin D, Cod-Liver Oil, Sunlight and Rickets: A Historical Perspective', *Pediatrics* 112(2): 132–5.

Ramos-Andrade, D., Ruivo, C., Portilha, M. A., Brito, J. B., Caserio-Alves, F., and Curvo-Semedo, L. (2014), 'An Unusual Cause of Intra-Abdominal Calcification: A Lithopedion', *European Journal of Radiology Open* 1: 60–3.

Rawson, B. (ed.) (1986), *The Family in Ancient Rome: New Perspectives*. Ithaca: Cornell University Press.

Rawson, B. (ed.) (1991), *Marriage, Divorce and Children in Ancient Rome*. Oxford: Oxford University Press.

Rawson, B. (1997), 'The Iconography of Roman Childhood', in Rawson, B. and Weaver, P. (eds.), *The Roman Family in Italy: Status, Sentiment, Space*. Oxford: Oxford University Press, 205–32.

Rawson, B. (2003a), *Children and Childhood in Roman Italy*. Oxford: Oxford University Press.

Rawson, B. (2003b), 'Death, Burial, and Commemoration of Children in Roman Italy', in Balch, D. L. and Osiek, C. (eds.), *Early Christian Families in Context*. Grand Rapids: William B. Eerdmans Publishing Company, 277–97.

Rawson, B. (ed.) (2011), *A Companion to Families in the Greek and Roman Worlds*. Oxford: Wiley-Blackwell.

Rawson, B., and Weaver, P. (eds.) (1997), *The Roman Family in Italy: Status, Sentiment, Space*. Oxford: Oxford University Press.

Redfern, R. C. (2007), 'The Influence of Culture upon Childhood: An Osteological Study of Iron Age and Romano-British Dorset', in Harlow, M. and Laurence, R. (eds.), *Age and Ageing in the Roman Empire* (JRA Supplement 65). Portsmouth: Journal of Roman Archaeology, 171–94.

Redfern, R. C. (2010), 'A Regional Examination of Surgery and Fracture Treatment in Iron Age and Roman Britain', *International Journal of Osteoarchaeology* 20: 443–71.

Redfern, R. C. and Gowland, R. L. (2012), 'A Bioarchaeological Perspective on the Pre-Adult Stages of the Life Course: Implications for the Care and Health of Children in the Roman Empire', in Harlow, M. and Larsson Lovén, L. (eds.), *Families in the Roman and Late Antique World*. London: Continuum, 111–40.

Redfern, R. C., Gowland, R. L., and Powell, L. A. (2013), 'La santé des enfants sous l'Empire romain', *La petite Enfance dans le Monde Grec et Romain* (*Dossiers d'Archéologie* 356): 80–3.

Reilly, J. (1997), 'Naked and Limbless: Learning about the Feminine Body in Ancient Athens', in Koloski-Ostrow, A. O. and Lyons, C. L. (eds.), *Naked Truths: Women, Sexuality and Gender in Classical Art and Archaeology*. London: Routledge, 154–73.

Rémy, B. (1984), 'Les inscriptions de médicins en Gaule', *Gallia* 42: 115–52.

Rescigno, D. (2009), 'Un bosco di madri. Il santuario di Fondo Patturelli tra documenti e contesti', in Chirico, M. L. (ed.), *Lungo l'Appia. Scritti su Capua antica e dintorni*. Naples: Giannini Editore, 31–42.

Reydams-Schils, G. (2005), *The Roman Stoics: Self, Responsibility, and Affection*. Chicago: University of Chicago Press.

Ribichini, S. (1990), 'Il sacrificio di fanciulli nel mondo punico: Testimonianze e problemi, in *Riti funerari e di olocausto nella Sardegna fenicia e punica*. Cagliari: Edizioni Della Torre, 45–66.

Ricciardi, L. (1992), 'Canino (Viterbo): Il santuario etrusco di Fontanile di Legnisina a Vulci. Relazione della campagno di scavi 1985–1986: L'altare monumentale e il deposito votivo', in *Notizie degli Scavi di Antichita* (1988–1989), 42–3: 137–209.

Riches, G. and Dawson, P. (1997), '"Shoring Up the Walls of Heartache": Parental Responses to the Death of a Child', in Field, D., Hockey, J., and Small, N. (eds.), *Death, Gender and Ethnicity*. London: Routledge, 52–75.

Riddle, J. (1994), *Contraception and Abortion from the Ancient World to the Renaissance*. Cambridge, MA: Harvard University Press.

Ridgeway, V. (2009), *Secrets of the Gardens: Archaeologists Unearth the Lives of Roman Londoners at Drapers' Gardens*. London: Pre-Construct Archaeology.

Riquier, S. and Salé, P. (2006), 'La nécropole du Haut-Empire de Tavant (Indre-et-Loire)', in Ferdière, A. (ed.), *Ensembles funéraires gallo-romains de la Région Centre I* (Revue Archéologique du Centre de la France, Supplément 29). Tours: FÉRACF, 7–108.

Rissanen, M. (2014), 'The *Lupa Romana* in the Roman Provinces', *Acta Archaeologica Scientarum Hungaricae* 65: 335–60.

Roche-Bernard, G. (1993), *Costumes et textiles en Gaul Romaine*. Paris: Errance.

Rogers, C. H., Floyd, F. J., Seltzer, M. M., Greenberg, J., and Hong, J. (2008), 'Long-Term Effects of the Death of a Child on Parents' Adjustment in Midlife', *Journal of Family Psychology* 22(2): 203–11.

Rose, A. J. (1923), 'Noctural Funerals in Rome', *The Classical Quarterly* 17(3–4): 191–4.

Rose, C. B. (1990), '"Princes" and Barbarians on the Ara Pacis', *American Journal of Archaeology* 94(3): 453–67.

Rose, M. (1997a), 'Ashkelon's Dead Babies', *Archaeology* 50(2): 12–13.

Rose, M. (1997b), 'Origins of Syphilis', *Archaeology* 50(1): 24–5.

Rosenwein, B. H. (2006), *Emotional Communities in the Early Middle Ages*. Ithaca: Cornell University Press.

Rossi, F. (1993), 'Deux poupées en ivoire d'époque romaine à Yverdon-les-Bains VD', *Archäologie der Schweiz* 16(4): 152–7.

Rossini, O. (2006), *Ara Pacis*. Rome: Mondadori Electa.

Rothe, U. (2011), 'Der Grabstein der Severina Nutrix aus Köln: Eine neue Deutung', *Germania* 89: 191–214.

Rothenberg, B. and Blanco-Freijeiro, A. (1981), *Studies in Ancient Mining and Metallurgy in South-West Spain: Explorations and Excavations in the Province of Huelva*. London: Institute for Archaeo-Metallurgical Studies.

Rotili, M. (1972), *L'Arco di Traiano a Benevento*. Rome: Istituto Poligrafico dello Stato.

Rouquet, N. (2003), 'Biberons, les tire-lait ou les tribulations d'une tubulure', in Gourevitch, D., Moirin, A., and Rouquet, N. (eds.), *Maternité et petite enfance dans l'Antiquité romaine*. Bourges: Éditions de la Ville de Bourges, 171–8.

Rouquet, N. and Loridant, F. (2000), 'Note sur les Biberons en Gaule Romaine', in Rivet, L. (ed.), *Société française d'etude de la céramique antique en Gaule: Actes du congrès de Libourne, 1er–4 juin 2000: productions régionales et importations en Aquitaine: actualité des recherches céramiques*. Marseilles: Société Française d'Etude de la Céramique antique en Gaule, 425–40.

Rouvier-Jeanlin, M. (1972), *Les figurines gallo-romaines en terre cuite au Musée des Antiquités Nationales*. Paris: CNRS.

Rouvier-Jeanlin, M. (1995), 'Les jouets en terre cuite de la Gaule romaine', *Bulletin de l'Association Guillaume Budé Année* 1(1): 77–84.

Rubel, A. (2013), 'Infant Burials in Iron-Age and Roman Europe: Prolegomena to a Comparative Analysis, Roman Dobruja and Iron-Age Germany', *European Journal of Science and Theology* 9(6): 233–41.

Ruiz, M. P. (2013), 'Domestic Cult and Ethnicity: Surveying Local Identity and Cultural Interactions through Private Religion in the Provinces *Baetica* and *Terraconensis*', in Bombardieri, L., d'Agostino, A., Guiarducci, G., Orsi, V., and Valentini, S. (eds.), *SOMA 2012, Identity and Connectivity: Proceedings of the 216th Symposium on Mediterranean Archeaology, Florence, Italy, 1–3 March 2012* (BAR International Series 2581). Oxford: Archaeopress, 1001–9.

Russell, J. C. (1985), *The Control of Late Ancient and Medieval Population*. Philadelphia: American Philosophical Society.

Rustico, L. (2013), 'Giocattoli', in Capodiffero, A. (ed.), *Evan Gorga: La Collezione di Archeologia*. Milan: Electa, 243–57.

Sadurska, A. and Bounni, A. (1994), *Les Sculptures funéraires de Palmyre*. Rome: Giorgio Bretschneider Editore.

Sallares, R., Bouwman, A., and Anderung, C. (2004), 'The Spread of Malaria to Southern Europe: New Approaches to Old Problems', *Medical History* 48(3): 311–28.

Salowey, C. A. (2012), 'Women on Hellenistic Grave Stelai: Reading Images and Texts', in James, S. L. and Dillon, S. (eds.), *A Companion to Women in the Ancient World*. Malden: Wiley-Blackwell, 249–62.

Salvadei, L., Ricci, F., and Manzi, G. (2001), 'Porotic Hyperostosis as a Marker of Health and Nutritional Conditions during Childhood: Studies at the Transition between Imperial Rome and the Early Middle Ages', *American Journal of Human Biology* 13(6): 709–17.

Sánchez Romero, M., Alarcón García, A., and Aranda Jiménez, G. (eds.) (2015), *Children, Spaces and Identity*. Oxford: Oxbow.

Sanders, H. A. (1927), 'The Certificate of Birth of a Roman Citizen', *Classical Philology* 22: 409–13.

Šašel Kos, M. (1999), 'Nutrices Augustae Deae', in Šašel Kos, M. (ed.), *Pre-Roman Divinities in the Eastern Alps and Adriatic*. Ljubliana: Narodni musej Slovenije, 153–92.

Scattarella, V., Sublimi Saponetti, S., and Selvaggi, A. (2006), 'I resti scheletrici umani', in De Juliis, M. (ed.), *Catalogo del Museo Nazionale Archeologico di Taranto, II, 2 Rutigliano I: La necropoli di contrada Purgatorio Scavo 1978*. Taranto: Scorpione Editrice, 615–26.

Schallmayer, E. (2006), 'Gräber von Kindern und Jugendlichen in römischer Zeit', in Seitz, G. (ed.), *Im Dienste Roms: Festchrift für Hans Ulrich Nuber*. Remshalden: Verlag Bernhard Albert Greiner, 55–69.

Schauerte, G. (1985), *Terrakotten mütterlicher Gottheiten: Formen und Werkstätten rheinischer und gallischer Tonstatuetten der römischen Kaiserzeit*. Cologne: Rheinland Verlag.

Scheid, J. (1984), '*Contraria facere*: renversements et déplacements dans les rites funéraires', *Aion* 6: 117–39.

Scheidel, W. (2010), 'Greco-Roman Sex Ratios and Femicide in Comparative Perspective', *Princeton and Stanford Working Papers in Classics*, Version 1.0, January. https://www.princeton.edu/~pswpc/pdfs/scheidel/011003.pdf.

Scheper-Hughes, N. (1989), 'Death Without Weeping', *Natural History* 10: 8–16.

Scheper-Hughes, N. (2013), 'No More Angel Babies on the Alto', *Berkeley Review of Latin American Studies* Spring 2013: 25–31.

Schmidt, J., Kwok, C., and Keenleyside, A. (2016), 'Infant Feeding Practices and Childhood Diet at Apollonia Pontica: Isotopic and Dental Evidence', *American Journal of Physical Anthropology* 159(2): 284–99.

Schultz, C. E. (2006), *Women's Religious Activity in the Roman Republic*. Chapel Hill: University of North Carolina Press.

Schultz, C. E. and Harvey, Jr, P. B. (eds.) (2006), *Religion in Republican Italy*. Cambridge: Cambridge University Press.

Schulz, F. (1942), 'Roman Registers of Births and Birth Certificates', *Journal of Roman Studies* 32: 78–91.

Schulz, F. (1943), 'Roman Registers of Births and Birth Certificates', *Journal of Roman Studies* 33: 55–64.

Schulze, H. (1998), *Ammen und Pädagogen: Sklavinnen und Sklaven als Erzieher in der antiken Kunst und Gesellschaft*. Mainz: Verlag Philipp von Zabern.

Schwartz, J. H., Houghton, F. D., Bondioli, L., and Macchiarelli, R. (2012), 'Bones, Teeth, and Estimating Age of Perinates: Carthaginian Infant Sacrifice Revisited', *Antiquity* 86: 738–45.

Schwartz, J. H., Houghton, F. D., Macchiarelli, R., and Bondioli, L. (2010), 'Skeletal Remains from Punic Carthage Do Not Support Systematic Sacrifice of Infants', *PLoSONE* 5(2): 1–12.

Schweder, B. I. M. and Winkler, E.-M. (2004), *Untersuchungen zu den Gräberfelden in Carnuntum: Bd. II. Die menschlichen Skelettreste des römerzeitlichen Gräberfeldes Petronell-Carnuntum südlich der Zivilstadt (Notgrabungen 1984–1986)*. Vienna: Verlag der Österreichischen Akademie der Wissens.

Scott, E. (2001), 'Killing the Female? Archaeological Narratives of Infanticide', in Arnold, B. and Wicker, N. L. (eds.), *Gender and the Archaeology of Death*. Walnut Creek: Altamira Press, 3–21.

Seitz, G. (ed.) (2006), *Im Dienste Roms: Festchrift für Hans Ulrich Nuber*. Remshalden: Verlag Bernhard Albert Greiner.

Selzer, W. (1988), *Römische Steindenkmäler. Mainz in römischer Zeit*. Mainz: Verlag Philipp von Zabern.

Sengupta, S., Carrion, V., Shelton, J., Wynn, R. J., Ryan, R. M., Singhal, K., and Lakshminrusimha, S. (2013), 'Adverse Neonatal Outcomes Associated with Early-Term Birth', *JAMA Pediatrics* 168(1): 1053–9.

Sestieri, P. C. (1954), *Il Nuovo Museo di Paestum* (Itinerari dei Musei e Monunenti d'Italia). Rome: Libreria dello Stato.

Sestieri, P. C. (1955), *Paestum: The City, the Prehistoric Necropolis in Contrada Gaudo, the Heraion at the Mouth of the Sele* (3rd edn). Rome: Istituto Poligrafico dello Stato.

Shapiro, H. A. (2003), 'Fathers and Sons, Men and Boys', in Neils, J. and Oakley, J. H. (eds.), *Coming of Age in Ancient Greece: Images of Childhood from the Classical Past*. New Haven: Yale University Press, 85–111.

Shaw, B. D. (1991), 'The Cultural Meaning of Death: Age and Gender in the Roman Family', in Kertzer, D. I. and Saller, R. P. (eds.), *The Family in Italy: From Antiquity to Present*. New Haven: Yale University Press, 66–90.

Shaw, B. D. (2001a), 'Raising and Killing Children', *Mnemosyne* 54(1): 31–77.

Shaw, B. D. (2001b), 'The Seasonal Birthing Cycle of Roman Women', in Scheidel, W. (ed.), *Debating Roman Demography*. Leiden: Brill, 82–203.

Shaw, B. D. (2013), 'Cult and Belief in Punic and Roman Africa', in Adler, W. (ed.), *The Cambridge History of Religions in the Ancient World, Vol. 2: From the Hellenistic Age to Late Antiquity*. Cambridge: Cambridge University Press, 235–63.

Shepherd, G. (2012), 'Women in Magna Graecia', in James, S. L. and Dillon, S. (eds.), *A Companion to Women in the Ancient World*. Malden: Wiley-Blackwell, 215–28.

Shelton, J. (2013), *The Women of Pliny's Letters*. Abingdon: Routledge, 125–7.

Shumka, L. (1993), *Children and Toys in the Roman World: A Contribution to the History of the Roman Family*. Unpublished MA thesis, University of Victoria.

Sigismund-Nielsen, H. (1990), '*Delicia* in Roman Literature and in the Urban Inscriptions', *Analecta Romana Instituti Danici* 19: 79–88.

Sigismund-Nielsen, H. (1997), 'Interpreting Epithets in Roman Epitaphs', in Rawson, B. and Weaver, P. (eds.), *The Roman Family in Italy: Status, Sentiment, Space*. Oxford: Clarendon Press, 169–205.

Sigismund-Nielsen, H. (2013), 'Slave and Lower-Class Roman Children', in Evans Grubbs, J., Parkin, T., and Bell, R. (eds.), *The Oxford Handbook of Childhood and Education in the Classical World*. Oxford: Oxford University Press, 186–301.

Sinn, F. and Freyberger, K. S. (1996), *Vatikanische Museen, Museo Gregoriano Profano ex Lateranese. Grabdenkmäler 2. Die Ausstattung des Hateriergrabes*. Mainz: Verlag Philipp von Zabern.

Sintès, C. (ed.) (1996), *Musée de l'Arles Antiques: Collections archéologiques d'Arles*. Arles: Actes Sud.

Slim, L. (1983), 'A propos d'un cimetière d'enfants à Thysdrus', *L'Africa Romana* 1: 167–77.

Small, A. M. (ed.) (2012a), *Vagnari: Il villaggio, l'artigianato, la proprietà imperiale*. Bari: Edipuglia.

Small, A. M. (2012b), 'The Kilns', in Small, A. M. (ed.), *Vagnari: Il villaggio, l'artigianato, la proprietà imperiale*. Bari: Edipuglia, 231–77.

Small, A. M. and Small, C. M. (2007), 'Excavations in the Roman Cemetery at Vagnari in the Territory of Gravina, Puglia, 2002', *Papers of the British School at Rome* 75: 123–229.

Smith, A. C. (2012), 'Personification: Not Just a Symbolic Mode', in Smith, T. J. and Plantzos, D. (eds.), *A Companion to Greek Art*. Oxford: Blackwell, 440–55.

Smith, P., Avishai, G., Greene, J. A., and Stager, L. E. (2011), 'Aging Cremated Infants: The Problem of Sacrifice at the Tophet of Carthage', *Antiquity* 85: 859–74.

Smith, P. and Kahila, G. (1992), 'Identification of Infanticide in Archaeological Sites: A Case Study from the Late Roman–Early Byzantine Periods at Ashkelon, Israel', *Journal of Archaeological Science* 19(6): 667–75.

Smith, P. and Kahila, G. (2005), 'The Use of Dental Criteria for Estimating Postnatal Survival in Skeletal Remains of Infants', *Journal of Archaeological Science* 32: 83–9.

Smith, P., Stager, L. E., Greene, J. A., and Avishai, G. (2013), 'Cemetery or Sacrifice? Infant Burials at the Carthage Tophet: Age Estimations Attest to Infant Sacrifice at the Carthage Tophet', *Antiquity* 87: 1191–9.

Smith, R. R. R. (1987), 'The Imperial Reliefs from the Sebasteion at Aphrodisias', *Journal of Roman Studies* 77: 88–138.

Smith, R. R. R. (2013), *The Marble Reliefs from the Julio-Claudian Sebasteion: Aphrodisias 6*. Mainz: Verlag Philipp von Zabern.

Smith II, A. M. (2013), *Roman Palmyra: Identity, Community and State Formation*. New York: Oxford University Press.

Sofaer Derevenski, J. (ed.) (2000), *Children and Material Culture*. London: Routledge.

Soren, D. (2015), 'The Children's Cemetery of Lugnano in Teverina, Umbria: Hierarchy, Magic, and Malaria', in Coşkunsu, G. (ed.), *The Archaeology of Childhood: Interdisciplinary Perspectives on an Archaeological Enigma*. New York: State University of New York Press, 235–50.

Soren, D. and Soren, N. (eds.) (1999), *A Roman Villa and a Late Roman Infant Cemetery*. Rome: L'Erma di Bretschneider.

Sourvinou-Inwood, C. (1983), *Reading Greek Death*. Oxford: Clarendon Press.

Southern, P. and Dixon, K. (1996), *The Late Roman Army*. London: Routledge.

Southwell-Wright, W. (2014), 'Perceptions of Disability in Roman Britain', in Carroll, M. and Graham, E.-J. (eds.), *Infant Health and Death in Roman Italy and Beyond* (JRA Supplement 96). Portsmouth: Journal of Roman Archaeology, 111–30.

Sparreboom, A. (2014), 'Wet-Nursing in the Roman Empire', in Carroll, M. and Graham, E.-J. (eds.), *Infant Health and Death in Roman Italy and Beyond* (JRA Supplement 96). Portsmouth: Journal of Roman Archaeology, 145–58.

Spatafora, F. (2014), 'Seppellimenti infantile nella necropolis punica di Palermo', in Terranova, C. (ed.), *La presenza dei bambini nelle religioni del Mediterraneo antico*. Rome: Aracne, 291–309.

Speidel, M. A. (1996), *Die römischen Schreibtafeln von Vindonissa: Lateinische Texte des militärischen Alltags und ihre geschichtliche Bedeutung*. Brugg: Gesellschaft Pro Vindonissa.

Spieser, C. (2008), 'Cercueils d'enfants dans l'Egypte ancienne et tardive', in Gusi, F., Muriel, S., and Olària, C. R. (eds.), *Nasciturus, infans, puerulus vobis mater terra: La muerte en la infancia*. Castelló: Servei d'Investigacions Arquelògiques i Prehistòriques, 513–50.

Stager, L. E. (1980), 'The Rite of Child Sacrifice at Carthage', in Pedley, J. G. (ed.), *New Light on Ancient Carthage*. Ann Arbor: University of Michigan Press, 1–11.

Stager, L. E. (1982), 'Carthage: A View from the Tophet', in Niemeyer, H. G. (ed.), *Phönizier im Westen*. Mainz: Zabern, 155–66.

Stager, L. E. (1991), 'Eroticism and and Infanticide at Ashkelon', *Biblical Archaeology Review* 17(4): 35–53.

Stager, L. E. and Wolff, S. R. (1984), 'Child Sacrifice at Carthage: Religious Rite or Population Control?', *Biblical Archaeology Review* 10(1): 30–51.

Stavrakopoulou, F. (2004), *King Manasseh and Child Sacrifice: Biblical Distortions of Historical Realities* (Zeitschrift fur die Alttestamentliche Wissenschaft 338). Berlin: Walter de Gruyter.

Stefan, A. S. (2015), *La Colonne Trajane*. Paris: Picard.

Stevens, S. T. (2013), 'Stages of Infancy in Roman Amphora Burial', in Evans Grubbs, J., Parkin, T., and Bell, R. (eds.), *The Oxford Handbook of Childhood and Education in the Classical World*. Oxford: Oxford University Press, 625–43.

Stewart, A. and Gray, C. (2000), 'Confronting the Other: Childbirth, Aging, and Death on an Attic Tombstone at Harvard', in Cohen, B. (ed.), *Not The Classical Ideal: Athens and the Construction of the Other in Greek Art*. Leiden: Brill, 248–74.

Strong, E. (1937), 'Terra Mater or Italia?', *Journal of Roman Studies* 27: 113–26.

Stroszeck, J. (2012), 'Grave Gifts in Child Burials in the Athenian Kerameikos', in Hermary, A. and Dubois, C. (eds.), *L'Enfant et la mort dans l'Antiquité III: Le materiel associé aux tombes d'enfants. Actes de la table ronde internationale organisée à la Maison Méditteranéenne de Sciences de l'Homme (MMSH) d'Aix-en-Provence, 20–22 janvier 2011*. Arles: Éditions Errance, 57–75.

Struck, M. (ed.) (1993a), *Römerzeitliche Gräber als Quellen zu Religion, Bevölkerungsstruktur und Sozialgeschichte*. Mainz: Institut für Vor- und Frühgeschichte, Universität Mainz.

Struck, M. (1993b), 'Kinderbestattungn in romano-britischen Siedlungen – der archäologische Befund', in Struck, M. (ed.), *Römerzeitliche Gräber als Quellen zu Religion, Bevölkerungsstruktur und Sozialgeschichte*. Mainz: Institut für Vor- und Frühgeschichte, Universität Mainz, 313–18.

Subirà, M. E. and Molist, N. (2008), 'Inhumacions perinatals múltiples i espais de treball en els assentaments ibers', in Gusi, F., Muriel, S., and Olària, C. R. (eds.), *Nasciturus, infans, puerulus vobis mater terra: La muerte en la infancia*. Castelló: Servei d'Investigacions Arquelògiques i Prehistòriques, 365–85.

Susini, G. (1973), *The Roman Stonecutter: An Introduction to Latin Epigraphy*. Oxford: Blackwell.

Talvas, S. (2007), *Recherches sur les Figurines en Terre Cuite Gallo-Romaines en Context Archéologique*. PhD thesis, Université de Toulouse II.

Taylor, A. (1993), 'A Roman Lead Coffin with Pipeclay Figurines from Arrington, Cambridgeshire', *Britannia* 24: 191–225.

Tentea, O. (2012), *Ex Oriente ad Danubium: The Syrian Units on the Danube Frontier of the Roman Empire*. Bucharest: Mega Publishing House.

Terranova, C. (ed.) (2014), *La presenza dei bambini nelle religioni del Mediterraneo antico*. Rome: Aracne.

Teyssier, E. (2014), *Nîmes. La Romaine*. Nîmes: Alcide.

Thompson, N. (1997), 'Masculinity and Loss', in Field, D., Hockey, J., and Small, N. (eds.), *Death, Gender and Ethnicity*. London: Routledge, 76–88.

Thylander, H. (1952), *Inscriptions du Port D'Ostie*. Lund: C. W. K. Gleerup.

Tibbetts, B. (2008), 'Infant Burials in Iron Age Britain', in Bacvarov, K. (ed.), *Babies Reborn: Infant/Child Burials in Pre- and Protohistory* (BAR International Series 1832). Oxford: Archaeopress, 189–94.

Tocheri, M. W., Dupras, T. L., Sheldrick, P., and Molto, J. E. (2005), 'Roman Period Fetal Skeletons from the East Cemetery (Kellis 2) of Kellis, Egypt', *International Journal of Osteoarchaeology* 15: 326–41.

Tomas, A. (2009–10), 'Reading Gender and Social Life in Military Spaces', in Stepniowski, F. M, *Swiatowit: Annual of the Institute of Archaeology of the University of Warsaw VIII (XLIX)*. Warsaw: Instytut Archeologii, 139–52.

Tomei, M. A. (ed.) (2006), *Roma: Memorie dal sottosuolo, Ritrovamenti archeologici 1980–2006*. Rome: Electa.

Tomlin, R. S. O. (1997), '*Sede in tuo loco*: A Fourth-Century Uterine Phylactery in Latin from Roman Britain', *Zeitchrift für Papyrologie und Epigraphik* 115: 291–4.

Tomlin, R. S. O. (2008), 'Special Delivery: A Graeco-Roman Gold Amulet for Healthy Childbirth', *Zeitchrift für Papyrologie und Epigraphik* 167: 219–24.

Torino, M. and Fornaciari, G. (2001), 'Paleopatologia degli Individui nella Casa di Giulio Polibio', in Ciarallo, A. and De Carolis, E. (eds.), *La Casa di Giulio Polibio: Studi Interdisciplinari*. Tokyo: Centro Studi Arti Figurativi, 93–106.

Toynbee, J. M. C. (1954), *The Ara Pacis Reconsidered and Historical Art in Roman Italy*. London: G. Cumberledge.

Treggiari, S. (2007), *Terentia, Tullia and Publilia: The Women of Cicero's Family*. London: Routledge.

Trumm, J. and Fellmann Brogli, R. (2008), 'Mitten im Lager geboren: Kinder und Frauen im römischen Legionslager Vindonissa', in Brandl, U. (ed.), *Frauen und Römisches Militär: Beiträge eines Runden Tisches in Xanten vom. 7. bis 9. Juli 2005* (BAR International Series 1759). Oxford: Archaeopress, 102–19.

Turcan, R. (2001), *The Gods of Ancient Rome: Religion in Everyday Life from Archaic to Imperial Times*. New York: Routledge.

Turton, P., Badenhorst, W., Hughes, P., Ward, J., Riches, S. and White, S. (2006), 'Psychological Impact of Stillbirth on Fathers in the Subsequent Pregnancy and Puerperium', *British Journal of Psychiatry* 188(2): 154–72.

Uhlenbrock, J. P. (1990), *The Coroplast's Art: Greek Terracottas of the Hellenistic World*. New York: Aristide Caratzas.

Uncini, A. (1995), *Bildkatalog der Skulpturen des Vatikanischen Museums: Museo Chiaramonti* (Teilband 3). Berlin: Walter de Gruyter.

Uzzi, J. D. (2005), *Children in the Visual Arts of Imperial Rome*. Cambridge: Cambridge University Press.

Uzzi, J. D. (2007), 'The Power of Parenthood in Official Roman Art', in Cohen, A. and Rutter, J. B. (eds.), *Constructions of Childhood in Ancient Greece and Rome* (Hesperia Supplement 61), Princeton: Princeton University Press, 61–81.

Van Andringa, W., Duday, H., Lepetz, S., Joly, D., and Lind, T. (2013), *Mourir à Pompei: Fouille d'un Quartier Funéraire de la Nécropole romaine de Porta Nocera (2003–2007)*. Rome: École française de Rome.

Van Driel Murray, C. (1994), 'A Question of Gender in a Military Context', *Helinium* 34(2): 342–62.

Van Driel Murray, C. (1995), 'Gender in Question', in Rush, P. (ed.), *Theoretical Roman Archaeology: Second Conference Proceedings*. Aldershot: Avebury Press, 3–21.

Van Driel Murray, C. (1997), 'Women in Forts?', *Jahresbericht der Gesellschaft Pro Vindonissa* 1997: 55–61.

Van Gennep, A. (1909), *Les rites de passage*. Paris: Nourry.

Van Hoorn, G. (1951), *Choes and Anthesteria*. Leiden: Brill.

Van Minnen, P. (1994), 'House-to-House Enquiries: An Interdisciplinary Approach to Roman Karanis', *Zeitchrift für Papyrologie und Epigraphik* 100: 227–51.

Van Sleuwen, B. E., L'Hoir, M. P., Engelberts, A. C., Busschers, W. B., Westers, P., and Blom, M. A. (2006), 'Comparison of Behaviour Modification with and without Swaddling as Interventions for Excessive Crying', *Journal of Pediatrics* 149(4): 512–17.

Vandervondelen, M. (2002), 'Childbirth in Iron Age Cyprus: A Case Study', in Bolger, D. and Serwint, N. J. (eds.), *Engendering Aphrodite: Women and Society in Ancient Cyprus*. Boston: American Schools of Oriental Research, 143–55.

Varner, E. R. (2004), *Mutilation and Transformation: Damnatio Memoriae and Roman Imperial Portraiture*. Leiden: Brill.

Vassallo, S. (1993–4), 'Ricerche nella necropolis orientale di Himera in località Pestavecchia (1990–1993)', *ΚΩΚΑΛΟΣ: Studi pubblicati dall'Istituto di Storia Antica dell'Università di Palermo* 39–40: 1243–57.

Vassallo, S. (2010), 'Himera alla luce delle recenti indagini nella città bassa e nelle necropoli', *Mare Internum: Archeologia e culture del Mediterraneo* 2: 45–56.

Vassallo, S. (2014), 'Le sepolture dei bambini nelle necropoli di Himera: dati preliminari', in Terranova, C. (ed.), *La presenza dei bambini nelle religioni del Mediterraneo antico*. Rome: Aracne, 257–90.

Vassallo, S. and Valentino, M. (2012), 'Scavi nella necropoli occidentale di Himera, il paesaggio e le tipologie funerarie', in Ampolo, C. (ed.), *Sicilia occidentale: Studi, rassegne, ricerche*. Pisa: Edizioni della Normale, 49–71.

Vedder, U. (1988), 'Frauentod-Kriegertod im Spiegel der attischen Grabkunst des 4. Jhr. v. Chr.', *Mitteilungen des DeutschenArchäologischen Instituts, Athenische Abteilung* 103: 161–91.

Vermaseren, M. J. and van Essen, C. C. (1965), *The Excavations in the Mithraeum in the Church of Santa Prisca in Rome*. Leiden: Brill.

Vertet, H. (1974), 'Pauvres potiers, pauvre misère', *Sudan: 5,000 Ans d'Histoire* (*Dossiers d'Archéologie* 6): 85–9.

Vierneisel-Schlörb, B. (1979), *Glyptotek München: Katalog der Skulpturen, Vol. 3. Klassische Skulpturen des 5. und 4. Jhs. v. Chr.* Munich: Beck.

Vlachou, V. (2007), 'Oropos: The Infant and Child Inhumations from the Settlement (Late 8th–Early 7th Centuries BC)', in Mazarakis Ainian, A. (ed.), *Oropos and Euboea in the Early Iron Age: Acts of an International Round Table, University of Thessaly, June 18–20, 2004*. Volos: University of Thessaly Publications, 213–40.

Vlachou, V. (2012), 'Death and Burial in the Greek World', in *Thesaurus Cultus et Rituum Antiquorum VIII*. Los Angeles: J. Paul Getty Museum, 363–84.

Vokotopoulou, J. (1994), 'Ancienne nécropoles de la Chalcidique', in de la Genière, J., *Nécropoles et sociétés antiques (Grèce, Italie, Languedoc): Actes du Colloque International de Lille III: Lille, 2–3 Décembre 1991*. Naples: Centre Jean Bérard, 79–98.

von Gonzenbach, V. (1969), 'Der griechisch-römische Scheitelschmuck und die Funde von Thasos', *Bulletin de correspondence hellénique* 93(2): 885–945.

Wahl, J. and Kokabi, M. (1988), *Das römische Gräberfeld von Stettfeld I: Osteologische Untersuchung der Knochenreste aus dem Gräberfeld* (Forschungen und Berichte der Vor- und Frühgeschichte Baden-Württembergs 29). Stuttgart: Konrad Theiss Verlag.

Walker, P., Bathurst, R., Richman, R., Gjerdrum, T., and Andrushko, V. (2009), 'The Causes of Porotic Hyperostosis and Cribra Orbitalia: A Reappraisal of the Iron-Deficiency-Anemia Hypothesis', *American Journal of Physical Anthropology* 139(2): 109–25.

Warden, P. G. (1983), 'Bullae: Roman Custom and Italic Tradition', *Opuscula Romana* 14: 69–75.

Weber, T. M. (2006), *Sculptures from Syria in the Syrian National Museum at Damascus, I. From Cities and Villages in Central and Southern Syria*. Worms: Wernersche Verlagsgesellschaft.

Weigel, R. (1992), 'Lupa romana', in *Lexicon Epigraphicum Mythologiae Classicae*, Vol. VI. Zurich: Artemis, 292–6.

Wheeler, S. M. (2012), 'Nutritional and Disease Stress of Juveniles from the Dakhleh Oasis, Egypt', *International Journal of Osteoarchaeology* 22: 219–34.

Wheeler, S. M., Williams, L., Beauchesne, P., and Dupras, T. L. (2013), 'Shattered Lives and Broken Childhoods: Evidence of Physical Child Abuse in Ancient Egypt', *International Journal of Paleopathology* 3(2): 71–82.

Wheeler, S. M., Williams, L., Dupras, T. L., Tocheri, M., and Molto, J. E. (2011), 'Childhood in Roman Egypt: Bioarchaeology of the Kellis 2 Cemetery, Dakhleh Oasis, Egypt', in Lally, M. and Moore, A. (eds.), *Re-Thinking the Little Ancestor: New Perspectives on the Archaeology of Infancy and Childhood*. Oxford: Archaeopress, 110–21.

Whitehouse, R., Wilkins, J. B., and Herring, E. (2000), *Botromagno: Excavation and Survey at Gravina in Puglia 1979–1985*. London: Accordia Research Institute.

Wiedemann, T. (1989), *Adults and Children in the Roman Empire*. London: Routledge.

Wierschowski, L. (2001), *Fremde in Gallien- 'Gallier' in der Fremde: Die epigraphisch bezeugte Mobilität in, von und nach Gallien vom 1. bis 3. Jh. n. Chr.* Stuttgart: Steiner.

Wigand, K. (1915), 'Die Nutrices Augustae von Poetovio', *Jahreshefte des Österreichischen Archäologischen Institutes*, 18: 188–218.

Wild, J. P. (1965), 'A Roman Silk Damask from Kent', *Archaeologia Cantiana* 80: 246–50.

Wild, J. P. (1970), *Textile Manufacture in the Northern Roman Provinces*. Cambridge: Cambridge University Press.

Wileman, J. (2005), *Hide and Seek: The Archaeology of Childhood*. Stroud: Tempus.

Willfong, T. G. (2012), 'The University of Michigan Excavation of Karanis (1924–1935): Images from the Kelsey Museum Photographic Archives', in Riggs, C. (ed.), *The Oxford Handbook of Roman Egypt*. Oxford: Oxford University Press, 223–43.

Wilson, M. (1997), 'The Subjugation of Grief in Seneca's *Epistles*', in Braund, S. M. and Gill, C. (eds.), *The Passions in Roman Thought and Literature*. Cambridge: Cambridge University Press, 48–67.

Witteyer, M. and Fasold, P. (1995), *Des Lichtes Beraubt: Totenehrung in der römischen Gräberstrasse von Mainz-Weisenau*. Wiesbaden: Reichert.

Wittmann, A. (2009), 'Les vases-cercueils de bébés', in Goudineau, C. (ed.), *Rites Funéraires à Lugdunum*. Paris: Éditions Errance, 179–80.

Wood, C. (2004), *An Investigation of the Prevalence of Rickets Among Subadults from the Roman Necropolis of Isola Sacra, Italy*. MA thesis, McMaster University.

Wood, S. E. (1992), 'Messalina, Wife of Claudius: Propaganda Successes and Failures of his Reign', *Journal of Roman Archaeology* 5: 219–34.

Wood, S. E. (2000), 'Mortals, Empresses, and Earth Goddesses: Demeter and Persephone in Public and Private Apotheosis', in Kleiner, D. E. E. and Matheson, S. B. (eds.), *I Claudia II: Women in Roman Art and Society*. Austin: University of Texas Press, 77–99.

Wood, S. E. (2001a), *Imperial Women: A Study in Public Images, 40 B.C.–68 A.D.* Leiden: Brill.

Wood, S. E. (2001b), 'Literacy and Luxury in the Early Empire: A Papyrus-Roll Winder from Pompeii', *Memoirs of the American Academy at Rome* 46: 23–40.

Wrede, H. (1981), *Consecratio in formam deorum: Vergöttlichte Privatpersonen in der römischen Kaiserzeit*. Mainz: Von Zabern.

Wrede, H. (1990), 'Der Sarkophagdeckel eines Mädchens in Malibu und die frühen Klinensarkophage Roms, Athens, und Kleinasiens', in True, M. and Koch, G. (eds.), *Roman Funerary Monuments in the J. Paul Getty Museum*. Malibu: Getty Museum Press, 15–46.

Wright Jr, J. R., van den Hof, M. C., and Macken, M. B. (2005), 'Prenatal Infantile Cortical Hyperostosis (Caffey's Disease): A "Hepatic Myeloid Hyperplasia-Pulmonary Hypoplasia Sequence" can Explain the Lethality of Early Onset Cases', *Prenatal Diagnosis* 10: 939–44.

Xella, P. (2010), 'Per un "modello interpretativo" del tofet: Il tofet come necropoli infantile?', in Bartoloni, G., Matthiae, P., Nigro, L., and Romano, L. (eds.), *Tiro, Cartagine, Lixus: Nuove acquisizioni. Atti del Convegno Internazionale in onore di Maria Giulia Amadasi Guzzo Roma, 24–25 novembre 2008* (Quaderni di Vicino Oriente IV). Rome: Dipartimento di Scienze Storiche Archeologiche e Antropologiche dell'Antichità, 259–78.

Xella, P. (ed.) (2013a), *The Tophet in the Ancient Mediterranean. Studi Epigrafici e Linguistici* 29–30.

Xella, P. (2013b), 'Tophet: An Overall Interpretation', in Xella, P. (ed.), *The Tophet in the Ancient Mediterranean. Studi Epigrafici e Linguistici* 29–30: 259–81.

Xella, P., Quinn, J., Melchiorri, V., and van Dommelen, P. (2013), 'Cemetery or Sacrifice? Infant Burials at the Carthage Tophet', *Antiquity* 8: 1199–207.

Zanier, N. (1992), *Das römische Kastell Ellingen* (Limesforschung 23). Mainz: Verlag Philipp von Zabern.

Zanker, P. (2000), 'Die Frauen und Kinder der Barbaren auf der Markussäule', in Scheid, J. and Huet, V. (eds.), *Autour de la colonne aurélienne: Geste et image sur la colonne de Marc Aurèle à Rome*. Turnhout: Brepols, 163–74.

Zanker, P. (2016), *Roman Portraits: Sculptures in Stone and Bronze in the Collection of the Metropolitan Museum of Art*. New York: Yale University Press.

Zupan, J. (2005), 'Perinatal Mortality in Developing Countries', *The New England Medical Journal* 352(20): 2047–8.

Zwierlein-Diehl, E. (2007), *Antike Gemmen und ihr Nachleben*. Berlin: Walter de Gruyter.

Index

Printed and bound by CPI Group (UK) Ltd, Croydon, CR0 4YY